Cuba and the Fall

New World Studies

# Cuba and the Fall

## Christian Text and Queer Narrative in the Fiction of José Lezama Lima and Reinaldo Arenas

Eduardo González

University of Virginia Press
Charlottesville and London

University of Virginia Press

Printed in the United States of America on acid-free paper

*First published 2010*

9 8 7 6 5 4 3 2 1

Library of Congress Cataloging-in-Publication Data
González, Eduardo, 1943–
Cuba and the Fall : Christian text and queer narrative in the fiction of José Lezama Lima and Reinaldo Arenas / Eduardo González.
p. cm. — (New World studies)
ISBN 978-0-8139-2981-1 (cloth : alk. paper) — ISBN 978-0-8139-2982-8 (pbk. : alk. paper) — ISBN 978-0-8139-2987-3 (e-book)
1. Gay men's writings, Cuban—History and criticism. 2. Homosexuality in literature. 3. Fall of man in literature. 4. Homosexuality—Religious aspects—Christianity. 5. Homosexuality and literature—Cuba—History—20th century. 6. Christianity and literature—Cuba—History—20th century. 7. Lezama Lima, José—Criticism and interpretation. 8. Arenas, Reinaldo, 1943–1990—Criticism and interpretation. I. Title.
PQ7382.G64 2010
863′.6409352664—dc22

2009047695

Julieta Campos
*in memoriam*

For my mother Delia

For Steve Nichols

Whatever pure thou in the body enjoy'st
(And pure thou wert created) we enjoy
In eminence, and obstacle find none
Of membrane, joint, or limb, exclusive bars:
Easier than Air with Air, if Spirits embrace,
Total they mix, Union of Pure with Pure
Desiring; nor restrained conveyance need
As Flesh to mix with Flesh, or Soul with Soul.

(Raphael explains to Adam before the Fall how
unfallen angels enjoy sex in heaven)

*Paradise Lost* (VIII.622–29)

# Contents

# Preface

> Can one say what the Christian has to say about the human condition as fallen, and yet mean it otherwise?
>
> Stephen Mulhall, *Philosophical Myths of the Fall*

THIS BOOK has a predecessor and companion in *Cuba and the Tempest: Literature and Film in the Time of Diaspora* (University of North Carolina Press 2006). Both books invest in the comparative interpretation of literature written by well-known Cuban authors related to authors and film directors from abroad. Each book develops themes guided by the saturated allegorical symbols and tokens of *Tempest* and *Fall.* In the first book, saturation comes from what some might consider the mythical and archetypal resonance of the Storm that splits apart and at times reunites peoples and fortunes in works such as Homer's *Odyssey* and Shakespeare's *Tempest.* The theme of the first book is exile from the inside and the outside. The storm in question batters a spiritual and material Island besieged by politics—but for all that never to be confused with Cuba.

Nor was politics to be confused with politics. The aim was vain, as if the reader in the writer himself could be left to fathom the nasty stuff beneath the Tempest allegory. (But when or where was there ever a storm worth its salt not spun by politics?)

The capitalized word *Fall* in the present title echoes the Christian conception of disobedience to God's command as the cause of human grief and proof of wickedness and severance from grace. The book is informed by the Christian perspective not because of the author's religious beliefs but in order to reflect and interpret moral problems at the core of the fictions and characters examined. These problems are in most instances caused by conflicts related to sexual morality and its defiance. More specifically, the three Cuban writers under discussion in this book were either self-avowed homosexuals (Reinaldo Arenas and Virgilio Piñera) or were (José Lezama Lima) consumed in what they wrote by the moral and theological consequences of male homosexual desire rendered in extravagant words and misdeeds.

Rather than considering the issue of homosexuality as a political means to achieve moral autonomy from social prejudices or to gain a high moral ground of ethical exemption from such forces, the interpretation offered here attempts to demonstrate the opposite. It tries to show how male homosexuality in its complex manifestations in fictional form generates in this case moral compulsions and ordeals of its own, which are certainly queer, but not on that account different from other instances of human subjection to the force of character under pressure by the social constraints and forms of hate that shape it.

Recognition of such shaping negative forces upon character in society represents the nonreligious—but mindful of Christian belief—version of falling from grace. Here is then one answer to Stephen Mulhall's question in the epigraph: "Can one say what the Christian has to say about the human condition as fallen, and yet mean it otherwise?" Yes indeed, but grounded on the condition that disgrace—as manifest in the capital notion of human Fall—is not blamed on humans only without God's responsibility in the affair. Human Fall entails God's eternal stumble.

Interpretation in this book takes grace to imply the common hope and illusion that each time a new life begins it does so free from the proneness to fall in the ordinary form of human error. This is an upbeat belief as common as the disenchantment it so commonly fosters when things turn bad. The fictions studied here walk the line between the early hopes and illusions sought in grace and the melancholy of fallen disenchantment that often follows disgrace.

The word *Cuba* in the title represents the actual but also imaginary realm where the force of character and social constraints just mentioned are located at specific moments in history directly or indirectly rendered in fictional form. Although not in any remote sense a study of the Antillean or Caribbean world at large, the book recognizes the force of that imagined and actual presence as a territorial blessing and a burden loaded with great suffering for which literary fictions could not atone even if they tried. The force of regional territoriality above and beyond particular nations is thus acknowledged and enjoined as the informing whole lying beyond the locations of character and conflict. In fact, contrary to a good many recent and worthy interpretations of the region's literature and culture, my own effort finds no benefit and a great deal of wasted imagination in trying to *deterritorialize* the national and regional locations where actions of human—and hence political—consequence take place.

Nietzsche's sense that morals had a history and his attempt to provide one in *The Genealogy of Morals* comes to mind when considering attempts to escape from Caribbean territoriality. Human actions do not so much require as create territory in the archaic mode of *nomos* made graphic in charting and mapping. It was Nietzsche's philosophical intent (and Carl Schmitt's fascist political will) to prove that such a charted map *had* to be missing (or withdrawn from sight) in order for European morals to take flight and act as if they required no history in order to take effect anywhere. In this crucial regard, Nietzsche's *Genealogy* was decidedly against *deterritorializing* the grounds of human action and its entrenched justifications mapped and charted (chartered) by the apportioning force of conquering *nomos.*

Insofar as history is territory, this book would provide at its best a means to chart some of its fictional character maps on Cuban soil, as well as within and beyond the Caribbean sphere, through the intervention of writers such as John Milton, Nathaniel Hawthorne, Charles Dickens, John Ruskin, William Faulkner, and James Joyce, among others—as well as two films by Guillermo del Toro. The book does not do two rather large and fine things recently accomplished in the field. It does not and could not attempt the in-depth examination of particular authorships further situated in the wider Caribbean realm achieved in Silvio Torres-Saillant's *Caribbean Poetics: Toward an Aesthetic of West Indian Literature* (1997). Nor could it match the exuberant scanning of Caribbean desires and rituals of self-fashioning managed by Antonio Benítez Rojo's *The Repeating Island: The Caribbean and the Postmodern Perspective* (1996).

"For sin will have no dominion over you, since you are not under law but under grace" (Romans 6.14). Once again facing—now in Paul's echo—Stephen Mulhall's question on the human fallen condition when not judged from the Christian perspective, it should be asked how Lezama, Arenas, and Piñera face up to it—at least within the covers of this book.

First, Piñera, whose *La Isla en peso* represents *Paradise Lost* in miniature and with the blasphemous sight of the Lord taking a stroll in the early evening breeze into the banana grove with sin on His mind and loins. Second, Arenas, whose fiction on the whole reminds me of Felipe Guaman Poma de Ayala's wondrous letter, but in this case written to himself as if to his mother and the huge old tyrant she comes to represent and in such accursed trinity of hybrid authorship thus issues a testimonial blast cursing so cruel a God as the one invented by Christians. And third,

Lezama, whose belief in the resurrection of the flesh and the Catholic dispensation of grace in sacraments that put no curbs on the magic of being surprised by sin with honest chances to repent, I fully acknowledge: for to doubt that he upheld such truths in his heart and only wrote about them to pleasure himself in the mirror of words would truly disgrace any faith in the meaning of reading him. Any consideration of the three queer authorships in question that does not consider them in the purview of Christian belief in grace or disgrace seems banal.

# Acknowledgments

Thanks are due to Cathie Brettschneider and the three readers of the manuscript for the expedient and painstaking care given to its evaluation. George Roupe and Morgan Myers put the manuscript in final shape with consummate skill, and Heather Dubnick created the index.

I must mention at least Jorge Olivares and Francisco Soto and Rafael Ocasio on Arenas; and Enrico Mario Santí and Gustavo Pérez Firmat on both Arenas and Lezama and countless other things. Among the long-established readers of *Paradiso,* I have learned much from Emilio Bejel, Gustavo Pellón, Arnaldo Cruz-Malavé, and Alberto Moreiras. Among recent critics—but too late to be integrated into a bulky manuscript—I have encountered in César Augusto Salgado's work on Lezama's foot tracks back into Joyce a powerful case of literary history at its best. Three friends in Havana offered through the years between 1996 and 2004 what in retrospect now feels like a live YouTube on the Trocadero Maestro: César López, Chinolope, and Miguel Barnet. I enjoyed their voices often in the company of my wife Fifi, to whom everything that survives in me for the better is owed.

This book is dedicated to the memory of a great writer named Julieta Campos; to my mother Delia Castellón de González and to Stephen G. Nichols—at both ends of a biography lengthened by the power of love.

# Abbreviations

THE TITLES of the following works frequently cited are abbreviated within parentheses and followed by page numbers, separated by a slash ("/") where applicable: the first number refers to the English translation and the second to the Spanish original.

**Reinaldo Arenas**

*BNF* *Before Night Falls/Antes que anochezca*
BAF "Bestial among the Flowers"/"Bestial entre las flores"
*OR* *Old Rosa*/"La vieja Rosa"
*PWS* *The Palace of White Skunks/El palacio de las blanquísimas mofetas*
*SW* *Singing from the Well/Celestino antes del alba*

**José Lezama Lima**

*EC* *Paradiso: Edición Crítica*
*P* *Paradiso/Paradiso: Edición Crítica*
*OL* *Oppiano Licario* (my translation)
*OC* *Obras completas* (my translation)

# Cuba and the Fall

# Introduction

## Personal Character, Authorship, and the Incidental Caribbean

There has been romance, but it has been the romance of pirates and outlaws. The natural graces of life do not show themselves under such conditions. There are no people there in the true sense of the word, with a character and purpose of their own.

James Anthony Froude, *The English in the West Indies; or, The Bow of Ulysses*

I have English, Dutch, and nigger in me,
And either I'm nobody, or I'm a nation.

Derek Walcott, "The Schooner *Flight*"

---

ALTHOUGH IT may cause quite a different impression in the reader's mind, this book is intended as an old-fashioned study of literary character in the mold of the British Victorian invention of an impossible craft: to bridge the gap between character upon the page and on stage and the evanescent ghost of authorship that placed it there. For the moment, let us note the issue of character explicit and implicit in the two epigraphs. In the one by the English historian James Anthony Froude, character gives no purpose to West Indian lives, whose lack of aim and grace seems exhausted in the wake of the predations of commerce carried out by pirates and outlaws in early colonial times. Romance is gone, only business remains. Accordingly, one could say of the West Indies that there is no business in character there except business itself. But a counterclaim about such lack of character is implicit in Derek Walcott's "The Schooner *Flight*." As argued by Paul Breslin in *Nobody's Nation,* Froude's late-Victorian moral judgment about the absence of character among West Indians is rebutted in Walcott's seafaring manifesto. Personal, national, and regional character sounds off in the sailor's poet's throat as his umbilical cord with nobody's nation is cut. The cut severs the sailor-poet from his nation, but sutures forever their scarred twin birth. Just as the sailor character of the poet Shabine remains one with the afterbirth and stillbirth of himself and his nation, the poet Walcott and his character and their nation stand inseparable.[1]

This troubled birth counts as our first encounter with personal character and the imperative of regional nationhood in the framework of an author's fugitive claim to authorship. Imperative in how much and how earthily and radically the incidental location of character is recognized even in surrendering to its national and regional fixations. Fugitive in how authorship attempts to run away from the author's own fate so fixed. The incidental nature of character to nation and region in the pages ahead shows up each time the author behind authorship hides behind his characters in search of a character of his own. The use of the masculine pronoun here falls in line with the author's male gender, but not with the deep absorption of that gender's character in womanhood, as each of the authors in question plays himself out in a sex he is not when writing in a room of her own. Roomed but unsheltered, the three Cuban authors dealt with in this book (extensively in the case of Arenas and Lezama and briefly in the case of Piñera) are queered beyond their sexual orientation by their writing in a room first rented by Virginia Woolf.

## No Judgment, No Character

Virginia Woolf tenders the wrong birth clue when she famously quips: "On or about December 1910 human character changed"; but had she been more precise—or more mistaken—about issues of her concern in London and written instead, "on December 19," her errant proclamation of the birth-and-death of something earth-changing in human character might have proven a bit Christ-prophetic: like the telepathic singsong about a child soon to be christened "José María Andrés Fernando Lezama Lima," born in remote Havana and destined to cross planet orbits with a man named Reinaldo Arenas Fuentes, born on July 16, 1943, in the even more remote-from-London Cuban province of Oriente.

In what we are about to examine next, Lezama and Arenas meet as film characters just as they frequently did outside the magic reel when they crossed paths in Havana. Also, in line with Virginia Woolf's unintended zodiac echo of character world-change in Havana, Arenas forecasts the past by populating the constellation of his own personal character in alignment with the path of Halley's Comet in the spring of 1910. He does it in the 1986 story "El Cometa Halley" by transporting the lives of García Lorca's Bernarda Alba household into exile in Cuba and casting the story in the mold of his often retold fictions about female domestic imprisonment among his own women kinfolk. In so doing, the character demographics of the Arenas zodiac house constellation aligns itself with the unmentioned and hidden influence of Lezama's birth late in 1910, whose conception in mid-March anticipates the comet's perihelion by about a month.[2]

When in *Before Night Falls* José Lezama Lima and Reinaldo Arenas finally meet on the big screen (and afterwards on DVD with behind-the-scenes commentary by director Julian Schnabel), the issue of interpretation comes to the fore. In the scene, before nibbling croquettes with Arenas (Javier Bardem), Lezama (Manuel González) imparts a quick ironic lesson on beauty and transcendence based on the short documentary *PM*, which was banned by the Revolution in 1961: "It was a simple film," he says: "just about a group of people dancing and getting drunk"; as such, "it made no judgments," but he adds that "people who make art are dangerous to any dictatorship," for "they create beauty. And beauty is the enemy," and "artists are escapists. Artists are counter-revolutionary, and so you are a counter-revolutionary, Reinaldo Arenas, and you know why? Because there is a man that cannot govern a terrain called beauty, so he wants to eliminate it. So, here we are, four hundred years of Cuban culture about to become extinct and everybody applauds."[3]

Apparently, censors in 1961 banned the *PM* documentary by Orlando Jiménez Leal and Sabá Cabrera after either finding or implanting judgments of their own making in a film that they considered counter-revolutionary. The film showed people "dancing and getting drunk" and thus bore witness to a scene of low morals and bad behavior from a past that the new political culture wanted to snuff out. But if *PM* does not judge, but simply shows things as they are, what does it show besides the judgment of censors who turned its contents into politics? Was politics of the wrong kind in *PM* only in the censors' minds? And, by contrast, is the mind of those who defend the film a clean slate without traces of any judgment bearing on politics?

Perhaps Julian Schnabel mistakes Lezama's moral intent as an author as much as he mistakes the creation of beauty as moral disengagement from judgment. His director's comments on Lezama's words take the claim of aesthetic disinterest to an extreme point worth considering. Schnabel recalls his love for Marlon Brando's phrase "they made no judgment" in *Apocalypse Now* and says he actually wanted him to play Lezama, but it did not work out.

The words of Brando's Colonel Kurtz are no small matter when it comes to judging actions so monstrous as to defy judgment: In his close-up soliloquy Kurtz tells captain Willard (Martin Sheen)—who he knows will kill him—that

> Horror has a face. And you must make a friend of horror. Horror and moral terror are your friends. If they are not, then they are enemies to be feared. They are truly enemies. I remember when I was with Special Forces . . . Seems a thousand centuries ago . . . We went into a camp to inoculate the children. We left the camp after we had inoculated the children for polio, and this old man came running after us and he was crying. He couldn't see. We went back there and they had come and hacked off every inoculated arm. There they were in a pile . . . A pile of little arms. And I remember . . . I . . . I . . . I cried . . . I wept like some grandmother. I wanted to tear my teeth out. I didn't know what I wanted to do. And I want to remember it. I never want to forget it. I never want to forget. And then I realized . . . like I was shot . . . Like I was shot with a diamond . . . a diamond bullet right through my forehead . . . And I thought: My God . . . the genius of that. The genius. The will to do that. Perfect, genuine, complete, crystalline, pure. And then I realized they were stronger than we. Because they could stand that, these were not monsters . . . These were men . . . trained cadres . . . these men who fought with their hearts, who had families, who had children, who were filled with love . . . but they had the strength . . . the strength . . . to do that. If I had ten divisions of those men our troubles here would be over very quickly. You have to have men who are moral . . . and at the same time who are able to utilize their primordial instincts to kill without feeling . . . without passion . . . without judgment . . . without judgment. Because it's judgment that defeats us.[4]

It should be clear that it is not judgment overwhelmed by what he witnessed, but judgment disavowed by blind faith and by robotic action, that Kurtz wants us to be capable of admiring—as much as he learned to admire it—in the perfect enemy he faced. Perfect inside a fatal moral circle: *because one's ultimate enemy teaches by example how to become one's own worst enemy in order to best defeat one's most perfect enemy.* A tight hermeneutic circle obtains in the form of an injunction bearing on character: *be the worst enemy of all you love and hold dear if you want to act at your own best in cloning and killing your worst enemy.*

Julian Schnabel must love Brando's words as something not as horrible and senseless as what Brando's Kurtz actually praises in the enemy horror he witnessed. It cannot be the total absence of judgment made (of judgment as the necessary condition to comprehend actions, even if blindly executed) that Schnabel's aesthetics of disinterest judges exemplary. But if he is wrong in casually comparing *PM*'s presumed abstention from making judgments with Kurtz's bedazzled adoption of the perfect enemy's terror actions, could Schnabel also be wrong in having Lezama say that the simple film actually made no judgments? It is this seemingly small claim, thoroughly dwarfed by Brando's perfect enemy analogy on "no judgment," that I wish to contest.

The absence of judgment impacts and defines Colonel Kurtz's judgment on character in the perfect enemy as it actually blunts and voids character's personal will to action and thought. One might call *Satan* such absence of character as perceived in the oldest and most perfect enemy.[5] Indeed, one aspect of Christian Satan—the absence of moral judgment and reflection—erases conscience at the core of character. Hence, when Froude removes people and character from the British West Indies, he might as well have said: *there is no conscience there* (which is a covert or at best unwitting way of saying *all there is there is Satan's*). So, in the Bermuda Satan broad Atlantic character void a pregnancy of unburied but fathomed-resting bones animates the Devil's person in Milton's *Paradise Lost.* William Spengemann sees in Satan "the seeker of [America's yet unnamed] undiscovered land," bearing "the traits that readers of Hakluyt and Purchas had come to associate with New World voyagers" ("*Paradise Lost:* Milton's American Poem" 107).[6]

On the side of character void (caused by the removal of judgment as the basis of character) a similar vacancy in conscience would be implied about the authors studied in this book if they were not interpreted and judged by their fictions in reference to religion, belief, and unbelief. For as important as the issue of their sex and their queerness is in their work, and as hard and doggedly as their sex is examined in this book, the queerness at hand in properly judging their art is written with religion, not just sex, in mind. Questions arise: Who writes in queerness—the author or the interpreter? Who raises the stakes from issues in queer sex to confronting God's judgment as a matter of conscience? Who connects God with Satan with conscience at stake?

The queer choice of "sex" over "sexuality" is meant to reject the abstract discursive numbness of *sexuality* in gender politics in favor of the more colloquial and concrete *sex*. The polemical claim is that there is character at stake in sex but not in sexuality. Furthermore, when Heraclitus is quoted claiming that "Daemon is character—character is daemon" (Fragment 119; quoted in Lukacher, *Daemonic Figures* 7), sex and not sexuality would possess character in the daemonic switch that makes this fragment notorious as the one where the ghost of *ethos* in troubled (queer, perverse?) ethics is laid upon personal fate.

## Character and Commodity

Not that anyone need worry, but imagine the characters about to be discussed in this book (Comus, Noah, Ham, Samson, Satan; Bestial, Pearl, Hester Prynne, Celestino, Old Rosa, Arturo, Fortunato, Dreamerica, Linda Snopes; José Cemí, Eugenio Foción, Ricardo Fronesis, Farraluque, Godofredo the Devil, Laocoön, Finnegan; Sor Juana, John Ruskin, Danae, Effie Gray—and the sublime anal diva known as Ynaca Eco Licario, among others) being trademarked or registered as the intellectual property of their respective authors (the case of the Bible representing a peculiar legal challenge). As such, these characters would be the equivalent of songs registered as found on a Web site (such as *www.CarlosValera.com*), so that *Bestial*—in the non X-rated version—would become a rock ballad video hero in the retro style of Pink Floyd, and *José Cemí* a New Age one-hour rhapsody upon *Vieja Trova* queer themes with vocals by Pablo Milanés in the mood of *La novia que nunca tuve.* So imagined, digital characters would grow in various directions of their own marked off from their previous seamless function in the textual production of their authors. For instance, Bestial and his nemesis—either as Old Granny or Old Rosa—could become duet musical characters in *Bestial among the Flowers,* either as the aforementioned video rock ballad or as brand-name players in a video game about the life-and-death struggle between a bestial rural brat and the mother of all mothers. So fashioned, the characters would become market brand-name icons for our pleasure as consumers.

Such marked enhancement of character within and beyond the realm of a given authorship resembles in odd fashion—if not in reverse—the autonomy that Miguel de Unamuno claimed for characters in some of his novels and in Cervantes's *Don Quixote.* Taken out of the strict textual mold in which they exist in literary fiction, the new autonomy or freedom to evolve in interaction with extraliterary players and consumers would set these digital or electronic characters at odds with the ontology of freedom conceived by Unamuno, who would have considered it insane to associate commodity status in such characters with his brand of existential self-determination and ontological anguish (conditions he refused to entertain unless related to the larger issue of belief in God and the character of God as the ultimate object of one's belief). But rather than gaining existential freedom from the determinations of authorship under which characters by definition are cast, the outcome pursued here is far less ontologically ambitious. Carrying characters to the extreme of brand-naming in our consumer use of them simply marks or indexes them in the singular. Rather than contesting their author or—as in Unamuno—rebelling against authorship or claiming it as their own, our imagined characters would simply be characters—but characters no more exclusively marked by the illusion and judgment of authorial mastery.

In this regard, two options exist in the order of illusion rarely if ever considered concerning how Miguel de Unamuno could prove his author status to Augusto, his own fictional main character in *Niebla*—but not himself, the author Unamuno, as a fictional character in the same novel. On one hand, instead of writing about Augusto's death, Unamuno could just stop writing altogether and inform Augusto in a letter that he is done as a writer. On the other, Unamuno could instead kill himself, leaving behind a suicide note to Augusto and others, including Víctor Goti, the writer of the novel's prologue and fellow fictional author of the now dead Unamuno authorship. These two rather absurd, unthinkable, though quite logical possibilities give a twist to *Niebla* and its in-the-abyss or *mise-en-abyme* structure, wherein Augusto is either "killed" by the author named Unamuno or kills himself. The over-the-abyss situation obtains once author and character communicate and break the firewall illusion that formerly separated them as long as their respective "real" and "fictional" positions were strictly segregated from each other. But once the wall is breached, author and character keep in touch over the abyss of a curiously bipolar and certainly ironic relationship. Readers who do not understand or who refuse to acknowledge the ironic nexus and binding ties between author and character are left hanging in free fall in a limbo abyss of their own making.

Yet most readers—of the kind desired and sponsored by Unamuno—will not know *where* exactly Unamuno ends and Augusto begins; but if they are playing along, they ought to know that there is irony at work in how the author and his character confront each other over the abyss of their separable yet inseparable lives. My point here lies in claiming a double meaning for "character" as just written: meaning that Unamuno's fictional character named Augusto Pérez is also an intractable part of the author's own character and that the intractable character of their relationship is not limited to the writing effects or rhetorical ironies created by the author—but are to be further interpreted in ontological terms. The issue of character is then ontological and not restricted to either individual psychology or writing practice. The writing of character reflects the question of being and the being in question, but it does not originate or invent either question. It rather raises the question of conscience to the level of being in excess of the common moral sense adduced by conscience in the grounding of character.

When Unamuno creates the over-the-abyss ontological mousetrap where he and his characters become suspended, he is framing in Christian theological and existential terms the ancient affair between character and daemon and the less ancient but rather old kinship between Christian person and guardian angel. As Ned Lukacher writes:

> The daemon as guardian of the soul, the silent inner voice, the figure of the language of moral judgment, describes a fundamental relation of language to self-consciousness which exceeds the very limits of the self-relation. . . . The topology of the daemon lies somewhere between our experience and our reflection on it, between the way we feel about our actions and our sense of how we might have acted, between . . . our "pathological" existence and our existence as moral beings, our sensible existence and our supersensible being. Conscience is a figure for the difference between the way things appear and the way they might actually be, between the being of what is or has been and what might be, what *ought* to be. Through the silent speech of conscience, the realm of moral values seems to put pressure, to exert its force, upon the frailty of merely existent being. (*Daemonic Figures* 2)

Although the relationship between Unamuno's author persona and his characters may seem pathological, their mutual embedment and reflecting consciences—placed over the abyss of a single conscience mirrored and split—translates into the artifact of representational illusion known as *mise en abyme* the ancient question of character and its duplicate companion, daemon, inner voice, and the ensuing bite of conscience. It is in this guise that psychology turns into ontology as personal character finds incidental all locations and geographies of being other than the turf where it carries on its own conversation with God and/or Christian Satan. Needless to say, the conversation is haunted by the ghost of conscience in the voice of God and/or Satan, even as the voice remains soundless.

Likewise, in the fictions by Arenas and Lezama examined in this book, the relationship between character and double—occasionally heightened to daemonic companionship—proves relentless. Part of what is meant by *Fall* in the title concerns self-proof of imperfection, wanting, fractured being, queerness of character—not only in sex, but in not belonging where one nevertheless much belongs. Though not present on every such occasion, when being as character refracts its own fallen condition under self-questioning, the *mise-en-abyme* structure remains latent. It shadows and informs the defense system of doubles as either contrarian or acquiescent surrogate characters deployed in the fictions of Lezama in order to keep closeted the author's tricks in playing the slippery morals of personification and *personation:* when the voicing and staging of character by literary fictional means stages a further transference of itself into the realm of spiritualist listening and speaking. In the case of Arenas, the over-the-abyss gap comes into play at its most invisible instance when in *Otra vez el mar* the murder plot and the involved characters (including the protagonist's wife) are deleted. In cutting off characters from the plot (who up to that point were what his own character contents were all about) the main and now sole character achieves through negation and disavowal a deletion of selfhood akin to an act of self-creation in absolute egoism.

Such a deletion bears uncanny resemblance to the author in Unamuno's God-related dealings with his characters set over the abyss of bottomless but also solipsistic conscience and beset by its own narrative devices. Threatened by solipsism, *mise-en-abyme* situations, on the one hand, cannot but reflect the ancient dialogue of character with daemon (or the one between Christian Satan's power and the personal conscience it tries to enslave). But, on the other, *mise en abyme* actually mimics the Devil's tricks by creating, not the abyss it renders visual through illusion, but the *missing abyss* that lies in how that same illusion represents a time depth of virtual historicity that it simply lacks. If the Devil lies hidden in the mirror over the abyss, then the missing but actual depth of time in the stories and histories that hang over the abyss become false—and all the more truthful in the haunted actuality of illusion.

The *mise en abyme* as *missing abyss* visual and lingual conundrum takes us to the next step in approaching historicity in Caribbean terms as rendered in the character of Robinson Crusoe foiled by the daemon ghost of Adam as conceived by Derek Walcott. In "The Muse of History" (just after the author has quoted Neruda) the "awe of the numinous" and the "elemental privilege of naming the New World" are said to annihilate history and to represent "an elation" common to all "our great poets"—whether "they are aligned by heritage to Crusoe and Prospero or to Friday and Caliban" (*What the Twilight Said* 40). Walcott claims: "A political philosophy rooted in elation would have to accept belief in a second Adam, the re-creation of the entire order, from religion to the simplest domestic ritual" (40). Implicit in such claim is the notion that the renewed Adam must still answer to God and perhaps to other polymorphous manifestations of Deity. This implies that the elation in question is also in some minds an illusion, which means that, whether as elation or illusion, the Caribbean vision so defined either transcends or falls short of what Heidegger labels *Entgotterung,* or the decoupling or vanishing of the gods from modern existence under the rule of the World as Picture: *Weltbild.*[7]

The plural in Heidegger's *Entgotterung* points at multiple gods and sacred ensembles not foreign to Caribbean religious polymorphism—although the gods he has in mind are quite alien to the region, but not to Walcott's epic syncretism. The region's various belief environments are rich in manifestations of daemonic companionship dwelling in the numinous so dear to Walcott. As alien or incidental as the Caribbean might be to Heidegger's geopolitics of Being (*Dasein*), something of equal transcendental earthiness seems implicit in Walcott's own poetics and the New World poetry of naming he defines as enraptured by elation. Moreover, Heidegger's conception of encountering language—among other altering or uprooting contingencies manifested in *Erfahrung*—as an ordeal beyond mere experience connotes the numinous as embodied in a person, or something involving altered personhood, at once alien and personal (*unheimlich*): "To have an experience with something, be it a thing, a human being, or a god, means that it goes against us, that it affects us, throws us over and changes us" (*Unterwegs zur Sprache* 149). This includes encountering home language as strange and truly uncanny—as when second Adam finds in Robinson his own being thrown beside itself in loneliness and bare life:

> So from this house
> That faces nothing but the sea, his journals
> assume a household use;
> we learn to shape from them, where nothing was
> the language of a race.[8]

## Bare Life and *Nomos* and the Daemon of Character

Perhaps the most utterly incidental character in the whole Caribbean is Robinson Crusoe stranded on the island of Juan Fernández. Derek Walcott places him there—in Adam's shadow—as if the couple roomed together inside a single though divided soul. Robinson's solitude on the island of his second birth mimics Adam's loneliness in Paradise in the absence of Eve, distracted as he—Adam—is by the knowing noises made by animals all around him. Uncharted temptations crowd the path of Adam's *rooted uprooted-ness,* a vintage uncanny condition for which Heidegger would have invented a meaty German neologism. Rooted on home turf yet uprooted to the core is second Adam the moment he shares character partnership with Robinson and plays his daemon. But who of the two pair-bonded men proves incidental and thus perhaps daemonic to the other?—who's the other's shadow, and who is the solitary dude who casts it? Second Adam must represent the autochthonous element (*nomos-grounded* and *pleasured*) as the *ruler-force* in the pair; his ancestry in colonial time warp belongs to Caliban's progeny in the just sense of being there even before there is a there there.

On the opportunistic issue of the *just* elevated to *justice*—as if moonwalking by Adam's siesta—the shade of Odysseus rises in the opening of his own poem of return (*nostos*) as "the man of many ways (*polutropos*) who was driven far journeys" and who "saw" many "cities" whose "men's minds (*noos*) he learned of" (*Odyssey* 1–4). The foursome of bare life on Crusoe's insular *nomos* niche gathers in Adam, Robinson, Caliban, and Odysseus, and the key words at the start of the poem in which Pietro Pucci underlines "the implicit idea of survival" that goes "hand in hand with the notion of *nostos,* 'return,' whose etymology means 'return to safety, to light,' and with the *polytropy* of Odysseus. . . . For *polutropos* indicates that Odysseus is the man of many travels and many turns of mind and language. The etymological connection of *noos,* 'mind,' with *nostos,* 'return,' confirms the double meaning of *polutropos*" (*Odysseus Polutropos* 49). Yet Carl Schmitt argues for *nomos* (law) in place of *noos* (mind) at that same point in the *Odyssey* as he wishes to establish *nomos* as lynchpin of the *fundamental process of apportioning space.* Schmitt remarks "that only in modern psychological distinctions—relating to 'spirit' or *esprit*—can 'spirit' be a historical and social-psychological theme that can be applied to cities and citadels" (Nomos *of the Earth* 77). He finds in Herodotus descriptions of different customs and habits and norms among diverse peoples always under the guiding maxim (Pindar's) of the ruler of laws (*nomos basileus*), and he argues that Hellenists would not have related "these differences to *noos,* rather than to *nomos*" (Nomos *of the Earth* 78). Mind (*noos*) "is universally human—common not just to many, but to all thinking people," argues Schmitt as he comes to the main grounding point in *nomos:* "something walled or enclosed, or a sacred place"—contained in the word *nomos* expressing "the divisional and distinguishing orders whose particularity necessarily would be of interest to a perspective and 'very wily' seafarer" (78). Granted that there are no high walls or citadels or enclosures visible on Crusoe's island, but the whole idea in having him there (with Adam on his second coming to earthiness and shades of Caliban with Odysseus also in the picture's ghostly pixilations) seems driven by the *telos* of building and settler development (it being rare in such circumstances to find solace in playing second to a founding *cacique*).

Redundancy conspires with incidental character in the second comer's blurring of who plays heresy to whom on Crusoe's island. So, as in the "second Adam since the fall," corruption is borne as a "congenital heresy" in human descent inside Robinson's Adamic cloning: the craftsman, the castaway, conspire as one man inside a single head, paired into infinity, yet hopeful they remain distinct as each other before their Maker:

Craftsman and castaway,
All heaven in his head,
He watched his shadow pray
Not for God's love but human love instead.
(*Collected Poems* 69–70)

There is a sense in which the pairing between the second Adam and Robinson proves dissociative, a case of multiple personalities held at bay by the spell of elated poetics threatened by the Frankenstein factor: Adam engenders Caliban, who engenders Philoctetes, who engenders Robinson, who is reborn in Odysseus. Yet this prolific and stitched-up but sutured relationship with second Adam as nonincidental main character fashions and potentially trademarks authorship in Robinson the craftsman of prose and maker of the Book where Creole Creation exudes from carpentry matter. "Like those plain iron tools" salvaged from the shipwreck and shaped by the adze into prose from the odor of "raw wood" (*Collected Poems* 92), friction from Robinson's tool applied upon virgin wood brings forth timber and scripture. Wood and word are thus shaped by Adam into a first book and further into poetry as his voice echoes back and surprises his own hearing:

out of such timbers
came our first book, our profane Genesis
whose Adam speaks that prose
which, blessing some sea-rock, startles itself
with poetry's surprise.
(*Collected Poems* 92).

From this platform out on some Caribbean beachhead survey is taken in introspection of the need to improvise in incidental prescriptions a plural character.

First, from newcomer Robinson, haunted by second-comer Adam, we may reread in his household journals how "to shape from them, where nothing was/the language of a race," in which, as Paul Breslin points out, the absent comma after "was" allows us to read that "nothing was the language of a race" or that "before Robinson's coming this people spoke Nothing, but now they have acquired English" (*Nobody's Nation* 110).[9] By such reasoning, it might well be denied to second Adam the gift that first Adam had, the ability to actually speak *nothing* while he spoke a tongue that even animals understood. But for others, either speaking the tongues that Robinson brought to Juan Fernández or the ones Juan Fernández had incidentally spoken on his island, masking seems congenital with language:

> and since the intellect demands its mask
> that sun-cracked, bearded face
> provides us with the wish to dramatize
> ourselves at nature's cost.
> (*Collected Poems* 94)

Self-creation with irony as midwife is the issue in second Adam poetics and the writings found in Robinson's journal of colonial self-imprisonment. Not autochthonous rooting but incident, as subject-noun grounded in the *incidental* and *incidentality*—a sort of indigent, incurably ironic, postcolonial condition nowadays more than ever facing compelling political claims from *indigeneity*. Yet, could it be said that, rather than questioning or opposing such claims to original grounding (as first-right apportioning *nomos*) belonging in the indigenous, the incident host (as in dissident) within the incidental should help understand that incidence existed and still exists at the very site of origins and origination? This augurs a zone of contestation and even bloodshed between primal characters on the island.

## Bare Queer

Second Adam Robinson poetics of authorship (with Adam as main ghost character and Robinson as carpenter author) soon dovetails back to Friday—once Caliban quits the island to get prosperous. It could even be argued that Friday is Adam who *second-comes* out of the hiding place where his original tenancy on primal grounds had lapsed in need of renewal—until this queer fellow showed up. For Friday, too, may have a first Adam, though not by the same name: a first Friday to whom his own indigenous life once proved incidental and perhaps quite bare—besides his naked or skimpy manner of dressing up his loneliness.

But poetics—whether elated by the numinous or relieved of primal burdens by the rustlings of incidentality—may still run into foul dealings on the issue of preterritorial law or the primordial assumption of constituting *nomos*. Aboriginal second Adam and incidental Robinson might clash to death over the power to enslave the other beyond the cocoon of character and daemon wherein they nestle as in homoerotic bliss exempt from any female presence but the Earth's bare back. The need to go forth and engender their respective breeds or races in the absence of woman puts them face to face with mythical parthenogenesis or procreation out of oneself or by a single parent only. (Even if this were not a book mainly about queer writers, the poetics of revenant Adam and parvenu Robinson with Friday's date looming over the horizon would suggest the makings of male parthenogenesis on some tropical and volcanic *Brokeback Mountain.*)

Giorgio Agamben's *Homo Sacer* provides the framework for setting up the potential struggle between second Adam and Robinson over the question of claiming and ruling the island land through the constituting powers of justice or violence, either with one force opposing the other or one winning over the other, or with *nomos* laying down norms of legal mediation between justice and coercion. The issue of a grounding threshold between the legal and the nonlegal is not faced in Walcott's poetic fable, as it need not be, considering that his recourse to Adam's second coming (itself a Christ-like event) is meant to heal wounds open and festering in the person of Caliban. In fact, behind Adam and Robinson and the indigenous presence of Friday, the sibling characters of Caliban and Philoctetes are visible in Walcott's redeeming fable. Both are distinctly marked by Agamben's corporeal signs constituting sacred and political sovereignty in the body of a man who is ruled sacred and thus designated as unfit to be sacrificed, but who is not spared from being killed:

> *Homo sacer* presents the originary figure of life taken into sovereign ban and preserves the memory of the originary exclusion through which the political dimension was first constituted. The political sphere of sovereignty was thus constituted through a double exclusion, as an excrescence of the profane in the religious and of the religious in the profane, which takes the form of a zone of indistinction between sacrifice and homicide. *The sovereign sphere is the sphere in which it is permitted to kill without committing homicide and without celebrating a sacrifice, and sacred life—that is, life that may be killed but not sacrificed—is the life that has been captured in this sphere.* (*Homo Sacer* 83, emphasis in the original)

We might regard under such perspective both Caliban and Philoctetes as characters whose lives are deemed worthless, but who go on living as prime chosen prey; eternally marked for control or extinction by intruding powers. Except that in their case, as conceived by Walcott, the life of each character—reinforced in the epic poem *Omeros* through the allegorical resemblance between them—stands apart from that of other social beings. Jointly, in one allegorical figure, but in two different bodies, Caliban and Philoctetes put their mark upon the sacred and political grounds where the presumptive social order originates in *foundational* and *nomic* terms—terms that Agamben considers far from being easily bonded (by sheer force) or mediated (by instrumental legality) with respect to the constitution of sovereignty.

Welcome or unwelcomed, Agamben's moral genealogy of sacred man forces upon the allegorical couple between second Adam and Robinson the political issue of resolving either through violence or through legal negotiation the primordial constitution of sovereignty. Regardless of what other politics may already exist in the character coupling of Adam and Robinson, under Friday's coming shadow, the question of the sovereign constitution of politics seems absent from the poetic fable created by Walcott.

In the character of Philoctetes in *Omeros,* as Paul Breslin points out, the "amnesiac" Adam-Crusoe "acquires a visible wound, as if Walcott were now acknowledging openly the formerly tacit ironies of his Adamic stance" (*Nobody's Nation* 246). I have suggested that the initial stance in the Crusoe poems attempts to heal injury and rage in Caliban's body and soul insofar as Robinson rewrites upon second Adam's reborn conscience a forward-looking and fresh-naming rapport with his renewed native surroundings (an indigenous landscape to which he comes almost Ariel-like, as if for the first time, as if being exuded by birthing from Robinson's solitary thoughts). But in *Omeros* Philoctetes is all flesh and wounded soul and soil; he incorporates affliction in his flesh and the island's earth substance, affliction of the sort attached to shame and to location. As Sophocles' hero's bow is to his wound, the foul "radiant anemone" in Philoctetes' leg is to St. Lucia's Homeric armature and soil. It embodies memories of a substance drenched in historicity—insofar as such a notion might not seek autonomy from mythic nourishment. The wound in Philoctetes casts the "antipodal odour" of "a flower, its gangrene, its rage/festering for centuries," bearing all "the unburied gods, for three deep centuries deep" and nursed by a "caverned prophetess" drawn to the wound like a "spidery sibyl," a prophet mother named Ma Kilman who almost kills her man when she plucks clean his flaming shin:

> and as he surrendered to her, the foul flower
> on his shin whitened and puckered, the corolla
> closed its thorns like the sea egg. What else did it cure?[10]

The split question between political and sacred sovereignty lies in whether such *kill-man* cure can cure the need to cure again.

On one hand, Philoctetes is all memory taught by wounds; on the other, amnesia can only exist in Adam once he is reborn from his earlier birth out of God's breath, with no memories, with no preexistence except in the measureless caverns of God's streaming thoughts. But even if first and second Adam and Robinson are insulated in more ways than one from the status of being gods of their realm, their nearness to Deity becomes enshrined in Caliban and Philoctetes. In these two bare lives sacred adhesiveness to the indigenous grounds they bless and curse with their step takes root. The character of historicity zigzags through whatever foreground zone holds together Adam's and Philoctetes' disjointed but communicant memories about who brought them where they are as if to block off from their ancient conscience the begging thoughts of a prior incidental residence elsewhere.

## Gothic as Migrant Accident

Just as if it had been by Occidental accident instead of design that Count Dracula had landed on English soil rather than on the island farther west where promise of his own native land across the forest was held out to him, beyond the pale, let us read of another such queer landing as told in Matthew Lewis's *The Monk:* "by the sudden effects, I suspected that the Abbot was stung by a Cientipedoro" (*Monk* 72). (One should hasten to add Cientipedoro's birth rights on Cuba's soil, long before it found itself by accident in Gothic Spain after sailing the Atlantic as if in reverse aboard the vessel of Columbus.) One hundred tiny legs undulating in a crawl at the end of which a poison dart enters your flesh and kills you as you turn green reads like an incident of the most awful kind, for which no vampire would be blamed.

It would be only by such an accident or by the meandering incidents of reading while becoming a writer—as in the case of Jean Rhys and *The Wide Sargasso Sea*—that the workhorse genre of modern scare- and horror-mongering known as Gothic might have anything indigenous to do with the Caribbean. But if such were the case, it would result from imported Gothic horrors having fled after confronting the cultivation of living horrors already settled on some of the sugar islands. Moreover, a genre that has given the modern world such permanent characters as the pastiche monster Adam called Frankenstein and the prosthetic God of international sexual politics and empire known as Dracula must by force compete with voodoo forces and obeah and santería offices of sacred possession and demonic healing.

Throughout this book the incidence of strong character in uncanny circumstances resonates in the space consecrated by Gothic conventions. The following passage from *Oppiano Licario* is one among many in Lezama in which the agencies of magic filter through images of persons out of character upon being invaded by the demon of character. Person-to-person character contact proves invasive to the individual it penetrates erotically as if sex were where the tissue of existence was nurtured and properly poisoned:

> When the curtain went down Fronesis resembled Icarus; he walked over river water, slept on tree tops, came near Palmiro without talking to him. When Palmiro saw the shadow of the body hiding behind the curtain, a truce ensued. Like a mirror image, the body of Fronesis entered his own ecstasy without harming him; it lent him a humid shadow. When the body was not behind the curtain, pulling at it delicately, then it became a war image, a restless trident wielded by a hidden little devil. (*OL* 153)

Nowhere else is Fronesis accountable as a vampire (a fallen solar false bird Icarus perhaps tricked by his own father into reaching the sun) or as a man who possesses other men and their wives (Palmira is included next as being much possessed by the erotic intruder in Fronesis as is her husband and virtual brother and also male double Palmiro). Likewise, the incidence of Gothic hunger for possessive companionship with other bodies and souls through erotic spiritualism is so pervasive in the fictions of Reinaldo Arenas examined here that this and other passages—quite frequent in Lezama—help create extended character kinship between their respective authorships.

Two aspects of Gothic recently studied are relevant here. Peter Brooks argues that Romanticism dealt with the *desacralization* of European culture emanating from the Enlightenment. Romanticism, he writes,

> reasserted the need for some version of the Sacred and offered further proof of the irremediable loss of the Sacred in its traditional, categorical, unifying form. Mythmaking could now only be individual, personal; and the promulgation of

> ethical imperatives had to depend on an individual act of self-understanding that would then—by an imaginative or even a terroristic leap—be offered as the foundation of a general ethics. In fact, the entity making the strongest claim to sacred status tends more and more to be personality itself. From amid the collapse of other principles and criteria, the individual ego declares its central and overriding value, its demand to be the measure of all things. (*Melodramatic Imagination* 16)

Besides the emphasis on personality and character in ready-made and archetypal images, Brooks notes with approval Devendra Varma's notion in *The Gothic Flame* (1957) concerning "a quest for the numinous" and sees in Gothic literature and its dissemination high and low the discovery that the Romantic "reassertion of spiritual forces and occult issues hidden in the phenomenal world cannot lead to the resacralization of experience. The status of the Sacred . . . as a realm of being and value recognized to be apart from and superior to man, is gone and is irrecoverable" (*Melodramatic Imagination* 20). This seems to imply that the reproduction and recycling of character in machine, typographic and technological modern culture has its beginnings in the Romantic reaction against unplugging personality from sources in magic and in the ritualized influence of personal character out to possess other characters through the infusion of erotic charisma. Beyond its machine conventions, Gothic pervades figurations of character whenever—as is the case in the fiction of Arenas and Lezama studied here—the story is told of how persons cannot go on living unless reproduced in other persons in the name of passions harmful to their own character integrity.

The crisis of character lies in the compulsion to transfer itself or migrate to other characters, compromising as a result the homeland that character keeps in the host personality where it supposedly originates. Dracula's nomad politics of parasite insertion into other lives is the winning personality in this arena. In his *Vampires, Mummies, and Liberals* (1996) David Glover demonstrates how Bram Stoker's creation altered the Victorian reliance on character in strict moral commitment to narrow self-interest, self-control, and the articulations of worldly enterprises. He mentions how John Stuart Mill proposed the science of *ethology* to study the formation of character.

A contemporary of James Anthony Froude, Mill would have recommended a sustained dose of this science of character building to West Indians, unless their very lack of character according to Froude might have persuaded Mill that perhaps the single-minded devotion to trade and business in the area meant a potently minimalist handle on the personality requirements of entrepreneurship across the Caribbean.

In any event, Dracula's business in transporting to London Transylvanian topsoil in which to nourish the blood of his ancient regional soul puts him dead set (but in complicit fantasy nurturing of harsh governing realities) against the emerging biopolitics mentioned by Glover (in the study of degenerationism, mental physiology, criminal anthropology, and psychical research). These objects of research (think of Lombroso and his impact on early Fernando Ortiz) brought what Foucault calls biopolitics into play on the side of plugging character into scientific regimes that disproved any sense of personal autonomy in impersonal social energies. Various forms of environmental determinism were established in which the idea of public character and citizenship—as self-governed and regulated by individual personality—vanished into political mythologies nowadays stereotyped as *neoliberal.* As Glover claims with insight, one of the remarkable features reflected in Dracula is how Stoker "attempts to hold on to the older notion of character, while being completely transfixed by the findings of the modern sciences and parasciences" (*Vampires* 60). Yet the obverse side of vampire magic shows to the unblinking eye of the analyst how character is forever nothing if not *the older notion of character* falsely begging for a new science of character to give it back its youth.

Although no such fascination with scientific discourses is in evidence in Arenas and Lezama, the forces of character that their literature unleashes seem inseparable from disciplinary vested interests in figuring out the inner and outer reaches of male homosexual desires and actions with obvious political consequences. What would otherwise be construed as the peculiar accident of being virtually normal in being queer turns into a potentially infinite series of incidents through which issues of conscience and character are summoned into confession.

Writing as they ultimately did at a time when revolutionary sovereignty enforced ruthless allegiance to a militant conception of national character, their fiction calls upon us to test our own sense of personal integrity in trying to understand and to voice the mysteries they dispelled and those they reinvented. Insofar as such endeavor may presuppose a transcendent view of personal character, their incidence in our lives as readers may in fact resemble the love that promises to make vampires immortal with our cooperation—if not our consent.

# Part One

## Castle Dismal

### Reinaldo Arenas as Boy and Girl

It is no small satisfaction to know that Mrs. Hawthorne's remainder of life will be glorified by the presence of these children and of her own son. I am so glad to win her out of the Castle Dismal, and from the mysterious chamber, into which no mortal ever peeped till Una was born and Julian—for they alone entered the penetralia. Into that chamber the sun never shines. Into these rooms in Mall Street it blazes without stint.

Sophia Peabody to her mother

# 1 A House in the Woods

Sophia Peabody wrote of Castle Dismal, the domestic dark cell in which her mother-in-law dwelled, being herself a former addict to the cloistered bedroom. Sophia had suffered from invalidism more than a decade earlier as a result of severe migraines and had found occasional solace in opium while bedridden. Seeking a cure, she was sent to Cuba in late 1833 to undergo treatment at the coffee plantation La Recompensa, west of Havana, where she stayed until returning to Boston in May of 1835. Besides sketching and drawing in precise detail plants and trees and wildflowers, she wrote letters in the form of a log called "Cuba Journal" by her family. As her biographer Megan Marshall writes, had these impressions been published at the time of their writing, "Sophia would have been counted among the earliest practitioners of literary Transcendentalism" (*Peabody Sisters* 278).[1] Settled, at least spiritually, above the rank of incidental tourist, Sophia absorbed the landscape of western Cuba ("the vast garden of the island") as if the earth itself had risen transcendent from the soil. Calling upon her romantic soul mates everywhere, Sophia claimed possession of the earth around her in order to enjoy it, "not in proportion to the revenue of gold it yields," but in "infinite proportion" and beyond the appropriation that only its "immaterial pleasure" pours into the heart. The highest phrase in Sophia's Cuba Earth aria comes next: "We it is who possess the earth. It was mine that morning—I was the queen of it all" (quoted in Herbert, *Dearest Beloved* 55). At a stroke of the pen, she became queen of the coffee plantation, monarch of the elevated tropics, and mistress of the unbound soul.

The grounds around the slave plantation and the receding woods beyond its six-mile radius (an expanse of landed property Sophia had never seen in her native New England) could well have served for a staging of

John Milton's masque best known as *Comus,* which was first presented in 1634 on the grounds of Ludlow Castle on the Welsh colonial border with England. Sophia must have known *Comus,* if not before reading her fiancé's *The Blithedale Romance,* certainly afterward, after reading or hearing from the author's own mouth the "Modern Arcadia" chapter, in which the girl Priscilla's possible bewitchment hearing voices in the woods on Brook Farm's fictional grounds is compared by Mr. Cloverdale (Hawthorne's mouthpiece) to "'the gift of hearing those "airy tongues that syllable men's name"—which Milton tells about'" (*Blithedale* 60). (Priscilla's spiritualist attunement to voices in the woods is thus enshrined by allusion in Milton's girl Lady's virtuous perils while she is lost in the night forest possessed by the sorcerer Comus.) Nathaniel had joined the Brook Farm enterprise in communal living in April 1841, hoping to find a space in which to write and settle with Sophia, but soon found too much human ferment around him—and too much work shoveling manure—and by the end of the year had quit Arcadia and by next July had married her and found a home in ancestral Salem.

The respective sojourns by Sophia and Nathaniel (hers at a coffee plantation in Cuba sustained by slave work, and his at Brook Farm, a commune supported by peers in utopian labor and passionate turmoil) will index in disjunctive fashion my approach to pastoral dark romance and haunted social realism in part 1. In what lies ahead new grounds are plotted for the early fiction of Reinaldo Arenas and the childhood it recasts in elements of romantic myth. Such grounds are new only as far as the connections made here between his childhood fiction and fictions by Milton, Hawthorne, Faulkner, and Dickens, and two films by Guillermo del Toro should follow a script of my own making.

But such a script or plot harks back to the ancient art of pastoral and its unfolding connections with the spirit of Nature in Renaissance, Baroque, and Romantic sensibilities: those mixed pastoral-spiritualist human echoes; the so-called Gothic or darker side of pastoral rising as sublime sensations turn horrid; and—last but not least—as the familial regression of passions to origins in pastoral gear, Christian or pagan, takes on incestuous primal colors.

The twin protagonists in part 1's evolving pastoral script are the ruins of childhood and the natural deities such ruins harbored in the child's invention of the sacred: the sorrows shed and the ghosts planted in living souls. The sex-gender of biographical character in the whole affair is mixed, even when it implies queerness. If it were up to pastoral to account for the reticulations of gender in the network of biographical character, it would perhaps declare that there are of course only two genders: young and old.

## Older Than Little Red Riding Hood

While facing nocturnal threats to his sister's and his own chastity, the Second Brother in *Comus* considers foul invasiveness by victim's consent:

> but when lust
> By unchaste looks, loose gestures, and foul talk,
> But most by lewd and lavish act of sin,
> Lets in defilement to the inward parts,
> The soul grows clotted by contagion,
> Embodies, and imbrutes, till she quite lose
> The divine property of her first being.
> (lines 462–68)

In Milton's mind, as written into the brother's understanding of his sister's imperiled chastity, the girl lies besieged by foul hunger: "savage hunger" or "savage heat" (357). She is assaulted by the sort of craving that will clot the soul and render her beastly, gross, and ghoulish—render her brute and potentially brutal to herself, even in her own (fallen) victimhood. The soul's gender in this case lies not only in grammar but in the sexual essence: in the ontological proneness to sin embodied in (and emanating from) the chaste sister woman who is at risk of defilement if her will is ever broken by allurements. Brotherly panic threatens two boys of noble parents for whose "unowned" or lost sister they search in the dark, in "the close dungeon of innumerous boughs" (193) enshrouding the wild Arcadian night wood.

The lost girl (or Lady) in the masque known as *Comus* is called "a hapless virgin" by her older brother, but she is a virgin well-armored by the "hidden strength" found in chastity:

> 'Tis chastity, my brother, chastity:
> She that has that, is clad in complete steel,
> And like a quivered nymph with arrows keen
> May trace huge forests, and unharboured heaths,
> Infamous hills, and sandy perilous wilds,
> Where through the sacred rays of chastity,
> No savage fierce, bandit, or mountaineer
> Will dare to soil her virgin purity.
> (419–26)

Yet panic threatens. It is prompted in the younger brother's imagination by the suspended spectacle of his sister's Girl Lady's surrender to wantonness. (She is a virgin girl playing an ageless and larger-than-life Woman Lady.) Comus the night prowler is out to seduce and ravish her—both girl and Lady. He, the "sorcerer" who dwells in "the navel of this hideous wood" (520), who, aided by his "monstrous rout" (530) of howlers and orgy makers

> By sly enticement gives his baneful cup,
> . . . whose pleasing poison
> The visage quite transforms of him that drinks,
> And the inglorious likeness of a beast
> Fixes instead, unmoulding reason's mintage
> Characterd in the face.
>
> (524–29)

In such fashion, Comus draws out the beast in you and carves it right on your face. As Stephen Orgel wisely advises: Comus "enables people to be what and where they want to be—and that is construed as a bad thing"; Comus, the wild thing, he adds, "in fact is a pleasure principle" ("Case for Comus" 35). Although one may not want to awaken Freud's ghost any more than Orgel gently does, the Lady will overcome her ordeal face to face with the (pagan unprincipled) pleasure (principle) before (and inside) her.

She negotiates the pleasure principle with unbending Christian mastery, while glued to her "venom'd seat" (916) and ogled and pricked by the wizard's visual wit and weapons: "Nay lady sit; If I but wave this wand,/ Your nerves are all chained up in alabaster" (658–59). She endures her triumph, if not for the pleasure of her own masochism (a supportive affliction yet unheard of) perhaps for our own sake as readers and viewers. We are—those of us who are thrilled by *Comus*—her eventual ethical and perverse witnesses in pleasure and pain. But, if so, is our pain bound with pleasure only for ourselves? Is such spectator masochism possible unleavened by sadistic pleasure, by our own displeasure turned into another's pain?

Although such questions may originate and remain within the rehearsal of Milton's masque in one's own mind, my response finds them snarled in the fictions of Reinaldo Arenas. These fictions are autobiographic and confessional, which means that setting Milton's masque in rapport with some of them yields a picture of Arenas in self-fashioning display. (But obviously not in the same manner in which such display is enacted by the author all by himself when there is no intrusion from Milton.) In being made to bind his biographic fictions with the figures of ordeal in *Comus* the written Arenas sheds skins once again. The encore Arenas becomes Comus as the central peacock character in *Comus*. His fictions of self-display represent a theater absorbed in the drama of how, once upon a time, his innocence and his malice made love to each other like two entwined serpents under Eve's enthralled gaze. It all begins at birth: a second birth, naturally.

### Earth's Birth in Dirt Hunger

At the start of *Antes que anochezca*, or *Before Night Falls*, a child of two stands in the past tense bent over the dirt floor he is tongue-licking. He recalls the taste of earth as the taste he first knew. He was eating fresh dirt with his cousin Sweet Ofelia (Dulce Ofelia) of kindred age. Although the author known as Reinaldo Arenas was his mother's only child, he grew up in plenty of sibling traffic. The dirt soil eater was skinny, but swollen at the belly, on account of the earthworms grown in his gut thanks to such eating habits. The siblings ate inside the "ranch" or animal shack, next to the house where the barnyard beasts and poultry lived. Someone among the family elders, now lost to memory, scolded the pair: "My mother, my grandmother? One of my aunts? Or maybe it was my grandfather?" (*BNF* 1/17). Then one day an awful bellyache gave the boy no chance to run for the outhouse, and he emptied himself in the pot kept under the bed where he slept with his mother: "The first thing that came out was a huge worm, a red creature with many legs like a centipede. It was jumping up and down in the pot, no doubt enraged at having been expelled from his home in such a violent way. I was deadly afraid of this worm, which now appeared in my dreams every night trying to get into my belly while I embraced my mother" (*BNF* 1/17). A primal pastoral moral on the birth pains of love for mother against the dread of engendering one's own siblings rises from the affair. Something like: *worm birth and worm fear and the fear of mothering the next worm bind together inside the only son his mother-clinging to his mother-love.* A polemical question follows: *is the receptive queer love in the descendant of the only child, so reared and so wormed, his own adult way of mothering himself in siblinghood with each successive male mate's mating?*

### Desire as Mother Illth and Son Health

In Dickens's *Our Mutual Friend* John Harmon's false death puts a mortgage on his life made worse in more ways than one by the loss of his father's inheritance. Indeed, a condition worse than death itself comes with the *illth* of Harmon's acceptance of his father's wealth only if he married a woman he has never met and would meet only after coming back to life: John's false dying would allow him to live through his certain moral death if he sold out to inherited money. Writing about the posthumous state (and estate) of the son's predicament, Catherine Gallagher applies John Ruskin's coinage of "illth" in *Unto This Last* to John Harmon's inheritance condition: *illth* means being opposite to wealth and well-being—with or without material wealth. What degree of animation, Gallagher asks, "in the formerly dead man [Harmon] would be necessary to render possible his possession of (instead of by) his money?" (*Body Economic* 87). If under such conditions Harmon came back to life, reanimating himself, "gradually working his way from dead to ill to well, could he change illth to wealth?" (87). A comparable threefold illth condition exists in the Arenas fiction. It combines the son's foundational lack of money, his father's kidnapping away through abandonment his son's spiritual or material wealth, and the illth carried in such loss when blamed by the son solely upon his mother's bequeathed resentment toward his father as laid upon him by her hatred.

The mother was very beautiful and very lonely. She knew only one man whose love she enjoyed for only a while before he ran off in less than three months and left her pregnant in his own parents' house. The three-month-old abandoned bride's "fruit of her failure" child grew up stewed in hatred for his unknown father. He used to sing a hero's hate ballad to the enthralled ears of the same relatives from whom he had learned it: "*The boy grew up and became a man and to the wars he went to fight, in vengeance he killed his father. The sons who love will do what's right*" (*BNF* 2/18). No one would have guessed that the singer trained in the primal form of love known as hate would spend his spiritual and physical energies the rest of his days bringing back to life (in illth) the father he might—and should have—killed.

Then the day came when, by the river, child and mother ran into a man on horseback who was tall, dark, and handsome. The mother threw stones at the man as he got closer, gave the child two pesos, a pat on the head, and galloped away. This would be the one and only time father and son ever met outside the fictions of remembrance. The abandoned mother never found (or thought herself that she had found) a serious man in any other man. Her grown-up author son writes: "My mother was always faithful to my father's infidelity—and she chose chastity; a bitter chastity, unnatural, and cruel, because she was then only twenty years old." Her chastity was "worse than that of a virgin, because she had known the pleasures of love for a few months and then gave all of it up for the rest of her life" (*BNF* 3/19). In the mirror of her son's desires and demands, the mother's desire was throttled by pride, fear, and inherited guilt: it was sheer illth.

In one of his mock-wisdom learned asides, Jacques Lacan spoke of the mother's role "as her desire," a troublemaking and often unbearable desire: "The mother is a big crocodile" (he said) "you find yourself in her mouth. You never know what may set her off suddenly, making those jaws clamp. That is the mother's desire" (Fink, *Lacanian Subject* 56). By contrast, in the Arenas case lady crocodile opened her jaws and dropped the kid on the earthen floor. But if it were only that easy to get a handle on desire, when it comes to the mother and her desire, it would be easy to say who or what made those jaws let go. But it is not: it is not so when it becomes painfully clear that the mother's grinding role in desire is clamped tight upon her own flesh and only as such upon her son's primal wants.

That jawed desire should be so ingrown and twisted upon itself, so deliciously hard to chew—all at once self-inflicted and imposed by others—was something that the son must have understood from the mother's unheard laments and blasted cursing (and yet also missed in his own knowledge about himself). He then dedicated a good deal of his fiction and his posthumous autobiography to grappling with the borrowed nature of desire. This is how the son's fiction turns upon what Lacan defined as *méconnaissance*, going further than ordinary neurotic self-knowledge or ignorance: "Misrecognition is not ignorance [but] represents a certain organization of affirmations and negations, to which the subject is attached . . . it cannot be conceived without correlate knowledge. . . . There must surely be, behind his misrecognition, a kind of knowledge of what there is to misrecognize" (Evans, *Introductory Dictionary* 109). In the Arenas case, not only the mother as such, but the very issue of "as such" itself implies misrecognition: as lynchpin for any recognition of oneself besides oneself—in working through oneself on behalf of others, in being author of others besides oneself.

The Arenas fiction amounts in some fashion to allowing the mother the chance to tell her tale through her son's wounded and rebellious heart. In a lover of women, rather than a lover of men as lovers in kind, such wounded rebelliousness might have produced the scandalous memoirs of the mother as a libertine, a Don Juan penned by her son's life in authorship. But, instead of the mother sharing in his lover's quest, her son takes over the seducer role all by himself and leaves the mother imprisoned (*dismal-castled*) in renegade chastity against absent father rule, as he (her son) romps with a host of male siblings: of fathered-but-fatherless sons and brothers of a kind. Through him (the only son-among-all-sons) the mother forecloses on her own mortgaged desire and leaves herself one unique son to spend the wealth—and the illth—of mothered desire in counterfeit alms of random sex and pieces of memorable literature. He is saying: *Yes, you see, there's charity after all in queer sex with perfect strangers.*

We come to a twist in the wealth-and-illth relationship as conceived by John Ruskin that proves relevant to the fiction of accursed mother inheritance in Arenas. Again, Catherine Gallagher's commentary proves useful. Ruskin, she writes, "begins his investigation into the nature of economic value with death in order, it seems, to root wealth in bodily well-being. Wealth, he concludes, is the possession of useful things by those who can use them. Useful things are those that nurture life, and those who can use them are those who are (at the very least) in a state of bodily animation. To the degree that possessions cause bodily harm [and] to the degree that they incapacitate or make people ill, they are 'illth'" (*Body Economic* 87). The example in mind is that of John Harmon in *Our Mutual Friend*, the man who must return to life in order to claim his father's wealth (now in someone else's hands) and who, by accepting money in exchange for marriage, would cause his own moral death. With so much money at hand in reward for so easy and customary a step as a marriage of convenience, Harmon's predicament in moving from ghostliness to illth-wealth seems almost offensively irrelevant to the young man at stake in the Arenas fiction of starved inheritance.

What would young Arenas have done if measurable wealth had come his way, but only upon his promise of marriage to a landowning young woman who later on became known as Old Rosa? Could the vital powers in both bride and groom have resisted the load of illth that his marrying her in spite of his own desire for men had dumped upon both of them? By the same token: could his wife Rosa's unbending dislike for sex of any sort beyond procreative agency have caused anything but harm and the turning of landed wealth into ruinous illth through their accursed marriage? What would seem like a marriage made in hell could well lead to each spouse's accommodation, respectively, to his own queer desires and her own no less queer sacred and living widowhood in illness and in wealth.

Such is the situation turned tragic narrated in the story of Old Rosa (examined later in chapter 4) as the limits of egotism and honor invested in the ownership of land take a catastrophic twist under the Cuban Revolutionary Law of Agrarian Reform, except that in the story the young queer man (just imagined as young Arenas as bridegroom) is Old Rosa's queer son, not young Rosa's frustrated and sex-starved husband—who ends up hanging himself. The power of illth in wealth binds together the young husband whose frustrated lust for Rosa ends in suicide and his queer son, the young man whom Old Rosa will try to kill after finding him in bed with a male friend. Queer desire (known as the *Arenas* literary authorship) lies in both young men, groping for health in the animating substance of mother illth.

## God Lives Eternal in Cursing

In her son's eye his mother never had much of a practical sense about childcare and thus adapted herself to her own mother's rule "at the helm of the house"—where she lived "attached" as a sort of taken-back devalued token of shame. The writer remains uncertain about her love for him at the time, but not about her anger. He writes of how she rocked him in the sackcloth hammock so hard he would fall to the floor (he survived with only bumps and scratches because the surface was made of earth and not cement).

The mother was not the only rejected or unused household item in marriage exchange. There were other unmarried and returned brides living in the house among the dirt-eating boy's aunts besides a daughter-in-law (Sweet Ofelia's mother) who was abandoned by one of the boy's uncles. At the childhood heart of this bloated Noah's Ark of ruinously communist maternal desire, there lived a nucleus of kinship, a couple of cross-cousins, boy and girl siblings born of fugitive fathers (those siblings of a kind in flight from a common father of men like themselves whose legacy they avoided like the plague).

The other and larger heart of the household belonged to the grandmother, who "peed standing up and spoke with God," or perhaps she spoke not with but *to* God and the Virgin Mary and called them into account for all the bad things that befell humans, plants, animals, and all things around her. She talked of her own beatings at the hands of her drunken husband, about their brood of eleven unmarried daughters and abandoned brides and their ephemeral husbands on the run and the pregnant bellies left behind.

The grandmother's husband spoke only to himself and never to God unless to swear to heavens. He had sired children in the neighborhood who in time had found shelter in the house ruled by his wife. And as the

Ark filled up in kindness to strangers, "my grandmother decided not to sleep with my grandfather again, and so she also was celibate and as frustrated as her daughters" (*BNF* 5/20). Old grandpa—this Noah of a man whose Christian name is never disclosed, this professed atheist who cursed God's Mother with a load of his own shit, just to see his wife fall to her knees as she often would to pray for something never granted, this reprobate man of ill fate—he too once had a mother. Cursing God (as if to put life back into Him) seals a kind of dissonant verbal incest in this grandparents-marriage version of Adam and Eve.[2]

## Ham Repeats Noah Who Repeats Ham

Old houses like fallen arks that once floated are left standing to tell the story: "There was a house. And in the house someone was dying. There was always someone dying in the miserable houses. *We are all always dying in the miserable houses*"(*PWS* 19/29). These old haunts and stranded boat carcasses might have been the site of crimes across species. For just as God's old promise of wrath before the deluge might have been soon forgotten, it seems hard to believe that no one got killed inside Noah's Ark. After all, God decided to "blot out" the race and all living things because of "the wickedness of man" and because "the earth was corrupt" and was "filled with violence" (Gen. 6.1, 11). And indeed, except for Noah and his sons and his wife and his sons' wives, "all flesh died that moved upon the earth, birds, cattle, beasts, all swarming creatures that swarm upon the earth, and every man; everything on the dry land in whose nostrils was the breath of life died" (Gen. 7.21–22). A total wipeout, except for those crammed onboard that huge balsa made of gopher wood that went nowhere but in circles and rested on a mountaintop not that far away from where home might become home once again.

No one died in the Ark, and by some traditions, such as the *Babylonian Talmud*, there were three who mated and were all punished. The dog did it and doomed himself to be chained. The raven did it and ever since he pukes his seed inside his mate's throat. Ham, or Cham, did it and paid with his own skin. His skin turned black, but that was not all. The youngest of Noah's sons built a reputation akin to that of Bacchus and Pan. And just as these pagan revelers and sex engines either evoked animal lust or were themselves animals in godly shape, Ham was black and guilty of incestuous sodomy with his father and of bestial rapport with his animal partner in sin, the raven. Sometime after the flood ended and the family became tillers of the soil, Ham caught Noah drunk and naked and forced himself upon the old sire. In some traditions Noah did not mind being so abused, and in others Ham did not stop with the father but had his way with one of his wives or even with his own mother among them.

Looking back in time into Noah's place in the Arenas tale of family origins, the view starts at the well that stood a bit far from the boy's home. Gone to fetch water one day, the son sees his mother's father naked bathing by the well. When the old man turns to him, he sees the man's huge and hairy testicles and prominent penis, and he rushes back home flustered and without the water. He then feels jealous of his mother with her father as he imagines her "being possessed by him, and him raping her with his big penis and huge testicles" (*BNF* 13/31). Later on, the boy could not tell whether he felt jealous out of desire for his mother or for her father: jealousy multiplied. He became jealous of his aunts. But also: "especially of my grandmother, who slept in her own bed, but had more right than anyone else to enjoy those testicles. Although all this existed in my imagination, for quite a long time I was obsessed with the vision of my naked grandfather" (*BNF* 15/31). In this case, Ham's actual trespass does not extend beyond stealing a quick look at his herniated grandfather's balls. Nevertheless, inside the boy's head the beholder in him behaves as Ham does in Genesis after seeing his drunken father Noah naked. Except that, in the eyes of the Arenas grandchild, seen as boy Ham, it is as if, instead of (but also besides) being raped by his son Ham, Noah himself (instead of Ham) had raped Ham's mother and mated with (or raped) everyone else in the crowded house besides his daughter. All of it happens only in Ham's spying mind, and it appears to exclude only Ham from Noah's Ham-like biblical-rampant sex.

Here lies a twisted or queered incest moral Ham Sandwich: *for just as Ham could not rape himself or freely abuse himself in Ham instead of in Noah, Ham could best rape as Noah on Ham's own behalf and, perhaps, since it is all in the mind, Noah could rape Ham, and only then, perhaps, Ham might impossibly rape himself—as Noah never could without being blotted out by God as old Noah: as the only one among his sons whom not even God would wipe out.*

Thus, on the near side of the Arenas family saga, in memoir as well as fiction, traces of son Ham splatter upon father Noah, who is now the grandfather in charge of the household in the absence of the son's father. As the sole male adult in the household, amid a cohort of females, the grandfather encompasses for the boy the long view of fathers-in-a-row. In the broad scope of biblical ageless living across generations, Lamech was a mere one hundred and eighty-two years old when he sired Noah, whose birth he outlived by five hundred and ninety-five years, and it was not until Noah reached almost that same age that he fathered his three sons. Regardless of how those immense lives of old are adapted to our diminished calendar numbers from cradle to coffin, their long shadows outplay understanding. Yet, without piling on years upon centuries, a sense of long duration may grow out of a particular ageless father's absence: for the mother of all ages is the age of the absent father whenever it is recognized as such by the son's desire. (And it goes without saying that his desire for the father continues nestled in the jaws of mother crocodile—even after her fallen son is dropped from them.)

On the mean barnyard side of splattered Ham behavior, bestiality couples with incest as a racist warning against blood mixing with strangers and blacks in the generation of Canaan, Noah's grandson. Ham's son in blackness was said to be the offspring of his father's copulation with the raven, an act of blood mixing or miscegenation against pure white bloodlines, as argued in Charles Carroll's 1900 tract *The Negro a Beast* (Sollors, *Neither Black nor White* 102). At the height of his first erotic fury, at age seven to ten, the remembered Arenas would put his pecker into any organic hole he found: dogs, pumpkins, whole trees. But it was not him but cousin Xavier who tried Ham's breeding antics on a rooster, who apparently died not as the result of the kid's penis size, said to be too small, but out of shame from being outraged by a young punk in the presence of his hens.[3] Rooster interspecies shame throws racial Ham against Noah's face as this foul act is linked with the shame suffered by the Arenas grandfather and grandmother in two fictions examined later in chapter 4, in both of which a daughter marries a black man. It proves of great interest—more so than the racial anxieties about the custody of family bloodlines—how in the humming beehive carcass of shame left by the absent father in the son's soul the grandfather occupies the paternal rank closest to the grandson in the order of family male behavior across generations.

## Myth and Memory Renewed

The Arenas mother-question begins with her father's own mother curse, with the death of her paternal grandmother. It happens near the beginning of *The Palace of White Skunks* when the man that became her father finds out his mother is dead by biting her in the ear before abandoning the ancestral house, built on what became arid and salty soil cobbled with rocks. From somewhere on the "abhorrent" Canary Islands "the old guy (then a young man) jumped to the island of Cuba" trailing after "the fatalism of islands" (*PWS* 19–20/29–31). He left home chasing the promise of Paradise across the ocean on a ship full of bootleg human cargo, poor men from many countries who tied themselves legally as chattel labor in order to escape slavery.[4]

Although it seems certain that this passage represents the beginning of the grandfather's life story in the family saga as told by his grandson, it should be properly framed at the start of the *old-man-to-young-man* transformation saga into a character myth prototype. Such a transformation, against the grain of generational time-passage (or from *old-age-back-to-youth*) actually moves in both directions at once: from the grandson's authorship present perspective toward the past, when his grandfather was as young and even younger than his grandson is now, and from that distant vantage point back toward the present. This double shuttle path from present to past and past to present unfolds in most family sagas stories. As such, the young man author and the old man character become instantaneous to each other in storytelling and mythmaking time warp. They bond together upon their common line of ancestry in the shape of a *trans-parental* figure. This is a narrative figure within whose purview (all at once) memory registers its remoteness, actuality, and currency across generations. This compound *transgenerational* figure could not be more real or testimonial than it already is in the represented fictions and woven memoirs written by Reinaldo Arenas. Its testimonial effect works by virtue of accessible vividness, a quality already and forever available to narrative in character prototypes readily found elsewhere. Such live and ever-present current value (as narrative and as testimonial impact upon imaginable lives) is anything but original. The seeming originality and freshness of testimonial narrative actually represents acts of renewal in which old modes of narration are recycled. Ancient originals in storytelling are renewed from hardwired sources in the craft of narrating across millennia and cultures.

In *Work on Myth* (1985) Hans Blumenberg explains the renewal of narrative freshness in terms of how the art and wisdom of storytelling grew through accretion as a testing process of choice-and-discard akin to Darwin's theory of natural selection. Apprenticeship in narration lasted thousands of years and became perfected as a well-tested craft much before Homer, Hesiod, the *Ramayana,* and the Bible. Blumenberg writes at great length, thus the usefulness of Robert Wallace's introductory remarks on the growth of storytelling wisdom:

> The mature mythology that we know from Homer, Hesiod, the *Ramayana,* from our informants in "primitive" cultures, and so on, must be imagined as the product of thousands of years of oral storytelling, in the course of

> which vastly greater quantities of stories, figures, and variations on earlier stories and figures were tested on audiences upon whose active approval the storyteller's success, perhaps even his livelihood, depended—and as a result of such "testing" most of these were discarded as not having the impact that the surviving material has. In other words, the stock of myth that has come down to us is the product, not of a reverent process of handing down (such as comes into play with written texts, and above all with Scriptures), but rather of an unsparing process of "natural selection," which Blumenberg in fact entitles the "Darwinism of words."[5]

Such interplay between preliterate or unrecorded storytelling, on one hand, and written collections and script-to-scriptural recordings, on the other, has ceased to be a factor in how past and present are currently collapsed in the multimedia creative cosmos in print or online. For better or for worse, the world's time zones currently at work repossess the past in illusionist depth in ways well advertised by Norman M. Klein's witty commuter's cosmonaut quip: "Driving Two Hundred Years a Day in Los Angeles" ("Vatican to Vegas" 363).

It is the unoriginality (rather than originality) of episodes as searing as the beginning of ancestral trauma in the Arenas family saga that establishes vividness and truthfulness beyond particular truths or lies. The narrative of trauma survives on the wings of its own rhetorical and storytelling powers, not because its contents could be truth-tested or corroborated. The gluing together of the often hated and heinous and heroic old man and the routinely self-punished and self-aggrandized nonheroic hero grandson stands for their mutual and reciprocal truth in authorship. This one-sided-double-faced testimony of general truthfulness in the author's voice and its lying beyond any particular truth is what binds together in a grand gesture of self-fashioning the grandfather's transoceanic passage from the Canary Islands to Cuba and the grandson's crossing in 1980 from Mariel to Miami. Novel and memoir are, in the voices and figures of allegorical and fictional representations, superficially segregated by genre from each other. Yet, glued chimerically, they speak to each other's autonomy as the one binding truth that opens up authorship to the warfare of disparate readings in ever-present partisanship. This mirror play finds its best representation in the visual perspective box known as *mise en abyme.*

## The Mirrored Missing Abyss

First, the *mise en abyme* occupies a stellar place in the art of showing off the conundrum picture of two jammed-into-each-other and in-flight reiterations of identical images tunneled deep in eternal time. Second, in related though not identical fashion, *placing-over-the-abyss* shows present actuality regressing or framing itself back into infinity and boomeranging from the vanishing past into an equally vanishing present. In line with such regressive/progressive reiteration, the recourse to allegory presently at work in this chapter is meant to come into transparent focus in the following scene of mirrored crisis. The scene centers on the passage from *Comus* in which truth-bearing Minerva wins the Gorgon's head to wear on her chest shield as part of her own war embodiment. Minerva's bosom signature goatskin aegis or *Gorgóneion* carries into the adversary's sight the awful truthfulness borne on the Gorgon's face:

> What was that snaky-headed Gorgon shield
> That wise Minerva wore, unconquered virgin,
> Wherewith she freezed her foes to congealed stone?
> But rigid looks of chaste austerity,
> And noble grace that dashed brute violence
> With sudden adoration, and blank awe.
>
> (C 446–51)

Milton depicts the Gorgon's loss of her snaky locks and "rigid looks" as well as her whole head to Minerva's chest gear as the war trophy turns into a weapon of lethal arrest. Decapitated blind brute force is now captured and embossed on the shielded bosom of warring and unspotted wisdom. Even though the technical placing of a whole image into one of its constituent parts (in *mise en abyme*) is not wholly present here, in the Gorgon's loss of her lethal head to Minerva's lethal chest, something in the seizure evokes the shuttle effect of the mirrored original (Gorgon) still at work inside the empty and now filled frame that captured it (Gorgon's image on Minerva's chest shield).

Hans Blumenberg lends great ontogenetic significance to the way in which Greek myth "tried to concentrate the world's alienating quality [*Befremdlichkeit*] into forms," and how myths translated this alienating quality "into the optical realm, and hardly ever alluded to the tactile aspect" (*Work on Myth* 14). He zeroes in on how the Gorgon sisters were descendants from the sea depths (were he locates "resistance to form" in the shapes of "monstrous gods") and were inhabitants of the world's oceanic edges. Among the awful sisters, Medusa would have concentrated in herself all the "unapproachability and intolerability" present in the archaic world's alienating quality. Blumenberg calls "the absolutism of reality" the archaic point in the evolution of human consciousness when groups "came close to not having control of the conditions of [their] existence" and believed they "simply lacked control of them" (*Work on Myth* 3–4). Material and cognitive defenses were built to ward off a reality routinely perceived as lethal. As divine actor in the drama of defending against archaic terror and rising on a curve away from such archaic thralldom to primal fears, Pallas Athena "has already moved too far from this quality in the direction of pleasantness and friendliness to culture" (15) as she wins Medusa's head for her *Gorgóneion* chest piece.

It might be added, in line with Blumenberg's speculations, that Athena's or Minerva's victory over invasive monstrousness from the archaic depths is itself allied with the enemy terrors it defeats and incorporates as trophies. In A. B. Cook's account, Athena's sacred animal past, as snake and owl, splits into two different types of cloak, one scaly and the other feathered, with the chest *Gorgóneion* on each one "wearing the *exuviae* of the animal that once she was" (*Zeus* 837). Moreover, in a typical accretion in myth stories, Apollodorus includes in his account of the war among giants (Gigantomachy) the story of Athena's killing one giant, her father Pallas, flaying him and using his skin as a shield after he tried to rape her virginity (Cook, *Zeus* 842; and Gantz, *Early Greek Myth* 84, 837n30). The archaic interspecies nature of mythic divine beings such as Athena (reptile, bird, giant deep-sea creature) mirrors in wondrous form the unbound type of cognitive overreach associated with Freud's notion of the *omnipotence of thoughts* in childhood and neurotic obsessions—as well as with Blumenberg's own adaptation of it as *the absolutism of images and wishes.*

Freud associates the play of thoughts in children, neurotics, and "savages" and underscores the psychic or magical power to annul distances: "Since distance is of no importance in thinking—since what lies furthest apart both in time and space can without difficulty be comprehended in a single act of consciousness—so, too, the world of magic has a telepathic disregard for spatial distance and treats past situations as though they were present" (*Totem and Taboo* 85). Blumenberg selects childhood psychic dominion and neurotic fantasies and suggests "imagining the absolutism of wishes and images as that of products of the caves, in isolation, at first, from the absolutism of reality," so that, "in the hunting magic of his cave pictures the hunter reaches, from his housing, out and across to the world" (*Work on Myth* 8). Yet the exemplary value of either claim (associating psychic overreach in children and patients with stone-age hunting magic) lies not so much in anthropology or archeology as in appreciating the temporal articulation of *present-ness* or actuality (of accessible vividness) in storytelling. Allied with mythmaking and invested in the management of morals in family stories as a retelling of the ordeals of surviving origins, a foreshortening of time frames or scenes inside spatial dimensions takes place: though seemingly infinite, time is boxed in and displayed in virtually identical confronting images. Time becomes—at least for a time—a live myth frozen in mirrored space. The abyss of time fits in the nutshell inside which, housed as much as imprisoned, the storytelling mind spins off her tales.

At this point (with respect to the fictions and memoirs of Reinaldo Arenas and later on when dealing with the ordeal of purity in the film *El laberinto del fauno*) the question of truth-telling being framed as mirrored images in face-off will involve an altered take on the *mise en abyme* as just sketched. A face-off takes place between the hunting war goddess of civilized wisdom, Athena, and her monster and primeval sister, Medusa. We may label as *missing abyss* the truthfulness-to-image that recedes and advances within the common *placing-over-the-abyss* of narrative illusion. The *missing abyss* illusion springs from inherent falseness in visualized and narrated temporal depth obtained in *mise en abyme.* Its illusion-bound past empties into false infinity when mirrored in the boxed-in tricks of visual perspective best captured in *mise en abyme.* Whether unrecorded or historical, the past lies beyond particular visions and envisioning; and yet, any past is not, is nothing, unless it is rendered by agencies of imagined sighting or viewing. This is the case in the fictions examined here, where all is vision and all is viewable, or else false, lame, limping in shadows and worse than a ghost that won't be seen. The past issues from a present claimant's stake in singularity as based on bold and retooled visual commonplaceness. The moral obtained from setting side by side a missing temporal abysmal depth as the picture of the whole lodged inside one of its own parts may read: *This is how it seems whenever something happens and it really looks nothing like it should ever look when it actually happens.*

But moral can turn into legend and the missing abyss into childhood-telling: the child seen or played as the older man reflected inside himself but larger than himself, yet smaller and receding and touchable as the boy whom Arenas remembers in *Before Night Falls* playing at large in the grove near the house, the space where and through which he roamed in "splendor" and in "absolute poverty but also absolute freedom," surrounded by "trees, animals, apparitions" and by people oblivious of him, whose own existence "was not even justified, nobody cared" (*BNF* 5/22). There and then (but also here and now) inside the grove, the boy one day found the fetus of an unborn child either miscarried or somehow aborted by one of his resident aunts. During his childhood, mostly spent sheltered in the grove's wild freedom, and thanks to the arts of Arcadio, the spiritualist psychic, the boy survived meningitis and falling from trees and horses. He took to the trees and roofs as he tried to live in loftier wildness, above animals and phantoms, such as the cannibal hag with giant teeth who came at him from both sides at once honed in on her next human meal. The bad angel image of hunger herself came after the boy who had learned in the grove to surpass hunger and who lived suspended and wild and nursed inside his private Arcadian games.

## The Arcadian Roost

In *The Cult of Pan in Ancient Greece* Phillippe Borgeaud reminds us that "humankind in Arcadia has not yet completely broken its links with its savage origins: with the *theriodes bios,* the bestial life that endures like a nearby frontier of sinister memory, which requires only some transgression to be revived" (19). Such is the space where "Bestial entre las flores" occupies a spot of iridescent fantasy in the early fiction of Reinaldo Arenas and more so in the cosmos in fission it generates. Idioms of forces in expansion seem appropriate to capture on paper the multiple self's fragmenting growth and the iconography of passion and strife in which it aims to absorb the viewing reader's gaze as accomplice Narcissus. The figure of the youth who in Ovid's *Metamorphoses* pays with his own life for his captivity to the flower in whose petaled flesh he was born seems equally appropriate to Bestial's agony as he struggles with the witch grandmother gardener over the keeping and nurturing and rebirth of a bed of flowers in whose cycle of renewal from death to life the child remains forever caught.

The archaic bucolic setting of Arcadia on ancient Greek soil in Western art and the pastoral genre in literature will function in this section on "Bestial among the Flowers" and the following chapter on *El laberinto del fauno* as envelope for the interrelated interpretations of the story and the film. This same ancient Arcadian frontier domain, layered over the sorcery and enchantment of the allegorical forest in which three children lose their way home in Milton's *Comus,* maps itself over the grounds on the borderland marshes between England and Wales where, in Ludlow Castle, the Earl of Bridgewater and his family were entertained by the masque, which they eventually would join at the processional finale. When connected to "Bestial among the Flowers" the embedded mapping of this dual frontier of representation deploys a joint and fluctuating landscape animated by pastoral and rural figures in dissonance. The bucolic mode shows in bold relief shapes of intense visual impact etched in arrested motion. The theatrical illusion of stilled action at peak breaking-point instances of conflict and aggression melts back into the background of rural life and its crawling routines for subsistence. The counterpoint bucolic and rural iconography of Arcadian origins in archaic Greek legend and myth combines with Ovid's and Milton's reworking of these figural prototypes as frames for the action in "Bestial among the Flowers" and its imaging of character in particular.

The paired wild boy called Bestial is, on one hand, the heads-or-tails flip self of the boy self from whose viewpoint the tale is told, and, on the other, he (or it) acts as the zero-sum equalizer of their game of turbulent mutuality. Their *doppelgänger* hookup is turbulent in strict rapport with motion and rest, wakefulness and dream, aggression and passiveness, freedom and bondage. But this bipolar duet *pas de deux* between the bestial male self and its human brother defies the dualism that sets it in motion and renders it viewable, a *viewing* notion used here as distinct from visible, stressing the *mise-en-scène* effect of staged iconography. Set side by side with *Comus*, what happens in "Bestial" is seen here as a masque that would be staged before the extended family of the boy, his mother, and grandmother—with the boy Bestial acting as a descendant of Comus himself: *Bestial among the Flowers: A Masque Held at a House and Surrounding Woods in Perronales, Oriente Province.* Such a theatrical stage device serves as climax in Reinaldo Arenas's first two novels. In both *Celestino antes del alba* (*Singing from the Well*) and the extension of its protagonist's life from childhood to youth in *El palacio de las blanquísimas mofetas* (*The Palace of the White Skunks*), the family ensemble cast performs a play in which the boy/youth is caught as both witness and accused scapegoat victim on trial. What the satyr play was to tragedy in ancient Greece this type of trial play masque is to plot at large in both these novels. The masque element comes into play in inverted fashion. Rather than celebrating and performing itself before its live constituents, the family revels in its passions, hatreds, and aborted loves and mixes them up into a kind of macabre epithalamium or wedding feast in ritual awareness of death. The masque becomes a widow's witch sacrifice as well as her family's ensemble wedding to the judgment trial of its own past and any future departed progeny. Though live and played by the living, the Arenas boyhood masque takes place among the departed.

William Kerrigan claims that Milton "inscribed three images of himself in the Ludlow masque" and that in such "cryptography" he becomes "a certain shepherd lad"—and also the Elder Brother as well as his sister the Lady (*Sacred Complex* 38–42). But Stephen Orgel finds it "tempting to think that as the Attendant Spirit was written for Lawless [the Masque's musician] to play, Milton wrote Comus for himself" ("Case for Comus" 31). Since it is impossible in theater, though not in film or video, to play both the boy's role and Bestial's, Reinaldo Arenas would be more than just tempted to play the feral beast boy visitor from Arcadia in his own heads-or-tails masque.

*Heads:* "With Bestial, things were different. He could make his eyes change color; he ate quails raw; one time he told me: 'Get down on all fours and I'll show you what'll feel good.'" (BAF 321/123). (Bestial hated the boy's grandmother as did the boy himself; he climbed tree tops, said he could fly, blew up live cats in midair, bathed himself in the river, peed in the cistern tank, and knew how to read.) *Tails:* "Without Bestial, things are the way it looks like they have to be. Nobuddy can't read or write a thing; Nobuddy doesn't climb up on the roof of the house or hold wasps' nests in their bare hands; Nobuddy is got no eyes (not even eyes that are just of one color); Nobuddy doesn't eat lizards; Nobuddy's nobody" (BAF 321/123). A figure of primal animation, Bestial puts life into things and destroys them, as when he walked into the house and the house shrank like a dog about to be whipped; or when he dropped from the hands of the man who brought him to the boy's house and left just as the brat ran into the dinning room and grabbed the kerosene lantern and smashed it on the floor. The boy's grandmother took him by the neck and held him high like a dead chicken. "'Bestial is his name'"—said the boy's mother, who had heard everything about the orphan from voice noises inside the talking well. Prompted by her words, Bestial asked the boy with a look of disgust if he too had a mother and vomited before hearing the answer and said that he killed his own mother a long time ago. (The report about Bestial's mother's death comes from the boy's mother, who says that it was her sister Angelina who hanged herself.)

Bestial's tale is a story of generation emerging from decay. It is at heart the story of three-women-in-one and one-boy-in-two and of their threesome combined into the shapes of countless lives held over the abyss of time—time flattened into a short season of strife between the manifold threesome of grandmother-mother-boy who fight over the care and command of a plot of marigolds in whose fate their own lives (and the grandmother's and Bestial's in particular) hang in the balance.

The tale of generation combines story shreds from Noah's Ark and the Tower of Babel. Bestial speaks in nonverbal or extralingual ways outside or beyond his mother's tongue. When he snores he exhales (into the grandmother's ears) the grunts of a frog being swallowed rear end first into a snake or (in the mother's hearing) the bird-singing of a train's brakes and the cuckoo's call. His mouth mimics the housebound sounds and noises of nature and machine amalgamated into a jubilant mimicry of chaos and lingual crossbreeding. As Bestial snores, outside the Ark house the deluge rages on and lightning blasts the ivy on the porch and burns the mirror in the bedroom and he hears the thunder's waking call and decides to run to the roaring river. He rides the current jumping and gamboling from floater to floater with and against the flow until he drowns. But when the boy who witnessed the death of his daemon playmate returns home with the news, he learns from the women in the house that Bestial has been asleep in his own bed for hours. And when the boy goes in to check on snoring Bestial and wakes him up, he jumps out of bed and runs into the women who want to hurt him, but he pulls them by the legs and they fall to the floor.

The animation action loop (*from bed-to-river-to-bed and from snoring-to-swimming-and-drowning-to-snoring*) encircles within its round trip from Ark to Deluge the absent presence of the combined boy's father. (Namely: the father who abandoned the boy and his mother and who was seen only once in the boy's life crossing the river, and the father whose flight might have cause Bestial's mother's hanging.) The absent presence of that combined father in the dual boy is set against the present absence of the mother who hanged herself and who is embodied in both the terrible avenging grandmother and her daughter. The combined father ghost roosts himself into bed companionship with the lost boy and his found but lost sibling.

The women who emerge from the boy's confession to Bestial seem like the same person split in two generations sitting at each end of the table. The boy's grandmother is sly and brutal, the mother just brutish. His mother is a lump of earth upon which her own mother spits or else plants a tree. When young, the spitting gardener mother was a witch who brewed love potions and was said to have been in bed with a singing crocodile. She might have buried a pot of gold coins under a ceiba tree, but her sole treasure now and until death is in the marigolds she guards from dawn to dusk:

> The outline of my grandmother still hanging over the marigolds would be something wonderful then, and it would have the strangest effect on me; it looked like she was actually spilling right onto the flowers, like some strange

> kind of tree sentenced to grow upside-down, with its leaves and branches in the mud and the dark, dark trunk sort of fading out up into the sky. In a little while my grandmother would come into the kitchen; then we'd light the oil lamp and she would pass out the plates, with her hands still covered with dirt. There would invariably be a moth from the leaves outside stuck in her hair, and it would fall in the soup. (BAF 329/133)

The smell of the marigolds lifts and floats from the surface of this painting-in-motion in the style of animation. As when, one evening, already after dusk, the boy returns to the plot to absorb the emanations of marigold essence rising from the ground into the night air like green firebugs and the painting-in-motion settles into another instance of arrest: "Just then, without knowing why, I looked around: like a bird with great motionless folded wings, there stood my grandmother, right behind me, wrapped in the darkness and a sheet. She stood there and held her eyes on me for a long time. On her face and all over her body I thought I could see great sadness, though it might have been from the effect of the night. 'Child,' she said, 'you go to your room and go to bed'" (329/134). Unsure whether the scene had been a dream or not, the boy returns to the plot the next night and smells the scent again but sees no emanations of light from the soil. He stays in vigil all night, and when he tries to rise up at dawn the grandmother holds him down with hands made of earth and tells him that she might have to kill him: "'I believe I'm going to have to kill you'" (330/134). The lethal struggle sets in and for a moment the grandmother's death threat aims her guardianship of the marigolds at her grandson rather than Bestial, but the heads-or-tails game between the two boys tied up in dual personhood begins to collapse: her menace has made them interchangeable.

Their fusion is sealed during a week spent away from the house alone in the woods. In what will become a mute dialogue of telepathic oneness, requiring no speech between them, Bestial begins asking questions about the grandmother, it being possible to surmise that his voice may also be the boy's own, as the latter remains silent while answering the questions posed by his bestial soul mate. As it turns out, the secret that Bestial wants to unlock will allow him to destroy the enemy gardener who controls the marigolds, as nearly happens when the woman begins to shrivel and die like a withering plant resting next to the flower bed. But before her death-by-nature and the fire that seems to incinerate her like a burning witch, something else happens, a species of birth that takes place as if twice in the order to time: the birth of Bestial from the grandmother.

The birth scene unfolds as the boy and his mother rush back to the house after hearing the grandmother yelling and find her in apparent pain caressing her dress and putting on a shoe. A strange hunch makes the child play the scene of the sitting old woman over in his mind—as if he had direct command over it—and now he uncovers the unseen or screened-off gesture from before, as the grandmother's hand reaches down and comes to rest on "that unmentionable area of her body" below her underbelly and between her legs (334/140). The dirty war between her and Bestial over the marigolds centers on two navel points: the flower bed itself and the old woman's body, oddly capable of birthing as if sprouting another offspring. In her struggle with Bestial, as he tries to uproot the flowers, the woman turns into a beast who tries to crack his head with an ax, just before the birth scene recurs: "I watched my grandmother gasp and breathe deep and put her hand on that part of her body again, like it was that part of her body, and not the flowerbed, that the flower had been pulled out of" (335/142). Near the end, both the grandmother and Bestial become in the boy's mind foot soldiers and "slaves to a higher power"—a power embedded in the flowers and ultimately in Nature herself (343/152). The powers of generation and decay limn their original and terminal shape in the seamless yet gnarled life of Nature herself illuminated and consumed by fire: "Just as the fire was beginning to be the same all over, and the whole country around had turned into one huge monumental pyre, Bestial loomed up out of the flames like some triumphant demon" (343/152). Both enslaved foot soldiers—the witch woman and the feral child—prove immune to fire in the same measure in which their ability to rise from its ashes eternally and cyclically consigns them to it.

When the grandmother emerges from her shriveled marigold death and rises from her own cinders, she carries a book and places it next to the stalk of a new nascent plant. The book acts as bait as Bestial becomes absorbed in its reading. Absorbed and consumed, because Bestial grabs the book as it lies on the grown plant and reads and reads squatted over the flower bed as he begins to change shape and substance and becomes a flower plant: "his body had turned into a long slender stalk pushing up out of the ground . . . his arms were two bright shiny leaves . . . his head was getting soft and satiny like petals" (BAF 346/156). The next morning, the boy reader consumed in reading and turned into a flower will be eaten: "I watched her, bathed in the morning brightness, plunge her hands into the marigolds like a thirsty horse dipping his muzzle into the clear quiet pool of water. With all her might she grasped the stalk the book was still leaning up against and with one tug she pulled the flower in the air for a second, showing it to the sun. And then she brought it to her lips and with perfect aim she popped the flower in her mouth and swallowed it in one gulp (346/156). With the witch woman in digestive and gestating arrest, the boy picks up the book that was not swallowed and takes it down to the river, walking over the cinders and mud of the burned woods, and throws into the stream.

But the story is unfinished, as the spiral cycle is about to restart. The boy returns to the flower bed and acts as if mimicking the grandmother's gardening duties, but this time with cannibal fury, as he uproots the plants as if to eat them, and then hears his mother moaning and sees her reaching for that "unmentionable part of her body"—as it happened when her mother seemed to be giving odd birth to her grandson Bestial. It is then that the boy remembers and understands the words once uttered by Bestial: "kill her before she kills you" (BAF 336/143). But why kill her? Why kill the mother in the grandmother and the grandmother in the mother? Here we come to the next moral: *because killing becomes the son's duty the moment he hears from his mother that she loves him and that if he were to disappear or die she would kill herself. In response, the son aborts the death pact with mother-love, as if he preferred to owe her death to himself and his own murder of her, rather than to her and her suicide.*

It is the mother's abnegation and disavowal of herself in her love for him that the son truly hates forever. His own disavowal of that fibrous bundle of love and hate will clear the way for his love of himself—best felt in symbiotic company with Bestial. For it was his beastly alternate boy-self who brought him the freedom to experience hatred for the gardener grandmother and eventually for his own mother through his heads-or-tails actions with the wild boy. They learned how to cry together "in one single rhythmic and harmonious sound" (337/143), and with that they built up a "tiny happiness" that climbed over the world in lordship of it and went up so high it ended up "instalándose entre las estrellas [installing itself among the stars]".[6] The word for such installation in ancient Greek myth and afterward is *catasterism*, an action in which the starry heavens are peopled, as it happens over Arcadia when Arcas (Arcturus) and his mother, the nymph Kallisto, are turned by Zeus into stars.

When the boy feels that he is returning to his companionship with lost Bestial, he hears his mother's horrible scream, "que provenía como de un tiempo despoblado" (*Termina el desfile* 158), which came as if from a time unpopulated or without people—and in Thomas Colchie's translation: "some prehistoric time before anybody was alive" (BAF 347). It is a time as old as Noah's was before it was "blotted out" by God's punishment, a time as old as the origins of Arcadia and of humankind itself. It is an abysmal womb time of sacrifice and child murder, as when a boy named Arcas or Arcturus went hunting and killed or mated with his own mother, who had been turned into a bear, and both of them were, by the mercy of Zeus, her ravisher of old, turned into stars. And so they remained perhaps unseen, either as two people or a single one: in Arcturus, the brightest star, watched by many eyes within and without the fictions of Reinaldo Arenas.

# 2 Pan's Labyrinth

In the brook beneath stood another child,—another and the same.
*The Scarlet Letter*

. . . the radiance and innocence of reinstated infant divinity.
John Ruskin

BOTH HAWTHORNE and Ruskin see two children where there is only one. In the first case, the girl Pearl sees her reflection in the water, and the adult writer who tells her story sees her twice: as one child other than just either as herself or as her figure in the water. There are two Pearls in the adult's sight besides the girl who bears her name and the reflection she casts in the brook. That Pearl sees herself in the same manner is highly probable, as is the chance that she might have encountered in the forest, in a story untold by Hawthorne, a wild mate alternate companion much like the one the Arenas boy finds in Bestial. Pearl has after all met someone in that same forest, a black man, whom we as readers may well recognize as none other than the Devil.

Although not as obviously, Ruskin, too, sees at least two children. He sees the radiance of the lost child restored, and he also sees in that fashion a child besides the one once upon a time known in childhood.

In moving further along in our surveying of the imaginary sphere of refuge and imprisonment and double exposure named Castle Dismal, we will examine next two sibling films by Guillermo del Toro, *The Devil's Backbone* and *Pan's Labyrinth*. We will examine them in reference to Milton's *Comus* and the death of innocence and what may or may not survive the ruins of childhood under the spell of adult pressures and worldly cruelties. These moral issues find common ground in the Arenas fiction to which we will return in the next chapter. In seeing double exposure (besides refuge and imprisonment), we become aware, as already examined in the Arenas childhood's rural nest, of how feelings of entrapment in the mutual and embroiled lives of children and adults can create the exposure in double shape of the young self to the surrounding world.

A third realm besides del Toro's films and Milton's masque also related to the Arenas fiction is found in the Victorian environment of literature written for children and constructed childhood where Ruskin lost and recovered a divinity he could not, in saneness or in madness, find anywhere else. It is not, however, any children's fiction in particular that will occupy our attention. We will look into a character construct within Ruskin himself being haunted "phantomwise"—as Lewis Carroll said he was by the living memory of a certain dream-child. We will see through John Ruskin's narrative eyes in the role of cinematic ghost as if he were watching with us scenes from these two films—films seen, then, as if from the past and in that manner screened in the present. For, with or without any given foreknowledge of film, Ruskin's vast imagination created mazes in writing and drawing, and he would certainly have pricked up his ears like an old faun had he heard of a girl being lured into a labyrinth by a creature resembling Pan, the god on whose hairy shoulders Nature herself in her boundless desire was made to rest.

## Pan at Large in the World Wild

Among the pagan and largely vanished gods Pan stood the largest and most boundless in Milton's sight:

> The Birds thir choir apply; airs, vernal airs,
> Breathing the smell of field and grove, attune
> The trembling leaves, while universal *Pan*
> Knit with the *Graces* and the *Hours* in dance
> Led on th' Eternal Spring.
>
> (*Paradise Lost* IV.264–68)

He wrote paradoxically about the gap (and the joint) between a wild shepherd (hoofed) god sexually conjoined with animals and nymphs and the newborn Christ at rest in the manger. The universal Pan emanates from the doctrinal mind's need to have such a double creature in both bestial and sacred places at once, as in Milton's "Nativity" ode:

> The Shepherds on the Lawn,
> Or ere the point of dawn,
>     Sate simply chatting in a rustick row;
> Full little thought they than,
> That the mighty Pan
>     Was kindly com to live with them below;
> Perhaps their loves, or else their sheep,
> Was all that did their silly thoughts so busie keep.
>
> (lines 85–92)

Milton was well aware of the other, wild and brutal god of herdsmen, when he pictured him in the person of Christ at birth. This was not original, since in Christian allegory the *Deus Faunus* had been typed for long as Nature in her primordial Love-and-Lust. This is something to keep in mind when hearing Pan speaking to the Night about the meaning of allegory in Pedro Calderón de la Barca's sacred play *El verdarero Dios Pan:*

> Allegory is nothing more than
> A mirror that translates
> What is with what is not;
> And all its elegance rests
> Upon the copy on the slate
> Being so much like the original
> That looking at one
> Seems like looking at the other,
> So evenly runs now
> The look-alike look
> Between what's alive and its own cast.[1]

Although faded in most minds, the thrill of translation here lies in living up to both live copy and live original. Or in Pan's case, keeping both pagan and nonpagan divine persons alive and kicking. For instance, Andrea Alciato gives us the essential cast or stamp behind Calderón's learned though, one presumes, biased goat speaker: "The people reverence Pan (that is to say, the nature of things), a man who is half-goat, a god who is half-man. He is a man down to his loins because the virtue implanted in us, rising from the heart, is seated in the high citadel of the head. Below, he is a goat, because nature continues us through time by means of copulation, like birds, fish, brute animals and wild beasts. Because this is common to other living creatures, the goat is the sign of lechery and bears the open marks of Venus. Some give wisdom to the heart, others to the brain. No moderation or reason rules the baser things" (*Emblemas* 98). Indeed, when it comes to the divine goat, the loins rule, and to their reign we owe all we owe to ourselves and more.

Pan's blessings are mixed the wilder things get. Philippe Borgeaud, the foremost scholar of the archaic Lord of Arcadia, finds in him "the symbolic embodiment of the repressed," and he adds that "everything man flees and rejects in order to distinguish himself from the animals makes him like to the gods"; thus, Pan's myths seem to say that "if we refuse the beast, we shall never know to resemble a god" (*Cult of Pan* 54). This is different from claiming that Christ's divine and human dual nature and his boundless kindness toward all creatures on earth makes the Lord Jesus in some sacred fashion bestial. The human-beast borderline stands unbroken since Eve's interspecies errant and disobedient knowledge of the snake's counsel. What separates the oldest brute and sacred Pan from the Christian version of his universal rule over humankind in nature cannot be breached except by doctrinal fiat and in disobedience of the same ancient wisdom thus tapped and adulterated. When the "Truest God Pan" proclaims Calderón's doctrinal universal truth on the workings of allegorical copying-in-likeness, the god speaks of his own makeup wherein the beast has been lost in translation. And when Ruskin summons himself and others to rejoin "the radiance and innocence of reinstated infant divinity," it may well be asked if childhood's divine innocence in this instance encompasses energies consubstantial with Pan's sacred beastliness.

A twisted (if not queer) answer of sorts lies in Pan's double childhood genealogy. For as the ordinary child may split at least once in childhood's sacred precincts, gods may manage even better, as they often live their infant and early growing years all at once in places somewhat remote from each other. Pan's double childhood location places him in the mountain regions of Arcadia and on the island of Crete. In Arcadia, he is the son of Zeus and the nymph Kallisto and twin brother of Arcas, the eponymous founder of the ancient realm. In Crete, he is established as son of Cronos and thus as contemporary and child-mate of Zeus and as the love child of the god's Cretan breast-mother, the Aix or she-goat monster later on assimilated into Amalthea and her custody of the horn of plenty. In rural Arcadia, Pan is son of Zeus and twin brother of the ancestral hero whose name is given to the region, while on the island of Crete, he is both half brother and foster brother of Zeus, who happens to be the only Olympian survivor not devoured by Cronos (the Mighty Father and god behind the breast-feeding affairs of the goat-mother Aix/Amalthea).

In the mountains and valleys of Arcadia, Pan and Arcas grow up entwined in mutual kinship with animals. Pan the herdsman's brute intimacy with his own animals is notorious. His sexuality, writes Borgeaud, "seizes whatever is available, or becomes perverted. It is by definition perverted and wild. The poets call him . . . 'unlucky in love.' . . . The Shepherds practice two expedients that they share with Pan, who may even have invented them: onanism and bestiality" (*Cult of Pan* 76). For his part, Arcas the hunter will chase his own mother Kallisto, not knowing that she has been transformed into a bear. In some accounts the hunter kills the nymph mother who was turned into a beast, while in others he mates with her.[2]

## Childland Postage

In what it partakes of sacred affairs, the magic found in and through children's literature by adult authors and their readers of all ages enters a fractured realm sutured by balms and tricks of perspective and by the alchemy of pristine lying. What binds together Hawthorne's Pearl into one double child lies beyond and yet almost on the same spot with her as she is observed by her allegorical fiction maker in Hawthorne. Whatever double dealings in play and games Pearl may have treasured and feared, in company with her live reflected stamp in another child's embodiment, the author who devises her cannot exclude himself from knowing. He knows through her own knowing, as if he, too, were a conspirator in the girl's twin character. This is far more complex than saying that childhood's double nature is mainly the adult invention of someone who conspires with innocence against acts of defilement and ruin caused by aging time.

The microcosm postage stamp for children's literature as *adult-authored-for-the-adult-child letters* may be found in *The Scarlet Letter*'s chapter sequence "The Child at the Brook-Side" (chapter 19) and "The Minister in a Maze" (chapter 20). Hester Prynne and Arthur Dimmesdale have met in the forest in Pearl's company after Hester has removed the scarlet letter from her chest, worn in pride and shame for some seven years. When Pearl is summoned to join them from across the pool formed by the brook, the girl refuses to come across and the "sensitive minister" tells Hester that "'this brook is the boundary between two worlds . . . thou canst never meet thy Pearl again'"; and he asks, might it be that she is "'an elfish spirit, who, as the legends of our childhood taught us, is forbidden to cross a running stream?'" (*Scarlet Letter* 133). It is the mother, from whom the child seems so suddenly severed, who divines Pearl's reason for her refusal to join them: "'Children will not abide any, the slightest, change in the accustomed aspect of things that are daily before their eyes. Pearl misses something which she has always seen me wear'" (*Scarlet Letter* 134). Put otherwise, the child misses the One Letter of her Universal Literature; she misses the Symbol learned outside school training as if from Mother's Law as a rebellious modulation of Patriarchy. She misses the *A* of Allegory in the Gothic character in whose sole hieroglyphic rubric Shame is embroidered with Pride—its occult moral and religious twin.

Arthur Dimmesdale leaves the meeting in the forest infused with mad pride, in full-blown allegorical exuberance. He walks the streets of Salem having to represses his wish to scandalize each parishioner he runs into with news of the most shameful and blasphemous lies—shouted and whispered in their ears as if such blasphemies were his own heartfelt message of moral truth. His repressed confessional outbursts amount to the only moments of outright humor in the haunted novel. The humor is produced when a sinful adult man reenters the maze of childhood and leaves it and feels like releasing upon his suddenly older adult brethren from the outside world the energies of untrammeled eloquence he found there, in Childland. He becomes a postal emissary, a letter in his own adult flesh postmarked from the land of children. That such temptation to regress to "the innocence of reinstated childhood divinity" should come on the eve of Dimmesdale's delivery of the Election Sermon and his subsequent public shame and dying confession of guilt, adds the last note of closure to Arthur's sudden return to and resurrection from the realm of Childland.

## The Devil in Gothic Illth

As we enter Gothic latitudes, a basic issue of proportions and power comes into view, as when we first hear of Mr. Pontifex's sizable almighty spouse in Samuel Butler's *The Way of All Flesh:* "His wife was said to be his master; I have been told she brought him a little money, but it cannot have been much. She was a tall, square-shouldered person (I have heard my father call her a Gothic woman)" (33). The impression of a cathedral-size wife seems inordinate to the husband's fortunes and of such disproportion to his domestic means as to implant in them the divine and demonic illness of the grotesque.

Such confusion between Godly rule and Devil craft informs the view of childhood treasured in the Gothic legacy of spookiness exploited in the two films we are about to review assisted by John Ruskin. One issue of the grotesque we will keep in mind is the disproportion between passions and fears in children as enshrined in the Gothic and the adult want for such thrills that animates their renewed and retro viewing in fiction and cinema.

In his director's commentary on *Pan's Labyrinth,* Guillermo del Toro introduces the film as the "sister" of *The Devil's Backbone,* and it is along such sibling lines that both films will be examined here: not exactly bloodlines in strict kinship terms, but cruel lines of spilled blood and of blood gestating in the womb before birth and still boiling up in ghostly flesh after violent death. From the theme of children's abandonment during the Spanish Civil War—whether by dead parents or desperate ones—we will glimpse back in time to the Middle Ages, through the

Gothic rebirth moment in history which del Toro foregrounds, in allusion to Giovanni Battista Piranesi's *Carceri* and Horace Walpole's *The Castle of Otranto*. And then, from the modern Gothic Romantic milieu haunted by unquiet ghosts and its Victorian aftermath, the abandonment of children will be reset in reference to the widespread custom of casting off unwanted progeny to the kindness of strangers during the European Middle Ages.

Such historical travel in time will allow us to hit a sort of ground zero for the connected themes of affinity between house and womb and architectural ruins and ruined ghost-bodies, which the evocation of Gothic horror plot effects and decor in *The Devil's Backbone* already entertains as virtually medieval in origin. But the idea in that film is not to turn to medieval themes for aesthetic pleasure, but rather to frame the question of ghost fears and unsettled deaths in the old domain of Christian religion and its attendant superstitions as presumed remnants of the medieval past. In addition, beneath the universalism of recycled medieval themes, the world-reach of the modern Gothic horror machine, and the worldwide politics of the Communist cause against fascism during the Spanish Civil War, the film unearths the living fossil of a particular ghost nurtured in soil and nation. It should then be asked: in what sense and manner are the two most visible personal ghosts in the film natives and nationals of fractured and invertebrate Spain? And how are the soil and its nation housed in the orphanage still haunted by ghosts?

It is discovered at the end of the film that the epigraph and epitaph words that frame the action have been spoken by the ghost of Dr. Cáseres, an Argentine physician, child mentor, and Romantic memory teller of songs and poems and custodian of the ghastly folklore of the unborn. A "man of science" by his own description, he names the film by retelling the folk belief of how the spinal deformity known as "the devil's backbone" comes in punishment against the accursed population of *nobody's children* who should have never been born. He rejects the people's superstition and attributes the congenital defect to poverty and disease and then proceeds to drink the rummy spiced liquid called the "Water of Limbo" in which the fetuses are preserved. He does this to scare away the orphan child Carlos from believing in the ghost that the boy and the film viewers have seen and whose presence the doctor firmly disavows with a touch of bawdy irony as he swallows the mildly cannibalistic tonic to restore his potency. However, his earnest rejection of the devil's backbone superstition (supported by the scientific knowledge that the birth defect is caused by humans and not by God's design or the Devil's signature) comes from the same mouth that at the start and at the end of the film speaks to the living enigma of the ghost's refusal to forget the dead as most people who are not ghosts actually manage to do—people who, in getting over the dead here and there and everywhere, could possibly be implicated in the long-term historical abandonment of children and child-murder.

The enduring human ability to outlive or leave mourning behind is not unrelated to the infinite capacity to give birth to departed persons in their local and haunting shapes (persons commonly known as ghosts). The doctor's final ghost words outline a credo or minimal elegy for the otherwise obliterated and local singularity of each and every dead person who has not yet managed to leave the scene: "What is a ghost? A tragedy doomed to repeat itself time and again? An instant of pain, perhaps. Something dead which still seems to be alive. An emotion suspended in time. Like a blurred photograph. Like an insect trapped in amber. A Ghost. That's what I am."[3] Earlier, he has diagnosed Europe's ills, besides those for so long present on "superstitious" Spanish soil: "Europe is sick with fear now, and fear sickens the soul" (scene 11). Dr. Cáseres is portrayed—and so named in del Toro's words—as a left-wing revolutionary and a Romantic who does not dare to take up arms. Even before turning into a ghost wielding a shotgun, the learned physician would have scoffed at the trivia of the earlier published term "hobgoblin" ("'a frightful hobgoblin stalks throughout Europe'") being dropped from the final English version of *The Communist Manifesto* in favor of *spectre* (Linebaugh, *Magna Carta Manifesto* 144).

As an armchair political philosopher of material ghostliness, Dr. Cáseres would have found further amusement in Peter Linebaugh's comments on the first English translation of the *Manifesto:*

> The translator was Helen MacFarlane, a Lancashire Chartist, whose choice of words derived from the forest commons—"Hob" was the name of a country laborer, "goblin" a mischievous sprite. Thus communism manifested itself in the *Manifesto* in the discourse of the agrarian commons, the substrate of language revealing the imprint of the clouted shoon [those who wore patched shoes studded with nails for rough ground work] in the sixteenth century who fought to have all things common. The trajectory from the commons to communism can be cast as the passage from past to future. (*Magna Carta Manifesto* 144)

In the film, the barren and dusty lands that encircle the orphanage render testimony to the void left by the flight of fruitful labor, an absence in turn mimicked by the remnants of industry seen in the ragtag menial jobs carried out by the few laborers on the scene. The vacancy left by the drainage of communal endeavor from local living is the reigning specter of the place.

In this emptied-out setting, a census of dead souls will haunt whatever democracy or tyranny may rule among the living dead left inside the desolate orphanage beyond the film's ending. Hence the questions: Who remains—and who remains not—a ghost among those violently departed persons who are still awake and walking in such abandoned dwellings? And: Can ghosts haunt other ghosts? Questions of the sort (such as the hobgoblin query as to whether there could be ghosts walking among the living who have never been dead) may be said to *haunt-back* at the ghosts in their perennial haunting of survivors. A haunting ironically summoned, though much in earnest, by Marx and Engels in their *Manifesto.*

The Gothic microcosm left at the abandoned and ruined orphanage shelters a physician turned custodial ghost and two murdered fetuslike living corpses for whom the building serves as native soil and amniotic habitat. Together, the amphibious ensemble of afterlives (in the womb waters of the cellar pool and in the life of the guardian ghost doctor) set up an alternate historical scenario besides the Gothic horror of Piranesi's maze labyrinth imprisonment highlighted in del Toro's DVD commentary.

For the Gothic fashion among elite and popular cultures in Dickens's England often associated the fate of dead children turned goblins with the accumulated dead generated by a surplus of poor minors among often migrant and homeless people. According to Josephine McDonagh, the uncanny *unhomeliness,* or *unheimliche,* reiteration of dead lives in the affairs of the living re-created the figure of the fairy as "a way of memorialising the surplus population of the poor" (*Child Murder* 119). The Victorian Gothic sensibility reached beyond novels and poems and essays into the gossip machine, pamphlets, and the press, and the phenomenon of burial societies, rumored and denounced by many as a means for poor parents to kill their children for money. The full spectrum of Gothic consciousness in its Victorian heyday involved body counts in children and the traffic from pauper flesh to buried corpses and unquiet ghosts and goblins. In the film's afterimage, the ghost of the doctor is shown walking among several unburied people (beginning with Carmen, whose corpse is seen covered with a bedsheet lying on the floor) and followed also by the children who died instantly in the gasoline explosion and the woman who burned in the storehouse. Their unresolved burial fate adds a truly invisible ghostly view to the story's ending.[4]

It may be asked whether it stretches things too far to incorporate such larger themes as Victorian child-murder into the film's elegantly stark plot. The answer lies in the transcendent and universal consequences of the Gothic vision itself as drawn as well as pillaged from the medieval Christian heritage and its modern Catholic legacy. Among the various Gothic styles, Spain's unique brand is hardly in dispute when it comes to the European traveler's salvage hunt for remnants of decaying faiths amid ruins or in convents, abbeys, and other sites in a sublimely backward land as seen in the eyes of those "Northern hearts" (Ruskin's phrase in "The Nature of Gothic") among Romantic tourists, pilgrims, and culture gawkers (a land in that sense more Goth than Gothic). Dr. Cáseres himself is a disenchanted throwback to the milder antiquarian Romantic soul, content with relics, old books, poems, and ballads, instead of the imaginary Byronic fare sought after in the flesh of Don Juan's Seville. Cáseres has settled next to Carmen, the widow of an officer of the Republic, herself maimed and harnessed to a wooden leg. Carmen runs the orphanage and supports her sexual appetites with Jacinto, the oldest orphan at the convent, whom she has been using in bed since he turned seventeen. We will next look at her in the mold of a medieval abbess who cares for abandoned children.

In prelude to viewing her in that role, the only shot we will examine comes after Jacinto eats with Marcelo and the Pig, on whose help he depends to escape with the gold bars that he thinks Carmen keeps in a safe. In the scene, we see Jacinto's dismissive treatment of Conchita and learn of her marriage plans to move with him to Granada and buy a *cortijo*, or small farm with a house. Her high hopes are not pinned on Jacinto's plot to steal the gold, but on the iffy chance that he will make something of himself and break his bondage to the orphanage. The next scene shows Conchita acting wiser than Jacinto in her loathing of the pair of men whom he blindly trusts and in whom she intuitively senses the danger of her boyfriend's own corruption. At that point, under the bluish moonlight, we also learn from her that Jacinto has in fact returned to the orphanage of his youth, but driven by bad motives she obviously still ignores. He then remembers his old wish to buy the place where he once was held for fifteen long years so he can tear it down. He speaks of looking at the sky when he said those words and, after a pause, a flapping noise directs his gaze up into the next, higher crane shot, high from where the aerial bomb that did not explode lies stuck in the middle of the courtyard. The couple is seen heading back into their room from the courtyard, where the scene has taken place, as the shot widens and circles to the left in suspense and to the sound of ghostly music and wind noise.

We have moved in dialogue from the kitchen out into the yard in middle-range shots that frame the couple in tight, and then the visual sweep starts, as if pivoting on the bomb, and the shot moves in closer to the figure of Carmen, who has watched and heard the scene hidden in the shadows, and the camera glides into the children's dorm as her troubled face dissolves mirrorlike, and through her ghostlike vanishing the shot advances and turns to the right inside the dorm toward where Carlos's sobs are heard and he is seen from slightly above his bed lying in tears. Next, Carlos traces with his fingers and pronounces the name "Santi" carved on a wood panel as the ghost's sighs are heard from behind the curtain that flanks the bed.

The shot has fused in one slow sweeping motion the wretched remnants of an extended holy family haunted by war and the specter of hunger and death. One senses that the marriage promise between Conchita and Jacinto is doomed because he is shackled to the place by more than gold hunger. Although Carlos is the one reading a comic-book version of *The Count of Monte Cristo*, it is Jacinto who is best fit to get his share of the curse that hangs upon Edmond Dantès and his wealth in that novel. For even if Jacinto did not die in the attempt to grab it, gold would make him worse than he already is from the sickness of incurable hate it renders palpable. John Ruskin's moral view of the Gothic makes Jacinto a sinner more than a criminal in a world long ago deserted by the Christian God. Yet the Gothic sinfulness attached to wealth would not originate in Jacinto's theft of gold but in the illth carried in wealth itself—whether stolen of not. For, mysteriously and mystifyingly, in the Gothic view, sinfulness lies not in what is done with wealth but in what illth in wealth does to the wealthy. The Gothic view of wealth is Christian-primitive and it goes a long way in robbing the Church of the spiritual richness it claims to have needed in order to house such golden treasures in proper medieval splendor. The Gothic mystery of accursed wealth, always in the wrong hands, mirrors in mystified suspense the corresponding mystery of child abandonment, not out of awful necessity, but for only God or the Devil knows what illth motives.

Gothic horror may well be regarded as one specific aesthetic mode in which to hold mysterious and to nurture in ghostly suspense the wondrous human capacity for inflicting and tolerating cruelty. There is no mystery on strict Christian grounds in the exposure, abandonment, and eventual death of children as the direct result of their parent's actions. The attrition rates of the phenomenon throughout histories and cultures would be attributed in Christian terms to human nature and base instincts acting in clear violation of God's command and in disobedience of His rules. The melodrama of exploitation and the spectacle of sadism upon abused innocence in Gothic horror add an ineffable, grotesque, and darkly sublime aura of mystery to the affairs of the human will, of which the abandonment of children is one among many recurrent ills.

John Boswell summarizes in *The Kindness of Strangers* the circumstances of abandonment in the European ancient and medieval contexts:

> Parents abandoned their offspring in desperation when they were unable to support them, due to poverty or disaster; in shame, when they were unwilling to keep them because of their physical condition or ancestry (e.g., illegitimate or incestuous); in self-interest or the interest of another child, when inheritance or domestic resources would be compromised by another mouth; in hope, when they believed that someone of greater means or higher standing might find them and bring them up in better circumstances; in resignation, when a child was of unwelcome gender or ominous auspices; or in callousness, if they simply could not be bothered with parenthood. (428–29)

Christianity is believed to have increased cases of abandonment with its rigid enforcement of exclusive and legitimate procreative ends in all human sexual practices as well as by allowing lasting shelter in churches and monasteries, through so-called oblation, for the humane disposal of unwanted infants. It has been established that the death rate among children who went on to live in such places and in foundling houses was staggering. In antiquity, under non-Christian norms and laws, children were exposed or released and not left at specific institutions. Their survival was thus diverse and routine, as they simply found new parents and occupations. But, writes Boswell: "The intricate, gentle complexities of the systems of transfer developed in ancient and medieval Europe were transformed into a simple technique of disposal—in a hauntingly literal sense. Entrants to foundling homes were removed from the population by isolation and death. A minority returned to society in their teens, anonymous and stigmatized, but more fortunate than the greater numbers who died in infancy or early childhood" (*Kindness* 432). Died, that is to say, in harsh—though by Christian norms benign and charitable—confinement.

The practice of doctrinal charity on the rise during the Christian Middle Ages was driven by the will not to allow children to die of hunger, be eaten by beasts, or fall prey to unwitting incest with a relative in a brothel. The medieval Christian European system of charitable confinement evolved in the context of heightened worries about preserving lineage ties intact and fending off the religious stigma upon bastards. The perils and moral and physical horrors invoked against outright child exposure of the non-Christian or pagan kind were awful enough to be seized upon as strong plot elements for use in the modern Gothic horror genre.

It seems apt to take into account the role of Christian virtue, as opposed to sinfulness, in the abandonment of children at the height of the Middle Ages. Two cases among several discussed by Boswell should suffice to illustrate the issue. He quotes the twelfth-century Benedictine Guibert of Nogent, who wrote of being dropped from his mother's interests as she embraced her religious calling: "'She knew that I would be an orphan with no one at all on whom to depend . . . she knew for certain that she was a cruel and unnatural mother. Indeed, she heard this said aloud, as she had in this way cut off from her heart and left bereft of succor such a fine child'" (*Kindness* 285). In the case of a husband pilgrim to the Holy Land, Boswell quotes testimony that a child born in the man's absence should become a monk, and that if the wife "does not have a child and she herself wishes to become a nun or to place another of her children in monastic life, the same agreement should be made" (301). The focus in our looking at the role of Carmen as head of the orphanage in the spectrum of the medieval confinement of abandoned children heightens the issue of such pious intentions.

In Carmen's case, her faith for "the Cause" ("la Causa") and her embattled moral altruism should compel us to consider her the mother superior of the film's spectral communism. However, she is not a Communist, in the same mirrored and spectral manner in which she is not a Catholic abbess either. What she actually is can be established by *negating* (or bringing back from disavowal into full figural exposure) what she may or *ought* to be. (In this allegorical fashion one is outing Carmen's Christian ghost from its Communist closet). She is the spectral negative of a Communist and Socialist woman committed to a cause as universal in scope and faith-expansion as was the medieval Church. Her true *Gothicness* (to use the term coined by Ruskin in "The Nature of Gothic") transcends the atmosphere and plot elements skillfully deployed in the film. But the best view of Carmen's Gothic role (in the house where her corpse will fester indefinitely and her soul will wander imprisoned) is best obtained in retrospect from the sibling del Toro film *Pan's Labyrinth* (*El laberinto del fauno*).

## The Gothic Soul Maze and the Girl in the Faun

On the potentially morbid kinship between excess in architectural fantasy and the grotesque, Ruskin wrote in "The Nature of Gothic" that "the tendency to delight in fantastic and ludicrous, as well as in sublime, images, is a universal instinct of the Gothic imagination" (*Unto This Last* 105). But it takes only one among many memorable sentences in that essay to separate Ruskin's conception of Gothic from any association with horror or sickness of the spirit. One such sentence comes as a gloss to "I have given thee every green herb for meat" (Gen. 11.30), part of which reads: "The proudest architecture that man can build has no higher honour than to bear the image and recall the memory of that grass of the field which is, at once, the type and the support of his existence; the goodly building is then most glorious when it is sculptured into the likeness of the leaves of Paradise" (*Unto This Last* 105). In the same spirit, what Ruskin wrote in *The Stones of Venice* chapter on Gothic architecture is meant to endure on account of the character and scope of communal life it envisions. No one has defined the vision better than John D. Rosenberg: "The burden of Ruskin's social criticism, beginning with "The Nature of Gothic," is the mutual dependence of all upon all, rather than the legally sanctioned war of each man against his neighbor. To redefine that larger identity of interest required that Ruskin redefine wealth not as indiscriminate production at any cost to life, but as the wise consumption, and just distribution, only of those things which sustain the fullest possible life" (*Darkening Glass* 100). This is why Ruskin's absorbed reaction to the death toll in *Pan's Labyrinth* and its retroactive effect upon *The Devil's Backbone* would return him to the sentence "There is no Wealth but Life," on which the social vision of *Unto This Last* actively rests against the baneful will of illth.

We will next examine mainly one shot from *Pan's Labyrinth* in order to establish the umbilical matrix that links the film with its sibling, *The Devil's Backbone,* in a way in which architectural space and the human body, in room and womb, build themselves into a microcosm of female anatomical power and vulnerability. This sort of dissection will offer further passage into the maze where girl and Faun combine their souls and minds. The search will bring us to the marrow of Gothic as conceived by Ruskin, our precinematic witness to the film and to the adult involvement in children's literature. The idea is to imagine, as in full kaleidoscopic exposure, the sibling films' thematic integrity combined, as only the visual imagination can, in response to cinematic stimulus and aided by reviewing and clipping film images. Obviously, no such synthesis is possible upon first viewing both films. But the same impossibility informs the kind of inspired contemplation and rebuilding of Gothic architecture and many other art objects textually composed by Ruskin as if casting a single glance at such creations. His beautifully balanced sentences of visionary prose would have to translate nowadays into visual video work with verbal counterpoint.

As in the previous shot studied in *The Devil's Backbone*, a sense of place or site in which human lives are embedded is built through visual motion. In that instance, Carmen's presence in the shadows spying upon Jacinto and Conchita acts as the pivot point upon which the orphanage's divided zones turn and become for one moment continuous and contiguous. In fact, as her image dissolves and the shot proceeds into the dorm where the boys sleep, the object that glimmers and disappears last is the silver handle of her walking cane, gripped and nervously spun back and forth in winding motion in her right hand. At this point, the silver handle visually quotes her prosthetic right leg to which it is in a way attached, not only in function but in looks, as the metal knee part of the leg resembles it in color and texture. Next, we will see how Carmen's cane handle and Captain Vidal's silver watch serve as counterpart objects in the shot just examined from *Backbone* and related scenes in *Labyrinth*.

The prolonged shot early in *Labyrinth* follows a short one in which Ofelia enters the bedroom to join her pregnant mother in bed. It will last over two minutes, as underscored by del Toro in his commentary (scene 3). The camera moves closer to Ofelia and Carmen as they speak softly about the old house's noises and night growls and the girl complains that her mother should not have married Captain Vidal, because Carmen was not alone as she claims she was. Ofelia obeys Carmen and tells the story of the magic rose of immortality to her "brother" while resting her head upon her mother's pregnant belly. The shot descends into the womb where the fetus is seen and then moves to the right to where the rose grows above a thicket of poisoned stem thorns. The womb/fetus and mountain/rose spaces are both distinct and contiguous, and this hints at the implantation of such space-relatedness in the mother's pregnant insides through the magic of Ofelia's tale. The fairy-tale essence of the girl's story concerns wilted immortality as the rose fades and dies with no one ever taking the magical flower to claim the gift of undying life. Ofelia's voice is heard as the insect that will guide her steps into the faun's labyrinth flies from the stem of the thornbush and across the moon landscape and into the bedroom and brings to an end the scene's circle and cycle displacement as the shot blends with the next scene, in which Captain Vidal is seen cleaning his watch as the girl's words "until the end of time" are heard.

The passage from pregnant womb space to the rose space of immortal life and poisonous death implies the magical temporal realm from which Captain Vidal and his fetish watch are barred. Vidal epitomizes the unwillingness and inability to pluck the rose, and as such he embodies mechanical time as a realm strictly clocked by death. In his comments del Toro wants us to see Vidal inside the watch cleaning the watch, taking such *mise-en-abyme* cue from the wheels of the mill behind his back as if they belonged to the insides of a big clock: Vidal would be holding in miniature shape the big watch behind him with himself in repeated shape standing both where he is and within the same scene held in his hand. A struggle for the baby brother's fate beyond birth is taking place: a struggle between the father's mechanical timepiece—held over the abyss of its vanishing duplication attached to his own image—and the organic conception of time and person inside and outside the mother's womb space.

During the dinner with guests from the nearby town, the Captain will deny the existence of the watch when told the story of how his father smashed his against the ground to mark the hour of his death in battle. In professing that no such watch exists, the anxiously expectant father of a son in Captain Vidal denies the father-son fetish link that he harbors invested in the silver timepiece, seen in close-up at the start of the scene, and also the one, earlier, when his wife and stepdaughter arrive in the house. At dinner, Ofelia's father has just been mentioned by Carmen, who tells the guests that her late husband made the Captain's uniforms and that after his death she met Vidal again while working at a clothing store. Carmen speaks unaware of any mischief behind her husband's death, but the tense mood of awkward knowingness among the guests—and Vidal's embarrassed contempt for her words—seem to imply that murder might have occurred aided by the Captain's own involvement.

The deeper issue of fatherhood and murder is present at the dinner and banquet tables in unspoken and unspeakable ways. The Captain sits at the head of the dinner table just a few hours after he beat to death a captured man in front of his father, who denied his son's guilt in the insurgency by claiming he was just hunting rabbits. After the murder, Vidal found in the victim's pouch two rabbits, which he gave to Mercedes the servant to prepare for supper. She answered that they were too young for that purpose and he told her to use them for broth, but when she got to the kitchen she ordered the rabbits cooked. And so they appear—lean, roasted, untouched—among other dishes at the table. Later on, the dinner table transforms itself—inside the Pale Man's alternate world—into the opulent banquet setting as Ofelia grabs a couple of grapes against the Faun's orders not to eat from any of the dishes. Her disobedience causes the death by cannibalistic decapitation of two of the fairies who escort her in a scene associated by del Toro in his comments with Goya's painting of Saturn devouring his own children.

The umbilical link between the womb and rose shot just examined in connection with other scenes and the one discussed earlier involving Carmen and the holy family of lost children in *The Devil's Backbone* may be construed along sibling lines between the films. The axis of reference concerns generation and death as focused upon the womb and its biological and nonbiological or magical insemination. Carmen in *Backbone* is repeated by Carmen in *Labyrinth*. In the first case, the actual widow and spectral abbess is attached to and burdened by a prosthetic leg inside which she hides the gold bars that her equally attached lover boy Jacinto wants to steal. Folk themes about fertility/barrenness with respect to gold are present in the false but hyperreal prosthetic womb limb finally opened and emptied of its precious golden load by Jacinto while standing not far from where Carmen's corpse lies. The weight and illth of the gold bars doom Jacinto to death when he is speared by the boys in revenge for his murder of Santi—as ordained by the boy's ghost. Ballasted by pockets stuffed with the gold bars, Jacinto's body sinks in the pinkish amniotic pool water as he is embraced into drowning by Santi's ghost's body. The watery grave resembles in coloration the "Water of Limbo" liquid in the jars where Dr. Cáseres keeps his fetuses, including at least one marked by the devil's backbone. At the start of the film, when the words about a ghost being like an insect trapped in amber are heard, a boy's body is seen sinking into the bloodied water with a rope tied to his neck—we are being shown what will turn out to be Santi's murdered body being dumped in the pool. As credits continue, the figure of a fetus is seen rotating and suspended in murky liquid and showing a spiked or serrated backbone. The mysterious blend of different views of the same or perhaps multiple fetal bodies implants the first visual clue blurring the difference between intrauterine and extrauterine liquid realms. A grotesque overlap—in the form of visual and tonal links—is thus established between the sinking boy's body with an umbilical rope tied to its neck and the malformed horrific fetus.

If the orphanage building were viewed as homologous to the body, in cosmological fashion, its womb would reside at two locations: the jars in the lab and the cellar pool. Carmen's womb connection is attached to her gold-pregnant leg and the limb's distinct association with the aerial bomb stuck in the middle of the courtyard. At one point in his comments, del Toro speaks about it, and indeed both leg and bomb have insides that fascinate and invite prying and entry. The dud bomb falls from the night sky moments after Santi is accidentally killed by Jacinto's malicious fury and in conjunction with the birth of the ghost who will demand the killer's execution. All that happens in the plot beyond this point in time happens to people who live hostage afterlives: living persons who have become unfinished replicas of the undead.

Murder as ghost-birth seems related to Carmen's pedagogical role in patriarchy. Her illustrated lesson about prehistory implants in Jaime's imagination the spear-hunting and killing of the mammoth. He draws the hunting scene in his notebook in his role as the film's internal storyteller and visual artist. As if copying him, Jaime plots the spear-torture wounding of Jacinto and the offering of the body to the ghost of Santi in the cellar pool. Peer group action against Jacinto under Jaime's lead expresses the hierarchical imprint of Santi's death as the founding event of group solidarity. Jacinto is gravely but not fatally wounded when his ultimate death is offered as a gift to the ghost who inhabits the womb waters of the cellar pool. A circle is thus closed as the orphanage is abandoned by the seven child survivors and is left to whatever unfathomable fate may await its resident ghosts. On the pessimistic side, ghost afterlives do not appear likely to transcend the retributive cycles of political strife: the civil war goes on among ghosts in the afterlife.

Jacinto and Jaime's triangular and lethal bonding with Santi and his ghost carries over to *Pan's Labyrinth* and the issue of boy birth and girl death. Ofelia's death and transport into a magical realm ruled by her parents cannot be separated from the survival of her newborn brother and his removal from the fascist father under the lead of Mercedes as adoptive mother on behalf of the entire non-fascist group. And neither can Ofelia's mother's death while giving birth be segregated from the complex matriarchal role of Carmen in the previous film. But before aligning the films any further, let us look closer at del Toro's wish to have them considered as siblings.

He sees in *Labyrinth* a story of "choice and disobedience" about a girl who is "not dying but giving birth to herself the way she wanted to be" (scene 1). Her disobedience reinstates a central theme in *Backbone:* the rebelliousness of the abandoned children against Jacinto's juvenile and broken-hearted fascist abuse of their lives and the future of violence and resentment that his life as a "prince without a kingdom" poses as their own fate. I claimed earlier that Carmen's *not* being a Communist implies her spectral militant mother superior character in reverse allegorical terms. Carmen is what she is (not Communist) by means of not being what she is not (Communist) and thus embodying or *casting* in negation precisely this other alternate and disavowed way of being herself.

This is not exactly what del Toro means about the girl Ofelia, who, in not dying, is giving birth to herself just as she wills or wants herself to be. Nevertheless, my way of recasting his view of *Labyrinth* rests upon the claim of *affirmative negation* or *disavowal* that we see allegorically cast and embodied in the character of Carmen in *Backbone*. In this fashion, I take a parallel but opposite view of allegory with respect to the definition given by the God Pan in Calderón's sacred play. While agreeing with Pan's words to the Night about the fitness between a given person and its resembling cast or copy, I fall and—if you will—err on the side of the rule of difference (not similarity) in the articulation of identicalness and identity. In this view, the articulation of identicalness remains both unsettling and unsettled. This implies disavowal—and more pointedly *Verneinung*—in the casting of character in my understanding of both films.

Let us assume that Carmen in *Backbone* denies to her own conscience or to a questioner that she is a Communist. And let us further assume that her denial is not a neurotic repudiation implying the opposite of what is affirmed in what is denied. And let us finally assume that—going beyond any such denial—she disavows and deeply refuses any trace of the Communist in her. It is this highest degree of negating—more than just denying—that is reached in disavowal or *Verneinung* (thus she both denies she is a Communist and disavows that she is a Communist). For instance, in the case of Milton's Christian/Protestant *Universal Pan* and Calderón's Christian/Catholic *True God Pan*—both cast in Christ's image—it is like having God both ways at extreme opposite ends. In allegorical cast, the Christian universal and truest god Pan is definitely not (he refutes and disavows) the Arcadian brute shepherd who rapes nymphs and mates with goats and spills his seed on the ground. This seems a lot like a true instance of castration as the bedrock example of disavowal in Freud's theory. Goat-god becomes sublime/sublimated (is castrated) as his sexual grotesqueness expires (and is *sublated* or uplifted and taken beyond) in Christ's chastity. Likewise, mother Carmen, agent of patriarchy in denial, keeps her disavowal of herself as Communist inside the lost limb and detached womb in which the gold that she says is "for the Cause" is hidden. Jacinto (her abject Prometheus son figure and prosthetic love object and thief) turns incestuous as he is dropped into the breeding waters of the cellar pool, where the slugs gather seeking moistness like minute crawlers for the maternal touch. Thus, seen in terms of disavowal, the Gothic depths of *Backbone* reveal an unbroken nexus between Carmen's virtual (World) Communism and the broken mold of her communicant Catholicism, just as in *Labyrinth* the King and Queen parental couple who await Ophelia in her new life after death bear the stamp of being pastiche divine monarchs in a Catholic mold empowered in their rule by a faun named Pan.

In between Carmen in *Backbone* as Communist and communicant mother and Carmen in *Labyrinth* as sacrificial womb stand Conchita and Mercedes as younger instances of potential motherhood beyond Ophelia's truncated passage beyond puberty. Conchita is stabbed in the abdomen and killed by Jacinto under the sun's glare, and Ophelia is shot in the abdomen and killed by Vidal under the full moon at the labyrinth's mouth—but she is reborn beyond ordinary life. Her rebirth keeps her forever in Fairyland or Childland. It keeps the Gothic girl forever out of the reproductive charnel house where her mother Carmen has encountered the monstrous death that Ellen Moers identified in her 1976 classic *Literary Women* with mothers in Gothic novels who die in labor or after giving birth. Ofelia saves her newborn orphan brother, and he is carried away by Mercedes—who acts as a surviving version of Conchita, who is stabbed in the womb by the man she wanted to father her children—while Mercedes keeps hidden in her apron, folded over the upper abdomen, the knife she uses to rip open Vidal's mouth. Mercedes' role as avenging mother dominates the film's ending. She and her insurgent guerrilla brother are the main parent figures of the newborn boy taken from Vidal's custody and the rule of fascist paternity. In this sense, brother and sister repeat and redeem the Conchita-Jacinto fatal and broken union.

## The Girl in the Faun and the Double Child

The crux of the matter about the view of allegory and personification in both films brings us to what I call *the girl in the Faun*—not *the Faun in the girl*—as a more conventional view of Gothic and Freudian uncanny female powers might have it. In my view, it is Ofelia who inhabits (and in that manner haunts) the Faun, who in translation for the global film market consents to the greater universal name of Pan. Freud's version of Faun dualism would have the beast factor repressed in the girl's ageless and archaic unconscious. Indeed, in the film's earliest script sketch, as explained by del Toro, something of the sort happens in magical ways.

Ofelia's earliest avatar is a pregnant woman who moves into a mansion in northern Spain owned by "a fascist" that is being restored by her husband and who falls madly in love "with a satyr, with a faun," and has his child, whose blood, however, her faun beast lover claims as the price for her to be able to follow him into his kingdom—a horrid deed the adulterous interspecies mother is quite willing to perform. Such is the girl Ofelia in reverse: a mad woman crazy-loving the real magical and sexual Faun—as well as the Faun in her—and who is willing to sacrifice their blood-child for the reward of an infinite trip into the Other Side kingdom where her Faun rules.

Thus, in its earliest screenplay incarnation *Labyrinth* was a *sexually* adult film whose R rating in the U.S. market would have come from its strong sexual content and themes, rather than from the shocking violence that does not place its final R-rated version out of the reach of adult-accompanied minors as young as Ofelia. By the same token, the adult and unfaithful married woman protagonist in the original script represents a current cinematic market solution to the issue of female sexual precociousness and girl bondage to adult marriage norms latent in the social and political unconscious of Victorian children's fiction. For just as the adult wife who betrays her husband and has a child with a magical beast would break the R rating or young adult market niche mold if she were a minor, not much older than Ofelia, in Victorian children's fiction girl-latent sexual ordeals in minors do not require Freud to be placed in the foreground. The girl native in Victorian Childland possesses the pagan Faun beast inside her in refashioned and tolerable Christian shape and within a pastoral garden haunted by the perils of earthly paradise, which led to the primal parents' fall and expulsion from grace.

Seen in retrospect, the boy in childhood Arenas and his bestial alternate boy companion make up a Gothic ensemble cast that in my view stretches back to the night forest perils to chastity and selfhood staged in Milton's *Comus*. The two boyhoods share a virtual lost girlhood between them, perhaps an emanation of the host of betrayed witch women and female elders against whom boyhood struggles for emancipation from manacled maternity. An archaic modality of women communism stands at the vanishing point of the boy's complex melting back into his maternal origins and the paternal ghost that haunts them.

## John Ruskin's Girl Character

John Ruskin's social gospel against the abuses of wealth and the reign of illth has framed our cinematic allegory of Gothic fantasy pastiche in del

Toro's sibling films. In Ruskin's encompassing view, beyond architecture and in transcendent moral terms, Gothic does not obtain as a worldview if not compromised by poverty and squalor. Gothic rises from the transfigured awareness of the fallen condition, which could not be so materially overwhelming a factor in social existence without shaping the soul that in Gothic style and substance elevates humans to a God in whom Ruskin believed with every breath he took as he wrote in his spoken style. In this regard, the birth of Oliver Twist in Dickens's first novel is as exemplary a Gothic birth as any. It comes in the involuntary prescience experienced in the newborn against being born as "an item of mortality" who is "ushered into this world of sorrow and trouble" by the workhouse parish surgeon (*Oliver Twist* 45). Considerable difficulty occurs in trying to induce Oliver "to take upon himself the office of respiration," as for some time he lays "gasping on a little flock mattress, rather unequally poised between this world and the next, the balance being decidedly in favour of the latter" (45). But the Gothic we seek to visualize here lies not only in the horror finally dispelled by Oliver's birth, but in the fantasy twist of further horror also inherent in Gothic besides its own compromised birth in the midst of human poverty.

Turning back to *Pan's Labyrinth,* this further fantasy horror should be in turn dispelled and replaced by transforming its literal depiction as torture into its own figural mimicking of birth compromised by the sheer horror of being born. It happens when Captain Vidal tortures to death the stuttering doomed prisoner and promises to spare his life if he can count to three without halting. The second-degree fantasy horror comes if and when the stutterer is held in suspense by viewers before his assumption—like Oliver Twist's—of the "office of respiration," as if stuttering were to renew with its stammering pronouncement of the fallen condition the horror of being born. In the scene, once the prisoner's respiration officiously exhales the stammered number three, the Gothic reluctance to be born, once surrendered, ushers in the torturer's lethal confirmation of life's evil character. But Gothic hopelessness, in prescient reluctance of being born into a world ruled by evil, most often hides from view the specific human agencies in control of evilness. It is my claim that on the reverse side of Ruskin's sunny reinvention of Gothic, he uncovers the moral duty to reveal in a style of sublime grandeur life's grotesque subservience to the disaffection that in the management of wealth he associated with illth.

The Gothic birth precondition in both horror and primal disavowal of life, taken from Dickens in collaboration with Ruskin, is meant to inform issues of moral consciousness and conscience in the Arenas fictions examined thus far and in those addressed next. In its simplest form, the Gothic horror hesitation and disavowal of being born just sketched exists here as the foundation of the Arenas social unconscious and our own moral access to it. Furthermore, the still unfinished issue of the girl in the Faun will be explored in the next chapter by having episodes in Ruskin's life serve as figural elements of the Arenas social unconscious. Against the background of Milton's girl ordeal in *Comus,* Ruskin's own girl saga will represent for us how in the Arenas childhood the double child embodied in association with girlhood inhabits the Faun biography of the writer.

The question of embedded girlhood in a queer mode of masculinity will bring us face to face with gender issues nowadays related to the heated polemics surrounding the social and medical diagnostics of *sexual dysphoria* as a specific condition associated with self-choice by those who experience it as their sexual and personal and group identity. But instead of claiming that girl-embedded queer masculinity signifies a *dysphoric* or "hard to bear" gender condition in a man with "girl" character elements in his personality, I will illustrate how in the Arenas fiction the burden in question is previously borne by women among his inner family. It is therefore the "hard to bear" of dysphoric condition attached to the gender of these kinfolk women as embedded in his fictional personality that the Arenas character's specific queerness engenders (and struggles with) in his mode of masculinity.

# 3 Lady in the Hot Seat

To undo the charmed band
Of true virgin here distressed.
. . . . . . . . . . . .
Next this marble venomed seat
Smeared with gums of glutinous heat
I touch with chaste palms moist and cold,
Now the spell hath lost his hold.

*Comus* (lines 903–4,915–18)

THE MOST scrutinized passage in Milton's masque brings us back to it for a last glance, now in perspective from our examination of some central themes in del Toro's sibling films. We will look next at the ordeal of chastity in the Lady, who in the epigraph just quoted sits paralyzed before Comus's magical wand at the moment when the river goddess and virgin, Sabrina, releases her from bondage. The goddess restores the rule of chastity in a Lady figure who is being played by a thirteen-year-old girl named Alice, daughter of John, Earl of Bridgewater, President of the Council of the Marshes of Wales, in honor of whose family and under whose patronage the masque was performed, with his daughter and two of her brothers in the leading roles, besides Comus and the Attendant Spirit. Our brief survey of the scene will bring John Ruskin to bear upon issues it raises about the survival of innocence in girls and in virgins—Ruskin's presumed virgin condition not excluded. Needless to say, the Ruskin in question is himself a masque-allegorical character reduced to some bare essentials of his personification as the preeminent aesthetic and moral mind of the Victorian Age, and no less preeminent visionary critic of the British industrial order and its horrors. This historical and allegorical mirror will allow us to cast a final glance at the issue of embedded girlhood thus far developed in Castle Dismal in primary reference to the Arenas fiction.

## A Gothic Eden

Ludlow Castle is no terrifying house in the Gothic mood rehearsed in *The Castle of Otranto;* nor is it a Gothic villa such as the one built by Horace

Walpole on Strawberry Hill as citadel of the style of cultivated emotions in picturesque surroundings known as the Gothic Revival. The Ludlow estate does not—could not—belong to the class of "archaic toys in stone or prose" where medieval special effects were erected oblivious of the Gothic spirit later on recovered and reinvented by John Ruskin. Ludlow is no Gothic Eden, such as William Beckford's hulk at Fonthill Abby, where Paradise becomes a stone mass with huge twin towers designed and built by the author of *Vathek* with wealth inherited from his father's Jamaican slave sugar plantations.

The allegorical Arcadian horrors brought by Milton to Ludlow Castle for the installation of the Lord President of Wales and the enjoyment of his Bridgewater family were of a different vintage, but were nevertheless the ancestors of the Gothic capitalization of Evil in a realm belonging to wealth and surrounded by poverty. The masque presents a young girl as the Lady who with her two brothers becomes lost in a dark forest on the way back to their father's house. The Lady (played by Alice Egerton, the Earl's thirteen-year-old daughter) is left to rest while her brothers (played by two of Alice's siblings) go in search of refreshments, so she finds herself alone when Comus discovers her. He is the offspring of Bacchus the god of drunkenness and the witch Circe. Comus acts true to his breeding and takes the Girl Lady to a cottage hidden further into the woods, puts her in manacles, glued to a magical chair, and tries to seduce her with the spell of his magical wand. But the Lady resists Comus's attempts to have her "roul with pleasure in a sensual sty" (77) together with his rout of beastly followers. She is saved when the Attendant Spirit summons the goddess Sabrina from the waters of the Severn River, who unglues our virgin Girl Lady from her hot seat.

Curiously, the Bridgewater family had in the recent past experienced troubles adaptable to a filmed Victorian sensational novel of uncensored debauchery. Not long before the masque's performance on Michaelmas Night in 1634, two of the children actors were said to have been bewitched by a servant in the house, but the chances that Milton knew that the Bridgewater siblings had been associated with demonic possession are considered slim. However, there were other major sources of scandal among family relatives within living memory. The maternal aunt of our Girl Lady had been the guiltless victim of her husband's attempt to corrupt her into forced sex with a highly favored household servant. Mervin Touchet, the Second Earl of Castlehaven, was tried, convicted, and executed with two of his men servants on charges of sodomy with one or more of them, of helping one servant to rape his wife (the sister of our

Girl Lady's mother), and of allowing another to sleep with his adolescent daughter-in-law. He was accused of plotting to disinherit his own son in favor of his domestic favorites.[1]

Nothing in the affair's aftermath has yielded solid evidence that Milton intended to have his masque serve as means to dispel any apparent guilt of the Bridgewater family or to separate its members from the scandal. Stephen Orgel speaks for the dominant view among leading scholars when he writes that "the capital crime" that sent the earl and his men to the gallows "had more to do with subverting the concept of patriarchal authority than with kinky sex" ("Case for Comus 33). This holds true when the legal fiction known as sodomy proves kinkier beyond plain lust as a crime against the bounds of humanity. As Cynthia B. Herrup writes: "The danger of the sodomite was not that the focus of his attention was a man, but that his desires had no focus; they ran in indiscriminate streams that undermined allegedly categorical boundaries between men and women, humans and animals, nobles and commoners. Hence, the logic behind conflating sodomy and bestiality under a single legal category: buggery" (*House in Gross Disorder* 33). Such crimes are far from the allegorical perils envisioned in *Comus*, but that depends on who is envisioning them, and it does not take much imagination to regard the son of Bacchus and Circe as a beastly fellow ready to violate whoever is brought to wallow in his sensual sty with consequences well beyond what is nowadays called sexuality.

Debora Shuger has established with accuracy that Milton's famously suggestive lines on the "marble venomed seat/Smeared with gums of glutinous heat" echo St. Augustine's thoughts in *Confessions* (10.30–40) on nocturnal emission and other expressions of insubordinate sexual behavior in men as "the birdlime of concupiscence," or *concupiscentiae visco expedita;* birdlime or *visco* became the token for spilled semen in Patristic writing ("'Glums'" 2–4). While pinned down and bound in sleep, men were moved and ambushed into involuntary defilement by spilling their birdlime seminal fluid. Shuger quotes a letter by Gregory the Great that Milton is believed to have known, besides Augustine's *Confessions,* in which all the key terms for being tied down by ligatures or "birdlimed" as if in sinful consent to lust are present (4), from which, Shuger adds, it may be gleaned that "reading the birdlimed chair in terms of wet dreams entails that the Lady be, as it were, a man" and that this should not seem all that strange, since for most of the masque "Milton seems to have conceived the Lady's experience in male terms" (4). It should be borne in mind that the Bridgewater girl—copied in the Lady as the stronghold of chastity and staunch virginity—acts in words brought into her ears and out her mouth by a twenty-six-year-old virginal male poet, named John Milton, once known in derision by his rowdy peers at Cambridge as the "Lady of Christ's."[2]

Besides Shuger's historical and philological spade work on birdlime's involuntary sinful ties, the intuitive sense of Milton's resonant lines and their psychoanalytical echoes lie not too far apart. John Kerrigan follows Edward Le Comte's *Milton and Sex* on the echo of *gluteus* (buttocks) in "glutinous," and recognizes in the "hot gums" a sign of semen. But he further remarks that "the dominant iconography of paralysis on a throne is anal" (*Sacred Complex* 47). This comes in prelude to his useful inquiry into the girl's motives as Alice Egerton herself—the girl who plays the Lady as the daughter of the Earl of Bridgewater. This is useful because it allows us to pair off two couples face to face on the issue of Fantasy: Alice and Comus in Milton, and Ofelia and the Faun in del Toro's film. (Fantasy is capitalized in reference to its established cinematic genre.)

## The Gift in Horror Fantasy and Theological Evil

In Kerrigan's view, the Lady absorbs a heavy dose of guilt in figuratively drinking the venomed potion from Comus. He claims (playing analyst and confessor) that if the masque were "Alice Egerton's fantasy, the origins of this guilt would be fairly obvious," and further that "the tempter [Comus] with his wand, his throne, and his desire to make Alice 'my queen' (265) [would represent] a projection of her father with his 'new-entrusted Scepter' (36), his throne, and his 'Lady bright'" (*Sacred Complex* 48). Moreover, Alice faces her superego as she "relives the oedipal temptation, invited to usurp the throne of her mother. She chooses virginity, fortifying the lock of anal passions," but this does not release Alice from the power of the wand. Because "her virtue is bound to a repressed wish, she is fixed at the stasis of primitive superego formation, a captive of old love and old fear that have not dissolved into the mobile self-possession of intra-psychic structure"; so, Kerrigan concludes, "she must be forgiven by her rival, arrived on the scene as the virgin Sabrina," whom he portrays as "a pre-oedipal mother with no sexual entanglements, to give her [Alice] life once again through the sanctification of nourishment" (48). Yet the masque is not Lady Alice Egerton's fantasy in *Comus;* it is not unless a fiction or film corresponding to Kerrigan's Freudian reading would situate our view of the masque within Alice's otherwise unrecorded thoughts. What suggests itself is a *mise-en-abyme* situation in which the girl actor is situated both inside the play in which she is a character and outside as the unconscious agency through which the action takes ulterior shape in the budding guilt of a minor entering the world of adult sexual politics.

It is in similar fashion that Kerrigan's psychoanalytic rap sheet of pent-up guilty desires in Alice the Girl Lady would allow us to bring the spoiled-rotten gift of the unconscious to dwell within Ofelia in her dealings with the Faun in *Pan's Labyrinth*. Our need to introduce this "gift" presumes that the film disavows the unconscious or anything reflecting the specifically sexual contents in the girl's psyche that such agency entails and that the film leaves up to the audience to surmise or invent. Though in fundamental ways harmless and sinless (as a nontheological agency that is not linked to the conscious will to act or to any active imaginings), the "venomed" gift of the modern unconscious would come to Ofelia (as it would to Alice) beyond her own powers to reject it. In fact, the gift of the unconscious would enter Ofelia somewhat redundantly: right where film Fantasy replaces it while taking for granted that something like it already functions in the audience as the fountain spring of fantasies mirrored in the film. So activated, the unconscious brings about the agency of guilt mixed up with sexual fantasies. Ofelia's unconscious in *Labyrinth* acts as the carrier of guilt about her father's death and her mother's marriage to his murderer. Her unconscious could not escape informing—beyond her conscious will to do so—a socially and politically negotiated view of her father's death and its sexually tainted aftermath. For instance, when she visits the underground to meet the giant toad, from whom she must obtain the key that unlocks access to the dagger, Ofelia is wearing the dark green dress that her mother Carmen made for her with her own hands. This dress is soiled not only with mud but with the gluey (perchance "glutinous"?) emission from the toad's mouth before he empties himself of the blob ("gums" perhaps?) stuck with the key and then deflates like a flaccid bagpipe. Soiling her mother's dress could be seen as Ofelia's way of insulting the widow's talents as seamstress in reference to her late husband, the girl's father who was murdered by Captain Vidal, the man whose uniforms the murdered husband tailored and whom now her mother insists on naming as her new father.

As Kerrigan does with Alice Egerton's unconscious as the guilt carrier and ultimate author of *Comus,* we may for a moment posit Ofelia's film authorship, in the Fantasy genre, of a story about her ordeal in bondage to the man who would have killed both her father and mother. This girl-negotiated scenario would correspond to the earliest and discarded version of the film, in which the adulterous wife is ready to sacrifice her newborn child to the faun beast father in answer to his demand. Betraying a husband who is rebuilding a palace owned by a fascist and mating with a faun who demands the sacrifice of his own child reads much like a sensationalist psychoanalytic melodrama of surrender to the totem-and-taboo sources of murderous resentment commonly associated with fascism. It follows that the discarded story might have been written either by a woman who portrays herself as a nihilist killer of her own child or by one bent on exposing the rotten unconscious of patriarchy in fascism as embedded in her own psyche by creating such a fantasy of murder and sexual pollution. Likewise, in Ofelia's own authorship of *El laberinto del fauno*, her mother's death giving birth to a son would be shown as the girl's fantasized—but all too real—acting out of her matricidal revenge for the murder of her father. In the discarded early version, the brutal sexual component centers on the faun's sacrificial demand of his son's blood. While in the story that was made into the film—and that we are recasting in Ofelia's authorship—sex in the girl (so overwhelming a factor in the betraying adult wife) is absent and idealized in Ofelia's disobedient bondage to the old Faun—she ignores his command and tastes the fruit while still tied to his will. (The Faun acts as superego, demanding blind obedience while in fact granting the wish to obey one's driving wishes.)

The guilt burden implanted in the psychoanalytic unconscious as a fading representative of modern moral conscience brings us to a qualification of horror film Fantasy involving child characters in movies made by marketing design not to exclude minors from the audience by simply deleting the sexual components otherwise inherent in their actions and haunted thoughts. Fantasy of the sort filmed in *Labyrinth* may delete or obscure the sex-tainted guilt emanating from repression and linked to unconscious wishes in children. Instead, deletion and sublimation would be negotiated by the adult audience as it looks back upon childhood on the screen through its own grown-up (immoral) film fantasies and corresponding moral deflectors. However, adult fantasies of the sublimated sort do not release children from their own original share in such fantasies, as guiltless or innocent as they may seem—the very notion of guiltless innocence itself being an adult retroactive and wishful invention. In the hard-core Freudian view here sketched, the biblical "sins of the fathers" (Exod. 20.5) are indeed visited on "sons" and daughters, in whom Christian sinfulness and psychoanalytic guilt already lie in negotiated kinship.

Fantasies and guilt feelings shared between adults and children concern Ofelia's nascent sexual feelings at a deeply troubled moment of her entrance into puberty. The blood shed upon the blank pages of her magical book may have a menstrual meaning besides the frontal allusion it makes to her mother's bloodied pregnancy. It is therefore not innocent blood in the realm of film Fantasy, but rather a blood type that if Ofelia were a boy would be typed O—as in Oedipus—and thus bound to transgressions against parental authority. The same goes for the X-rated unconscious, in which, out of reach for most audiences, but quite in the tradition of uncensored Gothic melodrama, the girl Ofelia would be accosted by her stepfather Captain Vidal and would respond to his sexual advances with acts of rejection haunted by feelings and wishes of surrender. This is of course a primal scene unspeakably staged at the borderline overlap between the Freudian unconscious, the libertine fictions of Sade, and the wanton but doomed challenges to girl virginity and virtue performed in Milton's *Comus*. This is also the borderland where film Fantasy and Christian theological negotiations with evil intersect.

In the Christian theological domain present in Milton's masque, evil lacks ambiguity when it comes to punishment for what constitutes the sin of human disobedience to God. Evil is unambiguously punishable: either the Girl Lady falls to Comus and becomes his orgy whore in the magical forest and is damned forever, or she triumphs over evil—as she is certain to do from the start, not withstanding the doubts and guilt fantasies and double dealings uncovered by psychoanalytic readings. But a wholly different order of evil steeped in sentimental ambiguity obtains in film Fantasy as present in del Toro's *Labyrinth*. Pan dictates terms to Ofelia, which she disobeys. Her disobedience saves her newborn brother from Pan's veiled threat of infanticide. In choosing to disobey her Faun, Ofelia *gives birth to herself the way she wanted to be*—as del Toro explains in his DVD comments and many in the audience wish she would. Her wish beyond mortality is constitutive of Fantasy in this case as a system of rewarded disobedience based on "Gothic" sentimentality, and as such requiring girl sacrifice. On the unsentimental side of the older Christian theology—mimicked but supplanted by Fantasy—Ofelia's sacrifice could never atone for an act of disobedience against Milton's God. It should be obvious that Fantasy in *Labyrinth* reinvests its—and potentially our own—regard for authority of a transcendent, theological, and divine sort on the sentimental rule of an unbending but rewarding old Faun.

We claimed earlier that the Arenas biographical fictions resemble the figures of ordeal in *Comus* and that the written self in those fictions sheds skins: as if the encore Arenas were Comus acting as the central peacock character in *Comus*. In the light of Milton's masque and in relation to film Fantasy as just explained, the Arenas fictions of self-display represent a core scene of self-absorption and seduction between mother and child directed by the child's adult role as author of his own fictional self: a scene in which his innocence and his malice (entwined as dictated by original sin) clasp each other and cast a spell upon Eve as the primordial mother. (A species of queer love/hate bonding between the son and the mother is thus sealed.) It will be examined later how this double and entwined figure of self-absorption in display belongs in the realm of autobiographical Fantasy as the spectacle of having it both ways—both ways when innocence and evil are mutually elevated by sentimentality and by remnants of the sacred invested with sublimity in the reiterations of melodrama.

## John Ruskin Wishes and Wishes Not

At the opening of "The Roots of Honour" Ruskin calls "the most curious" and "least credible" among the delusions of political economists "the idea that an advantageous code of social action may be determined irrespectively of the influence of social affection" (*Unto This Last* 167). He means that for the political economists of his day social affections are, as he echoes their words: "'accidental and disturbing elements in human nature,'" whereas they claim that "'avarice and desire of progress are constant elements,'" and, therefore, that "the human being" should be regarded wholly as "'a covetous machine'" (165). One should study (these economists insist) "'by what laws of labour, purchase, and sale, the greatest accumulative result in wealth is obtainable,'" and once those laws are determined, "'it will be for each individual afterwards to introduce as much of the disturbing affectionate element as he chooses, and to determine for himself the result on the new conditions supposed'" (165). Affects can be bought and tempered and tampered with, but the math gets fuzzy when it comes to their deeper roots in the mind—in which they belong as if in a maze of their own making.

Ruskin had answers and social experiments of his own to supply in the helpless absence of solutions to social ills coming from political economists. He saw economists mute and in default when facing "the first vital problem which political economy has to deal with (the relation between the employers and the employed)" (*Unto This Last* 168). Such desertion of the poor by the political science of economics is analogous to the absence of transcendent political and religious authority at the orphanage under the rule of Carmen and Dr Cáseres in *The Devil's Backbone*. Besides the ruins of politics at the abandoned institutional microcosm representing the entire nation of Spain, the socialist allegory of a parallel ruin in the economic order would represent the orphanage as a ghostly factory emptied of productive life (one good analogy being the workhouse Gothic environment in Dickens's *Oliver Twist*).

Among Ruskin's visual responses to the failed science of political economy the one best suited to a theory of ghosts in Gothic comes as he contemplates a science of gymnastics based on the assumption that men had no skeletons. He proceeds in cartoon fashion by showing boneless gymnasts being rolled into pellets, flattened into cakes, stretched into cables, and then having their bones reinserted into the desired new shapes. To such admirable results, Ruskin compares the triumph of modern political economy in its assumption, not that the human being is boneless, but that it is all bone. Hence, in dealing with all-skeleton or only-made-of-bones humans, political economy, he writes, "founds an ossifiant theory of progress on this negation of a soul; and having shown the utmost that may be made of bones, and constructed a number of interesting geometrical figures with death's-head and humeri, successfully proves the inconvenience of the reappearance of a soul among these corpuscular structures. I do not deny" (he adds) "the truth of this theory: I simply deny its applicability to the present phase of the world" (*Unto This Last* 168). Ruskin's hungry factory ghost under political economy is all bones and no soul. Thus, the same mind that revived and rebuilt cathedrals in character and distilled their stone essence into a preciously animate quality named *Gothicness* would have taken the ghost out of all ghosts. But not for any lack of personal belief in them: for, at their prime, ghosts are ghosts in Ruskin only as the walking dead in the hunger demographics of Gothic horror.

Such is the minimalist hard-times view of Ruskin's emptied soul in the skeleton of exploited labor. Thus viewed, the Ruskin-Dickens factory and workhouse represent our Castle Dismal in combined relevance to the Arenas and del Toro fictions of haunted childhood. We will now look at Ruskin's contribution to the soul economics of the labyrinth, following John D. Rosenberg's words about Ruskin's own character: "No other major English writer is so persistently autobiographical or has so successfully transmuted private pathology into great art. When Ruskin's nightmares usurp his waking life, as they did increasingly after 1878, he becomes certifiably insane. Yet in the last decade of his writing life, he creates two supreme expressions of genius, *Fors Clavigera* (1871–1884) and *Praeterita* (1885–1889)" ("Devil and Mr. Ruskin" 31). Besides Ruskin's periodic working madness, the issue here lies in the definitive modern character stamp he puts on the labyrinth as the mind's soulful and bewitched ground site. With this he contributes to situating Fantasy and its genres in adult perspective and in the mirror of insanity—even if his actual writings on mazes and labyrinths might have been achieved in full control of his senses.

With Ofelia and her Faun in mind, I will proceed to sketch an album of women *loved-and-unloved and wished-and-unwished-for-and-disavowed* by Ruskin (in this hyphened thorn-stem-bramble word lies the maze) from his adolescence to old age. I have in mind three biographic lessons for Ofelia in whatever latitude she may find herself at this point and the next Fantasy instant (as if learning about Ruskin-in-love meant finding, upon the blank pages of Ofelia's magical book, a few lines on how the girl inhabits the Faun).[3]

### Ruskin's Ofelia and Ours
*Adèle-Clotilde Domecq*

Ruskin first met the daughter of Pedro Domecq in 1833 at age fourteen in Paris when she was thirteen. Domecq had been appointed wine merchant to the king of Spain and was a partner with Ruskin's father in that business. His family owned large vineyards in Spain. He was educated in France, as were his daughters. Two years after the Paris meeting, when Adèle and her unmarried sisters came to stay in England with her father, John fell in love with her, to such ill effects upon his mood, that he wrote how passion reduced him to ashes and the Ash Wednesday lasted four years (but in fact it lasted longer, perhaps a lifetime).

Adèle never fell for John, who wrote about giving her lessons on "the Spanish Armada, the Battle of Waterloo, and Transubstantiation" during their second meeting at the Ruskin house in Herne Hill (Hilton, *Early Years* 36). Ruskin's inconsolable and embittered young love for Adèle is enshrined as late as *Praeterita,* when he recalls their last season in contact: "'Every feeling and folly, that had been subdued or forgotten, returned in double force . . . and day followed day, and month to month, of complex absurdity, pain error, wasted affection, and rewardless semi-virtue, which I am content to sweep out of what better things I can recollect at this time, into the smallest possible size of dust heap, and wish the Dustman Oblivion good clearance of them'" (quoted in Hilton, *Later Years* 52). (In such words dust and ashes mix in funeral homage to love's debris.)

The first lesson that Adèle Domecq's case might have for Ofelia in her own labyrinth lies in the boy who encounters in pain a human object he could never possess. In *Ruskin's Poetic Argument,* Paul L. Sawyer has grasped the full force of this drama and its aftershocks in Ruskin's life; it is like tracing love's lost engraving upon the labyrinth features of his creative life. John Ruskin's teenage love goal was "less to win Adèle than to construct a drama" (23). He wanted to construct a drama—and a maze—in which to replay and suffer through once again an earlier love loss and to signal to his parents that the loss occurred on their watch. After a second and desolate period of failure during Ruskin's years at Oxford—in which Adèle was engaged to a baron she had never met but felt quite ready to marry—Ruskin took the wounding traces of her memory to Italy. Sawyer cites in the *Diaries* (split between entries under *Head* and under *Heart*) the lines in which Ruskin begins to trace the future *Stones of Venice* as if joyfully silhouetting Adèle's grief-causing love-shadow: "'I feel fresh and young when my foot is on these pavements, and the outlines of St. Mark's thrill me as if they had been traced by Adèle's hand'" (*Ruskin's Poetic Argument* 26). The loss that might perhaps explain the lasting hurt caused by Adèle would have been the final loss of Ruskin's child self. Here is a double lesson for our Ofelia in the architecture of wounded love: the life of overprotected and gifted childhood is all at once lost and recovered through the agency of sorrow and pain. The teenage Ruskin was destined to suffer pain in falling in love with Adèle even before he felt rejected by her. He was primed for this by what I will persist in calling the *genius* (also genie) that had taken root in him as implanted by overzealous and controlling parents. Much later in life, he would blame them—in the person of his mother—for the vulnerability that wounded his mature genialness. But these injuries may have infused his character with greater energies than the ones he would have earned without so painful a failure. He wrote to his father: "'Men ought to be severely disciplined and exercised in the sternest way in daily life . . . , but they should never have their hearts broken. . . . Mama and you . . . fed me effeminately and luxuriously . . . but you thwarted me in all the earnest fire of passion and life'" (quoted in Sawyer, *Ruskin's Poetic Argument* 27). This is one thorny way for the girl to take root inside the Faun as Labyrinth.

### *Rose La Touche*

Studying a tomb whose established fame his own writings would enhance, Ruskin wrote about the tomb of Ilaria di Caretto that "the sculpture, as art, is in every way perfect—*truth* itself, but truth selected with inconceivable refinement of feeling" (quoted in Rosenberg, "Devil and

Mr. Ruskin" 34). His enraptured absorption in Jacopo della Quercia's tomb of a young wife's last repose became confused as years passed with the image of Rose La Touche. He met Rose when she was almost ten and he was about to reach forty. Within two years he had fallen in love with the girl in a manner idolatrous and obsessed. Her age at the time makes Rose even closer than Adèle to being our Ofelia's peer and playmate. In the final pages of *Praeterita,* among the last sentences Ruskin ever penned, their first sight of each other is rendered: "'So presently the drawing room door opened, and Rosie came in, quietly taking stock of me with her blue eyes as she walked across the room; gave me her hand, as a good dog gives its paw, and then stood a little back. Nine years old on 3rd January, 1858, thus now rising toward ten; neither tall nor short for her age; a little stiff on her way of standing'" (Hilton, *Early Years* 264). In matters of love ruined and made notorious by its nonconsummation, Ruskin carried into his chaste obsession with Rose a lot of what is nowadays called baggage. His marriage to Effie Gray had been annulled in 1854, some four years before he met Rose, on grounds the wife remained a virgin after six years of union. But toward Rose, Ruskin would express worshipful yearnings to crawl to her gate like a serf begging for mastery: "'I am so sick already for the sight of her, that—if it were not that it would plague herself, I would go to Ireland now, and lie down at their gate—and let them do what they chose with me, but would see her'" (Hilton, *Later Years* 107). Such were the wishes of a love possessed by the girl's character imprint rising from a man's mother-smothered past.

Ruskin named Rose's mother "Lacerta" for *lizard* and often described her as reptilian evil. Tim Hilton explains that in some of Ruskin's writings Maria La Touche "was connected in his mind with some deep horror, only partly inherited from Genesis," and he goes on to link Maria and Rose in Ruskin's mind, issuing one of the hardest truths ever applied to him:

> It is possible that Ruskin wished that Rose had not been born of womankind, as all people are. Not only was she virginal: her nature was such that her mother had failed her by not being herself a virgin. Only a little evidence supports this speculation. We know of Ruskin's strange dislike of babies. He usually avoided the subject of birth, including his own. In all his life he never approached his own birthplace, 54 Hunter Street, though he paid many dozens of visits to the British Museum and other places in Bloomsbury within a few hundred yards of the place of his mother's parturition. After Margaret Ruskin's death in 1871 she was commemorated by her son as though she had

> lived and died a virgin. Perhaps Ruskin could not bear the thought that his beloved Rose had come into the world as the result of a sexual act. (*Early Years* 112–13)

Rose La Touche guards the Dragon Gates of Ruskin's gnostic apprehension of a woman's maternal insides.

Of the three love stories sketched here, the one with Rose La Touche at its center is most likely to engage Ofelia's passion. It is too complex for encapsulation, but foremost among the few essentials to be mentioned is Rose's intense religiosity. She was a devoted evangelical who moved among adepts to the cause from the upper classes; described by Hilton as a bizarre host of wealthy and titled converts to a revivalist faith at first glance better suited for people of humbler means. Rose's piety found an outlet in public praying. Ruskin responded by consenting to her saintliness in a letter to a friend in which Rose's prayers are given credit for suddenly restoring a sick girl to health (Hilton, *Later Years* 114). But the image of Rose as saint and her increasing frailty and eventual death—emaciated and maddened by some anorexia-related illness—should not stamp her as a victim or in any sense disabled or morbid.

Among Tim Hilton's insights into Rose's active mind amid her unhappiness is his emphasis on her search after the secrets of Ruskin's sexuality. Why was such a gifted older man so full of worship in his desire to marry her? Although barred by her parents from seeing him, Rose never dropped Ruskin from her life and had the moral courage to return to him her copy of *The Queen of the Air,* either, as Hilton wonders, in contempt, or perhaps to have him read her annotations on his text. Hilton observes that Rose tormented Ruskin with her contradictions, that she "was indeed an unpredictable young woman, especially now that she was in her early twenties," and that she "was demure but possessed an Anglo-Irish wildness," and—while being called a "'younger sister to Jesus Christ'"—could "fly into passions and had been known to strike her father" (*Later Years* 171). Rose stood up to Ruskin, even as his distant and ostracized powers of mind and spirit occasionally entered her dwindling existence and may have aggravated her food anxieties and health. This she accomplished while having to absorb the gossip about Ruskin's dismal sex habits in accusatory letters from his ex-wife, Effie Gray, and other sources of gossip. Reacting to such information, Rose wrote: "'If [Ruskin] had been a heathen it would have been different, but he who had been brought up in Christ's religion, who had been given by God such power to know and love what was divine to sin as he did while writing as he did—it utterly overpowers me with the mysterious ghastliness of it all'" (quoted in Hilton, *Later Years* 237). The passionate though unsentimental hard core of Ruskin's ghastly Faun example for our Ofelia would have to surge out of the labyrinth that Rose La Touche thought she had plumbed before writing this letter.

But Ofelia's reading of Ruskin—facilitated by her magical blank-page book—should center on the twentieth letter of *Fors Clavigera*. This magical operation does not entail her reading Ruskin in the bulk—which helps a lot; and it does not seem out of line with del Toro's film to imagine that Ofelia's reading of her magical book may include the telepathic absorption of stories that would land upon its pages. The importance of Ruskin's "Benediction" letter lies in its sermon texture and subject matter: the stark and harsh contrast drawn by him between a saintly girl, whom he studies in total immersion, and two American girls in whose insufferable company he travels by carriage from Venice to Verona.

It was in Verona that he had cloistered himself in prolonged and minute meditation upon Vittore Carpaccio's *The Dream of St. Ursula*. John D. Rosenberg draws the counterpoint between the saint on canvas and Rose La Touche: "Ursula had been courted by a heathen prince; Rose, much troubled by Ruskin's growing 'heathenism,' had deferred his marriage proposal for three years, as Ursula had deferred the proposal of her prince. In the rigid stillness of Ursula's unbending body, he saw the prefiguration of Rose's death. Upend Ruskin's 'sleeping' Ilaria or the dreaming Ursula and you see, unmistakably, the features of Rose, a triptych of sister faces" ("Devil and Mr. Ruskin" 33). Ruskin's epistolary sermon on benediction frames the meditation upon the dreaming St. Ursula in reference to the ancient and modern ways of cursing and blessing in religious practice. He first enjoins his reader to consider how "cursing seems at present the most effectual means for encouraging human work," and he asks us to ponder whether "it may not be conceivable that the work itself is of a kind which any form of effectual blessing would hinder instead of help" (*Genius of John Ruskin* 390). Ruskin then asks about "the faith in a spiritual world" involved—or not—in present ways of cursing through prayer. In one prayer, God is begged to damn someone's soul, and in another, He is asked to damn only parts of the body. Ruskin further asks what sort of mischief—other than in spiritual terms—is sought in damning only certain body parts and their faculties. He claims that we are for the most part unconscious of the spiritual thrust behind our cursing—in God's name—only the flesh and its motions. He doubts that such a split could actually occur in segregating body parts from the spirit through the efficacy requested of God in praying. Thus, before addressing benediction, Ruskin insists on finding God in cursing and questions the split sought in having the accursed so damned *only* in the flesh, but *not* in spirit (all this as if the vicious passion at work in cursing either way did not aim at manifesting the involvement of God in any manner of badmouthing in His name).

Ofelia's interest in so arcane a matter would quickly fade if it were not for those two American girls traveling by carriage from Venice to Verona, seated across from the professor, who are about to be condemned by him in his most foul Faun mood. Between Ruskin's teaching on cursing and the girls episode comes his sublime meditation on the saintly girl Ursula. So the girls from America are up against stiff competition from a great aesthetician and a Catholic saint. However, the central purpose in Ruskin's moral aesthetics fails if the painted St. Ursula and the living girls are isolated from each other—as we might now say—ontologically. (A big word for our Ofelia to learn, but she already knows the outcome of being dead and not being dead, on film, and that is the ultimate way of learning how to cope with ontological difference.)

The girl passengers on that fateful day were not the impossible Victorian precursors of the study-abroad U.S. undergraduates of more recent vintage, as they traveled with both their parents, unaware that across from them sat the recently appointed Slade Professor of Art at Oxford University. Nor could they have guessed, for lack of inclination or instinct, that he had just emerged from hours of meditation in recent days about a princess who had become a saint some centuries ago, or that they would find themselves, in proper anonymity, cast as the accursed and lazy and morose counterparts of the princess's industrious blessedness.

We will skip the most important part of the letter, the part most likely to go into the syllabus for a class on Victorian aesthetics, in which Ruskin scrutinizes the room and the dream state of the saint as she dreams the allegorical—and hence more than just real—figure of the intruding angel before her sleeping gaze. Except for: "So dreams the princess with blessed eyes, that need no earthly dawn . . . but the lovely characteristic of all is the evident delight of her continual life. Royal power over herself, and happiness in her flowers, her books, her sleeping, and waking, her prayers, her dreams, her earth, her heaven" (*Genius of John Ruskin* 394). In the meantime, the American girls in the carriage went on acting in blindness with their eyes open before Ruskin. They curtained the Alps from their own bored sight and fought Italian flies from landing on their flesh. They were, Ruskin writes, "two girls of about fifteen and eighteen," who had "evidently been indulged in everything (since they had had the means) which western civilization could imagine" and were "the specimens of the utmost which the money and invention of the nineteenth century could produce in maidenhood—children of its most progressive race," who enjoyed "the full advantages of political liberty, of enlightened philosophical education, of cheap pilfered literature, and of luxury at any cost" (394). It is hard to tell in hindsight in which direction Ruskin exaggerates about the girls' moral dereliction. A chiasmus in historical time emerges with respect to Ruskin's immediate and still current past and our own equivalent past in recent times. One may ask whether Ruskin exaggerates with respect to the civility attained by the battered and pillaged American country in the midst of Reconstruction and westward expansion, a nation not too far behind his own—and to him in this regard quite loathsome Britain—in producing the horrors of the poor, having already fostered those of the enslaved. Or does Ruskin exaggerate (quite fantastically) for us now, in particular, with respect to the current imperial and embattled nation, closer to us from our vantage point after the catastrophe of September 11, 2001? For this is the event that in del Toro's DVD comments compels him to write and film the story of choice and disobedience by *a girl who gives birth to herself the way she wanted to be.* In our quest for the Faun in the girl and for Ruskin in Ofelia, this dual perspective opens up: Ruskin's immediate and still present past and our own.

Let us get back to the future, as it were, between Venice and Verona. The two American girls "were neither princesses, nor seers, nor dreamers," like the sleeping saintly Ursula: "By infinite self-indulgence, they had reduced themselves simply to two pieces of white putty that could feel pain. The flies and the dust stuck to them as to clay, and they perceived, between Venice and Verona, nothing but the flies and the dust. . . . And so they went their way, with sealed eyes and tormented limbs, their numbered miles of pain" (*Genius of John Ruskin* 395). Now we reach—as would perhaps our Ofelia—the sermon's two examined moral conditions in clearest contrast: the "Blessed" and the "Accursed." In Ursula: "the happy industry, the eyes full of sacred imagination of things that are not." In the girls: "the tortured indolence, and infidel eyes, blind even to the things that are" (395). The words *tortured* and *infidel* coexist in this sentence: "tortured" is rendered explicit by "indolence," while "infidel" does not refer to those who might use the term against others deemed evil. Rather, "infidel" points at the unfaithful opposite of "such sweet *cosa è la fede*"—the phrase that illustrates how Ursula's sacred imagination grasps *things that are not.* The terrible moral for our Ofelia—and for her to fear, love, or hate—comes down to this: *it being inconceivable for John Ruskin to have cursed the girls, either by himself or by invoking God's name, he would be showing his readers how the accursed do curse themselves with no help from God or prayer.* The two girls before him *were* accursed, period. Such sharply edged reversal of Calvinist doctrines on election and damnation would have to work its way into our Ofelia's sense of her own disobedience to the Faun and the limits to His (or his?) unearthly powers to create and destroy.

### *Effie Gray*

In a letter to her mother, Effie Gray (at the time still Mrs. John Ruskin) writes about a friend's infant in her husband's regard: "'John allows it to be passable for a baby because it has eyes like rat's fur and he likes it a little because it is not like a baby at all, but has a black face like a mouldy walnut, which is a great deal for him as it is quite against his principles to admire any of them at all'" (*Early Years* 120). Our Ofelia knows quite well the difference between a baby fetus made from a mandrake root and the brother she believes her mother Carmen carries in her belly. The mandrake baby that Ofelia hides under Carmen's bed is linked by sympathetic magic to the human in the womb. Its removal from under the bed by the baby's expectant father causes the horror of the mother's death in giving birth to Ofelia's brother. No one knows exactly why a mind as complex as Ruskin's came to loathe babies before he reached middle age. Effie tells her father in another letter that her husband cannot "'bear lumps of *putty* as he terms babies'" (*Early Years* 120). Thus, when he writes that the two American girls had "reduced themselves simply to two pieces of white putty that could feel pain," Ruskin might be casting them as large overdone babies. (One assumes that seeing the Pillsbury Doughboy would have caused him to vomit.) To Hilton's suggestion that Ruskin's phobia could stem from his aversion to sexual intercourse, it may be added that he could have found loathsome some—for him—seemingly edible aspects of the newly born child, in its fresh emergence from the mother's oven maw.

Ruskin's dreadful fantasies about the business of birth and obstetrics might have been involved in the shock he experienced upon beholding Effie Gray's body on their wedding night, April 10, 1848. In a letter to her father, written shortly before her flight from Ruskin in the summer of 1854, Effie mentions that she "'had never been told the duties of married persons to each other and knew nothing about their relation in the closest union on earth,'" and goes on to explain that John talked about that relation with her, even as he affirmed his intention not to have them enter into it. She writes that "'he alleged various reasons, hatred of children, religious motives, a desire to preserve my beauty,'" and that just weeks before she wrote the letter, "'his true reason'"—to her "'as villainous as all the rest'"—was given. She writes that the reason that "'he had imagined women were quite different to what he saw I was, and the reason he had not made me his Wife was because he was disgusted with my person the first evening April 10th'" (*Early Years* 118). Even when not told about bedroom sexual intimacy (and perhaps due to such censored attitude) persons of either sex would appear odd when imagined as having a clean slate in their minds about such matters. Ruskin was immensely well read and possessed a wondrous imagination, so Effie's testimony about his having imagined women being quite different from how she looked that night could not mean he thought they were related to mermaids. Or, if he did, this particular mermaid sister proved rather odd. As stated in his deposition for the annulment: "'It may be thought strange that I *could* abstain from a woman who to most people was so attractive. But though her face was beautiful, her person was not formed to excite passion. On the contrary, there were certain circumstances in her person which completely checked it. I did not think either, that there could be anything in my own person particularly attractive to *her:* but believed that she loved me, as I loved her, with little mingling of desire'" (*Early Years* 118).

It is at this point that Ofelia should turn her attention to the married affairs of Mr. and Mrs. John Ruskin, and for that purpose it would be best if she found on the blank pages of her Faun's magical book a downloaded version of the book *Young Mrs. Ruskin in Venice,* edited by a certain Mary Lutyens—with a name written in pencil over the title by a librarian: *Millais, Euphemia Chalmers (Gray) Lady,* implying that there is not only life but even married life after being married to John Ruskin.

On faith that Ofelia would perform just such a reading, we will skip the intense, short Ruskin years in Rome and Venice, including Effie's romancing with Austrians officers, two of whom wanted to fight a duel on her account. (This reading by Ofelia would only serve as appetizer for her reading about the love affair between Effie and John Everett Millais—the love that allowed Effie to break away from Ruskin, annul their union, and marry, in less than a year after the annulment, the man who found her fit—as even certain mermaids are—for the love and motherhood of eight children.)

Once past the thrill and distraction of learning how a new kind of love freed a married couple from the habit of their mutual misery, Ofelia would discover that, before Millais used Effie to pose for the wife in *The Order of Release, 1745* and painter and model fell in love, he had done the death of Ophelia in *Hamlet*—based on Gertrude's words, fixed upon the oblivious girl's garments as they

> heavy with their drink
> Pulled the poor maid from her melodious lay
> To muddy death.
> (Shakespeare, *Hamlet* 4.7.181–83)

Mad Ophelia lies restful, half in and half out of the still water, as if enraptured, her mouth open, in numbness or in bliss, as the dress, in its dense and now drenched richness, pulls her body under by its lower half. (The painted scene would cast a spell upon our Ofelia even if the names did not match.)

We turn now to *The Order of Release, 1746* (figure 1). Millais had started painting it in late December of 1853 after asking Effie to sit for the Highlander's wife. He worked on her face first, after moving into the Ruskins house at Herne Hill, where painting sessions lasted from breakfast to dusk. As she sat before her painter and maker in oils and brushes, Effie was not chaperoned, which in Victorian manners was not strictly decorous. In pointing this out, Tim Hilton explains that "the only acceptable way to appear in painting was as the subject of a commissioned portrait" (*Early Years* 179). Her posing made Effie a model, and academy models were regarded as loose women—as in fact they often were. Yet the Ruskin family would not profess the belief that "the woman who was made an Academy model could not be a virtuous woman" until Effie fled from John (*Early Years* 179–80). Her flight took place in the spring of 1854. The summer before, Millais had joined her and John in a tour of Scotland, during which their growing devotion to each other's company grew intensely as Millais went about painting Ruskin's portrait by a waterfall.

The focus of interest in the notorious and widely admired painting *The Order of Release, 1746* narrows to the symbolic and allegorical meanings I wish to invest in its portrayal of a troubled family reunion. Specifically, I wish to focus on the quartet cluster of mother and child with the father and the figure of the jail guard. By virtue of the resembling—though slightly different—angle at which the reposing head of the husband and father rests upon the wife's and mother's shoulder, and the head of the jailer leans over the order's paper as he reads it, the heads and faces may be adapted into a kinship frame subordinate to marriage.

We will examine in the following two chapters of Castle Dismal the incestuous associations in the Arenas boyhood between mother, son, father, and maternal grandfather. Let us now establish the same association in the painting's cluster of heads, moving from left to right. A line of family succession appears in descending ages and ranks. The older—though

Figure 1. John Everett Millais, *The Order of Release, 1745*. 1853, oil on canvas. Tate Gallery, London.

neither actually nor pictorially old enough—guard would stand in this allegory as the wife's father—rather than her husband's. But in the incestuous warp that gives shape to the world of boyhood, Arenas would transform the father's father figure into *both* the releasing wife's and the released husband's father(s).

Such kinship convolution will prove relentless as we examine the incestuous imagination displayed in the fictions of Arenas. In this regard, two curls or loops can be traced in the painting. One curl begins with the dog's muzzle touching the couple's joined hands as it curls and climbs right, up, and then left, through the hands of the child, the father's, the child's head and the mother's and father's, his shoulder, her hand holding the paper, and the guard and his inspecting glance. Another and shorter loop moves from the dog's left hind leg to his right one, curling through the mother's bare feet and around and behind the rippled and rounding surface of her garment to the husband's obscured left leg and forward to his right, pillared leg, and to the guard's right leg, only in partial view.

Taking the hands as focal points directing our gaze into the scene, one should observe two starting points: her right hand joined to the guard's left by the soon-releasing agency of the paper note and her left hand joined to her husband's right as if reaffirming their sacred union. The dog's head and the guard's reflect each other in the angle at which they look upon different but related things. The jailer reads what he must obey and the dog "reads" what it cannot and does not need to read in obedience to its masters. This brings us close to the unwanted pathetic fallacy proscribed by Ruskin in painting and art in general. Even though the dog is no plant or landscape and has feelings cultivated by breeding and petting, such knowing feelings in this case actually resonate in the guard's attitude and status. The animal actively and spiritedly observes reunion. The guard submits his glance to a subaltern reading of the superior ordinance to release his prisoner. While the dog *knows* what he must know and thus knows that reunion has taken place beyond release, the guard only knows that the release must take place and knows—at that instant locked in pictorial time—nothing of union beyond what the order commands.

Two further points need to be made with respect to the woman. An interpretation once fashionable but now generally dismissed by art historians claims that she has paid for the release by offering herself to the releaser: not to the subaltern guard of course but to one of his superiors. What may seem a needless and redundant remark about the guard and his higher-up will find its niche in the incest-ridden realm of boyhood

Arenas. For it will become obvious that, besides the fantasies and desired actualities about sex between parental figures and their children in the Arenas boyhood domain, power—in its obsessed absence and obsessive presence—rules as the comptroller of incest: as seen from the desiring perspective of the controlled. Incest is thus welcome as the most intense and accursed mark of sovereign family Arenas rule.

Seen from the Arenas angle and as explored next, the gestures of release in the painting read as follows. She hands the order to her father. The piece of paper releases her husband from jail. Except that she never has had a husband. The figure that rests its head on her shoulder remains there—but it is also forever gone from her and the child's joint lives. The child asleep on her other shoulder has a father who fled and left both him and his mother stranded in her father's jaillike house. The child is about the age of the Arenas boy when his father exited his life and buried himself in his mind forever. From his present dreams the child will awake to tell and retell the family tale in voices that involve both genders and a host of relatives in awful assault of each other nerves, lives, and afterlives.

# 4 A House of Sand

> If you know anything of me, you know how I sprang out of misery, akin to none, a thing concocted out of the elements, without visible agency—how, all through my boyhood, I was alone; how I grew up without a root, yet continually longing for one—longing to be connected with somebody—and never feeling myself so.
>
> Nathaniel Hawthorne, *The American Claimant: Etherege*

THIS CHAPTER and the next rehearse the posthumous and otherworldly authorship connection between Reinaldo Arenas and Nathaniel Hawthorne with some help from William Faulkner, St. Augustine, and Milton. The Hawthorne authorship nexus begins with the words just quoted in the epigraph taken from the *Etherege* part of the most important among Hawthorne's unfinished romances. The bulky manuscript has been christened *The American Claimant* and its constituent parts are known as *The Ancestral Footstep, Etherege,* and *Grimshawe.* During his tenure as U.S. consul in Liverpool, Hawthorne envisioned and set to work on a romance or historical novel about the legal claims made by an American of his own New England Puritan ancestry upon his family's ancestral home turf on English soil.

Hawthorne's transatlantic historical family romance reclamation is comparable to the one established by Julieta Campos in her transhistorical 2003 family saga *La forza del destino*. The resemblance unfortunately lies in the unpublished monumentality of Hawthorne's grand carcass of a romance and the virtually posthumous quality of *La forza* as a historical project set to fiction as it might have been set to music. Posthumous in relation to the ancient, Jurassic-to-modernist, politically extinct *Cuba* memorialized in its symphonic pages and allegorical designs; posthumous in the epitaph characters it inscribes upon the author's ultimate vision of redemptive fiction-making confronting the Fall in its present though revocable causes and effects.

In this chapter, the Hawthorne connection concerns *The Scarlet Letter* and its core elements of adultery and split-parenting and haunted childhood. These elements will frame the examination of related themes in the fictional biography and experiments in alternate and multiple choral selves undertaken by Reinaldo Arenas from the early stories in *Comienza el desfile* (1964–68) to the novel *Otra vez el mar* (*Farewell to the Sea*)—the definitive posthumous work, having disappeared by various causes and means in its two earliest versions (1966/1970 and 1970–72) to be reborn in 1972–74 and revised into final form between 1980 and 1982.

## *NH* Written in the Sand

The confession of childhood loneliness and yearning for true connection with another "somebody" made by Hawthorne's late voice in *Etherege* will be stitched or monogrammed with the *A* or *Arenas*—the *A* of *Sand*. As a result, the text from *Celestino antes del alba,* or *Singing from the Well,* quoted next will be marked with the *NH* of Hawthorne under the sign of *A*—the *A* of Hester (Hester Prynne become Arenas Sand). A piece of narration or short story is born lost but lodged between two couples: mother Hester Prynne and daughter Pearl clasped together in *The Scarlet Letter* and the boy protagonist and his mother standing in front of their abandoned ancestral house and looking at it from inside and within poverty's foreshortened agelessness. Pearl Sand's name and her mother's are signed in the sand together with those boys who by alternate names like Celestino and Fortunato animate the loneliness of the singular sandman boy named Arenas in recognition of his vanished father.

Here, then, in a nutshell is *NH*'s story of *A* as told by Arenas and labeled "A House for Mr. A":

> And now the house is falling down. If it does finally fall down, what'll become of those voices I still hear saying "Christmas," "Christmas" over and over again. What'll become of me, still rolling around from being so happy, over there in the breeze way under the wasp-nest. If the house falls down, the water closet and the crocks will smash into a million pieces, and then I'm not going to be able to keep on living. If the house falls down, the big old cookstove, that's just slapped together out of wet ashes, will crumble to pieces too, and then I'm not going to be able to keep on living. If the house falls down all the jabbering and carrying-on of my cousins, who come to the Christmas Eve party, would come tumbling down too, and I'm not going to be able to keep on living. And the worst thing of all—if the house does finally fall down, we'd have to move away into another one, and then I'd have to start being born all over again, and find another word all over again to make me laugh out loud like that. And convince the wasps all over again to put up a wasp-nest in the breezeway. And keep after Grandpa all over again to pour some water into the washtub in the

> yard and to make a loblolly like the one there is now. And I'd have to wait for a long long long time for the roof to get black from the smoke and soot, like the one on our house is now, and maybe it wouldn't even get the way this one is if you waited a long time. And if the house doesn't have an old smoky black roof I don't want to live in it. And if the house doesn't have cracks in it all over the place and you can't see the same thing through every single crack that I can see through these ones, I don't want to live in it. And if the house doesn't have some goat's feet, up next to some ears of corn strung up, hanging from the ridgepole of the roof, I don't want to live in it, either. And if the house doesn't have a corner door and if there's not an old termite-eaten piece of palm thatch leaning up next to the corner door, I don't want to live in it. And even if it does have all those things—if the house doesn't have a well, full of maidenhair ferns and voices, then I'll never ever live in it. No, there couldn't ever be another house that would be like this one and hide all the secret things I've done in it. The other one would be strange for me, and I'd be strange for it, too.
>
> So then I cry, because I know the house doesn't exist anymore. But as soon as I start crying I stop again, because I remember I'll have to move away into a new house and there's no way it'll know about this crying. So I'm just wasting my time. (*SW* 137–38/120–21).

This is the type of falling house that never falls down perhaps because it does not stand or exist in the manner houses and humans and things organic or inorganic do. It is the house of here and there, the house in the mind and of the mind and its attributes and places here and there and everywhere the mind in spirit dwells. It is the place where mind encounters feelings, passions, home roots, and their inherent contraries, anomie, numbness, vacancy, a house always here as well as elsewhere, much like the one a certain Mr. Biswas at long last bought for himself.

When commenting on the passage from Hawthorne on childhood loneliness placed at the head of this chapter, T. Walter Herbert calls it a "wrenching lament" and finds it "spectacularly at odds with the story of Hawthorne's boyhood" (*Dearest Beloved* 59). Herbert reminds us that Nathaniel junior (who later in life added a letter to his father's last name) "grew up in a welter of kinfolk" and was born "in his Hathorne grandmother's house . . . where his mother and older sister crowded in with . . . his two Hathorne unmarried aunts" (59). His father and his uncles lived there too, but sea captain Nathaniel senior spent only seven months at home during his seven years of marriage before dying of yellow fever in Surinam after seeing his only son for the last time when the child was three years and five months old. After his father's death, Nathaniel junior was moved by his mother with his two sisters into her Manning clan household adjoining the Hathorne home. The increased Manning home became a full house in which fourteen people shared their lives across generations in varying degrees of acquiescence and reclusiveness.[1]

At first glance, the Hawthorne childhood loneliness lament expressed in *Etherege* seems mismatched by the feeling of crowded encroachment that permeates the fallen and abandoned houses in the Arenas boyhood fictions. But, just as the adult writer's lament proves "spectacularly at odds" with Hawthorne's own crowded surroundings in childhood and adolescence, the corresponding human saturation in what I call the House of Sand turns into a vortex of loneliness for the child in Arenas. Hawthorne achieves loneliness while in plenty of company as an orphaned boy, while boyhood in the fictions of Arenas regains solitude amid the fury of adult bad company. Conjured together, the remembered boyhood and joined lives of *NH* and *RA* take shelter in the sandglass of solitude. Boyhood absconds itself in loneliness against claims on behalf of aging often made by adults who are themselves aging badly.

Dreams transport solitude first-class into further allegiance with the omnipotent mind all at once asleep and wakeful. The same house enlarged in life and larger still in dreams is revisited by the teenager who daydreams while at work hammering together a thousand guava craters, "so as not to starve to death" (*PWS* 176/183). The dream house returns in sleep, this time to him, to his mother, and one of many aunts. The small-town neighbors have returned to the boarded-up hulk of the giant *bohío* shack abandoned by the owners, who had bought it from the grandfather in a bad deal—an ill-fated sale that uprooted the family from its country roost and the boy from the feral mythical sites of his childhood. The insides of the house have been partitioned, and the kitchen now lies halved. The cookstove, a cheaper one, stands no longer at the center but shoved against the wall. The "enormous pile of palm branches and palm thatch and boards cut from palm trees, . . . the sun, the wind, the rain had faded into gray" (*PWS* 178/185). All of it has lodged itself in the mind of an all-seeing blind seer shuttered from the past he knows he must escape.

## Arenas and Faulkner in Male Singular

The house shack was made of something besides dirt and sand stuffed by mind and spirit. As shown in the dream just examined, it was a huge *bohío* walled with palm wood bark and thatched with palm branches that grew in the manner in which the early settlers of Faulkner's Frenchman's Bend in *The Hamlet* built their shelters: "They took up land and built one- and two-room cabins and never painted them, and married one another and produced children and added other rooms one by one to the original cabins" (*Hamlet* 4). But the house in the Arenas boyhood is filled with rejected brides and not with a cast of inbred clan nesters of the Snopes family kind. Yet Flem Snopes's face does strike a twisted and queered resemblance to a grandfather trait in boyhood Arenas: "the face of the breathing archetype and protagonist of all men who marry young and father only daughters and are themselves but the eldest daughter of their own wives" (*Hamlet* 9). The Arenas *abuelo* old sire (whom we have seen earlier in the Noah role reflected in Ham's or Cham's eyes) fulfills now the young marriage likeness to Flem Snopes and also the even harder to prove eldest daughter's role to his own wife as indexed by Faulkner.

Proving the myth narrative DNA of such an odd sibling nexus between husband, wife, and first child involves showing how the boy grandchild in Arenas is part of a similar husband-as-eldest-daughter lynchpin tie to his mother as his own wife. In childhood Arenas, the grandchild boy asserts himself as a male singular person made up of several boys, girls, women, and men. This is how the husband in the father (who is also his own daughter to his wife) becomes the future grandfather to a boy who now repeats his role in reverse: being like the eldest daughter of his grandpa, who is like his oldest aunt, as if she were his mother and his mother were in twisted/queered ways his own grandmother.

Among these boys and men and girls and women clustered under one singular person, three pairings stand out: the one between Bestial and the boy already examined ("Bestial entre las flores"), the one between Celestino and the cousin in whom he dwells as resident alien self (*Celestino antes del alba*), and the one between Fortunato and the boy perspective from which, as in the previous two cases, the boy singular person performs in alternate counterpoint with his other persons and roles (*El palacio de las blanquísimas mofetas*). These boyhood persons in Arenas represent the *A* of *alternity* stamped by the girl Pearl upon her mother's *A*-branded bosom in *The Scarlet Letter.* The *A* of adultery stitched on Hester's dress with its "fertility and gorgeous luxuriance of fancy" (*Scarlet Letter* 40) becomes in Pearl the *A* of double paternity keyed by the alternate male parenthood shared by Hester's husband, Roger Prynne, camouflaged under the name Chillingworth, and by her lover Arthur Dimmesdale.

A similar paternity overwritten by alternity exists in the Arenas boyhood. It exists not only in his having to put up with more than one father in the absence of his father, but also in having to face up to the alternate involvement in his life of siblings, such as sisterlike cousins, aunts, and grandparents, all of whom nurse the singular male child's character at home in jubilant despair. Alternity operates as a function of paternity. It works as the alternative to the father implanted in the child without his own choice or recourse. The boy male singular carries with it a *-like* hookup indexical mark wherein each family relative acts as (or like) the type of relative in question, but indexed as such, as in quotation marks. Likewise, being *sisterlike* or *motherlike* also implies the boy's own hook-up role as: *my mother is as motherlike to herself and to me as I myself am to her and to each sibling and parent rank*. As such, the indexical pointer *-like* that links together all such kinship markers of incrusted identities pivots on *father* as the axis term.

The indexical character and force of the sibling ranks examined here transform the word *father* (and its contextual and connotative and unexpressed shifting status throughout the narratives in question) into the equivalent of a first-person speech-act proposition. That is to say, the term *father* (uttered or written or silenced) is to be heard as "father"—as something being said (or not said) as well as being intended (or implied or unintended) *about father* and the contextual emotions and symptoms that the term absorbs into itself and generates.

In similar indexical hook-up manner (and above and beyond particular instances of difference between them) Bestial's and Celestino's dead mothers are *-like* instances or indexical alternates of each other. Bestial's mother hangs herself and drags in the wake of her suicide the boy's own motherlike selfhood gift to her as well as hers to his. Bestial's hanged mother is to her son what Celestino's hanged mother Eulogia is to herself and her son and the father, who in the boy's understanding raped her as anyone might have due to her dumbness. The *-like* indexical circle comes around as the grandfather, who rapes his daughter in Eulogia, rapes another daughter in the boy's imagination—as told in *Before Night Falls* and *The Palace of White Skunks*.

Such reoccurrence of characters and scenes bound to reiteration implies that they are different only as indexical alternate figures of a fixed core of selfhood hooked up to the *-like* parenting mark that binds together all of those who alternate to and from a seminal mark in the boy's mind struck by default upon the father. Present in each shifting scene, fatherhood becomes the indexical clone effect of itself as a hidden first cause in which, generationwise, all siblings lie stuck and vibrating queerly.

Rather than being just a matter of repeated narratives in alternate shapes, the story of Bestial may be seen as its own sibling and parent cloned in Celestino's scenes and later on in Fortunato's. *A rose is a rose is a rose* resonates here as kinship repetition among gathered stories of boyhood singularity. We have seen Bestial and his boy host playing heads-or-tails adventures with death and resurrection and caught up in a war of flowers and ages in which the witch woman gardener of plants and babies dies and is reborn with all of the above as the mother of all of the above and whatever may follow below. Now, Celestino is seen by his boy host and cousin as he stumbles over a rock and hurts corn plants and grandpa chases him with the ax and mother turns into a huge corn plant and is eaten ear by ear and grandpa plants Celestino and expects a harvest. Mad capers follow as the *grandmother-mother-double-son* cluster in "Bestial" now includes the old man who kills roosters and would kill grandma if he could only catch her. We are on the same turf where Bestial and the old witch fought over the marigolds: "Then Mama got down on the ground and the two of us started pulling up marigolds, until there were too many to hold anymore so we started making a mountain of marigolds. The mountain was so big that it reached all the way to the sky and broke a hole in it" (*SW* 55/59). And when plants are not used as human flesh or grown all the way up to where God might be hidden, two-boys-in-one mirrored in Celestino will then build a Red Dirt Castle with a hundred bedchambers filled with people they themselves have created.

Fragments of an epic saga screened inside the mind of the male singular double boy punctuate these passages from *Celestino antes del alba.* The double boy saga begins with the corn-weeding season followed by encounters with the bad corn mother who is eaten. These are followed by flight to the dry river, uprooting of plants by the grandmother, death and burial of the kingbird, climbing the marigolds mountain, mother's falling into a hole while chasing them with a whip, deluge and fish swimming in the bedroom, run to the river chased by lighting turned into a snake, hiding in a tree trunk when grandpa chases them with the ax, spider woman and her brood, Red Dirt Castle, lying together inside a big tomb flowered by a choir of witches, flight over fields and forest, running into Old January on the road acting like a dead man, seeking shelter from house to house until finding home. At the end of this earth-water cyclical territorial saga the boys have reached the first THE END sign in a story with more than one such ending.

In the midst of all this, surrounded by live architecture, plants climbing skyward, and a palace microcosm, the mother's room inner sanctum is peeked into by the double boy host and his playmate. Life and death share the room half and half. A lit candle, a rock for a bed, chickens, roosters, hens, bird shit, the mother hanged by her own hands swinging from the roof beam. This place is the navel of the double boy territorial saga (the hanging mother possibly the specter of a lost girl sibling of similar age to theirs).

One traditional way in which boy sibling orphans like Celestino and Bestial and Fortunato are gathered into a single orphaned son (and spectral daughter) can be traced back to the ligatures of mother death caused by grinding toil and poor people sickness. Innocent of suicide, the universal mother-of-many, the everywhere-mother, also dies elsewhere and away from the Arenas boyhood vortex. She dies a slow death from which she and some of her boys and girls have not or could never have escaped.

For instance, in Russell Banks's *Cloudsplitter* (a novel about John Brown, last surviving son of America's most notorious biblical avenger abolitionist) Brown's son Owen remembers how, being too young to join his brothers at the father's tannery and too old to stay at home keeping after the babies, he once came upon an imaginary boy on his way to school. The boy was like a twin brother to him and soon became his constant companion. He named him Frederick, the name given to one of his brothers from a lost sibling dead not long before his birth. Owen's new companion soon became like Fred, the brother with the borrowed and healing name. The dead sibling's name christens the living sibling singularly. For Fred felt odd and felt things oddly, such as the heat or cold, and he was thus treated in special ways on orders from his father. The shedding process of one dead sibling turning into another sibling's mind, and the mind's living surroundings, and the growth of this same double sibling into a single odd one, comes to an end with the mother's death. For it was only with his mother that Owen had shared the life of his sibling Frederick, and it was she who in dying took him away—or took them both: "She was gone. Gone. And in that instant, although I was still a child, I understood to the bottom of my soul that I was now alone. I knew, too, that I would remain so for the rest of my life. . . . I never saw my mother again. I never saw my imaginary companion, my poor lost Frederick, again, either. My father would soon remarry, as you know, a good woman whom I called only Mary, never mother, and she would provide him with eight more children. But nothing would be the same for me, ever again. I mark the end of my childhood from that day" (*Cloudsplitter* 39). In such fashion, the sense of witchcraft or saintly healing, manifested all around the many lives of male singular personhood, swings back and forth between the living and the dead in a passage such as this one, that for some boys, if not for many, runs through the mother's demarcation of one boy's sense of enabling loneliness etched in another's passage into definitive singularity beyond death.

But, as already suggested in reference to Hawthorne's remembrance of childhood loneliness and the crowded solitude of his and Arenas's boyhood lives, such demarcations are in essence porous contact points in dealing with encroaching living elders. T. Walter Herbert studies how, in Hawthorne's case, the encroachment came, not only from the maternal uncles in whose lives the lost agency of his dead father still ruled, but also from the lost father himself, who in the testimony of Ebe, his eldest daughter, appears as the source of his son Nathaniel's invention of "'long stories, wild and fanciful'" (*Dearest Beloved* 68). Herbert points out that the main source for such stories was "the logbooks of his father's voyages, over which Nathaniel dreamed for hours on end" and notes that "the son's effort to ground his own identity in these traces of his father's life appears most poignantly in his profuse marginalia, often his father's words copied in elaborate script like his father's" (68). Likewise, Celestino's writing on tree barks and other surfaces as mad poet and internal poet at work—*mise en abyme*—over the *missing abyss* of his father's all too recent vanishing act, too fresh to truly be abysmal, traces the shadow of the symptom-maker lost father ghost. At the same time, the lost mother, upon whose death her son—like Owen Brown in *Cloudsplitter*—becomes a new and different son, is like the mother who does not die in boyhood Arenas after being returned to her father by her would-be and now late husband, from nearby or somewhere else: a late husband who lives on inside the son's mind. He lives inside the same place where she is now lost and where never again will she be as she was before the father quit on both on them. For each living but lost-to-father mother in boyhood Arenas, there is one who hangs dead from the roof beam and keeps her company. (The possibility of a specter girl sibling attached to that same mother and to the son's queerness remains haunting.)

Owen Brown tells the story of how after his mother's death he stole the gold watch from his father's father, also named Owen. He took it as if it were a "talisman, a magical amulet . . . as if it were the legendary sword, Excalibur, instead of a mere man-made timepiece" (*Cloudsplitter* 47). He took the watch from his own father—or from the giving of it as a gift to him or perhaps to himself by old grandpa Owen. When the watch is returned to its proper owner, the grandson is whipped by his father twelve times for each of the twelve hours engraved in Roman symbols upon the timepiece. But then, to his amazement, John Brown tells Owen that just as he failed him as a son, he too failed him as a father. And he gets on his knees and tells him that they are as connected as their sins are connected, "in the same way as the sixty minutes and the twelve hours on the face of Grandfather's watch are connected" (51). And he asks the son to place sixty lashes on his back. So the boy Owen learns "how it is between God and man," as when the Bible says, "Jesus wept," meaning that he wept for our sins as John Brown wept while being lashed by his son Owen as a slave might when punished by his master.

The graffitilike frequency of epigraph use in *Celestino antes del alba* renders uncertain such textual pieces and their implications and allusions. But when one reads, "Do not ask her whence she comes. Her history is of little account. In their poverty, her parents sold her for a bag of white rice" (*SW* 47), as quoted in an epigraph from *The Magic Mirror,* women and mothers in boyhood Arenas seem unavoidably implied to be like sold, unsold, or returned property. As chattel in their own paternal house, these women kinfolk toil like slaves in a struggle against hunger out of which their further matrimonial sale to an actual owner and master of their bodies seems likely. Sold, if not to a business buyer, certainly to a husband on the make who, in returning the poor bride-wealth daughter, gives back what once had a barter price on it or worse.

The Hawthorne connection pursued here would imply how in *The Scarlet Letter* the specter of child killing by the mother hangs over Hester and Pearl. Leland S. Person perceives "infanticidal mothering" in the opening scene at the market place and Hester's "state of nervous excitement that demanded constant watchfulness, lest she should perpetrate violence on herself, or do some half-frenzied mischief to the poor babe" ("Dark Labyrinth" 668). Person then argues with persuasion in favor of Hester Prynne's embodiment of "racial doubleness" and cites as Hawthorne's most intimate acquaintance with chattel slavery, beyond his reading of abolitionist tracts, the Peabody sisters' testimony of the sexual exploitation of slave women in the Cuba Journals, including the "frequency of infanticide—twenty or thirty deaths on the plantation where they stayed" (664).[2] Whatever polemics may surround Hawthorne's placing of Hester in lineage with enslaved women and their fate as exploited and besieged mothers, the connection with boyhood Arenas seems compelling. The connection comes with the confined existence and spiritual and material misery of women and the binding ties these trapped lives place on the male singular mind.

Also, as we are about to see, the story of old Rosa provides further evidence of the ties between the potential killing of children, race enslavement, and female bondage in the Arenas fiction. Rosa represents the hateful outcome of female resistance to the subordination of women in that fiction as a core element in the boy's development into queer manhood. She rebels against subordination and becomes a tyrant to others and to herself. This makes Old Rosa the largest manifestation of the hateful mother prototype in the Arenas world. Her tyranny reaches catastrophe with three events: the loss of her farm to the Law of Agrarian Reform, the marriage of her daughter to a black, and her discovery of her son Arturo in bed with another young man. This last event is implicated in the link between the troubled status of women's restricted freedom of action and race prejudice against blacks as descendants of slaves. Just as Rosa's daughter betrays family honor by marrying a black, her queer son Arturo raises the issue of getting rid of children considered harmed at birth or during early childhood. When Rosa goes after Arturo with her shotgun and tries to kill him as she drives him from her farm, her act signifies retroactively her wish to have gotten rid of her defective son the moment she had known he was homosexual.

## Personation: Old Rose Is Old Rose Is a Rose Too Old

It must be the agelessness of God hanging over the aging family that makes the choral voice in *The Palace of White Skunks* say that "God was He Who at the most unbearable moments of their lives would take up the burden of their terrors" (*PWS* 206/216). Next to God stands Old Rose, and upon her dwells the aging mind. For the rose that ages into *a-rose-is-a-rose-is-a-rose-too-old-Rose* does not age as the same rose of old, but as the aging mind as a person grasps it. For the ageless rose in the mind is not ageless forever, as even the mind fades off and dies as Old Rose perforce will.

Herein is found in full force the issue of *personation.* Nowadays—in circumstances that need not be entertained here— *personation* legally defines fraud in the assumption of personal identity for electoral or business gain. But in the golden age of spiritualism, and not unrelated to business, as Daniel Cottom writes, to "*personate* was to assume an identity, and much spiritualist discourse turned upon the problems raised by the invisibility of spirits. To put it simply, one could not be sure of a spirit's identity and so could not know how its communications should be interpreted. The medium's and the spirit's integrity were radically distinguished and yet inextricably knotted together in this issue of personation" (*Abyss of Reason* 69). Accordingly, distinctive literary bugs such as "plagiarism" (or sibling hoaxes such as authorship fakes) could thrive beneath what a pregnant phrase might call the ghostly abyss of false personation, a phrase written by Cottom but used here without quotation marks to underscore what "Daniel" the author (in quotes for lack of direct personal acquaintance) goes on to describe as the "common habit in nineteenth-century literature . . . to sprinkle one's writing with unattributed quotations from writers of the past both famous and obscure" (71). In Cottom's view, just as in those floating quotations uncoupled from authorship and copyright, "the dead that spoke in spiritualism" rose from a created or re-created living past increasingly owned by literary authors—named and unnamed—trained in the business of better understanding—or misunderstanding—the living: "In claiming that the dead yet lived, spiritualism did not really claim more than did laborers in the mainstream of literature" (71).

Personation resists aging and total oblivion even when it voices or embodies a person in a shape older than the one it assumes in dying. This is perhaps why Fortunato (the next-age spiritualist avatar of boyhood-to-manhood Arenas in the wake of Celestino and Bestial) finds a way to hide from aging by playing the mimicry of "not-living" (*novivir*) with Death "himself" as his playmate (*or* "herself"—as "la muerte" is gendered feminine). Except that such play happens whenever Fortunato becomes what Adolfina (a mad serial practitioner of personation) turns into or *personates* when she becomes him: an occurrence beyond mere impersonation told from her person- (indexical) perspective—but with no ontological grounds on which to eliminate all possibility that the plural shifting into other persons achieved by Adolfina (in a family permeated by *espiritismo*) is not being reciprocated by Fortunato in some transpersonal spiritual and *personating* fold. Such spiritualist shifts in personhood running in more than one direction between kinfolk, domestic objects, and familiar animals represents how spirit-haunting intersects alienated madness in Adolfina and transforms it into a choral event.

An instance of such personal shift happens at the *mise-en-abyme* infinity point quoted next in matching originals. That is to say, in the Spanish written by Arenas: "Yo iba a los parques con la muerte; siempre sujetándome a sus faldas. Y le decía: siéntate aquí. Y yo, la muerte, me sentaba en un banco, y esperaba el tiempo, y veía cómo él me sangundeaba, y me sentía casi temblar" (*Palacio* 203). Or as translated by Andrew Hurley: "I would go for walks in the park with Death, who would constantly be tugging at my [*sic*] skirt, so I wouldn't stray too far. And he would say, Sit down over here. And Death and I would sit down on a bench and wait for the time to come, and I would watch how he'd push me here and pull me there and poke at me to be still, and I would almost burst" (*PWS* 213). Rereading should reveal how the translation has *queered* (an action chosen here in place of *erred*) as it shifts the action of who is tugging whose skirt: from having Adolfina doing the holding-on and tugging-at death's skirt to "Death" doing the action to and with Adolfina. This is how Adolfina madly lives life "noviviéndola"—written as a single word, best and awkwardly translated as *notlivingit:* "Adolfina sabe que la única forma de soportar la vida es noviviéndola" ("that the best way to bear life is by not-living it") (*Palacio* 203/*PWS* 213). It is Adolfina-as-Adolfina (as mad and/or spiritualist hyphenation) who assumes the condition of *notlivingit* as divestment or going naked gendered feminine: "Se desnuda una de todas las boberías y solamente se piensa en el gran problema" (*Palacio* 213). If the "big problem" should be death (as spiritualism no doubt identifies it in breaching the gap and healing the wound of separation that death creates), Adolfina is in physical and vested-divested touch with the great source of spirit negotiation walking and sitting in the park and holding skirts like gender-crossed lovers of a sort.

Personation helps us honor the boy Fortunato (or boy fortune as such) in Adolfina's shape and spirit shifting. The male gender and personhood switch to and from Death in this instance is part of the indexical shift into *not-living* through which the plural boy in male singular moves from being Adolfina to being Digna, but also from chameleon to kingbird to table leg. Fortunato plays with Death and with a chorus of aunts who are witches and who are as real as is his own talent for flying: "I would go flying, and I'd be hanging between heaven and earth for hours and hours. Like that, just hanging there—thumbing my nose at time and laughing at everything as loud as I could" (*PWS* 204/213). Now, it can be claimed that, right upon the page, the flying is done by Adolfina-as-Adolfina and not by Fortunato (when she becomes him). Yet such narrowing of personation to Adolfina's sole personhood remains blind and deaf to the fortunes sought in spiritualism as the animating core of biographic affect, emotionality, mourning, and jubilation in the Arenas fiction. The literary and narrative effects in play are in fact derivatives of spiritualist means of personating the departed (whether they are actually gone or not). But they are derivatives not on account of coming after spiritualist agencies of contact with alternate or departed beings, but because, to start with, in a loop: literary means perform all too well what spiritualists have in most instances learned to do from literature.

## American Boyhood Dream Fortunes

Fortunato's life is punctuated by the history of regional insurgency in the Oriente province locality of his birth and in the mountains farther south occupied by the rebels led by Fidel Castro in the Sierra Maestra. His life, combined with the lives of his entire family, as carried in his voice and patched-up textual quilt, is in turn folded like a flag at sunset into the single connected life of aunt Adolfina and grandmother Jacinta and Old Rose and his own mother Onérica (Oneida Fuentes being the name of Reinaldo Arenas's mother). *Onérica:* that O name that takes out the *A* of *América* and does not let go of it, and to the *Am-* beginning couples the dream particle hint of *Dreamerica: onírica onérica América. Dreamerica:* the mother who fled to Florida to find a job taking care of children from other families. Onérica: *One-rich* (*One-rica*). Oneida: *One-gone* (*One-ida*): *The Wondrous Long Life of One Gone Rich America.*

A conundrum is now reached about father-daughter sameness. In *The Hamlet,* Faulkner conceives the life of Flem Snopes as that of his wife's own eldest daughter. But not, apparently, in reverse, or as the eldest daughter's life being her father in his/her role as her mother's daughter now altered. (The husband plays eldest daughter to his wife, but the daughter in him does not play the father and husband role toward the mother and wife.) The actual conundrum daughter in question would be the future Linda Snopes, the child by another father whom pregnant Eula Varner carries into her marriage with Flem. So the actual eldest Snopes daughter—besides what her putative father Flem becomes in that same role—is none other than he himself as a girl child by a father other than him. Throughout the trilogy of *The Hamlet* (1940), *The Town* (1957), and *The Mansion* (1959), this father-daughter bastard loop stands as no obstacle to Flem's rise as financial wizard and exploiter of his unfaithful wife Eula and their daughter Linda. In addition to Eula's suicide to protect her daughter's good name, widower Flem benefits from Linda Snopes's mother-wealth as he manages to have her sign over to him all her stocks. Together, in nominal incest, banker Flem and Linda (the eldest daughter who he himself is according to Faulkner's twist to his genealogy) testify here to thorny issues of symbolic genealogy and fictional mythmaking in boyhood Arenas.

The thorns of the rose that repeats itself in the House of Sand that Arenas built are first felt in the eldest daughter of Fortunato's grandparents, Polo and Jacinta. Adolfina's life is encapsulated early on in *The Palace of White Skunks,* right after the account of her father's passage from the Canary Islands to eastern Cuba. It is preceded in the telling by the story of how Polo bought the piece of "eleven *rosas* of harsh rocky land" ("some ninety flinty acres") (*PWS* 46/57) and found himself a wife named Jacinta, whom he soon hated and beat up and got a child from. A child he knew was meant to be a boy named Adolfo, but who came out a girl, named Adolfina by default. Onérica, Celia, and Digna followed on the accursed line of daughters he cursed as "'whores'" before fleeing into the wild, "smashing himself furiously in the testicles" for not daring "to kill the four women that he had brought into the world" (*PWS* 48/59). The female infanticide death wish manifest in these ordeals of injured paternal masculine pride offer redundant proof of how boyhood Arenas represents a boy born as the exceptional character in a genealogy of previously failed boy births and frustrated wishes to kill the girls born instead.

The story of four-daughters-too-many comes right after the story of the faulty first child named Adolfina. She was labeled "*Tall, skinny and imperious* (or some said *bossy*)," and later on "*Tall, skinny, bossy*—and now *abandoned*" (*PWS* 22/33), after failing, not for lack of trying, to find herself a husband. In the process (after each of her sisters left with a man and each man brought the abandoned daughter back home) Adolfina took over the house, "cooking, dishwashing, childrearing, herding the animals from one pasture to another, and carrying the water, kindling firewood" (23/33), and forcing her father to put a new thatched roof on the house. To the indifferent young men who came to her door, Adolfina brought her "gathered up hair, which by now reached almost to her ankles" and was plaited into "two immense braids which she wound around and around on each side of her head so they projected forward like two menacing ram's horns, ready to butt" (24/35). This probably scared the men even more, and in the end she "grew extremely scrupulous and picky, extremely moralistic, extremely chaste and upright; a stiff-necked old maid. She was the exemplar of the family" (26/37). Her story repeats in the Arenas boyhood and adolescence the story of Old Rosa. But given the time loop in boyhood Arenas, moving back and forth in the same *a-rose-is-a-rose-is-a-rose* motion, when one reads in *Celestino antes del alba* about the boy being too scared to go to the privy anymore because of the white shape hiding in there, and his grandma says, "That's the ghost of Old Lady Rosa that walks around dragging her chains because they didn't say the novena when she died" (*SW* 38/44), the old Rosa of old becomes the Old Rosa of now: the Rose that dies more than once.

In the story that bears her name in *Termina el desfile,* Old Rosa sets herself on fire some three years after the Revolution comes into power and after the Law of Agrarian Reform issued in May 1959 results in the loss of her farm. Yet the Rosa of old who is the Old Rosa of now was already dead and improperly mourned when Celestino and his host boy played during the earliest years in boyhood Arenas in the late 1940s. But the age conflict vanishes in the back-and-forth motion of bewitched calendar time. Old Rosa is here to stay. She is the character cell in which the figure of the grandmother lies imprinted and imprisoned in boyhood Arenas, with all her daughters and the husbands and the children her daughters feared and dreamed of having and dreamed and feared destroying. It has been said that Old Rosa is "the deconstruction of the figure of the oppressor" (Soto, *Reinaldo Arenas* 33), but this could not imply the extinction of her character power as long as boyhood Arenas remains alive in the minds of its readers.

The Old Rosa witch pedigree of Fortunato's grandmother Jacinta attests itself as she goes out early one morning to get milk for "the beasts of the house" and muses about the whole sick crew of them, about each of her daughters and her halfwit grandson in particular, who is now making wine and creating filth under his bed. She is the only one besides her grandchildren who believes in the presence of the elf of the house. Jacinta returns to the house carrying a heavy load of milk mixed with water and triggers a chain reaction among her witch cohorts. Their reaction is told in Digna's voice, who rushes into the kitchen and tells her mother Jacinta that she has just seen her on the rooftop beating up on God with a stick and that, caught in the act, she flew away. Digna runs off to tell Fortunato and Adolfina and her father Polo and her sister Celia, who has gone mad since the death of her teenage daughter Esther and cannot tell her death from her own as she rebuffs Digna's report. Last in line come her own children, who also rebuff Digna because they know grandmother Jacinta is safe in the drawer where they have locked her prisoner until she lifts her armpits and releases God from under them. But, although in all of this the voice belongs to Digna, it also belongs to Fortunato. This is no mere narrative protocol. As already examined in reference to the spiritualist and literary issue of personation, the assumption of multiple perspective frames Fortunato's unbound omniscience in a way in which voice itself transcends each individual enunciation in a moral lesson aimed at what seems fit to call the *broken up socialism of souls.*

In the long passage quoted next the twin issues of belief and faith are related to plural personation in either spiritualist association between living and departed souls or, perhaps, in political mockery of socialist ideals. And although the voice perspective is not that of the first-person singular, the voice in question is that of injured Fortunato on the run and dying. It could even be said that it is more than ever a first-person voice as a result of being displaced to the impersonal register of a third-person speaker and observer. The result is a choral voice reminiscent of the Gothic Wanderer in Melmoth and Dracula: the vampire voice of ontological thirst in departed souls with whom a species of mating is required beyond anything sex could offer:

> He had no God, and he had no trust in His new representatives, either, who assumed (in all seriousness—passionately, even) the divine role of fraud on a grand scale. What was he doing there then, full of lead, sweating horribly, bursting inside, lurching through the grass, through screams, through the rocks? For somehow it did all matter to him; he actually had *faith*—that was the word; that was always the word. Many times he had been Adolfina—he had suffered as she had (or perhaps more) the urgent need to be embraced, penetrated, to have his throat cut, to be strangled and asphyxiated, to be annihilated in the name of love. Many times he had been Celia, and he had discovered the splendor of traditional sufferings, and of madness. Many times he was Digna, and he learned of the other faces of betrayal and of solitude, faces which he would have thought impossible, unbearable. Many times he had been Polo and Jacinta, and he had learned at those times the terrible extent of fury and of frustration, the necessity for rancor and for blasphemy. Many times he had been Tico and Anisia, and he realized that in order for a man to survive, he had to possess two essential qualities—innocence and cruelty. Many times he had been Esther, and like her he reasoned (not without terror) that voluntary death is the only pure, disinterested, free act a man may aspire to, the only act which saves him, invests him with a halo of fascination, and, perhaps, bestows upon him some tiny bit of eternity and even heroism. Many times—all the time, really—he had been all of them, and he had suffered for them, and perhaps when he had been them (for he had more imagination than they did, he could go beyond the mere here-and-now) he had even suffered more than they, deep within himself, deep within his own, invariable terror. And he had given them a voice, a way of expressing the stupor, the dull horror, the fear, the blind terror which they, surely, would never be fully able to know or to suffer. Because there was that, too, the bearing all the wretchedness of the others on his shoulders, the suffering for them, the trying to understand it all, the trying to understand *them*. There was that, too—the infinite transfigurations of terror. His vocation as interpreter, spokesman, unblinking observer,

> scrutinizer . . . God, God—still without being able to invoke Him fully—and what about himself, when had there been time for himself? He had always yearned for time for himself, his own time, to howl in, and in which to howl his own particular howl. (*PWS* 234–35/241–42)

One could underline in red ink passages in this soliloquy and in fact take the whole of it and park it in the text of Charles Robert Maturin's late Gothic *Melmoth the Wanderer* (1820) or even Mary Shelley's *Frankenstein* (1818). In either instance, it would reiterate the wounded and searching spirit of congenital but also ontogenetic and in the end ontological condition of Gothic anguish and the need for fusion with others expressed in those novels or late Romantic dispiritedness—after the fury of world conquest that preceded it in that same soul. In the Arenas Gothic, reflected in the passage, we witness the shamanistic high-flying by a near corpse carrying aloft the grief and fury of others in utter despair. Fortunato's near-death sublime and plural personification of all players in idolatry—God, witches, martyrs, and poets too—is nothing but his rapture and capture of all their combined persons into his own dying.

Figures of witchcraft occupy the forefront of Fortunato's spiritualist coven. It is not only that Digna—who would "swing on the devil's balls" (*PWS* 216/226)—along with her mother Jacinta may easily qualify as foul communicants or witches, or that the whole neighborhood should regard the family of "hicks" (*guajiros*) who moved into their township as a nest of "witches and voodoo doctors" (*PWS* 216/225). The issue rests in what may hide behind witchcraft in particular social circumstances at a given moment in history, which is the perspective that places the novella *Old Rosa* at the center of personal character issues in the stories of boyhood Arenas.

Old Rosa is first seen already engulfed in flames in the holocaust that she and her angel boy have made setting her house on fire in denial of the order to hand the farm over to the Cuban Revolutionary State. Rosa succumbs to her old phobias and huge pride led by the hand of the angelic fire demon in whose figure her own foreclosure of sex in marriage is stamped: "She thought she saw that figure of radiant youth raise one of its delicate hands to the region of the body where men flaunted their virility. And suddenly she remembered with terror that her husband had once made that same gesture. And a new fury possessed her. And she raised the two palm fronds and thrust them at the angel, and she saw it laughing, its hand placed over *that accursed region*. Then Rosa went about setting fire to the entire bedroom" (*OR* 42/80). Her marriage to Pablo had ended in enforced celibacy before his death by suicide right on Christmas Eve. Her sworn submission to "the words *honor*, and *family*, and *respect*" (*OR* 4/35) killed their union after the birth of two sons and a daughter and the rejection of what she felt was bestial lust with her husband in favor of the worship of saints and spirits on the bedroom altar's "monumental installation" (*OR* 8/39). Widow Rosa invests all her passion on her pampered son Arturo, who lives with her, but retired in his own tower, listening to the radio, while his brother Armando runs to the hills to join the rebel guerrillas. The return of Armando after the rebels win the war brings with it a new political order and Rosa's liquidation. The land will be owned by no one except by all the farm workers together organized into cooperatives run by the Revolutionary State in whose power the people's sovereignty rests. On the eve of such unforeseen changes, Rosa the widow had become in the eyes of her neighbors "one of the wealthiest women around. . . . The enormous farm that she had expanded little by little, buying land from her neighbors, assuming mortgages, was now known simply as *Old Rosa's Place*. The number of workers continued to grow, the harvest yielded more every year. Later on, Old Rosa leased all the properties adjacent to her farm and rented them to sharecroppers" (*OR* 14/46). Adding insult to injury, it was her own son Armando who brought home news of the agrarian reform and presided over the execution of the expropriating law.

Old Rosa loses to the Revolutionary State what women accused of being witches in the New England of *The Scarlet Letter* often lost to predatory neighbors—or might themselves have taken away from them in reverse. Witchcraft was the weapon of choice in fierce scrimmages among the neighbors of Salem Village and Salem Town. Factions within village and town life in colonial Salem and other hotbeds of witchcraft involved the communal life of small rural subsistence economies in conflict with the commercial interests based in townships. The split between village and town in Salem during the latter part of the seventeenth century is comparable to a similar split in colonial Cuba, also in the late 1600s, among the residents of Remedios—one of the first townships established on the island. While in the case of New England factions grouped against each other driven by economic conflicts between the older village and the growing new town, in Remedios and its environs the conflict involved land tenancy and the manipulation of ecclesiastical authority in favor of one faction of neighbors and settlers against another. As told in painstaking detail by Fernando Ortiz in *Historia de una pelea cubana contra los demonios*, a group of parishioners were led away from Remedios by a priest who wanted to establish the new parish on lands closer to where he held his own territorial interests.[3]

In being the aggressor in the business of land grabbing and the creation of dependent sharecroppers, old widow Rosa stands in counterpoint with Katherine Harrison, also a widow, a wealthy woman from Wethersfield, Connecticut, who refused to remarry and who, in the words of Carol F. Karlsen, "lived alone, managing her extensive holdings herself, with the advice and assistance of her Hartford kinsman, Jonathan Gilbert" (*Devil in the Shape of a Woman* 86). In response to witchcraft proceedings undertaken against her in 1668, Harrison presented evidence of vandalism and destruction of property and the harming and killing of her animals and livestock (*Devil in the Shape of a Woman* 86). The wealthy widow as witch prototype matches the lurid grandeur of Rosa's torched suicide figure hallowed in flames, "like a girl lost in the middle of one of those storms that only occur in hallucinatory illustrations accompanying stories of witches and other phantasmagorias" (*OR* 3/33). Rosa sets herself in flames as she might have set on fire a worthless land title. (Moreover, her "girl lost" in flames stamp represents indelibly the hagiographic image of the lost female sibling and alternate self embedded in the Arenas boyhood.)

The old woman child and witch and widow Rosa rules as tyrant of her own soul and of the Arenas authorship spirit as well. The Arenas authorship is inalienable from Old Rosa as the towering woman figure in his fictions besides his mother, of whom she is a huge avatar—but also, in the spectral field of the Gothic sublime, both figures join together in the lost childhood of themselves as girls and as the lost girl sibling in boyhood Arenas. In this regard, we may picture Arenas the author present at the trial of "old Mistress Hibbins, the bitter-tempered widow" (*Scarlet Letter* 37), who early in the novel stands by the grass plot to witness the release from jail of Hester Prynne and her child Pearl in June 1642, and who in actual history was executed as a witch in 1656. Though quite thrilled by the spectacle, the Arenas author—if placed at the scene—might have also bristled at John Cotton's charges against Mistress Hibbins for having made a "wisp" and a "cipher" of her husband and for "usurping authority over him whom God hath made her head," as well as "over God himself," and for pushing herself "'into God's throne and seat, to know the hearts of men'" (*Devil in the Shape of a Woman* 151). So imagined, Arenas becomes the author and witness of the witch charges uttered by Mistress Hibbins's inquisitor, the author and witness who is himself inalienable in spirit from the blasphemies denounced in the witch, but not himself immune to the avenging spirit manifested in the man who judges and condemns her to death. The same Arenas author, the one who in the case of Jacinta—Fortunato's raving and possessed grandma—wrote in the voice of one of his aunts the following about the old mother:

> And the old woman just keeps panting and bugging her eyes out and speaking in tongues, over any little thing, with the spirits. Why just yesterday a spirit caught her standing in front of the cookstove, and it made her blister her hands, but the spirit left before you could say "Shit," because she shrieked and howled like a banshee, and she even cursed [*sic:* "Se cagó," "shat on"] God Himself. Who believes in that stuff? Who—with the way things are, I mean—is going to waste his time believing in such nonsense? Me—I'll tell you, what *I'd* give good money to see is God showing His face around here. Let Him be a man and come in here, I'd show Him. I'd bust His face for Him. Listen, you old faggot, I'd say to Him—Why? Why? . . . I'd first say that to Him and then I'd jump all over Him, I'd kill Him and then I'd kill Him again. (*PWS* 130–31/140–41)

The author who wrote this at the old bitch knew there was not a sin Mistress Hibbins was not guilty of before the Lord, whose seat she disputed and denied to His face. The author's spirits should have lifted upon hearing the last accusation against her: that the one sin that drove all of Mistress Hibbins's other sins home was her "'great pride of spirit'" (*Devil in the Shape of a Woman* 151). For what else are the fictions of the one known as Reinaldo Arenas if not a bonfire for the holocaust of the Great Spirit's pride already burning inside himself?

# 5 The A-Frame Agony

> Once, out of pure boredom, I went to Holguín's cemetery and discovered that it resembled the entire city; the crypts were like the houses, bare and flat, only smaller; they were concrete boxes. I thought of all the people in that town, and of my own family, living so many years in those house-boxes, only to end up in these smaller boxes. I think right then I promised myself to leave that town as soon as I could, and if possible never to return. To die far away was my dream, but to make that dream come true was not easy.
>
> *Before Night Falls*

THE BIG Thing that Grandma Jacinta in her blasphemous cursing calls *God!*—and that both she and Old Rosa fear and in Rosa's case is actually hated in her desperate actions, though not in her expletives—a righteous killer named Mink Snopes calls "Old Moster" in Faulkner's *The Mansion:* "He simply had to trust *them*—the *Them* of whom it was promised that not even a sparrow should fall unmarked. By *them* he didn't mean that whatever-it-was that folks referred to as Old Moster. He didn't believe in any Old Moster. He had seen too much in his time that, if any Old Moster existed, with eyes as sharp and power as strong as was claimed He had, He would have done something about" (*Mansion* 5). What Rosa and Mink have in common, besides the same faith that Jacinta puts in God by cursing Him, is the will power to exact revenge in the name of honor. Mink kills—and so would Rosa—driven by earthbound honor based on land ownership. Honor is like the Big Thing Itself held accountable by a name other than God's. When dirt-poor Mink Snopes kills Jack Houston in *The Hamlet* over some cattle-feed money, he wants to leave the mark of justice hanging on the victim: "What he would have liked to do would be to leave a printed placard on the breast itself: *This is what happens to the men who impound Mink Snopes's cattle,* with his name signed to it" (*Hamlet* 222). Rosa's honor lacks the easy target that Mink finds when he kills Houston in ambush. Her wrath upon losing her farm to the Revolutionary State turns against herself, in her suicide by fire, but not before she blasts her son Arturo with the shotgun and runs him and his boy lover off her already lost property.

In the end, Rosa turns her anger briefly against God before she finds the Devil in place of God and then finds nothing in the Devil except Nothing itself. In utter despair, Rosa destroys the images of saints in the bedroom altar by hurling them against the wings of the angel of death who assists her in her disgrace and fall and suicide by fire. However, unlike Mink Snopes, whose human target for revenge is the man he thinks has insulted him in a dispute over a heifer's feed and care, Old Rosa's target is multiple: it is all at once familial and communal. Her sense of honor is thus both reflexive—or directed toward herself and her kinfolk—and expressive—or dependent upon the respect of social peers and inferiors alike. While Rosa's familial honor is self-punishing and prone to self-destruction in the judgment of her own conscience, communal honor is equally uncompromising and based on social and economic values attached to at least a worthy measure of wealth. Without property Rosa is worth nothing because, having earned land, by whatever means she feels she was entitled to, endows her with honor's wealth, but wealth measured by and dependent upon the threat of being shamefully damaged by others and as such possessed by what John Ruskin named illth.

## Honor as the Honor to Honor

The sense of honor as a social category in play here is informed by Frank Henderson Stewart's *Honor* (1994)—a cross-cultural, juridical, and anthropological study. The key element in Stewart's argument concerns the notion of personal honor as a right: "the right to respect as an equal" (*Honor* 145), which implies that dishonor comes from being refused the right to honor someone else as an equal; the reciprocal character of which is the same as that same person not granting another person honor as an equal through acts of disrespect. The difference in viewing the reciprocal relationship from the confronted points of view of victim and aggressor is as subtle as it is crucial. For it often happens that the refusal of honor through disrespect—coming from the offending person and presumed peer—is seen as the origination of dishonor. However, according to Stewart's ethnographic inquiry, it is in *denying the bestowed right to honor as an equal* that the question of dishonor rests. This perspective focuses on the originating position of the person who starts or activates the honor encounter by wanting to honor the right to honor, instead of on the person bent upon dishonoring it. (The great instance of honor denied in world literature is perhaps Shakespeare's Shylock: the Jew who is *denied the honor to honor* by those who despise him.)

It is obvious that Rosa believes that she is entitled to honor as the reward of virtue, and that virtue could well be lacking in a number of people around her including her own children. So conceived, honor represents the right to respect as an equal, which Rosa actually holds contingent on someone's ability to own or to respect the ownership of land as the prime manifestation of wealth and guarantor of personal worth. This is the right that the Law of Agrarian Reform denies her in the name of Revolutionary Justice as grounded on the principle that private ownership of land is questionable and contingent on specific limitations in regard to property size and other matters. Regardless of the picture of Old Rosa as tyrant, racial bigot, and single-minded monster of egotism, her sense of dishonor and outrage on being deprived of her land is never questioned in the Arenas fiction. Monstrously capable of feeling dishonored to the point of self-destruction and suicide, Rosa stands transcendent as the individual embodiment of honor in that fiction.

## *Dreamerica* to the Tune of Incest

The connection with Faulkner's plot in the Snopes trilogy allows us to properly account for the complex character of Old Rosa's self-annihilating revenge. Let us recall how Faulkner's rhetorical flourish in *The Hamlet* about Flem Snopes being "the face of the breathing archetype and protagonist of all men who marry young and father only daughters and are themselves but the eldest daughter of their own wives" (*Hamlet* 9) allowed us to grasp the intertwined relationship between Adolfina and her father Polo. This ingrown nexus (between father and daughter and father as daughter of his/her daughter's mother) is what binds them both to themselves as coupled in endogenous and virtually incestuous kinship—and in that encysted shape binds them to the entire string of living and dead family.

The encysted connection did not end with the father and the daughter—or the father as his own daughter or the daughter as her own father in reverse. Their nexus served as the knotted point through which the entire cast of family characters in *The Palace of White Skunks* became part of a single tissue or web spun in the mind of Fortunato. This brings us, as hinted earlier, to the fate of his mother Onérica—the family member who left for America and who writes a stream of letters to the folks back home. Her almost daily letters sent from the USA are read in one of her sisters' voices—possibly Digna's. The dissonant sister chorus carries forth the story as an ensemble of echoes and deictic pointers given personified resolution in Fortunato's claim to embody and to speak for the whole household.

Onérica's letters pile up unread and unanswered except in her sister's God-cursing reading of them and in her mother's spirits-possessed commentary. At some point Jacinta decides to write a letter to Onérica on paper stolen from Polo's fruit stand. Her letter is *voiced* as well as written—with the misspelled words shown in italics and the silent letter *H* in Spanish missing: "*a* [to]," "aora [now]," "ace [does]," "asta [until]," "ijos [sons]," "ubo [had]" (*Palacio* 144–45). Jacinta's letter to her daughter Onérica is thus voiced into script, and as such it represents a minimal instance of the language of inscriptions and incisions characteristic of the writing of both Celestino and Fortunato, who are the two budding practitioners of the peculiar art of letters known as *literature* in the fictions of boyhood Arenas. (Their writing at large on surfaces other than plain paper is emblematic and graphic as well as aural and loud.) It might be said that Jacinta's letter to her departed daughter is *littered* with phonetic errors as it is voiced into script. By the same token, Onérica's letters to her son written from the USA are *lettered* with her ritual formulas of desire. The mother's postal love for her son Fortunato arrives as a single serial letter deadened by ready-made phrases, but awakened into voice by Jacinta's furious reader's response. These bitter laments by the mother-grandmother interrupt the departed daughter's script with the sound and the fury of her rage against the flat sentences of written love.

The single letter from Onérica is parceled out into serial installments of unread but overheard mother's love. The unopened mail becomes the soundboard for the thrill of spirits in Fortunato's role in boyhood Arenas. Jacinta's dominant reader's response to the letters stresses the importance of spirits' hygiene or their presence in Onérica's life: "I wish if you could you'd have a cleansing session. Although I don't know what the mediums are like up there" (*PWS* 136/144). If not precisely a "science of ghosts" or *hauntology*—as coined by Derrida in *Specters of Marx*—the thrill of spirits in these letters from mother may be taken to represent what is further specified by Derrida as the "dimension of performative interpretation; that is, of an interpretation that transforms the very thing it interprets" (*Specters* 51). Although virtually unmentioned by critics as a core element in the ontology of representation in the fictions of Reinaldo Arenas (and as already examined in reference to the shifting and plural nexus between Adolfina and Fortunato), *espiritismo* may in fact constitute the jinnee in the author's cracked-up boyhood bell jar.

The combined thrill and threat of spirits resonates throughout the fictions of boyhood Arenas. Spirits are explicitly heard in the sections of *The Palace of White Skunks* named "The Life of the Dead." They enter Fortunato's mind mainly as fear and in two related instances as the shameful result of sexual experiences in reference to or contact with his mother. In *The Palace of White Skunks* the boy discovers masturbation and finds its repeated and draining pleasure a threat to his own life. But he soon recovers well enough to face the woman medium at the Arcadio Reyes temple of spirits while fearful that her falling into a trance might mean that God is about to use her to speak to the crowd about his foul habits. This happens as the boy feels jealous about his grandfather and his mother and decides to kill the old man with an ax. But the aggressor is frightened by the sight of the old man's huge nakedness and flees and imagines as he runs that his mother enjoys being brutally raped by her own father, a thrill he later envies her as he wishes to possess her just as her father did and as he also wants him to possess him. The redundant subject pronoun for both grandson and grandfather is meant to reflect the encysted figure of "some monstrous sort of love—a love so strong that it perhaps had never been felt before—the consequence of a violent, irrepressible, and irresistible desire to possess his mother, exactly as in his imagination she was being possessed by his grandfather" (*PWS* 41/52). Incest redundancy queers the relationship between love in innocence and fallen lust. The English version just quoted in "[a] monstrous sort of love—a love so strong that it perhaps had never been felt before" actually slants or mistranslates "un amor monstruoso, es decir puro, insólito," where what is monstrous is said to be both "pure and unheard of [or rare]" (*Palacio* 52). The monstrous purity in question is clearly of the ontological sort and as such so rare as to be pure or untried.

The Arcadio Reyes spiritualist temple is once again the site of powerful mediums, or *mediumnidades,* when visited by the boy Arenas and his mother during another big moment in his sexual coming of age. In Fortunato's case in *The Palace of White Skunks,* the son is afraid that God will use the woman medium as His mouthpiece to denounce the boy's masturbation. His deadly pleasurable occupation in solitary sex is then followed by the even deadlier and consuming, twisted, and double passion of playing both rapist aggressor and raped victim with his mother and her father. This double incest corresponds to the discovery of "mutual penetration" with his cousin Orlando in *Before Night Falls*—followed by a similar scene at the temple with Aunt Mercedita in the role of the possessed woman medium. The episode retold in *Before*

*Night Falls* is once again followed (as the temple episode is in *The Palace*) by the grandfather's being caught naked with the same impact of incestuous wishes upon the boy's imagination. The thrill and threat of spirits haunt the Arenas boyhood in conjunction with defensive sensations of scorn and unbelief, but also in conspiracy with the psychic forces it puts into the lives of characters in chaotic resonance with each other.

Plural incest bonding beyond sex is what the ambivalent thrill of dangerous spirits implants in the Arenas boyhood. The impact of spirits upon the author's character lies not in his adherence to the doctrine of spiritualism and its practices, but in the intertextual connectivity at work in his fictions. The Arenas written lives are text-plural, and in so being they are fierce in their solipsism against the alien presence of other neighboring lives within themselves. But these alien ingrown lives are also omniscient and native to each other in their plural occasional joys and constant agonies.

European and Russian spiritualism—as in the writings of Allan Kardec so influential in Cuba—anticipated intertextual narration in the way it made claims to person-specific omniscience concerning adepts who thrilled and rapped and rattled each other and who routinely appropriated writings regardless of copyright. As already examined in the previous chapter, Daniel Cottom brings to light the "common habit of nineteenth-century literature . . . to sprinkle one's writing with unattributed quotations from writers of the past both famous and obscure," as he further claims that "the dead that spoke in modern spiritualism should be compared to these literary voices. In both cases people created a living past; in both cases problems might arise in orchestrating the conflicting possibilities that the dead presented to the understanding of the living" (*Abyss of Reason* 71). In a similar vein, Celestino and his boyhood companions find themselves in the midst of a story in which the threshold passage between the living and the dead is haunted by the crowded demographics of spiritualist personation. Their story is framed by numerous and properly attributed epigraph quotations whose allusive or cryptic relevance to the main text remains up for grabs. The repeated epigraph opens up multiple doors into a realm of representations and personifications that, in being dead and past but also alive and present, is above all actual—and, in that rattled and resonant sense, ultrareal.

The specific spiritualist issue of *personation* lies implicit in Fortunato's claim to tell the whole story of his family. As Daniel Cottom explains, "This term [personation] sometimes applied to mediumistic possession . . . , but more often it described the behavior of the spirits. To *personate* was to assume an identity, and much spiritualist discourse turned upon the problems raised by the invisibility of spirits . . . one could not be sure of a spirit's identity and so could not know how its communications should be interpreted. The medium's and the spirit's integrity were radically distinguished and yet inextricably knotted together in this issue of personation" (69).[1] While obviously free from the interpersonal burdens of spirit personation of the specific spiritualist sort, Fortunato inhabits a community of persons in distress, some of whom have gone mad mourning for dead siblings and do not let go of the departed in their voices and bodies. This is why the boy assumes the life burden of carrying other lives and other voices in him and in the reader's mind. It should be noted that his role as internal storyteller makes Fortunato the first reader to respond to the stories being told in the literary creation that comes to a climax with his death and afterlife.

Fortunato survives his own death by torture in the multiple voices that tell the story. The question of his implicit omniscience may seem superfluous except in retrospect, for besides surviving his death in the narrative point of view as the main claimant storyteller in *The Palace of White Skunks,* Fortunato will reappear in the character of Hector in *Otra vez el mar* (*Farewell to the Sea*). As examined below, the issue of omniscience proves central at the end of this other novel, when it is learned from Hector's sole perspective that the character of his wife and her role in writing the text to which the reader has responded up to that point were all made up by the author to whom he seems omnisciently bound.

But before addressing the issue of Hector's wife's banishment and vanishing, let us assume for a moment that the sentence from Faulkner's *The Hamlet* that has played such a key role in the ongoing interpretation had actually appeared as an epigraph in *El palacio de las blanquísimas mofetas.* Taking the epigraph literary device strictly in earnest, we may ask what could the story of its relevance mean to the lives of Fortunato, Adolfina, and Onérica; or what could be made of the story behind the imagined presence in Arenas's original text of the epigraph from *The Hamlet:* "*El rostro del vivo arquetipo y protagonista de todos los hombres que se casan jóvenes y son padres sólo de hijas y no son ellos mismos sino la hija mayor de su propias esposas*" (my translation). The rehearsal of the story behind the epigraph leads us now to the complex character already mentioned above as Onérica and her nexus with Oneida. They are Fortunato's and Reinaldo Arenas's respective mothers, who become entwined with Faulkner's Linda Snopes by virtue of the epigraph. The nexus Onérica/Oneida represents the daughter/father conundrum in *The Hamlet* together with Adolfina—Polo's eldest daughter and principal alternate person and spiritualist personation agency of her nephew Fortunato. This knotted cluster of persons and personations represents here the character of *Dreamerica.*

Linda Snopes (the daughter whose own father she herself is, conjointly with him, as herself, as both his wife and her mother's eldest daughter) plots the murder of Flem Snopes—the father-who-was and neverwas: the all-too-fatherly-absent-father who haunts boyhood Arenas in his own departed person and in the person of the boy's maternal grandfather. Here are the steps and degrees of embedded personation: the maternal grandfather, his eldest daughter Adolfina, who doubles herself in mutual personhood with Fortunato, who in this manner adds himself to the father/daughter conundrum of Faulkner vintage. Linda plots Flem Snopes's death (whose daughter she finally learns she is not) in revenge for his treatment of her and of her mother Eula. Eula had killed herself to protect Linda's honor, and now Linda manages to spring Mink Snopes out of jail, where he has been for the last thirty-eight years for the killing of Jack Houston. Linda is a Communist who fought in the Spanish Civil War and who returns to Jefferson as a do-gooder who organizes the black workers and who is blamed as a "nigger lover" by the whites in town. This last racist trait binds her to Old Rosa's daughter, Rosa, who marries a black in what amounts to the worst and lethal affront to her racist mother and a main motive in her suicide. Racism against blacks brings us finally to Adolfina, whose last desperate act of liberation in counterpoint with Fortunato's own escape to the mountains to join the rebel army includes offering herself to a black stranger on a street corner.

So in the end, the Faulkner conundrum of terrible sameness between father and eldest daughter bears its own awful truth in boyhood Arenas. *Dreamerica* is the daughter and mother who moves to the USA seeking a livelihood; she is also the daughter who runs away and offers herself to strangers including a black man and who returns home defeated; she is the daughter whom her nephew personates and personifies among other aunts and their spirits dead and alive; and she is the mother who, God forbid, is never a Communist and who, may the spirits protect us, never kills her true and false father, but who will in fact, as Old Rosa does, chase her son Arturo aiming to kill him, and who later on, as the mother-of-all-mothers herself, will assault her son—her *A Arthur Arenas* son—in the future of dictatorial bleakness narrated in *The Assault.*

## The *A* of Arthur in the *A* of Sand

The interrelations between characters in Arenas, Faulkner, and Hawthorne pursued thus far require deployment as a *narrative monadology* along lines of descent sketched in what follows. The notion of *monadology* is only loosely associated here with the strict philosophical use given to it in Leibniz's 1714 *Monadologie.* In the present context a monad is simply a narrative character such as Old Rosa. But character is not a *simple substance* or *gram* thereof as each *monad* is in Leibniz. Instead, narrative character is monadic only by virtue of being complex and interlinked with other such monad characters forming a chain or tree. Literary characters are in this specific sense both *monadic* and *monist.* Their intractable relevance to the lives of authors and readers turns each character into a single substancelike cluster of signification in complex interrelation with other such characters with which it shares a uniform and intelligible signifying substance. This is how the *Character Monadology* looks:

ARENAS/FAULKNER/HAWTHORNE<br>
(FAMILY MONADOLOGY)<br>
*MONAD*<br>
Old Rosa<br>
*TRIAD*<br>
Polo/Jacinta/Adolfina<br>
(father/mother/daughter)<br>
Flem Snopes/Eula/Linda Snopes<br>
Onérica/Oneida/Linda<br>
*TETRAD I*<br>
Flem/Eula/Linda/Mink Snopes<br>
*TETRAD II*<br>
Polo/Jacinta/Adolfina/Fortunato-Hector<br>
*TETRAD III*<br>
Roger Chillingworth/Arthur Dimmesdale/Hester Prynne/Pearl<br>
(cheated husband/lover) / (cheating wife/lover's child)<br>
Roger/Arthur/Pearl<br>
(St. Augustine/Alypius) / (Pearl novel avatars)

*Old Rosa:* It opens up the MONAD as the masthead Arenas power character. It embodies the one-person widow, the family land property, and its loss to the Revolutionary State. *The Old Rosa monad and the State monad represent the core antithetical character dyad in Arenas.*

Rosa also stands for the ruin of character as personal character and honor bonded together in the chemistry of individual survival known in Arenas under the *A* of *agony.*

*Polo/Jacinta/Adolfina:* The TRIAD of grandfather and grandmother and eldest daughter dominant in the boyhood and adolescence of Fortunato as a character monad in the Arenas boyhood. Celestino's boyhood and Fortunato's adolescence are each coupled monadic manifestations of the boy and youth protagonist inferred to be Reinaldo Arenas in fictional biographic and monadology shape.

*Flem Snopes/Eula/Linda Snopes:* The TRIAD in Faulkner's Snopes trilogy consisting of the putative and false father of Linda Snopes and the husband of her mother Eula, who was pregnant by another man when he, Flem Snopes, became the beneficiary of Eula's father's (Will Varner's) apparent largesse when he shrewdly invested in his daughter's marriage.

*Onérica/Oneida/Linda:* The TRIAD of Fortunato's mother, Reinaldo Arenas's mother—as represented in his fictions and memoirs—and Linda Snopes, the all-too-true but false daughter of Flem Snopes. The three mothers combine into the Diaspora monad known here as *Dreamerica.* In Linda's case, she is the Communist and utopian "nigger lover" avenger who kills her finance wizard banker and false father Flem Snopes. In Onérica's case, all that is known are her letters to her son from the USA. In Oneida's case the fictions of Reinaldo Arenas and his memoirs tell the story of a woman who is a monadic relative of Onérica. Her related status as Fortunato's mother is thus bound in monadic kinship to Adolfina as her son's aunt, her sister, and her son himself as his aunt's double.

*Polo/Jacinta/Adolfina/Fortunato-Hector:* the MONAD goes from TRIAD to a twofold TETRAD as a fourth monadic character is added in Fortunato and Hector. The first TETRAD issues from Faulkner's rhetorical and genealogical flourish about Flem Snopes as "the face of the breathing archetype and protagonist of all men who marry young and father only daughters and are themselves but the eldest daughter of their own wives" (*Hamlet* 9).

This first TETRAD links together the TRIAD of father (Flem), mother (Eula), and false-daughter-to-the-father (Linda)—a father said to be his own wife's daughter, and hence his false daughter's sister—with the first TETRAD anchored by Mink Snopes, the avenger who, in killing Flem on behalf of his false daughter Linda (and perhaps on that account his *truest* one, his being her sister), cuts the Gordian knot of symbolic incest. This act of vengeance in Faulkner is certain to be admired and yearned for from the heart of the family fictions of Arenas.

The two-in-one TETRAD convolute brings in Fortunato as Adolfina's alternate and double—and hence as the *fourth* member of the TRIAD turned TETRAD. Hector is the character that Fortunato becomes in the afterlife continuation of *El palacio de las blanquísimas mofetas*—second among the five novels that make up the *Pentagonía*. This fourth Arenas monad character is homologous to Mink Snopes, who in Faulkner's *The Mansion* kills his cousin Flem as the avenging instrument of Linda's revenge against her all-too-true but false father, with whom she forms a triad together with her mother Eula. Although the figure of the avenger does not exist as such in the second and third novels of the *Pentagonía*, it does as a character in our monadology. For it so happens that Fortunato dies, but then becomes Hector, who is married to a nameless woman recognizable as the avatar of Adolfina, the aunt with whom Fortunato becomes an alternate or double as two-characters-in-one in *El palacio*. Her husband Hector in *Otra vez el mar* invents her as his wife (as Fortunato does when he doubles himself in Adolfina) only to delete the invented wife's name and her very existence at the end of the novel. (The implications of such deletion will be examined below.) The wife deletion by the Fortunato-become-Hector monadic character corresponds to Linda Snopes's elimination of her all-too-true but false father Flem Snopes, with whom she forms a dyadic monad in triad shape together with his wife and her mother.[2]

*Chillingworth / Dimmesdale / Hester Prynne / Pearl:* The third TETRAD involves the most famous case of adultery in American fiction. In *The Scarlet Letter*, pilgrim colonist Roger Prynne adopts the name Chillingworth as he reemerges in Salem after an absence of seven years and uncovers the secret that his wife Hester Prynne's daughter, Pearl, is not his but Arthur Dimmesdale's child. Dimmesdale's preacher-seducer ordeal as a repentant adulterous sinner under Puritan law will end with his confession to the community and his death before their eyes from an overburdened and exhausted heart, which is at last released from guilt. After the death of her biological father, Arthur Dimmesdale, his daughter Pearl goes abroad to the Old World and to a new and wealthy life made possible by the legacy that her mother's husband Roger (Chillingworth) Prynne bequeaths to her. Her mother Hester also leaves and is lost and after a few years returns to her cottage and spends the rest of her life counseling adulterous women who find themselves "in the continually recurring trails of wounded, wasted, wronged, misplaced, or erring and sinful passion" (*Scarlet Letter* 165). While Hester Prynne returns to her New England home, her daughter Pearl never does. This disjunction will be reconsidered later with regard to the unsettled issue of Pearl's maiden name. For the father's name that Pearl might have assumed before her marriage is a matter of great consequence when considering the aftermath of *The Scarlet Letter.* The wealth bestowed upon "the elf child" by the late Roger Chillingworth makes Pearl "the richest heiress of her day in the New World," and, had Pearl remained on New England soil, she "might have mingled her wild blood with the lineage of the devoutest Puritan among them all" (164). But her marriage history is forever lost to speculation.

*(St. Augustine/Alypius) / (Pearl novel avatars):* Besides Pearl's afterlife in literature, the last entry in the family monadology contemplated here concerns a somewhat odd trio. Odd neither in terms of the long-established relationship between Pearl and the two men who stand in different ways as her dual father figures, nor in terms of the women characters who become Pearl's monadic avatars in such novels as George Eliot's *Adam Bede* and Henry James's *Portrait of a Lady:* the oddity or indeed queerness of the last entry lies in the Augustine/Alypius monadic pair. How are these two men joined in the Arenas fictions? How and why is their monadic mutual male role cast in the mold of a marriageable or married or abandoned or betrayed woman?

## The *A* of Augustine in the *A* of Alypius

Our path into the character of Alypius begins at the climactic moment of conversion in Augustine's *Confessions:*

> A mighty storm arose in me, bringing a mighty rain of tears. . . . I rose from Alypius: for it struck me that solitude was more suited to the business of weeping. I went far enough from him to prevent his presence from being an embarrassment to me. So I felt, and he realized it. I suppose I had said something and the sound of my voice was heavy with tears. I arose, but he remained where we had been sitting, still in utter amazement. I flung myself down somehow under a certain fig tree and no longer tried to check my tears, which poured forth from my eyes in a flood. (*Confessions* 8.12.28)

Even without recognizing its queer textual cradle in the *Confessions,* "El reino de Alipio" (Alypius's kingdom) stands out because of its allegorical tenor among the early stories first published as *Termina el desfile.* Alipio gazes at the stars absorbed in their group names in such arrested detail as to suggest the possibility of fixing his own troubled location on earth by their present course. It is November as he gazes, so the cosmic hope of finding his current place on Cuban soil heightens just a bit—and this is worth mentioning because the man seems to embody dislocation from himself and his earthly surroundings. He is perched on a balcony suggesting an urban setting, perhaps Havana, if the star name "Coppelia" is to be taken from where it is mistakenly placed in the text—with a dose of irony—among the stars of the Charioteer or Auriga constellation, in whose company the celestial Goat shines brightly as Capella or Alpha Aurigae. Evidently, Capella (the goat nurse of child Zeus who is carried by the Charioteer next to his heart) has been transformed into Coppelia as she is brought down to rest on the busy corner of L Street and Twenty-third Avenue in the barrio of El Vedado in Havana. Alipio's "most beloved beings" are said to be "the bright constellation of the Dragon and Coppelia [*sic*], the Goat in the Charioteer Constellation," and Alipio knows this even without studying "the only career that ever interested him, Uranology," whose pursuit would have forced him to "abandon the true stars in order to gaze at them in photos from books" (*Termina el desfile* 110). Street-level uranology fixes Alipio's place on earth in reference to the Ice Cream Palace Park Coppelia, opened in 1966, two years before the story's writing and recognized as a place for gays to gather in the well-known film *Strawberry and Chocolate.*[3]

Alipio's plight has him gazing at the stars and in the end being hunted down by their heightened size and roaring noise. The dream space in which these paranoid experiences unfold seems boundless; its nomadic space encompasses city places as well as rural landscapes. In a story of involuntary male incontinence, space and time are, accordingly, not contained within their dimensional coordinates and zones. Alipio witnesses the celestial fire approaching as the cosmic lights descend upon the city and the fields and the stars devour each other: "Not only one star, stars in the millions devour each other, grinding themselves into minimal particles and possessing each other" (*Termina el desfile* 112). The sound and the fury of cosmic conflagration and fornication cause Alipio to faint and the story itself to experience syncope. When he wakes up, "The first light of dawn begins to settle upon the trees. On the almond tree the top leaves shine like metal sheets. Little by little Alipio begins to wake up restless and still asleep. He opens his eyes and finds himself in the middle of the field, lying in a gooey pool, his arms and legs drenched and his eyes splattered. He tries to get up, and a strange pain seizes his body. He looks around and realizes where he lies in the sticky mud. He puts his fingers in the thick sticky stuff and brings it to his nose: it is semen, he says" (113).

The umbilical presence of the almond tree in Alipio's crisis connects it with another story in *Termina el desfile,* "A la sombra de la mata de almendras" (In the shade of the almond tree). While in Alipio's case the reference to Coppelia would fix his actual location or desires somewhere in Havana, in this other story the cutting down of the last almond tree by the anonymous young man's mother and her sister occurs in synchrony with his walk along specifically named places in Old Havana while in eye contact with a woman. Less in pursuit of her than pursued by her, he nevertheless brings the woman home for sex. The chopping of the almond tree will take place in strict synchrony with failed sex, as the naked woman with whom he cannot make love and his mother blend into the same figure. The mother's ax blows against the almond tree and her heavy panting are felt as if side by side with the woman's naked body and her mounting sexual frustration, while Alipio expects her to insult him with the "brutal word" *pájaro!* (*fag!*). Throughout the story, birds sing on the branches of the almond tree and are left homeless after its cutting as the son himself feels he miserably is while trapped in a house ruled by a roost of tree-chopping harpies.

It is hard to imagine a more blatant tale of symbolic emasculation. Combined with Alipio's cosmic nocturnal emission and his cryptic uranographic frustration with the Coppelia Ice Cream Palace, the two stories map out a garden or *hortus conclusus* space (an incontinent dream of cloistered desire) connected to an extramural sexual misadventure that ends in domestic bondage to the tyranny of women. Female power brings down the tree as it stands in full splendor, "intensely golden, as if aflame" (*Termina el desfile* 87). The women act in implicit bondage to patriarchy while emasculating the son's truer desires as abominations, which they blindly seem to intuit in their fury against the tree in whose branches Aaron found his magic rod, as the tree "put forth buds, and produced blossoms, and it bore ripe almonds" (Num. 17.8). Besides other more shameful fluids, Alipio's story abounds with tears: "Alipio's tears, as he stares at the skies, reach shocking dimensions" (*Termina el desfile* 110); "Alipio's tears well up warm and roll down the sides of his nose and wet his pillow" (114). This brings us to the other Alypius—in the *A* of Augustine's *Confessions*.

Augustine arrives in Milan from Africa in late August 386 CE at age thirty-two as a teacher of rhetoric with a life experience rich in sexual activity. Reinaldo Arenas first visits Havana in 1960 at age seventeen and then settles there two years later to train in agricultural accounting. Augustine soon resolves to abjure an active sex life and to embrace strict Christian continence, while Arenas sets out to rewrite the record books in random and relentless sex—"in the City" and beyond. During that same period, Arenas also becomes quite a random and hungry reader at the National Library and starts writing some of his early and best work. But rather than tracing any scant references to Augustine among the trademark use of epigraphs and quotations in his fiction, one may simply point to the card-index borrowing of titles from all sorts of works used as chapter headings in *The Assault*. These chapter headings become twice-misplaced: lifted from the texts of origin and dropped in their new textual home, where they do not seem to match any given content or context. Such jarring uprooting and planting of texts into other texts without any obvious matching implications could well index with random fury the wish for the free use and public display of textual matter under a political regime of restricted or foreclosed access to unchecked reading and publishing. The bookstalls at the José Martí National Library remain open to the feral reader and future harvester, grafter, and shepherd of textual matter. Reading these grafts and implants, one is tempted to imagine not so much the readings done by the author as those missed or discarded by him after a quick glance and thumbing through the book. (Milton, Hawthorne, perhaps?—or if not, a book such as Augustine's *Las confesiones* with passages ripe for epigraph plucking.) A passage such as the one quoted in English at the head of this section—and now in Spanish:

> Estalló en mi alma una tormenta enorme, que encerraba en mí copiosa lluvia de lágrimas. . . me levanté de junto Alipio [*surrexi ab Alypio*]—pues me pareció que para llorar era más a propósito la soledad—y me retiré lo más remotamente que pude, para que su presencia no me fuese estorbo. Tal era el estado en que me hallaba, del cual se dio él cuenta, pues no sé qué fue lo que le dije al levantarme, que ya el tono de mi voz parecía cargado de lágrimas. Quedose él en el lugar en que estábamos sentados sumamente estupefacto; mas yo, tirándome debajo de una higuera, no sé cómo, solté la rienda a las lágrimas, brotando dos ríos de mis ojos. (*Confesiones* 8.12.28)

This happens just as the climactic point in the *Confessions* is reached, when Augustine hears a child's sing-song voice saying "'take and read, take and read' [Tolle lege, tolle lege]" (8.12.29), and he returns to Alypius's side and opens the Gospel seeking a divine command in the first passage he reads. And sure enough, the guided and providential smart queer reading—snatched up from the Gospel as one might an epigraph or juicy bit from a book, dirty or clean—yields its harvest for a lifetime: "'*Not in rioting and drunkenness, not in chambering and impurities, not in contention and envy, but put ye on the Lord Jesus Christ and make not provision for the flesh and its concupiscences*'" (8.12.29) [*No en comilonas y embriagueces, no en lechos y en liviandades, no en contiendas y emulaciones, sino revestíos de nuestro Señor Jesuscristo y no cuidéis de la carne con demasiados deseos*]. As Eric Jager puts it, when the story is read in proper exegetical context, Augustine and Alypius make up, at this moment in the former's conversion, "an emphatically asexual couple [who] together form a symbolic community of chaste readers seeking spiritual fruit in God's work"; they are "unlike their carnally minded first parents who, after enjoying the wrong fruit, went on to beget the race" (*Tempter's Voice* 94).

However, it should be kept in mind that by the time of his conversion Augustine had fathered a boy named Adeodatus ("God-send"), who would have reached the age of twenty-five when the *Confessions* were written, the same age by which Arenas had written his first stories and was writing some of the fiction examined here. But Augustine's God-send natural son died at about the age of eighteen, the same age at which his father had begotten him. James J. O'Donnell highlights Augustine's unwritten hopes about his son by citing Cicero on his own son: "'You're the only man in the world that I would want to outdo me in everything'" (*Augustine* 85). The son issue is momentous because, with Alypius's help and counsel as a friend already mature in the conduct of the continent and celibate life, Augustine, the powerhouse convert to sexual abstinence, promises his mother Monica in front of Alypius that he will observe the renunciation of the flesh: not only of the flesh in sexual terms, but in terms of that other, even more carnal way, the way of all flesh, the generation of children.

The Almighty "You" in whose grand presence Monica rejoices at the news of her son's celibate purpose is, all things considered, not unrelated in magnitude to Alypius, the faithful friend and good counsel and seasoned practitioner of chastity. Both friends concur, then, in Augustine's praise to the Almighty You—the Lord's voice and role in Monica's well-being. For, as Augustine is thrilled to write, "You changed her mourning into joy, a joy far richer than she had thought to wish, a joy much dearer and purer than she had thought to find in grandchildren of my flesh" (*Confessions* 8.12.30). Thus, unless one takes too provincial a view of Alipio's plight and tears of sorrow in the kingdom where Arenas places him, a view narrowly confined to the issue of his thwarted homosexual desires, the example of Augustinian Alypius should help frame some larger issues, including the role of women and offspring as citizens of that same kingdom of tears, semen, and misplaced stars.

This is how the monadic relationship between "El reino de Alipio" and "A la sombra de la mata de almendras" serves to frame the picture of the solitary stargazer in the larger domain of women as potential sexual mates and as enforcers of taboos against queerness. One such queer behavior would include the following intense kind of male friendship in Augustine's younger life: "All kinds of things rejoiced my soul in their company—To talk and laugh and do each other kindnesses; read pleasant books together, pass from lightest jesting to talk of deepest things and back again; differ without rancor, as a man might differ with himself . . . these and such like things, proceeding from our hearts as we gave affection and received it back, and shown by face, by voice, by the eyes, and a thousand other pleasing ways, kindled a flame which fused our very souls together, and, of many, made us one" (*Confessions* 4.8.13). How much more strawberry (queer) over chocolate (macho) can one get than this? Here is the question: Is chocolate in Augustine's experience—as seen from the Ice Cream Kingdom of Coppelia—less a matter of macho or queer rule than of the utter male freedom from women claimants who insist on a larger share in men's lives, and a better share, beyond baseline mothering, in the lives that men might engender through female agency? A long question, for certain, and one that hangs in the air and over the abyss left by the deletion of the wife and the baby child from the plot of *Otra vez el mar.*

## The Authorship of Wife Disappearance and Spouse Deletion

Writing about the wife's retrospective deletion from the plot, Francisco Soto claims, perhaps with untroubled assurance:

> While in the documentary novel the witness insists on the authenticity and verisimilitude of his or her story and takes the time and trouble to establish his or her concrete presence in the text, in *Otra vez el mar* the autonomy and integrity of the character of the wife is totally discredited when it is revealed that she does not exist. Yet, it is precisely through the negation of this developed and complex character, who narrates her memories, dreams, hallucinations, and fears over 193 pages of the text, that attention is called to Hector's need to invent, create and compose as a way to defend himself from a rigid and intolerant society that is extremely hostile toward transgressions from the norm and believes that order is to be found in the preservation of an exemplary revolutionary social consciousness. (*Reinaldo Arenas* 53)

But something about such sacrifice-of-the-other logic for making it right by adding wrong to wrong remains troubling. One wonders if a deeper self-annihilating dialectic of sacrifice might not prove truer to such character deletion, a deletion on the order of Hegel's *Aufhebung:* to *sublate* or *sublimate* something or someone while keeping the best of it. After all, to spirit away a wife or make her disappear *sublimates* her in the core sense of liftoff into thin air.[4]

A comparable deletion by way of contrast takes place in Augustine's monogamous life of thirteen years with the concubine with whom he fathered Adeodatus. He met her in Carthage, when he was eighteen, and left her behind when he moved to Milan, as a character in Arenas might have left behind a woman he met in Santiago de Cuba before moving to Havana. Peter Brown observes that Augustine's search for wisdom upon reading works like Cicero's *Hortensius* drove him to austerity and that he remained faithful to his concubine throughout, "which was more than his own father, Patricius, had ever done for his mother, Monica" (*Body and Society* 389). In his writings and interviews Reinaldo Arenas always affirms his mother's stubborn celibacy and chastity after being abandoned by his father, most memorably in this *Before Night Falls* epitaph: "I think my mother was always faithful to my father's infidelity—and chose chastity; a bitter chastity, unnatural and cruel, because she was then only twenty years old" (*BNF* 3/19). But Augustine's concubine of thirteen years and mother of his only known son was not a "fallen" or "abandoned" woman, as Oneida Fuentes is portrayed to be in the writings of her beloved son Reinaldo.

Augustine's woman was simply that, a woman. A woman of lower rank, certainly, about whom James J. O'Donnell writes that "she was his wife in the Roman sense, appropriate for a woman of lower social status who could be dismissed when a better marriage came along," and who was "probably a free woman" who "may have begun as a slave or come from slave parents" (*Augustine* 39). Though higher than her in social status, Augustine's mother, Monica, was no less subordinated to his father in ways that would seem most unfair to modern eyes on account of the ancient unbending rule of gender inferiority relative to a woman's gifts or inherent worth and her bondage to her predestined role in life as man's lower mate.

The moral object lesson on wife-use from Bishop St. Alypius of Thagaste to Alipio in his kingdom in Havana is encapsulated in Peter Brown's summary of Augustinian friendship: "Instead of early marriage, [Augustine] joined a circle of hard young careerists. His lifelong friend, Alypius, maintained as best he could a *de facto* continence. After one unhappy experience, he decided that sex was not for him. Committed to an active career in the late Roman administration, the public cruelty of the gladiatorial games fascinated and distressed him far more than did the prospect of a love affair. Unlike Alypius, Augustine plainly enjoyed sleeping with a woman. He opted for the next best thing to marriage—a strictly monogamous relationship with a concubine" (*Body in Society* 90).[5] Whether Augustinian or platonic, closet uranology could well fit into a bureaucratic career in Havana of the sort a happier Alipio could aspire to if he ever recovers from the funk in which he finds himself in his stargazing kingdom, with a little help perhaps from glancing here and there into Augustine's *Confessions* as he enters into a love partnership with a well-employed older man in the Lettered City.

Meanwhile, in the *Confessions* the ancient Alypius becomes "fatally devoted to the Games" (6.7.11); he attends the Roman Circus with eyes shut, until on one occasion, as the crowd roars, he opens them and witnesses the bloody lust that he had tried to screen out of his sight. A similar porno-carnage is shown in the text of *Otra vez el mar,* written, one presumes, by the deleted wife, as she—or her *mise-en-abyme* ghostwriter husband—paints a mural of warring soldiers in the *Iliad* banging each other to death and sexual bliss with phalluses for weapons in homage to the arrival of Helen of Troy.[6]

Other passages besides those telling of Alypius's career successes and his lustful fear and loathing at the games (seeing nearly naked men kill other naked men and beasts) could draw Alipio's attention in his Havana kingdom while reading into Augustine's book. For instance: "During the period in which I first began to teach in the town of my birth, I found a very dear friend, who was pursuing similar studies. He was about my own age, and was now coming, as I was, to the very flowering-time of young manhood. He had indeed grown up with me as a child and we had gone to school together and played together. Neither in those earlier days nor indeed in the later time of which I now speak was he a friend in the truest meaning of friendship: for there is no true friendship unless You [God] weld it between souls that cleave together through the charity which is shed in our hearts by the Holy Ghost who is given to us" (*Confessions* 4.4.7). However, this is not Alypius, but a lesser friend of Augustine from an earlier point in life in whose company a lasting brotherly Christian friendship did not mature. The absence of the Holy Ghost between them was determinative. For the presence of such a third factor in friendship (Third Sacred Ghost Factor) lifts things up to the highest and most sublime and yet burdensome Christian Love altitude. And yet, this love—minus God, in Augustine's terms—is the same up-and-flying, cosmic-high, star-size Love suffered at its joyful best by the likes of Bestial and his playmate Celestino, and by Fortunato, who in retrospect may now appear as the Alypius teenage version of the terrible and blissful infancy in the life of his own pagan child image incarnation as the bestial brother of marigolds.

## Felix Culpa

Set side by side with "El reino de Alipio," the moral character type of the Christian saint named Alypius takes us back to a pagan and beastly eternal past in boyhood Arenas, the time analogous to the Christian Fall, when a lost boy is left behind—and in Bestial's case dumped on the earthen floor of the *bohío*—by the man who engendered him. This same manly type runaway and his kid-left-behind son make up the incest couple who in *Viaje a la Habana* involves the homosexual father who returns from New York to Cuba and the gay son who seduces him. The imaginary nature of the father's return to the abandoned Cuban home may represent the fulfillment of Reinaldo Arenas's wish fantasy of love-mating with his bygone father and to have the union acknowledged by his mother as the man's ex-wife. (*Mating* is meant to signify in my view the wish not only to have sex with the father but to engender a child with him.)

Jorge Olivares interprets with stealth, accuracy, and brio the incest scenario as a bold switch in persons worthy of Menander or Plautus. Accordingly, the returning father comes home in the role of Arenas, the *son*, who is then seduced by his father in the person of the son whom he left behind, and who is thus *fathered*—in the sense of making him *the* father who never left home—as the father in the life of Reinaldo Arenas did. While, at the literal level, a father returns to Cuba and is seduced quite knowingly by his own grown-up son, at the juicier, one might say, Augustinian/Queer allegorical level, it is in fact the departed and prodigal *son* who returns from New York to Havana and is outed into the gay life that he has thus far betrayed. In such a happily twisted sense, the Arenas gay returnee is then *fathered* by the father from home. That is to say, he is fathered *in* the son whom he became while in Cuban residence with the abandoned mother/wife. The custodian of the mother's celibacy and her chaste fidelity to her husband's infidelity represents a triad coupled with the mother's monad: *father/son/husband—MOTHER.*

In the context of such monadic turmoil and complexity, it may seem trivial that the Arenas mother (Oneida Fuentes Rodríguez), who in real life was never married by her premarital lover (Antonio Arenas Machín), would appear in the story as his ex-wife. Trivial or not, the ingrown Trinity fashioned into incest-shape by the son, in the father, with the mother as Holy Ghost, casts a heathenish shade of dark splendor upon the sublime person of the Son thus transformed into a Higher Queer Person.[7]

### The *A* of Angel in Samson Satan

Samson crashes in Milton's tragic scene as hard as Satan does—though from a fall far shorter than the Prince of Darkness traveled as he plunged into Hell:

> See how he lies at random, carelessly diffus'd,
> With languish't head unpropt,
> As one past hope, abandon'd,
> And by himself given over.
> (*Samson Agonistes* lines 118–21).

That the self should bring down upon itself by implosion the temple of its doom and glory is what the will of Samson achieves in hidden kinship with Satan as fallen angels of a kind. Or at least such is the signature *A* of *Agony* that binds upon this page the angelic to the satanic Arenas. Reading Samson's agony in sodomite fashion, as he performs the slaughter among Greeks and Trojans, Arenas might have found the erotic grotesque he so relished when he wrote disfigurations of Homeric heroism for *Otra vez el mar* and the hellish labor camp Sodom murals for *El central.* Besides the wholesale circumcision of an entire army yielding a thousand foreskins to rot before the eyes of God, Arenas might have paused over Samson's lament for injuries in passage from flesh to soul:

> O that torment should not be confin'd
> To the bodies wounds and sores
> With maladies innumerable
> In heart, head, brest, and reins;
> But must secret passage find
> To th' inmost mind.
> (*Samson Agonistes* 606–11)

Through such passage, if not his own HIV-positive body, not so damaged, other bodies are implicitly made fraternal beyond one's will in the shared flesh of sickness.

And then, perhaps with bitter humor, Arenas might appreciate the Chorus's warning to Samson about a charging, hair-raising war hulk coming at him:

> Look now for no inchanting voice, nor fear
> The bait of honied words; a rougher tongue
> Draws hitherward, I know him by his stride,
> The Giant *Harapha* of *Gath*, his look
> Haughty as is his pile high-built and proud.
> Comes he in peace? What wind hath blown him hither
> I less conjecture than when first I saw
> The sumptuous *Dalila* floating this way:
> His habit carries peace, his brow defiance.
>
> (*Samson Agonistes* 1061–73)

This is not nearly as grotesque as the joining together in one huge mass of flesh of Fidel Castro and Mother in the final frames of *El asalto* as the Son penetrates with lethal joy her Plutonian ass. Or as when Old Rosa in giant shape charges after her son Arturo and his brightest gay star to lay him waste. If the grotesque could bring sweetness in its breath, so would the Giant Enemy's hurricane voice when honey-wrapped in Delila's war song. Yet such images assuage with their compound visual remedies the Son's undying despisement of the Mother's toneless lack of rebelliousness spiced with artificial kindness.

## The *A* in *To Do* as the *A* in *You Two*

The character associated here with the compound person named *Dreamerica* goes to New York in *The Palace of White Skunks* to "work like a dog" (like a "burra," or she-ass) and leaves behind her son Fortunato. She is gone "to die of cold and loneliness. To wipe squawking babies' asses. To live like an animal. To earn some money. To bring up children that aren't her own so her own children won't starve" (*PWS* 7). The original has it slightly different:

> A morirme de frío y soledad.
> A limpiarle el culo a muchachos llorones.
> A vivir como las bestias.
> A ganar dinero.
> A criar muchachos que no son míos para que el mío no se muera de hambre.
> A.
> A.
> A. (*Palacio* 16)

The Spanish preposition *a* coming before the infinitive verb compound for *to do* is capitalized as *A* at the opening of each phrase. It couples as it must in this case with the labor actions of a woman in what has become known as the service economy. It also stands by itself at the end, in sheer reiteration, as if resisting closure. This "A" becomes emblem and monogram. It turns into a repetitive particle like many others in the fictional writing of Arenas signifying desperation, fury, recalcitrance, bold device, and in some eyes an overdone storytelling gimmick. Standing by itself, the *A* of *to do* is also in Spanish ears—and their accent and dictation to the tongue—the *A* of *you* or *thou* or *tú,* of *two* as in (and with) *you.* It is the mute nonphonetic *A* in the number *two* or second-person *you,* too, *tú,* who ought to bind *to do* and *tú* into mutual dialogue. It is the hardest *A* in the presumptions of democratic discourse; harder than the *A* of Adultery and Agony; hardest of all in the *A* of Arenas as the *A* of Sand running through fingers in time toward, once again, the Sea.

Part Two

# The Lord's Envy

## Lezama Lima as Satan Knows Best

Envy is our first parent.
Miguel de Unamuno

# 6 Son of Gorgo

There are many kinds of conceit, but the chief one is concern to let people know what a very ancient and gifted family one descends from.

Benvenuto Cellini, *Autobiography*

LIKE DEATH herself, Gorgo is a thing past and present that won't go away. A parasite, Gorgo had and continues to have no children of her own except with men driven to make her their macho mother; luckily, this happens only one child at a time. Evidently, a horde or host of grown-up Gorgo babies born from one stroke of her parasite glance is too much to bear. Let us then for the time being set aside the nightmare of multiple Gorgo births gathered into virile armies and gangs and look at a miraculous only-child birth face to face with her presence in the story of *Paradiso*.

We will approach the scene under the useful counsel of Jean-Pierre Vernant concerning two kinds of radical otherness personified by Artemis and Gorgo in ancient Greek myth with respect to the ordeals of training in citizenship. Artemis, the huntress goddess of wild places, works at the margins of civic life as she trains the young in the rough arts of survival before they return to the heart of city space. Her extramural otherness works on behalf of civic rule from the untamed territorial outside. By contrast, the terminal otherness ruled by Gorgo works anywhere. Gorgo's alien power strikes in a flash as it creates a vertical axis of death. Her glance comes out of nowhere upon the unwary man and strikes him in horror and chaos with a designed-for-males hard numbness. How can such a lethal thing create progeny? It happens every time Gorgo comes through the eyesight of the male child of any age and finds in his mind a home as mother of death and ruler of enabling and disabling sexual fears.

The notorious eighth chapter of *Paradiso* makes graphic the lethal birth pangs of Gorgo as witnessed in the mind of the disembodied narrator of José Cemí's life. As such, a surrogate narrative agency laden with profuse mythological and pseudophilosophical knowledge directs the action from behind a virtual triple-X porn video camera. Throughout the first section of this chapter the name "Gorgo" is used instead of "Gorgon" in order to signify her proper name as a female and a woman, and not—as in "the Gorgon"—to represent her as a nonhuman monster. (In this domain *Gorgo* could well be the name of a porn star of ambiguous gender attributes specializing in sadomasochism videos.)

## An Adolescent Murdered by the Gods

The eighth chapter of *Paradiso* earned the novel an instant pornographic reputation. Leading to the story of Godofredo the Devil, scenes of classroom burlesque and stealth sex come in quick succession. These grotesque scenarios involve two punks named Farraluque and Leregas who play the role of schoolroom prick devils. Their exploits are ghostwritten and directed by José Cemí's retrospective narrative in ceremonious mockery, as when Farraluque—a skinny lad with large genitals—is labeled a "leptosomatic macrogenitosoma" (*EC* 204) [a skinny dude with big flesh in his crotch].[1] This happens at the onset of Gorgo's first parasite gestation in the captive minds of school kids fixed upon the mother of all pricks.

Things go wild when the mind-numbing geography class becomes a naked lesson in cosmogony and books are seen crawling atop Leregas's prick, like tortoises "in a Hindu myth about the origin of the world," rising up against the teacher's desk as if clapped by thunder, "a wind eddy that turns into a sand column" in "progressive swirling uproar" and "dry phallic splendor" (*P* 199/201). Whenever the teacher's "professorial sadism" denies permission to go to the toilet, he is reminded by the student that an earlier denial had resulted in a boy's death like "an adolescent murdered by the gods" (197/199). The ensuing parade to the toilet is policed by Farraluque. He uses the chance to mimic possession by a "priapic demon" and performs a dancing "phalloroscopy" in which he treats his prick "as if it were a suckling child," "scolded," "soothed," "cradled . . . on his forearm" (197/199). The scene is cast in the style of an archaic pantomime (part burlesque, part fertility ritual) in clandestine celebration of the birth of Priapus. Acting as demon god of satire, the Phallus-as-Priapus becomes the mirror of lewd fun: it reproduces the face as it might the whole body; the resulting miniaturized transposition of a person's body into another person's face amounts to a *mise en abyme* in which the whole is holed up or sucked into one of its mirrored parts as if kidnapped by envy's sheer visual lust from one body into another.

When the shamed teacher lashes out at the offending Leregas, his gestures involuntarily mimic the motions of Farraluque's phallic pantomime: "a sudden charge of adrenalin rushed into the teacher's arms; his right hand shot out like a falcon and resounded on Leregas's right cheek, and immediately afterwards his left hand crossed over and found the cocky vitalist's left cheek" (199/201). The windmill motion ("cruzándose en aspa") of the teacher's arms mimics the swirling and swaying motions of fire and wind that started during the phallic display and were reflected in the flaming imagery sparked by Farraluque's copulations. Whirling, rotating, crisscrossing, pivoting, and other such motions illustrate the magical powers attributed to fire, until the figure of the Gorgo appears to unveil the climactic iconography of igneous lethal play.

By means of transgression, punishment, and mimicry's archaic bonding, the reader *sees* the Gorgon on Leregas's face, where it mimics a genital mask:

> Leregas plodded on . . . his tongue hanging out. His tongue was a lively poodle pink. Now it was possible to compare the tegument of his glans with that of his oral cavity. Both were a violet pink, but the color of the glans was dry, polished, ready to resist the porous dilation of the moment of erection, while that of the mouth was brighter in tone, shining with the light saliva, as the ebbing tide penetrates a snail on the shore. . . . Leregas' mouth was receptive, purely passive, and there saliva took the place of maternal water. The mouth and the glans seemed to be at opposite poles, and Leregas' clownish indifference allied him with the hidden femininity of his mouth's liquid pink. . . . Cemí remembered . . . the wild provincial's mouth, inside which a small octopus seemed to be stretching, disappearing into the cheeks like smoke, sliding down the channel of the tongue, falling to pieces on the ground like an ice flower with streaks of blood. (*P* 199/202)

The mask fixes the Gorgo in her grin: her tongue hanging out, binding in resemblance maternal tokens embedded in the affair between face and genitals. Masked by Gorgo, Leregas emblazons child-mother incest coupled between his face and genitals.

Gorgo's grotesque head instills a vision of birth as sexual wound. A mask and shield, her face doubles up as trophy head seized in genital strife. The head/mask iconography binds into one the act of decapitation and the condition of oral sex-hunger aimed at the male genitals; it denies uninjured genital status to the female person: woman and sex-wound become one. After showing up on Leregas's face, the Gorgo returns as an actual woman, as a "mature madonna" (*P* 204/206) engaged in elaborate fellatio with Farraluque. In the preceding quotation the image of Leregas's Gorgo mouth and pendulous tongue was shown migrating into his genitals (as the genitals rose to his face resembling the mother's vulva, the seashore, and the snail octopus). Next, it is the woman's face that travels down to his genitals and anus: "exaggerating her ecstasy . . . directing the frenzy imperiously toward the sinister grotto. When she thought the coordinated nibbling and polishing were about to reach an ejaculative finale, she started to pull it toward the deep shell [caracol profundo], but [Farraluque] raised his right hand to the madonna's hair, pulled upward with fury and exposed the excited Gorgon, dripping with the sweat extracted from the depths of her actions" (*P* 205/207). A perverse image ensues: Cellini's Perseus with the Gorgon's severed head gripped in the hero's fist, but showing her genital maternal aegis over the birth of his actions. (Lezama knows Cellini's statue quite well and holds it in twisted focus here.)

As pictured in chapter 8, Gorgo is not just an androgynous or double-sexed male visual parasite. Her complex iconography is that of a spellbinding monster, lodged inside the woman whose Gorgo head is impossibly gazed at by the young man: face to face from the outside, but as if from *within* her. He also gazes at Gorgo's head as if it had been torn off from his own body. The trophy head seems born out of Farraluque's genital decapitation, even as the head/mask approaches him to apply a lethal caress against his genitals and anus.

The Gorgo nexus involves two other males, both homosexual (although the proper word in this context should be *sodomites:* the "monkey-boy" Adolfito and the husband of the madonna woman, the masked *carbonero* homosexual inside the coal house, where Farraluque is taken next. Their frenzied act of buggery in the coal house is more than just a mere pornographic interlude. The Adolfito episode acts as overture to the story of Godofredo the Devil. It anticipates the mythic motif of the missing eye and the motions of wind and fire in connection with the one-eyed redheaded devil Godofredo. In order to lure Farraluque into between-the-thighs (*inter femora*) coitus, the monkey-boy Adolfito uses "one uncorked and mischievous eye" (206/208). Matching Godofredo's one-eye facial split, Adolfito shows "an asymmetrical face," as he presents to his "sexual aggressor" only "half of a serpent's bifid tongue" (*P* 205/208). Such maneuvers entail repeated "rotations of the body," until Farraluque ejaculates. The monkey-boy acts as male bawd trickster between the schoolmaster's home and the coal house where his rampage ends as he hellishly buggers the older husband.

Adolfito's procuring sodomy lures Farraluque away from his passive oral sex in Gorgo copulation toward his active role in buggery with a man playing a besotted mockery of the father: "A man was inside, about fifty years old, naked, his shoes and socks on, and a mask that made his face completely unrecognizable. . . . He was plump, white, with small waves of fat around the stomach. . . . He envisioned those prints where Baphomet, the androgynous devil, appears, possessed by a toothless pig, his waist encircled by a serpent that crosses over the site of his sex, inexorably empty, while the serpent shows its flaccid head in oscillating suspension . . . its flaccidity disdained by the roots of life . . . his phallus [was] accustomed to ejaculate without the heat of carnal envelopment" (207/210). Frenzied and grotesque, coal-house sodomy sexualizes the creation and hoarding of fire in the black pit of the *anus mundi*. Inside the "Polyphemic grotto" (208/210) Farraluque's phallic misrule meets a man who is "like the priest of a springtime hierophany" (207/210). As a deliriously willing victim of buggery, the carbonero shares his ravisher's wasting of male seed with his own corresponding denial of maternity to his Gorgo madonna wife.

As bad as it may seem to those who insist on authorial distance by Lezama when he writes such grotesque sex scenes, the possibility of self-portrait caricature cannot be ruled out. Pushing fifty, the carbonero is ten years older than was Lezama when he started writing *Paradiso* in 1949, but not much older than he was, much later, when writing the scenes in question. Lezama's obesity and fair complexion could be cast in the man's physique: "plump, white, with small waves of fat around the stomach" (207/210). Writers are no less given to partial or total self-portraiture than are painters and caricaturists. In March of 1949, Lezama wrote to his friend and benefactor José Rodríguez Feo: "I grow fat and fatter, and I am left with only the solution to explode out of the skin as it bursts" (Rodríguez Feo, *Mi correspondencia* 116). (It is likely that, just as José Cemí's disembodied ghostwriting keeps him off frame and beside the action, Lezama's graphic gaze and palette draw him into absorbed embodiment in the narrated scenes.)[2]

The joint picture of Farraluque and the carbonero evokes Onan's sin and the crimes of Noah's son Ham. As already discussed in chapter 1, Ham sees Noah drunk and naked and is cursed by him (Gen. 9.20–27). But according to long-standing exegetical guesswork going back to medieval times, seeing "the nakedness of his father" is a formula implying that Ham commits the crime of incest by sexual assault upon Noah (and in some accounts castrates him). Onan's sin of interrupted copulation and the spilling of seed is evoked twice: when Farraluque leaves the Gorgo madonna and spills his "liquor" on Adolfito's chest, and when the buggered carbonero ("accustomed to ejaculate without the heat of carnal envelopment") inserts "his vacillating tool in a crack in the charcoal" (*P* 208/210) and brings down the load of sacks upon both of them.

Two iconographic correspondences to the carbonero sodomite appear in chapter 9 of *Paradiso*. Ricardo Fronesis illustrates with a few "malignant examples" (aimed at the mocking cynicism of his homosexual friend and interlocutor Eugenio Foción) how virile manliness can turn into voluptuous receptiveness:

> I see now in my memory a robust Spaniard, perhaps a charcoal-burner, who one day at the beach goes up to the gentle water lapping the shore. He drops his sandals on the sand and savors the warmth of the wave with his foot. He tingles with voluptuous delight, his body seems to have been traversed by a cramp that clears the channels of his veins, and he lets out an 'Ah!' in which all his virility collapses. For one moment he is a traitor to his habits of life. . . . Another case, a good father [preñador], liked to go to bawdyhouses to have a woman, like a masked Laocoön, bind him from behind. And only thus, possessed by a woman who did not possess him, could he release his happy liquid. (*P* 255/257)

The double image of a carbonero in voluptuous meltdown at the seashore next to a masked woman Laocoön in drag creates a striking visual affinity in reference to the eunuchlike, laocoönized husband (striking a stretched-arms pose gripping the snakelike ropes), as does the sodomized and doubly masked by soot and mask carbonero: "The apoplectic tone of this all-powerful incorporator of the outside world crescendoed in genuine oracular roars. *His hands held high, he gripped the ropes fastening the charcoal sacks* until his fingers began to bleed" (207/210, my emphasis). In retrospect, the earlier charcoal-burner's painful ecstasy now evokes—in added disfigurement—Laocoön's arm motion in the Vatican marble group (figure 2). The feminized and buggered Laocoön could well be *Paradiso*'s queerest and most perverse visual joke at the expense of mature parental manhood. Its triple burlesque exposure leaves a lasting imprint on the novel's image surface. The composite figure appears as a masked aging man roaring in pleasure while being buggered by a punkish boy inside a coal house; and then as the same man dipping his foot in the surf in a gesture of extravagant effeminacy; and last: as a mask-wearing woman in a brothel binding her male client from behind.

The sodomite humiliation of the father corresponds to the seemingly random image of the adolescent being murdered by the gods at the beginning of chapter 8. As will be examined below, the sacrificial and murdered adolescent reappears at the end of the chapter in the figure of Godofredo the Devil and his maddened complicity in matricide and parricide. In *Paradiso* the twin transgressions of killing mother and father are in turn entwined with incest wishes and scenarios involving the son and his father. Rather than being un-Christian, these high family crimes

Figure 2. Hagesander, Athenodorus, and Polydorus of Rhodes, *Laocoön*. The Vatican Museum, Rome. (Scala / Art Resource, NY)

epitomize all-too-Christian appeals to the values of asceticism against sexual passions unleashed. Suffering figures like Laocoön transport pagan (or un-Christian) passions in the narratives of Lezama into peaks of sublime aesthetic fixation in sadomasochistic bondage to Christianized gazing. Among the marginal characters in *Paradiso* who traverse the porous (and now queer) boundaries between Christian asceticism, pagan misrule, and family passions stands Benvenuto Cellini.

## Deep in the Closet with Benvenuto Cellini

Laocoön represents the closeted, incestuously humiliated, queered father in *Paradiso*. The iconographic father appears sodomized, under wraps, inside the marble Laocoön, inside the besotted husband, inside the grand sire at the seashore. He stands inside a narrative wax museum peopled by a host of paternal androgyny homos. These museum set pieces represent peephole idols in the worship of the passive/active and dominant/subordinate split obsessively attributed to homosexual relations in *Paradiso* and *Oppiano Licario*—in association with the son's affections and fears concerning his dead father.

The second and less violently staged act in which the client's possession is actually faked ("possessed by a woman who did not possess him") will be mentioned by Ricardo Fronesis among "malignant examples" of homosexual perversion in men, evils from which he draws a lesson on the *menoscabo* (impairment, lessening, defaming) of sexuality: "In all those transient little demons there is a reminiscence of the reduction [menoscabo] of sexuality, and yet all of them are distinguished men, with the gruff voice of a Sioux war drum. They swayed in a hammock; they were and were not homosexuals. But they were all creatures plagued by a deviation, even though the center from which the deviation had sprung could not be discovered" (*P* 256/257). Fronesis mentions Julius Caesar and the Etruscan kings as examples of men of royal and divine descent known to have practiced the "vice" or to have mated with nymphs. He proceeds by quoting from Benvenuto Cellini's twisted praise for sodomy among the mighty and godly in response to Baccio Bandinello's slur, which Fronesis quotes "'Oh, keep quiet, you dirty sodomite,'" as hurled at Cellini in front of the Duke of Medici, at the moment when Cellini was discussing with his patron how to restore "the beautiful antique statue of a little boy," to which he planned to add an eagle so they could "christen it" *Ganymede*. Cellini tells the scurrilous Bandinello: "'You madman, you are going too far. But I wish to God I did know how to indulge in such a noble practice [sodomy]: after all, we read that Jove enjoyed it with

Ganymede in paradise, and here on earth it is the practice of the greatest emperors and the greatest kings of the world. I am an insignificant, humble man, I haven't the means or the knowledge to meddle in such a marvelous matter'" (*P* 256/258).[3] Amid the ensuing laughter at Bandinello's expense, Cellini thinks that the one insulted by the slur is the Grand Duke himself, outside whose presence he would have instantly killed the offending rascal (as he had come close to doing a few days before).

In reacting to this scene from the *Vita*, Fronesis proves quite deft at naming those who, like Cellini, manage to artfully avoid disgraceful admissions in front of their patrons with the help of foolish rivals. He also mentions writers and sexual adventures who, like Casanova and André Gide, can afford to hide behind the mask of sincerity ("la máscara del sincerismo") in describing their boy-chasing affairs. Not seen by Fronesis, however, is how Cellini denies himself the status of powerful sodomite in front of the duke by confessing to the same lowly social rank that had earlier made him quite vulnerable to being entrapped on precisely the same charge of sodomy by the duke's own majordomo. The latter is said to have hired "the dishonest whore Gambetta" for the purpose of creating the impression that Benvenuto was sexually abusing his "shopboy" Cencio—Gambetta's little son—a crime for which Cellini could have been banished from Florence for life (Cellini, *Autobiography* 324).

At issue here is not only the affordable or unaffordable practice of sexual sincerity in fifteenth-century Florence, eighteenth-century Venice, or twentieth-century Paris or Havana—or Julius Caesar's playing the "Queen of Bithynia" to King Nicomedes, or Numa Pompilius's mating with nymphs in the Etruscan tall grass. Of equal or perhaps greater local interest is the scene of the father's humiliation in the theater of sodomy that the seemingly random Laocoön iconography has exposed in full view. Yet what matters most is neither the grand spectacle of (in Fronesis's words) "great warriors who were troubled by undeniable sexual deviation," nor the minor show (choreographed by Fronesis with sly descriptive condescension) of "men who cling to a halfway normal sexuality but who tingle and twist when their skin savors the insinuation of the marine algae, receiving with the splash of the waters the investiture of their maternal spirit" (*P* 257/258). Between the absence of modern sincerity in ancient love among the likes of Achilles and Patroclus—and the tremors of baptismal queerness in maternal waters among respectable Cuban men—lies the need, among the latter, to replace unaffordable sexual sincerity with the erotic devotion to secrecy elevated to sacredness in *Paradiso*.

Closet-devoted comments in the *Edición Crítica* of *Paradiso* underline Fronesis's contempt for sexual sincerity in Casanova and André Gide in connection with Lezama's unsigned newspaper column and moral vignette "El sincerismo o de la boca seca" (On sincerity or the dry mouth). But no comment is made about the anxiety that lies behind the exposure of cultivated sincerity as an object of social satire. Writing anonymously for the *Diario de la Marina* on November 25, 1949, Lezama acidly exposes the baited "rap" or seductive chatter ("el sonsonete y el anzuelo") of intrusive sincerity by which the virtual stranger spills his guts in exchange for the listener's reciprocating secrets. In the vignette's final sentence he goes beyond unmasking counterfeit sincerity and makes an impassioned apology for sacred intimacy among male friends. The unsigned newspaper columnist contemplates the inner space of ethical sublimity wherein male friendship attains the devotional status of love among the esoteric elect: "How far is such cult of sincerity from a friend's confession to another friend, or from addressing it to his own solitude, muttered, almost stammered [musitada, casi balbuceada], hardly at all expressed, but needed and welcome like a gift from grace; since the birth of acquaintance between two persons is so mysterious that it requires a counterpoint development between the artisan's craft [artesanía] and the ineffable."[4]

In response to the sidewalk ambush tactics of *sincerismo* in Havana, the elect few seek refuge in a space of partaken subjectivity between reflecting icons of mutual devotion inside the male-exclusive space nowadays known as the "closet," which near the end of *Oppiano Licario* is given the Greek cult name of *abaton,* or "sacred precinct." Benvenuto Cellini's double figure embodies in Fronesis's wishful imagination ascetic and profligate routines: as the foxy denizen of the sexual closet and as the habitual escapee from its whispering imprisonment in devotional friendship.

## Socrates by the Handle

Tensions run high between the treasured space of whispered ascetic inwardness and what Fronesis goes on to praise as its implicit opposite, the ancient Greek notion of "*dromenón*" ("thing performed"), which he calls "the realized fact" or deed, and describes as a space in which the "conversation developed like a dance . . . a race in which beautiful bodies were impelled by light" (*P* 257/258). One hidden thing certainly up for grabs in Fronesis's ineffable account of *dromenón* is the penis as phallus, three times linked by him to "lo inasible," the quality of that which—either as object or concept—cannot be grabbed/grasped/seized ("asir") by the handle ("asa"). Also, near the end of their convoluted dialogue on male homosexuality (and after comparing one of Foción's arguments to an inscription engraved by razor across the buttocks of a Byzantium eunuch) Fronesis soothes his anger by saying: "'You are my closest friend' . . . 'but you are also my closest intangible [inasible], and the more you unmask yourself, it seems *as if you're intangibly going along picking up* [*parece que tu inasible va recogiendo*] all those masks that you abandon'" (258/259, my emphasis).

Fronesis attributes to Plato's early Socratic dialogue *Charmides* several notions about the body. (In what follows Rabassa's translation is placed in brackets, preceded by my more literal translation in quotation marks.) The body ("el cuerpo") in *Charmides* is (a) "the sudden-ness of remembrance" ("es el súbito de la reminiscencia" [the sudden curve of remembrance]); (b) "what remains of countless waves" ("la permanencia de un oleaje innumerable" [the permanence of an endless wave]); and (c) "the form of that which is remembered, an image" ("la forma de un recuerdo, es decir una imagen" [the form of memory, that is, of an image]). In each man ("en cada hombre"), the body's image "crawls" ("repta") with "almost ungraspable mutations" ("mutaciones casi inapresables" [with mutations that are almost intangible]). But this ungraspable (residual remembrance) or crawling image bears the measure of each man's sexuality ("pero ese inasible tiene la medida de su sexualidad" [but it is just that intangible part which contains the measure of his sexuality]) (*P* 257/259). As either *inapresable* or *inasible,* the cause or the *why* ("el porqué") "in the phallic" ("en lo fálico") is always ungraspable ("es siempre inasible"). As such, this ungraspable thing or quality "is the dark color" ("es el color oscuro") that passes (turns) into the ecstasy ("que pasa al éxtasis") that pours out ("que se vuelca") over another ungraspable ("sobre otro inasible"). It seems that Fronesis either has no handle or too much of a handle on that which cannot or should not be grasped or handled. In response, Socrates' question might well be, Why deal with the ungraspable before dealing with the graspable? A further Socratic request would be to ask where exactly in *Charmides* is any of this found. Socratic, not only because none of it is found in *Charmides,* but because, strictly speaking, the physical object of Fronesis's verbiage happens to be Charmides'—or Plato's maternal uncle's—penis.

Plato wrote the dialogue about his uncle and future tyrant to whom Socrates is teaching self-restraint and reasoned thinking in full knowledge (Plato's) that the beautiful youth is too hot-tempered and not likely to learn much from philosophy. Thus, the hard-to-handle character trait in

Charmides concerns not his sexual but his political behavior in politics. Trevor J. Saunders comments on Plato's motives for choosing (in Critias and Charmides) two members of his own family to be Socrates' interlocutors. He questions why Plato should have honored them with praise for their noble ancestry, to which the philosopher himself belonged. The answer lies in the two men's subsequent careers. Critias went on to become the extremist leader of the Thirty Tyrants, who imposed a reign of terror on Athens at the end of the Peloponnesian War as they tried to impose their oligarchy upon the city. Charmides too became one of the Thirty, meeting his death, with Critias, in battle against the democrats. According to Saunders, Plato's aim is to release Socrates from any blame in the abuses carried out by his former companions and their lack of *sophrosune,* or self-control (*Plato: Early Socratic Dialogues* 167). It is unlikely that Lezama knew of the family link between Plato and his maternal uncle or about the specific issue of *sophrosune* (self-control or temperance) addressed by Socrates in *Charmides.* Yet, both issues (kinship and self-control) define the character of tío Alberto, José Cemí's maternal uncle in *Paradiso,* whose behavior is haunted by his charismatic (and spectrally queer) lack of self-restraint.

Restored to its proper Platonic context, Fronesis's verbal duel with Foción resembles by unwitting parody the bad arguments coming from several of the victims or potential beneficiaries of Socratic irony in its method of inquiry aimed at grasping a specific virtue through quick question-and-answer rather than long speech-making. For there is nothing less Socratic in method or philosophical import than the lengthy oratorical pieces traded between Fronesis and Foción, with the occasional help of José Cemí. (Socrates would have made short work of picking apart their arcane appeal to clouded thinking and sentimentality.)

The scriptwriter in Lezama stands behind Socrates in these pseudo-Socratic exchanges, but Socrates' method and spirit of inquiry and questioning are not at work in *Paradiso.* With strict Socratic irony it could be said that the nearest that a mind of Socrates' tenor and reasonable aims comes to José Lezama Lima's life is in the open letters that Jorge Mañach wrote to him in late 1949. We will look next at the hidden question of sex and politics in the affair prompted by these letters with the aim of creating a *Socratic Moment* or *handle* in the public biography of Lezama's authorship. But my aim is not to designate Mañach as Socrates and Lezama as a flawed version of Plato's philosophical teacher and possible target of Socratic wisdom in action. Both Mañach and Lezama align on the Socratic side of arguing for self-restraint, but in different styles.

The styles in question represent divergent ways of thinking that bring Mañach and Lezama face to face on the issue of bad behavior and the harmful consequences of political conduct.

The first element of our Socratic Moment concerns Aristophanes and his lampooning authorship against Socrates in *Clouds*. In that comedy, the allegorical characters of "Better Argument" and "Worse Argument" square off in combined banter against Socrates and his teachings and accuse him of fostering unbelief in the gods of the city. It is nowadays agreed that the object of Aristophanes' debunking was Socrates, as he was believed to have been at the center of a Pythagorean group devoted to such notions as the immortality of the soul, esoteric mathematics, and strict asceticism. This particular Socrates was seen as the cult leader of a group devoted to Pythagorean attitudes and beliefs. Such is the man (aged about forty-five) who in Aelian's anecdote stands up among the audience at the Theater of Dionysus during the performance of *Clouds* in order to show the public that he is—in actual life and beyond Aristophanes' lampooning—the man under attack on stage.[5]

It would be tempting to caricature Mañach as taking sides with Aristophanes against Lezama on the issue of esoteric practices and politics by the Pythagorean Socrates—along the lines of Lezama's well-known fondness for Pythagoras, which would thus yield the lampooned figure of an elite and esoteric Havana Socrates up in the clouds. Accordingly, Mañach would represent the early Socratic and Platonic side of accessible public discourse, transparent and unhindered by baroque pleasures of metaphor and allusiveness. In contrast, Lezama would represent the dysfunctional Pythagorean Socrates who under Aristophanes' assault would favor a discourse of clouded indirection, arcane elitism, and esoteric doctrinal goals. Yet both men would, paradoxically, take sides with Socrates against his lampooning by Aristophanes.

Let us then consider how the hypothetical Socratic Moment in Mañach and Lezama comes up short of the witch-hunt politics latent in Aristophanic lampooning. The Havana Socratic Moment centers on Lezama's life as a poet given to esoteric obscurity as he turns to writing the novel eventually known as *Paradiso* and exchanges polemical letters with Mañach in late 1949.[6] Although it was unthinkable for Mañach to address even with utmost indirection aspects of sex and eroticism in the indirectness that he decried in Lezama's obscure poetry, it is hard to imagine that his own intuition—if not something in the poetry itself—should not have alerted Mañach to what he in fact never openly ponders: namely, the nature and character of what escapes or avoids apparent utterance in Lezama's poetic obscurities. This is not to suggest that Mañach or anyone else close to him knew anything about what nowadays would be labeled Lezama's sexual orientation. Yet it seems quite possible that Jorge Mañach did read Lezama's unsigned (but unmistakably Lezamiana) column "El sincerismo o de la boca seca"—published in the *Diario de la Marina* on November 25, 1949, just a few weeks after his response to Lezama in mid-October. Two questions follow: Would Mañach have recognized in the essay's tremulous appeal to devoted intimacy between friends (as examined above) a reiteration of the subjective exclusiveness that he had attacked just a few weeks earlier in Lezama's poetry? And could Mañach have spotted a symptom of sexual anxiety in Lezama's allusive appeal to a shared "counterpoint development between the artisan's craft [artesanía] and the ineffable" among friends? (Such friends were likely to be seen by Mañach as exclusively male, as they certainly were when placed in their actual historical context.)

The Socratic Moment suggests a double response to Mañach's possible reading of the newspaper column. First, with regard to erotic self-sufficiency, Socrates was not only able to avoid reticence about his own and other people's erotic feelings, but in fact was able to exploit philosophical inquiry into such feelings, in himself and his interlocutors, in order to steer these men into a better knowledge and self-control of themselves. Self-knowledge in Socrates was all at once daemon-inspired and philosophical. Possession by a personal daemon allowed Socrates to lead his interlocutors by question-and-answer into strict self-scrutiny. In every important sense, erotic self-sufficiency in Socrates resulted, not in obscurity or indirection, as it happens with the faulty-Socratic speech of Ricardo Fronesis, but in articulate enunciation and ironic wisdom—as it rarely happens with Lezama's Socratic interlocutors and mouthpieces.

In contrast with Platonic social capabilities, enhanced by the Athenian male-exclusive access to erotic philosophizing, neither Mañach (whose polemic against Lezama's obscurities leaves eroticism untouched on grounds of decorum) nor Lezama (whose poetry and prose deal only indirectly with elite homosexual eroticism) are capable of acting the least Socratic with respect to Eros. For different reasons, both men must avoid engaging Eros in newspaper print: Mañach due to public correctness and censoring, and Lezama out of fear of his own sexual daemon and the homophobic penalties that a less obscure "Socratic Eros" poetry would bring against him.

Thus, the first response allowed by the Socratic Moment appears bound by polite social closet rules on homosexuals. But the second response brings us closer to the hazing cruelties implicit in Aristophanes' outing of Socrates' odd behavior in *Clouds* with respect to the political norms of the Athenian city-state. At about age forty-five, the lampooned Socrates philosopher in *Clouds* is virtually of the same age as were Oppiano Licario and his creator José Lezama Lima in 1953. The worst charges against Socrates stem from what different characters in *Clouds* do or advocate in claiming the influence of his teaching, including denial that Zeus exists, refusal to pay debts backed by oaths given in the god's name, beating parents, and incest. At the end of the play, one enraged father burns down the thought-mill prep school Phrontisterion (the so-called thinketorium) in revenge against Socrates' alleged corruption of his son. In *Clouds* Socrates does not give a hoot for the community on whose economic wealth his thinketorium depends. Instead, he relies for his pedagogical survival and that of his students on sheer hustle: his philosophical concerns are up in the clouds and do not concern real persons, laws, morals, or family. So each time Pythagorean Socratic students in *Clouds* come in contact with civic life beyond the walls of their thinking mill, the results are chaotic.

Aristophanes' picture of Socrates as a dysfunctional esoteric shaman or wandering Pythagorean priest temporarily settled in the echoing cavern of the Phrontisterion frames the second aspect of the Socratic Moment in reference to Lezama's self-invention in the character of Oppiano Licario. This character represents the esoteric, ironic, and satirical self-portrait by Lezama of himself as a heroic bachelor who observes what can best be described as a form of voluptuous asceticism. Oppiano amounts to the self-personification of authorship as a man who, instead of closeting himself in some academic niche in which to harvest a crop of erotic pupil zombies, takes off for Europe, but not without remaining at home in his dream nights of walking and vigil in Havana. Such exercise in ubiquitous wandering lust (being in Europe and in Havana all at once) rubs elbows with the unsocial obscurities condemned by Mañach in Lezama's poetry. It also sets itself at odds with efforts to accommodate Lezama at home, to domesticate whatever elite teaching on the homosexual erotic life his poetry and fiction might proffer under the radar of social respectability or, worse, under the State's normative political correctness as a commemorative *viajero inmóvil* or armchair fellow traveler.

## When Beauty Becomes Tyranny Posing as Truth

The paradox of pseudo-Socratic dialogue in *Paradiso* involves copious verbalizing of tabooed queer sex while evasively arguing for the elite respect that pseudosacred or daemonic queer sex deserves. At stake is not a plea for tolerance among common sex offenders or regular guys but a claim of higher sublime status on behalf of the love that dares not speak its name. Foción is the first to mention Socrates as "the lover of Charmides" along with Euthydemus, Agathon, and Alcibiades, as if to show "that through the body Eros produces the beautiful" (*P* 249/250). Although Foción attributes the claim to Diotima, it belongs to Alcibiades, who only half in jest charges Socrates with deception: "He presents himself as your lover, and, before you know it, you are in love with him yourself" (Plato, *Symposium* 222b). With great eloquence punctuated by the hiccups, Alcibiades demonstrates that he has fallen in love with the wisdom lover instead of wisdom, which is what Foción feels for Fronesis as he desperately wants his sex. However, Foción's lust for Fronesis differs from Alcibiades' love-lust for Socrates, though not in the sex it desires, but on how and where it wants it. In R. E. Allen's view, "Plato gives us in Socrates a union of lover and beloved, beguiler and beguiled. But the personification of *Eros*'s two aspects in Socrates inevitably leads further. Unlike Agathon's unthinking love for love, which makes *Eros* an end in itself, to love Socrates, as Alcibiades knows and makes clear to the company, is to love what Socrates, as *Eros,* loves: the possession of beauty, wisdom, and goodness. To love Socrates is to be a philosopher . . . this is exactly what Socrates wanted of those he approached in his direct yet ironic manner" (Plato, *Symposium* xxiv–xxv). But Foción does not seek wisdom in the man who bears wisdom's name, *phronesis;* and neither does Fronesis seek in himself or in Foción an explanation, in terms of wisdom, of his own refusing—and the manner in which he refuses—Foción's hot sexual pursuit.

Such a lack of engagement in the disciplined pursuit of wisdom as self-knowledge is what represents the least Socratic trait in the literary character known as Ricardo Fronesis. Yet the narrative strategy that represents Fronesis in *Paradiso* tries to achieve the opposite overwhelming impression: that his character is indeed open and committed to combined modes of burgeoning moral wisdom in Socratic terms. Such is the political tyranny of elite queer male beauty embodied and disembodied in Lezama's invention of Ricardo Fronesis.

The highest standard for wisdom above sexual love between elite older and younger men is set by Socrates' doctrine of *Eros.* As explained by R. E. Allen, among others, the hubris of Socrates in shunning sex with Alcibiades goes beyond temperance. If Eros aims at happiness and stokes desire for generation in body and soul, common lust among men for men is not Eros. Thus, Alcibiades' desire for sex with Socrates is not Eros, since it is barren. In response, hubris in Socrates consists in what Allen calls *principled disdain:* "If Eros is wish for what is truly good, then asceticism in respect to desire and specifically sexuality . . . is implied in the *Symposium* and at the core of its moral psychology" (Plato, *Symposium* 108). Indeed, "principled disdain" seems an apt phrase for what Fronesis exhibits in his dealings with his best friend and sexual pursuer and beguiler, Eugenio Foción.

In José Cemí's view, Foción always acts driven by envy and resentment when he turns against friends he has previously held as "lovers of wisdom: like Charmides in the presence of the Silenus [Socrates]" (*P* 282/281). Furthermore, Cemí knows that Foción regards Socrates (or Silenus) as Charmides' lover, and in the same speech he claims that "Silenus passes from the beautiful body to the universal ocean, the way a Catholic goes from the visible to the invisible" (248/250). As Lezama's principal surrogate, Cemí knows this much about Foción's Charmides, just as he knows, since reading *Charmides* in adolescence, about "the seduction of the relationships between wisdom and memory" and the "Delphic" notion of knowledge based on remembrance (328/325). It thus seems that Fronesis, Foción, and Cemí differ little in their awareness of male beauty in *Charmides,* although knowledge of their related awareness of such beauty could in fact differ greatly.

The three friends and polemical rivals seem to implicitly share in the knowledge of Charmides' beauty, which is such as to cause agitation in Socrates, though he finds nearly all young gymnasts uniformly appealing. Fronesis's mention of the body's sudden emergence from reminiscence in *Charmides* and its further connection with the "ungraspable" quality of "the phallic" corresponds to the reaction experienced by Socrates in response to the dialogue's outstandingly graspable body: "Everyone in the wrestling-school swarmed all round us. That was the moment, my noble friend, when I saw what was inside his cloak. I was on fire, I lost my head, and I considered Cydias to be the wisest man in matters of love. When speaking of a handsome boy, he said, by way of advice to someone, 'Take care not to go as a fawn into the presence of a lion and be snatched as a portion of meat.' I felt I'd been caught by such a creature. All the same, when Charmides asked me whether I knew the remedy for his headaches, I somehow managed to answer that I did" (Plato, *Early Socratic Dialogues, Charmides* 155d–e). It should not surprise us that Foción's insane pursuit of Fronesis should correspond to his false and uncontested assertion that Socrates is the lover of Charmides. But this does not mean that either Fronesis or Cemí understands his specific knowledge of erotic love, as when Socrates lusts for Charmides as does Foción for his beloved Fronesis. That is to say, in terms of their *shared* knowledge of each other, as a sign of erotic love becoming answerable wisdom, when it comes to distinguishing erotically between one another, a lot hinges on what sort of un-Socratic things Foción wants to do to his beloved Fronesis—in the name of Socrates, but not as the wisdom teacher whom Fronesis could ever accept as his master and lover.

The tyranny of male physical beauty, cast as the possible source of philosophical truth—but ruined by differences in social status between plebian (middle class) Foción and aristocratic (and presumably wealthy) Fronesis—creates the split Socratic image of homosexual queer love in *Paradiso*. Otherwise, ignoring the implicit tyranny of spiritual elitism in homosexual love as portrayed in *Paradiso* in favor of queer brotherly universalism or open communal bonding among men, regardless of differences in social class high and low, erases all friction in male-to-male erotic desire and the pursuit of wisdom and runs against the obsessed depiction of precisely such abrasiveness in the novel's sexual polemics. But, by the same token, *Paradiso* goes a long way in disavowing aristocratic spiritualism as a symptom of love, higher in philosophical value than anything that Fronesis could recognize as love coming to him from another man who is not his own look-alike soulful emanation. Thus, pursuing erotic wisdom in *Paradiso* reenacts the death of Narcissus in the split image of a young man's soul placed under the gaze of his older male teacher, a pedagogue spiritualist man who has already passed the prime age when he could act out a strong hormonal life capable of binding his male soul to younger male bodies. Such is precisely the tyranny of renewed masculine beauty in each successive pupil that old Socrates' armored asceticism—as the horny master of truth—has taught him to philosophically overcome.

This is how Foción's false claim that maestro Socrates is also the erotic and physical lover of his pupil Charmides goes unchallenged by his friends Cemí and Fronesis. The false claim dovetails with Fronesis's own fabricated and fantasized account of the body's rising suddenly from recollection in *Charmides* being like the oceanic image that remains from innumerable waves. In both cases, the oceanic image of the youthful body's inspiring beauty in ageless daemonic Eros bespeaks the older man's sublimated lust for the younger body reaching beyond the constraints of wisdom. More important than Lezama's mistake in recalling or misrepresenting issues and characters in *Charmides* is the question of how the aristocratic parity in social and generational terms among elite philosophical pupils and gymnasts depicted in Plato's dialogue about his maternal uncle and his oligarchic peers becomes subordinate in *Paradiso* to the older man's sublimated lust, as he acts as the maestro who would try to teach temperance to his pupils as an antidote to their youthful ambitions to become tyrants. Ignoring the tyrannical political context behind the beauty of young Charmides as scrutinized in *Charmides* (and felt by Socrates with a measure of philosophical double-acting in lust and restraint) constitutes the transcendent mistake in the Socratic illusions cultivated in *Paradiso*.

Political lessons of the sort drawn from *Charmides* mark the limits of our Socratic Moment. The beautiful gymnast and future bloody tyrant (the sight of whose genitals momentarily shakes up Socrates' sense of restraint as he readies himself to teach temperance to his pupil) proves to be an all too gifted student quite beyond teaching. Apparently, Charmides never takes Socrates seriously. As Alexander Nehamas reminds us, the identity of Critias and Charmides as "depraved, evil characters" should frame in established historical terms our judgment of their obliviousness to what Socrates taught them about restraint (*Art of Living* 42). But such historical certainty does not resolve the riddle posed by Plato about evil conduct principally in political affairs. One could ask: Was unconcern for Socrates and his teachings what led Charmides astray into tyranny, or was it something inherently spoiled in his character that caused his dismissal of Socratic wisdom even before he met the man whom Foción calls Silenus? The tyrannical sexual charisma that adheres to Charmides in the eyes of both desiring Foción and desired Fronesis proves ruinously unlike what Socrates aimed at teaching his pupil. In *Paradiso*'s Socratic Moment, sexual charisma—capable of overwhelming the teacher into becoming his student's actual lover—spoils Socrates' wisdom in how thoroughly it associates the beautiful gymnast with sexiness and kills any chance to philosophically examine such tyrannical erotic allure in the context of civic politics—taken beyond the specific appeal of sexual politics.

The unexamined Socratic connection in *Paradiso* between the allure of tyranny and the call to civic duty remains curious because the repeated epithet "ungraspable" (turned into the noun "inasible," or without handle) will actually bind together conspiratorial politics, homosexual passion, moral risk, and death in *Oppiano Licario*. When Mohamed conspires between the political realms of East and West Tupek, it is written that "he knew that the struggle for power depended upon his setting in motion many ungraspables [inasibles] and that among all those inasibles he had chosen Cidi Galeb" (*OL* 184). (As it happens, Galeb is the most sinister character in Lezama's fiction, to the extent to which his evil deeds bind together politics and sexual actions as criminal misdeeds.) Beyond the unfinished *Oppiano Licario* (and taking into account the "Esbozo para el Infierno" [Sketch for Inferno] that contains notes for the rest of the novel) Cidi Galeb is supposed to murder Fronesis, after a very queer mismatch with him in bed, and then turn blackmailer and conspirator against Foción back in Havana, before Foción kills him and then commits suicide. Together with Mohamed, Galeb belongs to the impossible-to-grasp and without-a-handle host of homosexuals whose ground zero of passion and catastrophe is occupied by the three dissonant Socratic friends whose verbal sparring we have just examined.

Beyond any of their differences—which at times sound like combined echoes inside the chamber of a single mind—the three friends share a tortured interest in bodies as splendid as Charmides' and always attached to an older tutor and potential lover who is alluded to but never shown as part of the picture. What proves hard to handle for lack of a handle in their dialogue is the invested rhetoric that obscures what so transparently involves plain lust by an older man for younger men—unresisting of his teachings. Nothing in what the three friends argue in *Paradiso* denies their shared desire in loving a mind and a soul through the erotic knowledge of a body such as the one possessed by Charmides and Fronesis. What breaks the friends' single mind apart is the issue of whose mind, body, and soul will become the object of desire and how the lover should be driven to act in response to such desire.

Taking Socrates by the handle about this issue would help us distinguish sexual politics from politics—from the political as such. That is to say: to distinguish sex from politics so far as the degree to which unsound and convoluted thinking about erotic passion and the kinds of knowledge it might set in motion should constitute an early warning sign of trouble ahead as the minds so engaged in bad thinking turn to politics beyond love's lust. The story of Godofredo the Devil dramatizes with the retrograde force of myth precisely this issue.

## A Mirror of Matricide

During a trip to the Tres Suertes sugar mill narrated at the end of chapter 8, Ricardo Fronesis tells José Cemí the story of how one-eyed Godofredo fell in love with Fileba. Their conversation constructs an allegory not unlike the ones often encountered in Plato's use of myth for the purpose of illustrating philosophical doctrines. The crime of matricide ingrained in the iconography of Godofredo's madness concludes chapter 8 by returning us to the lethal and parasitic relationship between the son and his Gorgo incest mother. The imperative of killing the mother as a monstrous rival simultaneously confronting the son's body image and lodged inside his father-wanting soul could well represent the myth of eugenic male queer character birth in the movement of chapter 8 from pornography to autobiography and from sexual waste to philosophical abstinence.

At seventeen, Fileba is two years older than Godofredo and married to Pablo, the sugar mill's machinist, who's twice her age and often drunk. Fronesis tells Cemí an evil-eye tale: Godofredo "knows he knows the story that ends with his blind eye," and this is why "he always keeps his head turned," with the empty eye showing, being afraid that if the one who knows the story stares at him, "he might lose the eye he has left" (*P* 216/218). Since the age of fifteen Godofredo "hallucinates" in love with Fileba and hopes to blackmail sexual favors from her. When left alone on Saturday nights, she dreams of "monsters carrying her away naked to the hill tops" while her husband gets drunk at the bar. On the night of his death Pablo is dragged from the bar by Godofredo to spy on Fileba as she enters a house in the company of a man. Staggered by what he sees, Pablo returns to the bar and drinks well beyond the tenth glass. He has seen his wife Fileba from behind a tree entering a house in the company of Eufrasio the priest. Soon after, Pablo kills himself while Godofredo spies on the lovers' sex ritual in peep-show fashion. This riveting one-eye sex scene screws Godofredo's gaze into the single-eye hole he has bored through the wall. The spying scene is shown in retrospect, after Pablo sees Fileba go into the house with Eufrasio and before she finds him dead with his throat slit upon returning home. Pablo was brought home drunk with the help of the rural police. He had unlocked the door at the same time that Godofredo stalked the lovers' nest and felt "around the walls and windows with his nails for a peephole" (*P* 218/221). Thus, the cuckolded husband kills himself in synchrony with the ensuing sex show between his wife and the priest being watched by Godofredo.

In the past, each time he helped drunken Pablo home, Godofredo liked "to hang around the house like a wolf cub who knows that the girl of the house has tied the dove to the kitchen table by its leg" (216/219). From the beginning, as he stalks Fileba, Godofredo's hallucinations match Pablo's polluted drunkenness. In the end, he lures Pablo to the peephole, which seems to have been bored by his own piercing gaze. The two men are bound together by the same spell caused by drinking and peeping. But Pablo actually *sees* what Godofredo's one eye can only blindly watch and surmise. The sex scene between Fileba and Eufrasio is shown in time arrest. Past and present are joined in synchrony: thus, when Pablo covered (and *covers*) his eyes with a pillow; when he fell (and *falls*) into drunken sleep and death. In such synchrony, Pablo's killing occurs in the past-present time frame as both murder and suicide. He cuts his own throat as if trying to achieve by decapitation in mirror fashion Godofredo's peeping eye loss. What the detached spying peephole is to Godofredo's attached evil eye the head-covering pillow is to Pablo's decapitated head. In each case the body finds a metonymic object or leaning point to match its symbolic missing attribute. The peephole fits Godofredo's spying eye just as the pillow's decapitated head image matches Pablo's expired mind. What is shown—the peep show narrated in the text—occupies the death scene's blind or never seen actuality. The real event shows up as attained by its being witnessed in the gaze, a gaze that never saw (and blindly *watches*) the event. The gaze never sees the event that nevertheless exists in the gaze and is fused with it.

Pablo's death promotes mystery because in killing himself he seems to act out his desperate wish to be killed (by another) in order to become martyr to his own ruined life. Led by Godofredo, he hides behind a parasite plant that in folk belief suffocates the tree as it would a human being. Pablo is "sucked" by the "octopus" tree when he sees the adulterous couple entering the house. Godofredo is the tree's daemonic surrogate agent. He is punished by "an implacable army of vines" coiled "like rearing serpents" round his body when one of his eyes is lashed and marked with a cross. In climbing up to his waist, the vines whistle "like a hurricane wind," a noise Godofredo will eventually transform into his maddened "zigzagging" walks, "like bolts of lightning" (219/222). He becomes a human spark point situated between vegetation and lightning on which "incessant rain" has softened "the flames of the red hair" and given birth to "the malignant flower of the crossroads" (219/222). His daemonic arboreal character clings to fire and endows his parasite radiance with the glow stolen from dying vegetation and renewing fire: "His face was very white, and the reflections of his hair's flame dimmed in a pink spiral that sank blushing into a chiaroscuro neck. . . . Cemí was able to see how the spiral that began with pink tones became sharper, until it reached a fruity red over all of his body, exposing the fortunate energy of the stain and the demons of that energy who where so dear to Blake" (214/217).

Godofredo loses both "reason" and right eye at the same time. So, when a vine brands "a cross on his right eye, the canon's eye," he becomes a fire demon. The vine's fury answers his hacking at it with the "guámpara"; the same tool found next to Pablo ("on the floor near the slit throat"). His blinding ties together myth motifs linking fire-motion with limbs in motion and the loss of eye symmetry (already present earlier in chapter 8 in the one-eyed phallus). He is compared to Polyphemus through antithesis: "Handsome adolescent Polyphemus, when he saw that everyone was looking at his one raised eye, cursed from every pore of his unreconciled beauty" (214/219). Godofredo's Cyclopean blinding binds him to the presence of ligatures and fire motifs in the adulterous scene obtained in peeping-Tom one-eyed gazing:

> Like a marine apparition contemplated through the tube of a telescope, a strange combination of figures rose to view: Fileba, naked, lay on the bed weeping, showing the fullness of her body. But it was hardly suffused with pleasure; rather, she seemed indifferent, frigid. Eufrasio, his pants off, was still wearing his shirt and undershirt. A string was tied to one end of the bed and stretched to wrap around his testicles, purple with the gradual strangulation, as Eufrasio drew back with an almost liturgical slowness. His phallus, in the culmination of its erection, looked like a great votive candle that had been lit for a very sinful soul. His scorched, rigid cheeks were receiving infernal slaps. When the seminal reason of Augustine finally came out, the testicular strangulation was as much as the string could stand, and a sweaty moan struggling for silence trembled through the disoriented man's body. (*P* 218/221)

In her study of archaic motifs in the story of Hephaestus, Marie Delcourt begins by referring to the mystery of sexual life's exposure "to the power of ties" and the link between ligatures and genitals as either maleficent or beneficent bundles. Magical ligatures bind at a distance. Fascination fastens and binds; as when sexual organs are flashed or the evil eye is shown against someone. Tying someone up risks being tied down in return" (*Héphaistos* 24–25).

In line with such motifs, Godofredo trains his missing or displaced (right-to-left) canon's eye to witness a spectacle of genital binding, which in turn binds and blinds the one gazing. His binding evil-eye peeping happens as Pablo is killing himself at home. The wasting of semen corresponds to the spilling of suicide blood. Likewise, Pablo's suicide weapon turns into the murderous machete used by Godofredo to "kill" the vine that blinds and maddens him. Godofredo spies on a binding scene involving bound genitals, and he does this with an eye that is and is not canonical (either right-for-left or left-for-right). Pablo's evil-eye haunted mind needs no spying in order to prompt his own throat-cutting. Godofredo has watched the scene on his behalf.

Pablo kills himself in complicity with those he would have named as his murderers. Fileba's role seems passive and marginal, but she is in the eye of the storm. The adulterous girl evokes a tableau by Artemisia Gentileschi: "She noticed that Pablo's hands weren't crossed over the pillow shield on his face, as usual in his Saturday-night exhaustion . . . she saw in a shock that the pillow was soaked with blood, his shirt still wet. The machete on the floor near the slit throat had begun to oxidize with the coagulation of the blood. . . . Fileba tugged at the pillow on the floor, but like a Gorgon soaked in somber purple, it began to cast off threads and spurts of blood" (*P* 222/219). Suicide and murder switch places like the canon's eye right-to-left tied to the evil eye. That which is one and single resists understanding unless cast in perplexing relationship with what is double and paired, as when Pablo's suicide mirrors Godofredo's lost-eye punishment and suicide binds itself to murder.

Magic binds Pablo's head and its shadowed decapitation to the Gorgon's mask-pillow; it binds Godofredo's left eye to his right eye and to the *right* (correct) missing eye; it binds a killing sight (mirrored in Godofredo's blind eye) to the blindness that kills on behalf of blinding fire; it binds a dull machete blade (used in suicide) to a lightning machete blow that transforms suicide into murder and produces Gorgo's blood in order to feed with it the fires of matricide.

Fire fires up the daemon inside every demon. Godofredo would not have gone mad and become a fire demon had he not replayed Pablo's death—yet, not as a single murder, but as *their* conjoined share in sacrificial matricide stamped upon the Gorgon head and the blood-soaked pillow touched and rejected by Fileba. Pablo cuts his throat in the same mirror frame in which his decapitation is shown in the bloody Gorgon pillow. Gorgon decapitation embodies matricide as the binding tie between the husband (Pablo) who dies without male issue and the fatherless and perpetual young man (Godofredo) whose own Cyclopean blinding gains the stolen gaze spying into Eufrasio's wasted-semen and votive candle peep show. The son's voyeur matricide *reverses* parricide even as it *duplicates* it in the Oedipus scenario. Reversal comes as matricide may sexually bind (rather than unbind) the son to the murdered-but-lethal female parent and her castrating desire. Duplication comes as love for the murdered male parent may repeat itself as sexual love between men. The proposed scenario hinges on the *inalienable homosexual matrix of masculine love,* rather than on love's further outgrowth in the heterosexual ontology athwart sexual difference.

Side by side with its seminal economy of waste, chapter 8 deploys a twisted—and queer—iconography of eroticism and sacrifice centered on Gorgon decapitation. David Napier has shown that the Gorgon is found at the bottom of some ancient Greek drinking kylix cups showing large eyes at the drinker. The "gargling" of wine when drinking from these cups vies with the *gharga,* "gurgling" (Spanish "gárgara") etymological family. According to Napier, the fact that "Gorgons are frequently shown in the tondo of the eye cup points to a specific correspondence between losing one's head and being out of it"—being quite drunk (*Masks* 102). The Greeks "were aware of the eye-cup Gorgon as an irreducible iconographic structure"; they saw in the Gorgon kylix "a kind of ethological homunculus" or "indicator" of "human sensory capacities" fragmented into humanlike body parts (103). In similar fashion, Godofredo's magical eye blindly fathoms the face missed by Pablo (drunk-blind and headless) at the bottom of every fourth glass.

Acting as illustrative myth, Godofredo's tale of metamorphosis brings into focus a knotted umbilical drama at the heart of *Paradiso* and its unfinished sequel *Oppiano Licario.* It is the drama of the extent to which passions, lusts, and petty emotions of hate and envy aroused by specific male homosexual anxieties play havoc with the political energies implicit in their own turmoil and emotionality.

In this regard, the following questions seem pertinent: To what extent do the narrow politics generated by sexual (masculine/male) anxieties and rivalries spill over and become the driving force behind politics at large beyond sexuality—and into the political as such? To what extent can Socrates, for instance, be grasped beyond the daemons of pederasty that haunt his extended cameo role in *Paradiso*? To what degree do folklore and illiterate characters such as Godofredo the redheaded, one-eyed fire devil become scapegoats and martyrs for the eroticized body-versus-mind conflict that literate elite characters like Ricardo Fronesis and José Cemí keep in containment within themselves—or release in showers of emotionality and cloudy rhetoric? Finally, to what extent can the son of Gorgo act by himself without the fire and blood and semen that her own sacrificial mother-arts infuse into a queer sex life absconded in the aesthetic (abstract) contemplation of erotic insurgency?

The frozen look in the eye facing Gorgo's male-exclusive death performance blinds all answers to what amounts to a political puzzle. A puzzle that consumes and exhausts political sanity in *Paradiso–Oppiano Licario* as it wrongly fixates sex at the heart of social and political thinking. Such implantation is made worse as it further binds the sexualization of the political to a retrograde religious view of politics—politics thus aestheticized.

If the sexual murder of mother Gorgo by her son should take us by bloodied hands to the recognition that masculine/male human sexuality issues from a homosexual matrix embedded in poisonous mother nursing, the eugenic birth of the son released from such blood marriage to incestuous murder emerges as the birthmark of patriarchal sexual hegemony in the son's blocked access to masculine/male parenthood.

An egregiously current political issue arises from within the vicissitudes of queer sex in the fictions of Lezama Lima: burdened by such sacred and daemonic/demonic prestigious baggage, it is no wonder that gays—in that retrograde mold—would find insurmountable roadblocks on their queer path by choice to marriage, generation, and adoption.

In *Paradiso* and elsewhere in Lezama's fiction, homosexual queerness associates itself with the ancient Greek belief in *daemonic* possession that inspires the teachings of Socrates with the force of the host daemon inside his soul. But at the same time, Christian belief in *demonic* or Devil-related sinfulness permeates the conduct of some demonized homosexual characters in his fiction: most notably Foción, to the point that no stable boundary is ever guaranteed to hold firm between *daemonic* election and *demonic* fall, insofar as Foción's spiritual, mad queerness remains at least partially ingrained in the erotic desires and anxieties of his closest male sexual peers.

# 7 Mother Nero, Uncle Orpheus, and the Unborn

> The Atreidai family, the very best, must endure an awful fate revealed to them by fire-carrying Prometheus. During this mythic phase and once his mother has poisoned his father [*sic*] and as he faces the task of destroying mother-rule [la matria] the son desires a substitution, a first lie, a revealed fate.
>
> "Las imágenes posibles"

THE *poisoned-father-by-his-wife's-mother-rule* ("matria") passage in the epigraph is taken from Lezama's thoughts on Aeschylus's *Oresteia* and Euripides' *Ephigenia in Tauris,* in which the murder of Orestes' father, Agamemnon, by his wife Clytemnestra and her lover Aegisthus is not, however, caused by her poisoning him as head of the Atreidai family dynasty. Likewise, the *Electra-dragon-birth-breast-feeding* in the following passage comes from Foción's mouth as he names Orestes' sister, instead of his mother Clytemnestra, as the one who gives birth and nurses the matricidal son:

> When Electra [*sic*] thought she'd given birth to a dragon, she saw that the monster was crying to be nursed; she gives it her breast without hesitation and the milk comes out mixed with blood. Even though she had given birth to a monster, something which must have disconcerted her, she knew that her response had to be to keep him from dying of hunger, because the greatness of man consists in his ability to assimilate what's unknown to him. To assimilate in depth is to give an answer. (*P* 247/249)

The error in the *sister-for-mother-birth-and-breast-feeding* phrase lies in Foción's agreeing with Electra's claim that she "nursed" her brother Orestes, rather than with the Chorus's report in Aeschylus's *Choephoroi* about Clytemnestra's nightmare and her giving birth to and breast-feeding a viper. In Sophocles' *Electra* (lines 1141–50), the sister addresses the urn believed to contain her brother's ashes and speaks of "her nursing of old days" and how no one else within the household would "nurse" him. True to the meaning of her name ("the unwedded one"), Electra is a virgin and nubile woman during Orestes' infancy; thus her nursing claim is commonly interpreted as sibling-care or *nurturing* (nowhere in the tragedies is a dragon birth ever attributed to her).[1]

### Lost Sister and Mother

At the beginning of Aeschylus's *Choephoroi,* Orestes comes back to Argos from exile and offers a lock of his hair to Inachus, the river-god king and father of princess Io. In related fashion, in Sophocles' *Electra,* the old slave welcomes Orestes to the "old Argos of [his] yearning, the grove of Inachus' gadfly-haunted daughter" (*Inachus* and the feminine variants *Inaca* and *Ynaca* are names of great genealogical importance in Lezama's fiction). Electra comes to the same ritual site to pour libations, finds the lock of hair, and realizes that it belongs to her lost brother. She sees "splendor" and "honor" in the hair brought to her father's grave (as when "one small seed" grows into a "mighty tree"). Addressing Orestes' funereal tokens, she says:

> You light to my eyes, four loves in one!
> I have to call you father, it is fate;
> and I turn to you the love I gave my mother—I despise her,
> she deserves it, yes,
> and the love I gave my sister, sacrificed
> on the cruel sword, I turn to you.
> You were my faith, my brother—you alone restore my self-respect.
> (*Choephoroi* 240–47)

Electra is alluding to Iphigenia's death by immolation at Aulis, but not to her father Agamemnon's role in it. In the same scene, the hated mother is kept outside the inner circle of kinship (*Choephoroi* 242). For her part, Clytemnestra does not plead Agamemnon's guilty role in Iphigenia's sacrifice as her avenging motive for having him murdered. But as Orestes' matricide begins to take shape, the avenging son reminds Zeus of his split double ancestry and the revenge cycle attached to it. In his words, the three orphaned siblings are:

> Fledglings reft of the noble eagle father.
> He [Agamemnon] died in the coils, the viper's dark embrace.
> We are his orphans worn down with hunger.
> (*Choephoroi* 251–53)

In ancient lore the female viper "was thought, while mating, to bite through the neck of the male, and to be, in vengeance, killed by her offspring as they bit their way out of her womb" (Garvey's comments on *Choephoroi* 247–49). As a son, Orestes splits in half as both the paternal eagle's nestling and the maternal viper's offspring. (Garvey comments that Clytemnestra's monstrous counterpart is Echidna, Typhoeus's spouse—a creature worthy of Foción's dragon fears.) It seems clear that Clytemnestra's crime regressively symbolizes in terms of cosmogony the breakdown of Zeus's cosmos when he defeated the dragon.

In *Choephoroi* matricide springs from the guilty mother's nightmare as gleaned by Orestes from the Chorus Leader's report: "She dreamed she bore a snake . . . she swaddled it like a baby, laid it to rest."

> *Orestes:* And food, what did the little monster want?
> *Leader:* She gave it her breast to suck.
> *Orestes:* And didn't it tear the nipple, the brute inhuman?—
> *Leader:* Blood curdled the milk with each sharp tug. (*Choephoroi* 516–21)

This is what Foción remembers, but attributes to Electra. Just as Orestes finds his killing of Clytemnestra hatched in her own bad dreams, Foción (as discussed later) nurtures thoughts about himself as a grown man *and* a dragon-child slayer of his dragon-mother. His praise for Electra's heroic nursing corresponds to Orestes' surmise of his own matricidal incubation in Clytemnestra's nightmare:

> If the serpent
> came from the same place as I, and slept
> in the bands that swaddled me, and its jaws
> spread wide for the breast that nursed me into life
> and clots stained the milk, mother's milk,
> and she cried in fear and agony—so be it.
> As she bred this sign, this violent prodigy,
> so she dies by violence. I turn serpent,
> I kill her. So the vision says.
> (*Choephoroi* 529–37)

## Nero's Mothering

On one occasion, while reading Suetonius's *The Twelve Caesars* in bed, José Cemí thinks that Foción is like Emperor Nero, or "Neronian" ("neroniano") (*P* 231/234). Suetonius reports that Nero acted in the operatic tragedy *Orestes the Matricide* and that graffiti lampooned him as matricidal, such as: "*Alcmaeon, Orestes, and Nero are brothers, Why? Because all of them murdered their mothers*" (*Twelve Caesars* 231). Cemí considers it "Neronian" to represent "the detumescence [desinflamiento] of a conduct without mystery, the biting, cruel, premeditated working on the defenseless, the spectator-actor, waiting coldly for the shadow of the gull to pass over its mirror" (*P* 231/234). His perception is well in line with Shadi Bartsch's view of Nero's acting "as captive audience for the will of his gathered subjects," when the emperor abandons his place in the audience and takes the stage himself, "so that the mutual gaze of emperor and spectators now transpires across the dividing line of the seats and the stage, across the boundary that separates the real from the representational" (*Actors in the Audience* 2–3). More than just crossing the line by climbing on stage to face the audience, Nero's attention-grabber defines theatricality. According to Bartsch,

> Theatricality makes actors out of human beings placed in situations in which they feel themselves watched, in which their performance is subject to the evaluation of a superior who must be watched in turn to gauge his reactions; and in those contexts in which there exists a well-defined, self-conscious audience (as with Nero's stage performances or in modern metatheater), it entails a reversal of the normal one-way direction of the spectator's gaze, so that they know themselves watched by the object of their view and respond accordingly even as the categories of spectacle and spectator lose all stability. (10–11)

The trope of *envy as first parent of humanity* in the Unamuno epigraph heading my reading of Lezama's fiction involves precisely this two-way snagging mirror obviously related to the illusion achieved in *mise en abyme*. Foción plays a central role in the burlesque mock tragedy of envy's theatricality. No real audience needs to exist for his performance to take effect in conjunction with actual or imaginary fellow actors, friends, and enemies. The impinging actions of external/internal spectatorship take control over the actor's mind and the fictions he wishes to incite about himself in order to swaddle his bursting and injured Nero ego as monstrous maternal afterbirth. Looking back at the Socratic Moment sketched in chapter 6, Foción's Nero-like tyranny over theatricality offers the missing link between the politics of statecraft and the politics of homosexual envy among those "ungraspable" men so ironically difficult to grab by the handle.

Foción's Nero predicament amounts to a life sentence, not because it may last a lifetime but because it makes a single instant of dread and hate last forever. It puts him in the role of Alastor, or spirit of vengeance (Orestes' defining role in archaic matricide). Mother and son are bound together and pulled by the spirit's ligatures of revenge. In *Agamemnon,* Clytemnestra proclaims that the Atreidai Alastor was inside her:

> Fleshed in the wife of this dead man,
> The spirit [alastor] lives within me,
> Our savage ancient spirit of revenge.
> (*Agamemnon 1526–28*)

Yet, as disclosed by her viper nightmare in *Choephoroi,* the dragon and Gorgo mother has also given birth and nurtured her own avenger spirit in Orestes.

One may opt to see in Foción's Electra allusion a pointed choice rather than a simple mistake—but, in either case, it matters to imagine *whose* choice or mistake it is. The easiest and probably correct answer involves author's error (there being several other instances of erroneous allusions to Greek myth in Lezama's writings). But a more interesting response would see the Electra *double* error as the author's pointed choice in trying to imply something remarkably awful in Foción's attitude toward his mother *and* his (real or imaginary) sister. The error is double, as it concerns Electra's nursing of Orestes in addition to his being dragon rather than viper. If this were the case, as the story of Foción as a whole seems to confirm, the author's (unmistakable) Electra error (implanted in Foción's words and mind) would be akin to a *lie:* the author replaces his accurate Clytemnestra knowledge with Foción's inaccurate Electra utterance—thus lying for the sake of character and theatrical spectator effect. It could also mean that Foción is distorting or lying about his own knowledge of the tragedies in order to express something about his own mother-tragedy or *matria.*

A pointed case of misunderstanding or *misrecognition* ensues upon assuming that the author's mistaken allusion bears proof of his truest design concerning his character's character (or upon assuming that Foción is intentionally lying about mother Electra). The presumed error is embroiled in a tangled web spread over several chapters in *Paradiso* and further entangled in the unfinished and fragmentary *Oppiano Licario.* Thus, Foción's character misadventures would represent the author's version of seriously flawed self-knowledge or *méconnaissance.* As in Lacan, Foción appears webbed, enmeshed in a large quest for self-understanding (the largest one in Lezama's fiction) upon which the possibility of character is itself dynamically grounded—and disabled. Dylan Evans has usefully reminded us that "misrecognition is not ignorance [but that it] represents a certain organization of affirmations and negations, to which the subject is attached. Hence it cannot be conceived without correlate knowledge. . . . There must surely be, behind . . . misrecognition, a kind of knowledge of what there is to misrecognise."[2] Foción's theater-of-the-mind representation of sexual identity would appear (*mis-*)cast in his desire for (*self-* as *mis-*)recognition: a desire viewed through archaic *infancy-images* (not actual memories). The switch from mother to sister in *viper-birth* and *breast-feeding* could represent Foción's wakeful spectator-on-stage response to his own mother's nightmarish character: his *imaged* fear of being poisoned by the milk from *her* nursing, as if caught in *mise en abyme,* within his mirror dread of repeating her into infinity.

Foción's mother-fear seems inalienable from his guilt-ridden wish to split apart birth-mother from breast-nurse. The son's dread of being breast-poisoned lies at the core of his belief that the Mother Queen poisons her husband King and condemns him (her son and Prince) to execute the revenge duty of matricide. Therefore, the allusion in "Las imágenes posibles" to "the first lie" established in the Atreidai family lineage after the father is *poisoned* by the mother refers to Orestes' *engendered fate* in "bringing to task the betraying acts of mother-rule" ("un destino . . . tiene que engendrarse en el pedir cuentas a las traiciones de la matria") (*Órbita* 156). Yet Agamemnon is killed neither by poison nor by Clytemnestra alone, but through the agency of her lover Aegisthus.

Later on in the essay about possible images, the *first lie* ("la mentira primera") is given extended dramatic embodiment by Lezama in reference to *Iphigenia in Tauris,* in whose recognition scene brother and sister meet believing that each other is long dead. Orestes is ordered to steal a statue of Artemis (a type of rough-hewed wooden idol known as a *xoanon*) from the Taurians of Scythia and take it to Halae to be worshipped as *Artemis Tauropolos.* He does not know that Iphigenia did not die at Aulis, having been instead sent to the barbarous Taurians as their priestess to rule over rituals of human sacrifice in honor of Scythian Artemis. Iphigenia learned from a dream that Orestes was dead, so when he is captured and brought before her to be sacrificed, neither sibling knows that they are at long last reunited. Thus, as she learns from the stranger that her brother is alive, Iphigenia does not know that it is Orestes himself who's speaking to her. Sibling recognition hinges on a letter (dictated by Iphigenia when she thought her brother was alive), the same letter that Orestes is now asked to take home to Argos. Not knowing that he is not "dead" (or that he would be carrying home a letter to himself, hinging on his prior knowledge that Iphigenia—also not "dead"—is the author),

Orestes rejects his freedom and hands the letter and messenger role over to his friend and lover Pylades, to whom he entrusts Electra's care and the building of his memorial tomb at Argos (Orestes' refusal to carry the message would transform his scheduled human sacrifice into a case of self-immolation). But the letter is never sent, being instead read aloud to Pylades by Iphigenia, in fear that the tablet might be lost at sea. Then, hearing that she is alive and speaking to him and Orestes, Pylades gives the letter to his friend in fulfillment of his vow to deliver it.

It might be said that by mutually disclosing to each other their lost siblinghood, brother and sister overcome matricide. They do it just at the point where the healing sister is about to reenact the mother's lethal intent, the one that gives birth to the matricidal fate of her son, a fate Emperor Nero was all too theatrically enraptured to fulfill. Nero's matricidal theatricality informs Foción's misrecognition of his fate in the mother who destroys the father's lordship. As it turns out, the maternal twist that implants in him his worst and oldest birth-enemy sends Foción's character into exile from the pastoral realm where the fabric of Cuba's green world is woven.

## Cuba in the Honey Womb

It is in the Orpheus figure recast in José Cemí's maternal uncle Alberto Olaya that the family's myth of green pastoral beginnings and eventual catastrophe can best be surmised. For this we need to turn to the story of honey and its contrasting origins in *Paradiso*. First, in the voice of Doña Munda, José Cemí's paternal grandmother: "My father would get up at five in the morning, for when the dawn was too far advanced, it would irritate the tobacco leaves to be watered by hand. My father did it with the care of a person who deciphers an ancient script. My whole family had become slow and mysterious: as in the care of leaves, invisibly obsessed, as in the marriage of bees" (*P* 68/70). Her words about pastoral nurture relate to Virgil's account of apian abstemious marriage rules in *Georgics:*

> This custom of the bees may cause surprise:
> They take no pleasure in the body's joys,
> Nor melt away in love, nor bring to birth
> Their young in labor; females pick their children
> Straight from leaves, or gather them by mouth
> From fragrant grass, maintaining by themselves
> The royal line and tiny citizens,
> Themselves rebuilt the royal waxen realms.

> They sometimes crush their wings on flinty rocks
> In flight, and freely, while still burdened down,
> Give up their lives; so strong in them is love
> For flowers, so keen their pride in making honey.
> And though their narrow life is quickly spanned
> (They never last beyond the seventh year),
> The race lives on, the household's fortune stands
> Through many years and many generations.
> (*Georgics* IV.196–211)

Virgilian bees harvest their offspring with the same care with which Doña Munda's family nurtures tobacco leaves. In avoiding cohabitation ("neque concubitu indulgent") and child bearing ("nec corpora segnes/in Vererem soluunt aut fetus nixibus edunt") mother bees in Virgil escape the same obsessive *amor* that glues together José Cemí's beelike brood of ancestors in his great grandmother's pastoral evocation of the wedding between honey and tobacco. Virgil's fourth *Georgic* narrates the rescue of Eurydice by Orpheus and his death at the hands of maenadic women. The myth of the poet-singer is told by Proteus to Aristeus, the Arcadian master of bees, who learns from the god of many shapes that he lost his swarms in punishment for chasing Eurydice and causing her death from a snakebite (the story also alludes to the generation of bees from a rotten bovine carcass, a magical phenomenon of institutional prominence in Roman ritual affairs known as *bugonia,* or "ox generation"). Although Virgil's *Georgics* are not mentioned in *Paradiso,* I will adopt the fourth one for comparison in order to illustrate certain mythic aspects of Alberto Olaya's life.

As Marcel Detienne tells it, the marriage of Orpheus to Eurydice creates a bond that is best formulated as that of a man who "cannot prevent himself from being the lover and seducer of a woman whose husband he also is" ("Myth of 'Honeyed Orpheus'" 105). The contradictory monogamous predicament leads to Eurydice's death in the underworld and to the murder of Orpheus at the hands of maenads after he rejects the company of women. The fate of Orpheus is relevant to Uncle Alberto's role in seduction and marriage through double antithesis. At issue is not so much the opposition between marrying and not marrying as the conflict between the roles of husband and seducer within and without married life. Unlike Orpheus, Alberto never obtains a wife, but, also unlike Orpheus, he offers a bride to another groom and rejects a false bride for himself. Alberto becomes the lover destined never to marry and instead to embrace a form of celibacy uncannily related to seduction and sexual mischief.

From adolescence, Alberto's Orphic life-path includes elements of Promethean shamanism. One day at school he is forced to take a cold shower in punishment for making his classmates laugh. As in a nightmare, the shower head turns into Angra Mainyu, the polymorphous Avesdan evil spirit, described as "the oil-seeking eagle of the Caucasus" who feeds on Prometheus' liver (*P* 93/95)—although associated with pestilence and destruction, Angra Mainyu is, like Satan, skilled in the arts of seduction and on one occasion takes the shape of a beautiful young man.[3] Alberto is portrayed "nakedly asleep," his back "propped against the wall," as "the lead sternum of the shower" grows tall. The scene hints at masturbation: between Alberto's "left finger and the ring of his hand" his "sex" dangles "in the ultimate boredom of nakedness" (*P* 92/94). Mandrake roots are part of Angra Mainyu's weapons; they are mentioned three times, once in connection with a dog and finally in reference to the hanged man's ejaculation: "Feeling that he was still advancing toward Angra Mainyu, that he was reacting against the death of the first drain," Alberto "could not taste the seed in its gelatinous shell, where light does not find it until it penetrates the successions of the earth, until the hanged man goes beyond his substance and reaches the hot exhalations of the beaten dog" (*P* 92/94). The boy takes flight, leaving behind cigarette butts as signatures of premature adult behavior and tokens of his kinship with the ravished maiden Io and Prometheus: "These were what remained of the darkly conjured daughter of Inachus, the maddened Io, caught between the memory of the showers' music and the cigarettes stamped on by [the teacher's] fury, the remains of Argos whose flight none had been able to impede. But the small one pinioned there [Alberto], conversant with the resentful love of the daughter of Inachus, had taken possession of the first day on which his ransomed fire would burn" (94/96). Many-eyed starry Argos burns in the light of each cigarette after Alberto, "pinioned there," flies off bearing Io's maiden's pain, which is immediately reencountered after he runs away from school into an amusement park and finds a girl who is being used as bait by the old man who runs the show. Both figures are surrogates of Io's pain: a sinister old pederast in kinship with his raped daughter. (As examined later on, Io's role as seductress and promoter of her own incestuous rape is central to the guilt syndrome affecting the interrelation between male and female homosexuality in Lezama's fiction.)[4]

Alberto's powers of seduction are best shown in the way he lures his brotherly neighbor José Eugenio Cemí into marrying *his* sister Rialta. The syntactical ambiguity underlined in *his* is meant to imply, not so much the chance of either man's marrying his own sisterlike bride, as their mutual and uncanny incestuous brotherliness. José Cemí's mother (Rialta), her brother (Alberto), and his future brother-in-law (José Eugenio) are like blood siblings in their upbringing and collateral affiliations. As a result, the avuncular ties between maternal uncle and nephew (Alberto and José) are infused with currents of erotic affect already nurtured in the male-bonding brotherliness between the sister's brother and her fraternal bridegroom—in which their triple siblinghood is founded.

Alberto's acting as nuptial conduit in his sister's marriage to the future father of José Cemí should be seen in contrast with his provocation of hysteria in women (perhaps a remnant—in the mythical layers of Alberto's character—of the maenads' dismemberment of Orpheus). He escapes marrying one of José Eugenio's sisters (in a variation of marriage between cross-cousins) by claiming it would amount to incest, since Alberto is the son of Doña Augusta (also known by the honey name of Mela), who becomes José Eugenio's surrogate mother after his parents die. However, Alberto's scruples seem odd when compared with the corresponding groom status of José Eugenio, whose own adoptive son sibling rank should render his marriage with his sisterlike cousin Rialta even more incestuouslike than Alberto's with one of his sisters. (As Alberto's adoptive brother, José Eugenio becomes also his brother-in-law by marrying his uterine sister.)

Alberto plays a less obvious nuptial role in the elegiac story told by Doña Munda to her grandson José Eugenio Cemí about his dead parents: "When your father packed us all up and took us to the Central sugar mill, he never imagined that he was ruining our whole family" (*P* 66/67). As she explains mixed genealogies, Doña Munda tries to exculpate her son Luis for his notorious weak character by blaming it on the ill-fated marriage between his sister Eloísa and the Basque José María. The marriage of José Eugenio's parents brings into focus the dominant and contrasting cultures of sugar and tobacco, mediated by the less prominent but powerfully mythic culture of honey.

Along the lines of the contrast established by Fernando Ortiz in *Contrapunteo cubano del tabaco y el azúcar,* the care required by tobacco harvesting in *Paradiso* is family-based, intensely personal, grounded on the sunlight-to-moonlight daily cycle, and favorable to inbreeding among cultivators. By contrast, the culture of sugar is plantation-based, massively industrial, seasonal (with a "live" period of harvesting and production known as *zafra* and a dead period of *tiempo muerto*), and in need of exploiting an itinerant male workforce at times made up of foreign cheap labor. In *Paradiso,* despite its taste, honey falls on the side of tobacco rather than sugar: beehives and sugar mills produce honey and molasses, with the former belonging next to tobacco, as in "We were used to the gentle labors of Vuelta Abajo, tobacco and honey" (*P* 66/67). Honey is placed at the opposite end of the kind of *mieles* industrially extracted from sugar molasses: industrial and proletarian, sugar molasses resembles—but opposes—honeybee, which is the product of ingrown and inbreeding family habits.

Two kinds of beehive honey related to family blood types are produced in *Paradiso.* The most precious kind is made as "bees suck only on the blue flower and produce a honey that competes with the most splendid Mediterranean varieties" (67/69). This honey would resemble the type made by bees in Virgil's pastoral. In the best ancient tradition of Greek *melissai,* these blue-flower (and blueblood) Cuban bees abstain from sexual flesh, from rotten or venereal things, and produce the purest nectar. But another kind of Cuban honeybees avoid "the comb" in exchange for "the hollows of certain varieties of palm," as they "leech off the palm's circulation and sink into its currents to draw out the ambrosia" (67/69). Honey from this kind of chthonian vampire bees proves poisonous inside the body of a pregnant woman. (The mythical relationship between bees and bats implicit in Doña Munda's story about the honey sucked from the lymph of the palm and risen from the earth deep beneath it resembles Roman beliefs on the animal shape adopted by the soul in quest of immortality.)[5]

This happens in Eloísa's case, who is not pregnant and becomes ill from the low-lying valley climate of the sugar mill and decides to move for a while to her sister's home in the Vuelta Abajo region of Pinar del Río, the province in western Cuba where the culture of tobacco is at its finest. She is warned against tasting the "very transparent, very light" palm honey, but her "magical loathing for all kinds of obscure, impenetrable foods" makes her avoid the darker blue-flower honey until she dies of "black typhus" (*P* 68/69). Contrary to what might be expected about the lighter-colored palm honey, its character is chthonic, it originates in the deep, dark, unclean underground. Asthmatics consume it because "its heat cleans the bronchial tree of its heaviness and tired branches" (65/67). In homeopathic resemblance to Eloísa and her miasmic and vapor-related typhoid illness, the palm tree "calls for a light humor, one sufficiently filtered to be able to rise up within," but the "climbing lymph" comes from where the roots "extend themselves to corrupt lands, where the humus has endured, mellowing and becoming more submissive to the invasion of those threads seeking its poison" (68/69). Corrupt germs from chthonic depths swim in the clear palm honey. (The virtues of homeopathic magic to heal tubercular lungs act like a mirror-agent of typhoid corruption in the wife's blood as she remains segregated from her marital and maternal duties.)

Eloísa dies as her sickness carries her off "to see Chancellor Nu, the victorious, the chief gatekeeper of the Egyptian underworld" (68/69). But not being an underworld goddess like Eurydice, the departed wife lacks a rescuing Orpheus—though her husband's death soon follows hers as in Orphic myth. In eating the wrong kind of honey, Eloísa refuses to taste of the best kind, like the one produced by Virgil's fastidiously chaste bees. Instead, the estranged wife feeds on a type of dangerous nectar likened to the strong honey that Aristeus (the Arcadian bee master) would have obtained by "The method long since used of breeding bees/From slaughtered bullocks' putrid blood" (*Georgics* IV.284–85). The *bugonia* method comes from "Green Egypt with a rich black sandy loam," on whose soil a slaughtered calf's carcass festers until "creatures fashioned wonderfully appear; first void of limbs, but soon awhirl with wings" (*Georgics* IV.293, 410–11). The rotten origins of Egyptian bees do not make their honey noxious but reflect something of Aristeus's adulterous pursuit of Eurydice and his causing her death from a snakebite. As Proteus informs the bee master and his mother Cyrene, the loss of his swarms was due to the anger of Orpheus for his starting the chain of events that resulted in the permanent banishment of Eurydice to the underworld.

Eloísa's husband groom combines the tenderness and vulnerability of nuptial Orpheus with Aristeus's wild lover abduction habits. The combination of husband and lover in the same man proves lethal to both bride and groom as if theirs were an eternal but brief honeymoon rather than a long-lasting marriage. Thus, José Eugenio's pastoral-destroying father (as José Cemí's long-lost paternal grandfather) acts as both husband and abductor of his bride and wife. The "brutal" Basque's totemic animal is the bull, with its powerful neck, to which his wife opposes the vibration of her delicate nostrils. The couple's related deaths bring to an end the paternal family's myth of Orphic pastoral origins. Doña Munda tells her orphan grandson José Eugenio: "There's no more struggle between landscapes, and the neck doesn't come alive again with the nostrils' vibrations" (*P* 69/70), this being her epitaph to the erotic tensions between the powerful bull-husband and a wife who is both responsive to his energies and mortally sickened by them (at seventeen Eloísa was younger than half her bridegroom husband's age). Her *honeyed* death harks back to the embowered pastoral loneliness of her family, to the isolation of those fragile souls who tend the tobacco leaf and who, even when not caring for the hive, go about "invisibly obsessive, like the marriage of bees" (69/70). The bride's poisoned honey libation rises from the uncultured wild, all the way up, from the chthonic cradle of the palm to the cosmic bullishness of her husband's neck.

Doña Munda's pastoral lesson to her orphan grandson and future father of José Cemí contains an untold tale of male erotic excess trapped in matrimonial decorum and resulting from a case of extreme exogamy leaning on bride abduction. The husband's bull-like excess is applied to the exogamous uprooting of the pastoral honey-tobacco legacy of his wife's inbreeding family and their abrupt transplanting to a sugar land where her death begins to take shape. But the wife's death is not consummated until she returns to where the two kinds of genealogical honey are made. The uprooted bride (now a mother) comes into contact with two different blood cognates and fluid foods endowed with medicinal and poisonous virtues that seem obsessively committed to endogamy and uncleanly married to each other's kindred breed. The wife-killing honey flows upward as it climbs inside the royal palm tree from the depths of uncultured soil, like a pillared womb, rotten and feracious and akin to the festering bovine carcass from which bees are magically born in the *bugonia*. Orpheus (musician and poet) and his rival Aristeus (mad hunter and bee master) meet in the totem figure of José Eugenio's prematurely dead father and José Cemí's grandfather.

The Orphic pastoral joins in symbolic focus spouse-loss and eternal honeymoon within a fixed period of bridal virgin expiration and death. Considering that Eloísa's marriage to the Basque Don José María Cemí lasted long enough to produce four children, Doña Munda's genealogical album story captures their union in arrest: husband at thirty-seven, wife at seventeen. The latent honeymoon motif (of time eternal and time expired) becomes critically manifest in another rural marriage, the one between Delfina and Palmiro placed at the beginning of *Oppiano Licario*. As in Eloísa's honeyed death, the maternal character of the royal palm tree and its womb symbolism act as focal elements. Palmiro (the palm's offspring) is wounded by the killers of his brother José Ramiro as he hides in the trunk's hollow where palm honey is made and stored. Palmiro replaces his murdered younger brother in the role of Delfina's groom in a manner resembling the proximate brothers-in-law and brothers-in-love relationship between José Eugenio and Alberto just examined. His magical descent into the earth through the palm trunk and his protective burial in honey are related to symbolic death and rebirth. The Delphyna role (in Greek myth identified with monstrous Echidna) makes the palm offspring's repossessed bride (from sister-in-law to wife) a potential dragoness in a story of spoiled honeymoon and unresolved erotic madness: a honeymoon that never ends, during which the Orphic groom is cast in the familiar homosexual tragic figure of the youth destined to be torn apart by orgiastic female madness.

As both Delfina and her substitute groom Palmiro fall madly and murderously in love with Ricardo Fronesis, another Orphic mystery-twist scroll peculiar to Lezama's fiction begins to unfold in the aggregate lives of Foción and Alberto Olaya, according to which *Orpheus marries in Eurydice a vanishing person-alternative to the matricidal death that his own murder by maenads so oddly resembles.* In other words: the pastoral founding hero splits into two Orphic-impossible husbands. In one case, he marries the ill-fated bride whom he is fatally involved in losing, instead of killing the awful mother, like the one who will tear him to pieces in the female group fury of the Dionysian maenads. In the event Orphic brother Alberto ever marries (as he in fact does by proxy in his adoptive brother and bother-in-law José Eugenio's marriage to his sister Rialta) he would marry into eternal contradiction: honeymoon—and bride loss. For, even when he marries, Orphic Alberto remains a honeyed lover as the eternal and always provisional husband. In the other case, and looking ahead to the next section, the matricide son in Foción is always-already-married as the born-premature husband in whose bride the mother has picked herself as her son's mother bride. On one side, Alberto is the impossible husband because he is the eternal lover; on the other, Foción is hand-picked by the mother into marrying her in double jeopardy: as her impossibly eternal husband and the lost queer mate to a tabooed friend and lover.

These two coupled instances of failed spousal husbandry compose the pastoral image of immunity against the exogamous marriage union between man and woman in Lezama's complex view of homosexual male bachelorhood. It's complex in its insistence to wed bachelorhood to marriage in the shadow of widowed mother love. The son is all at once the substitute of his mother's dead husband and the latent cause behind her dying a widow by his own matricidal hands.

## In the Shadow of Nijinsky

Just as the *first lie,* or *proton pseudos,* functions all too visibly in mythical shapes, some actual lives remain unseen and unspoken. This happens in Alberto's life as a master of eloquence haunted and ultimately killed by his taste for sexual banter and shadowy relations with pederasty. His love pursuits are as cryptic as Foción's seduction ploys are blatant. Commenting on Aristophanes' *The Acharnians,* Kenneth Dover explains *paiderastia* "as one appetite of the roguish, insatiable god [Dionysus] who personifies the penis, together with adultery (illegal, but nice if one can get away with it) and a pounce on a pretty slave-girl caught in a lonely place" (*Greek Homosexuality* 136). In such cases *paiderastein* represents rampant behavior not exclusively tied to male homosexuality.

A word is now in order on contextual pederasty in *Paradiso* as surmised and composed from incidents in the story. A man pursues sex with younger men, most often from a class lower than his own—in culture if not in wealth. He is often harassed by older men, also from a class inferior to his own (the pivotal age exception to the rule being Foción—hence his importance). But in order to understand Foción's exceptional role, pederasty in *Paradiso* must first be understood as a corruption of friendship and love between men: male lovers can't be friends, split as their mating is by the sadomasochistic rancor that animates sex between them as either active-phallic or passive-anal. The most singular friendship in *Paradiso* (between José Cemí and Ricardo Fronesis) entertains and rejects the notion of sex between men. It gives it rhetorical play in the name of Socrates and then spooks it in the name of Aeschylus and the terrors of matricide. Orestes' wandering madness in *The Eumenides* under assault by the Furies becomes Foción's flight from a mother he hates but does not kill, who either murders his father or renders him mad, creating the inaugural mystery for his troubled life. In Cemí's mind, Foción is a mad pederast in panic because of his desperate passion for Fronesis, who befriends him with a mixture of moral condescension and arcane sexual teasing. José Cemí's peerless love for his widowed mother requires the tainted background of betrayed and betraying parental love in the combined lives of his friends Fronesis and Foción.

The taint in question is sexual. During his youth in Vienna, Fronesis's father fought off Sergei Diaghilev, founder and director of *Ballets Russes* and sex master of the great dancer Vaslav Nijinsky. Igor Stravinsky's opinion of Diaghilev and his alleged contempt for Nijinsky's sister fits neatly into *Paradiso*'s Vienna pastiche and its foreshadowing of Foción's accursed homosexuality and lunatic androgyny:

> Poor Bronislava had no luck with Diaghilev . . . the Nijinskys—brother and sister together—were the best dancing pair imaginable . . . after Nijinsky's

> marriage, Diaghilev could not overcome his prejudice. She looked like Nijinsky, was even shaped like him—with the big shoulders. She was a constant reminder to him of her brother. It pained Diaghilev, too, that this person who dared look like Nijinsky was a woman. You can hardly imagine how indomitable Diaghilev's sexual prejudice was. He had argued for years to convince me that the exclusive love of women was morbid . . . , that I was an incomplete artist because . . . "morbid." He would draw cartoons on restaurant tablecloths of steatopygous and mammiferous women . . . argue about Socrates, Jesus, Leonardo da Vinci, Michelangelo (what a chaos of pederasty is Michelangelo's *Conversion of St. Paul*—even including the horses). . . . He would describe his own latest *mignon* in the most gratifying terms, and quote Verlaine: "*Démon femelle.*" (*Memories* 39–40)

Resistance to the foxy impresario's sexual predation injured Fronesis senior's virile pride. Ever since the Vienna episode, the father's legacy of having been chased by a pederast had haunted the sexually arrested and guilty friendship between his son Ricardo and Foción. The Vienna intaglio ended when Fronesis abandoned his wife (who had been used as bait by Diaghilev in trying to seduce him) and married her sister. As a result, Ricardo junior never met his mother, who became a nymphomaniac attached to Diaghilev. In a jarring coincidence not likely known by Lezama when he created the Diaghilev-Fronesis story, Vaslav Nijinsky's last dance recital and the first entry in the *Diary* that he wrote on his psychosis occurred in the afternoon and evening of January 19, 1919, the day when Lezama's father, Colonel José María Lezama Rodda, died in Jacksonville, Florida.[6]

Foción's luck with his parents is even worse than Fronesis's with his. He is raised in a made-to-order masquerade of tangled fatherhood as the son of a man who may or may not be his father, in a way known only to his mother, who killed her brother-in-law by having sex with him and thus caused the madness of her husband, the brother who survives as father of the boy born from the lethal maternal coupling with the other brother (in *Paradiso* the surviving Dr. Foción is a psychotic; in *Oppiano Licario* he becomes a stalking pederast). Once again, as in the relationship between Alberto and José Eugenio, related instances of brotherliness and sibling role-switch involve more besides virtual homosexual love between men. At stake is not gay love as such as much as its compulsory homosexual nexus with the institution and sacrament of marriage. Being gay in Lezama's fiction is refused autonomous existence from marriage—but someone else's marriage. It is as if being gay and unmarried amounted to a compulsory double fault in the genealogy of character.

Although narrated ahead of Foción's dismal life fragments, Alberto's life needs to be reexamined against the background of paternal failure as the cause for homosexuality in sons (a failure imagined and feared from the son's implied perspective). As examined thus far in Fronesis's case, the *proton pseudos* or first lie acquires regressive implications in the son's ashamed recognition of his *filial* homosexuality, shadowed in regression as the father's prior lying about his own sex life. (As such, the first lie resembles a *shadowgraph* in the mold devised by Kierkegaard in *Either/Or* to dissect what he diagnosed as the best European response to the mystery of love in Mozart's *Don Giovanni.*) Alberto's life can thus be sketched as a sort of *hieros logos* or sacred script overshadowed by the tutorial figure of Oppiano Licario (as a childless and unmarried paternal guardian encrypted in habits of pederasty never laid out in the open). Licario's posthumous scripture (the *Súmula, nunca infusa de excepciones morfológicas*) provides a parody formula for such *hieros logos:* "It had to be a sacred text, Licario had secreted it from his own body, like death's sweat or a teardrop oozing from the eye, like bone jell, amniotic juice, uric flow, salt, which in one instant turns the person into fish or fowl" (*OL* 324). In association with the cult of charismatic psychic healing in ancient times, the sacred script is transmitted from Oppiano to José Cemí (and to his poetic and philosophical lover, Ricardo Fronesis). *Hieros logos* also involves *hieros gamos,* a sacred mating of souls and bodies, such as the one undergone by Cemí and Fronesis with the help of Ynaca Eco Licario, female ritual double of her departed brother, hierophant, and master, Oppiano.[7]

## Marrying the Unborn

Alberto Olaya is José Cemí's maternal uncle and the earliest conduit between Cemí's childhood imagination and the figure of Oppiano Licario. His meeting with the young Oppiano takes place at the Kingdom of the Seven Months tavern, where, next to "four raffish grasshoppers," he "stood apart, comfortable, indifferent, prince-like; a mature and worn-out adolescent, four or five years older than Olaya"—Oppiano is also called "the only child [*unigénito*] of the seven months" (*P* 98/100), transforming the bar's name into his own and forever womb-related life condition and epithet. His premature birth origin is associated with Christ's nativity when Alberto sits down not far from the "only begotten [unigénito] child" (a better translation than Rabassa's "only child"). Oppiano's age is hence timeless as both extrachronological and extradimensional. It is the same as Lezama's age when Oppiano is first conceived as his fictional surrogate in 1953. But it is also older than Cemí's age and the author's own remembered father, the Colonel, when Oppiano visits him at his death bed in Pensacola in 1919. By the same token, José Eugenio and Alberto, in brotherly company, are the same age: "Suddenly he [the young José Eugenio] saw someone [Alberto] his own age come out the door on the upper floor opposite" (70/71). (This makes Oppiano a bit older than thirty-three when the Colonel dies in 1919, but also just about forty-three in 1953, when he is born into Lezama's fiction.)[8]

Under Oppiano's guidance, Alberto goes through a night-long ordeal at the Kingdom of the Seven Months besieged by four men ("raffish grasshoppers") who are later recalled as "low-lifes, semi-fairies, and professional cynics" (*P* 150/151). The affair is scripted in Oppiano's mind, when he is able to tell Alberto in advance what will be done to him once he is gotten drunk and taken into the hut of a woman "mermaid" in the adjacent shantytown. She will be replaced in bed by one of the ruffians, who will play devil to drunken Alberto, invoking the Latin phrase uttered earlier as the trap is being set: "*Osculum fine spine dorsalis*" [*sic: spinae fine*] (99/101). Indeed, the *kiss that travels to where the spine ends* marks the anal spot where the devil and his witchcraft adepts celebrate their nocturnal compact (and where Alberto is meant to be nurtured by the mermaid-substitute and half-queer cynic). All this is foreshadowed by Oppiano from the sidelines as he coaches Alberto out of being bed-tricked. He also knows enough Latin to have translated for the owner of the bar another key phrase in the episode: "*Porta mae* [*sic: portae meae*] *tantum regi*" ("'*I open the door only for the king*'"), hung on the tavern's entrance. References to premature birth, combined with Kierkegaard's notion of reaching old age while still in the womb, place Alberto's ordeal under the sign of death-by-imprisonment and betrayal. He overcomes such moral death with the help of male friendship, born from the same ritually marked actions by which amity transforms itself into gay love in the spectral presence of Oppiano Licario as José Lezama Lima's phantom friend.

The phantom-friend and uterine relationship hyphenates Alberto and Oppiano as if they were inside the same womb. They share a womb habitat surrounded by elements of premature birth and satyr sex with strong anal and unfertile elements centered on Oppiano's ageless genesis. Thus, imperiled and unborn, beautiful Alberto gets drunk:

> His eyes lit three times on the Dutch juices [gin cocktails]. Perhaps because of some joke the bartender made, perhaps irritated by the band of four united for a grotesque evening of satyrs [del grotesco y del caprípedo], he let loose the aromatic with an excessive lash [extra gin in the drink]. Then he heard or seemed to hear, for the first time: Why Kingdom of the Seven Months and not Kingdom of the Seven-Month Baby? The first is a parenthesis, the other a pragmatic sanction. The Bacchic house of bamboo is where one should distinguish between seven months and the seventh-month baby. *A seven-month baby is a monster and those seven months call to mind some words of Kierkegaard: The nine months I spent in my mother's womb were enough to make an old man of me.* And seven months is Osiris's kingdom of songs and novelties, of death in the drought and return in the floods. Horus, hiding at the crossroads, sings in the floods while Osiris passes on to the kingdom of the dead. As he [Oppiano] said those things (as if withdrawn from the black humors and the psalmodies) his voice remained merry, youthful, endowed with loving grace. By means of a non-casual series of interposed experiences, fragments, interpolations, later reconstructions, the arrangement of authorities, in transmission they were organized into exultant plasmas, sympathetic lymph that plucked his body [Alberto's] like a guitar. (*P* 98–99/100, my emphasis)

Oppiano's words have a placental effect upon the drunken Alberto. What is said acts like a counterdrug or *pharmakon* antidote against alcohol poison and the intoxication that would make Alberto a victim of the mermaid's false-bottom charms and a better victim of the cynic pederast's satyr weapons.

Meanwhile, the blind and pregnant reference to Kierkegaard hints at deeper and truly arcane mysteries inside the womb's cocoon. The virtually certain chance that what follows about Kierkegaard's mother was unknown to Lezama, the author who makes the allusion, opens the womb's site to the *Moiraï*'s mothering of allotments and lottery in the alchemy of unborn fate. For Kierkegaard in fact makes no reference to his mother in his writings. Biographer Joakim Garff points out that the mother's "unproblematic spirit has not inspired any literary or poetic portrayals and perhaps can only be glimpsed here and there in Søren Kierkegaard's writings, where a housewife is depicted as a useful, quiet factotum in her husband's home"; and he adds that "in his journals, Søren Aabye did not mention her name one single time" and that "he never dedicated to her anything he ever wrote—not even an edifying discourse" (*Søren Kierkegaard* 6). As it happened, Ane Sørensdatter Lund was made pregnant by Michael Kierkegaard while employed as a maid in his widower's household. Ane was already carrying their first child four months before marriage. The girl's birth and the guilt incurred by Ane's former master and present husband in his Christian conscience burdened their marriage, as it led to his transferring away his business interests. His actions proved of enormous consequence in Søren's extraordinarily pious religious upbringing. Mark C. Taylor is not exaggerating when he writes that the father's "religious outlook was the inescapability of human depravity. Sin, the father relentlessly impressed upon the son, is manifest most powerfully in sexual desire, the 'name' of sin is 'Woman'" (*Altarity* 155). Thus, Søren's mother-silence holds up as loudly as the chiming of a distant galaxy in the absence of his own mother's name and personal references from his writings.

The silence holds up until Oppiano sounds the depths of a seven-month-old mothering womb to protect Orphic Alberto from being anal-raped. The blind Kierkegaard quotation on womb imprisonment and premature aging in Oppiano's words becomes blind no more as found in *Fear and Trembling*—a text that Lezama is known to have read and consider highly.[9] The quotation surfaces in the third reference to Isaac's weaning: "When the child is to be weaned the mother too is not without sorrow, that she and the child grow more and more apart; that the child that first lay beneath her heart, yet later rested at her breast, should no longer be so close. Thus together they suffer this brief sorrow. Lucky the one who kept the child so close and had no need to sorrow more!" (*Fear and Trembling* 47). Kierkegaard's Isaac crosses time frames—from beneath the heart's clockwork placental nurture of blood into breast-feeding milk. As if by alchemy—maternal, resting against the uterine heart, lost to the breast's mimic womb—Isaac the eternal son remains tied down to patriarchal time and life's aging seasons in past births.

One final allotment of mothering fate in womb lottery space near the vanishing point of paternal entry needs inspection. Nothing is known in writing about the significance that seven-month premature birth had in Lezama's autobiographical mind in relation to the birth of his youngest sister Eloísa, some three months after the sudden death of their father. In her words, "The surprising death of our father was decisive for his childhood. I was born three months afterwards, a symbol that will remain [A los tres meses nazco yo, símbolo que quedará] in *Paradiso* like an epiphany after an absence" (*Paradiso* 1980, 18). It seems certain that the symbol in question is not that of Eloisa's own birth after their father's death, but the death itself from which her birth unborn is in symbol born again. (As examined in the next chapter, the symbolic debt to the born sister supports the ontology of grandeur in the brother's fictions.)

A HIDDEN *hieros logos* surrounds uncle and brother Alberto's life as Oppiano's precursor. The double ghost facemask of male erotic brotherliness in *Paradiso* is worn by Oppiano when he visits the dying Colonel and when he sees Alberto at a bar on the eve of his death. Alberto confronts a street-bum guitarist named Juan Charrasqueado and is insulted with dirty *coplas* by the "maddened, Bacchic" man ("moaning" like "an abortion of eggs and slime"):

*Look at us, buddy, boy,*
*as if on the cross of love,*
*one on top of the other*
*and a spike between the two.*

[*A vernos mañito, maño,*
*como en la cruz del amor,*
*uno encimita del otro*
*y un clavón entre los dos.*]
(*P* 187/188)

Oppiano is present at the bar where the insulting doggerel is sung. He has come to meet with his "friend" Olaya (whom he has not seen in quite a while). But even as they recall their first meeting on the night Alberto "had accosted those fiendish queers [maricas endemoniados]" (184/185), the reunion breaks off when Dr. Santurce arrives with news that Doña Augusta is dying. Oppiano ("the one who steps in front of *Ananke*") leaves the bar where he might have once again protected his friend, just as the *coplas* turn from sexual ribbing into death omens (Alberto will die at dawn in a car crash; Lezama's real-life uncle hanged himself on a similar night, while being held in jail [*Paradiso* 1980, 341n74]).

At the police station Alberto cries in catharsis while hearing the captain's story of how he was pardoned by Colonel Cemí one Christmas Eve, after he had left his post at the fortress to go see a girlfriend. The cadet had to risk death by descending through a tunnel hanging from the "sling that country people use to climb a palm tree" (*P* 190/192). (The escape had something of "the magic of the Christmas ritual.") Upon hearing that the Colonel pardoned the cadet by having him repeat the feat before his eyes, Alberto weeps "tears of shame and memory" (the cadet "had performed his deed at the time of the greatest rite of birth," on the night when the Colonel sat at the head of the ritual feast of *nochebuena,* like the "titanic and most Cuban of figures, the family's mainstay and his presiding happiness") (191/192). Thus, hours before dying in a car accident, the fictional Alberto eludes having to confess to itemized guilt. The story he is told becomes his own unspoken confession, as the real-life suicide, hanging in shame, turns into the poetic catastrophe of crashing at the tune of a dawn song against a rushing train. From this catastrophe, Alberto's steps lead backward through perils and guardianships into a seven-months-pregnant womb where love's siblinghood with female flesh becomes one's unborn consubstantial sister. This unborn ghost of compound origins in sister sex marks the living spot where the accursed birth from the mother as dragon is given prenatal burial by the expiatory queer narrative of a son turned into brother. The incest mark remains, except that now it is Antigone who nurses her brotherly son out of his fears of unmediated maternal desire. But: is the son's attempt to transform mother into sister a brotherly or sisterly act?

# 8 *Paradiso* as a Five-Star Inferno

Thou canst read nothing except through appetite.

Hart Crane

SOON AFTER its publication *Paradiso* was labeled a *Bildungsroman* and even before that—during its first season in hell under the eye of some in power upset with the sexual shenanigans in chapter 8—it was rumored to have been called by Raul Castro "un monumento al maricón" (a fag monument). High and low, whether at the prestige level of literary name-branding or down in the gutter of urban talk, the novel right from the start inspired architectural and sculptural associations among the happy few who had read it at least in part and the legions who would not—and acted as if they had.

In Lezama's fiction's thick symbolic armature, the joint figures of the ancient magical craftsman and maze builder Daedalus and his ill-fated son Icarus are linked with images of architecture and sculpture in support of the writing, building, and crafting of *Paradiso* and *Oppiano Licario* as imaginary structures that transcend mere literary textual fabric. The father and son's joint responsibility for the mythical texture of the two linked novels (imbued as both fictions are with the spirit of erecting live monuments honoring life in the otherworld) resides in the afterlife nature of their partnership and affiliation. A structure of mourning binds together the father who once dared climb near the sun by human flight and the son whose death by celestial fall was caused when he flew on wings designed by his father and master.

The bonds of mourning animating the structures and building designs of *Paradiso* are secured by a twist in the ligatures of creative alliance between master and pupil. For in the case of *Paradiso,* it is the father and master who has died and his pupil son who has survived and incorporated the paternal fall into his own creative life. While in the Daedalus myth and legend it is the son's celestial fall that causes paternal grief, periodically assuaged by ritual remembrance, in *Paradiso* the son's mourning, upon spiritually surviving his father-related fall, finds abode in his melancholic incorporation of the father as the ultimate survivor inside his own body and work. The ligatures binding the incorporated melancholia between father and son correspond to the analogously aggrieved and injured binding of the son with the building of his textual and sexual artwork. The injurious nature of the melancholy and incorporative binding between father and son seeks the outlet of repeated negotiations in fictions aimed at twisting (and queering) the sexual difference that divides them across the issue of homosexuality. Assuming the celestial fall when he fell from the skies as being caused by his father, the son restores his own person to life and relives his father's death as his own in his artwork—personified in winged ligatures and the flying contraption of dual bonding. However, the fall that joins both of them stands (in architectural and sculptural terms) as a monument to the son's sexual difference with the father, a difference disavowed and negotiated by their joint work in the son's authorship. Thus, apocryphal or not, Raul Castro's presumed slur about *Paradiso* being a fag monument stands the test of time as a fittingly gross speech act in asinine celebration of the novel's monstrous sublimity in support of the son's queerness.

## Ass Birth

Eugenio Foción is the only character in *Paradiso* in whose conception the parents are shown at work—as he, too, is shown trying to make his wife pregnant without having intercourse with her; hence the urgency to show the trick in the making. As we will see in a moment, Foción's womb fabric requires a father too many, while in his own fabrication of a child (certain to be a boy) the father to be attempts to annul direct carnal contact with the mother. I will parody a bit of wordplay gynecology in guessing that *annulment* comes into play in the work of conception in order to echo how Foción puns with words that begin or end with *anus*-sounding syllables as a way of foreclosing on his increasingly manic paranoid fears about his mounting homosexual desires. That is to say: his conceptive experiment in mother-bypass gynecology is cesarean, as it duplicates manic anal punning when the father is driven to annul all contact with the child's birth canal. On the eve of his breakdown and removal to a loony house, Foción puns madly with aberrant etymologies, such as having the name of the Egyptian dog-face Anubis "derived from anus" (as he puts it: "the worshiper of Anubis/god of the anal way" [*P* 352–53/347–48]). A sort of double anal trumpeting obtains, inasmuch as devils in Dante's *Inferno* are combined in his mouth with "Anubis" as they fart their foul tongue ("ed elli avea del cul fatto trombetta") at the wary visitors to the bulge for grafters and corrupt politicians in the Eighth Circle, once the poor souls refuse their escort services into the next section of Hell. Foción trumpets that: "'Fronesis the foot soldier advances with his javelin'" and says:

"But I belong to the *Oxyrhynchi* Greek tribe,
*My snout is point-sharp,*
*ed elli avea del cul fatto trombetta.*
But he does not advance before the wild boar.
Is he not the master of the golden javelin?
And I? A pig with tusks
for the hunting horn,
the worshiper of Anubis,
god of the anal way."

(*P* 353/347)

The grafting of Dante's Eighth Circle with Egypt's excremental underworld in Foción's celebration of the anal path to glory implies that his being guilty of insane envy surpasses in sinfulness Brunetto Latini's sodomy as the sin that presumably landed Dante's teacher among dwellers of the Seventh Circle. For as much as Latini is believed to have ran afoul of church doctrine for some unspecified heresy, and not just for sodomy, it remains to be seen whether Foción's undisputed mastery of sinfulness in *Paradiso* and beyond can in fact be reduced to his manic fondness for the anus.

## The Dragon Gospel Channel

Foción's birth seems prophesied in lines by Julián del Casal in his poem "Spurious Son": "I am the fruit begotten by a father's loathing and a mother's obscenity." Accordingly, his future father (a physician named Nicolás) lived with his younger brother Juliano. He married a girl named Celita and the three shared a house. Nicolás went on long tours to visit patients while Juliano became addicted to laudanum and his bedroom was changed into a "labyrinth" with him in the role of Minotaur. On one occasion, while he sleeps drugged, "bullman" Juliano, instead of goring his bother in the groin ("as if seeking out and enshrouding the secrets of his sperm") takes away "the trophy of his reason" in his horns (*P* 315/313). In such fashion the sleeping and brotherly and unconscious Minotaur rapes and abducts his brother's reason in an act in which injury to paternal fitness by goring the brother's groin is cognate with the wound to paternity caused by sodomy. Juliano (a name suffixed by *anus*) had already allowed Celita to enter the labyrinth of his sleep and to make of himself her victim's body: "soft with the timidity of adolescence," his eyelids "like a lock made constant by laudanum" (315/313). It is then that the triumphant lethal mother "unveils" the lover's dying and impregnating body: "Celita was closing her eyes in sleep; moments later Juliano was opening his in death. They had both incorporated themselves as happiness in eternity. Celita had ascended through ecstasy to sleep. After seeing her face, Juliano had descended to the cold grottoes of Persephone" (316/314). By being essentially raped in sleep, the Minotaur has found two victims in himself and his brother. Although Juliano's drugged state puts him in the unconscious role of the horned man-beast Minotaur, and although his brother Nicolás loses his reason to the same horns that do not injure his groin, both brothers fall victim to the same evil woman. The doctor goes mad upon discovering her infidelity with the unconscious patient whom he assists too late. Hence the uncanny and coiled inversion: the Minotaur as the cause of death to both Theseus and himself is also itself the woman and phallic mother in the evil role of Ariadne.

In the making of his father's madness in synchrony with the conception of Foción, wife infidelity proves less wounding to the father than the annihilating discovery that she raped his brother while he lay unconscious: that she raped him into becoming the father of a son who should be his own. Later on, when "Celita turned out to be pregnant, it was impossible to tell which of the brothers had been the archer" (318/315). Meanwhile, Dr. Foción goes mad, changes Celita's name to Eudoxia, and makes her his nurse. For many years he practices at home, first with patients, then without them. In the alchemical dragon-making scenario, the younger brother who dies in narcolepsy while in the womb-and-tomb maze of Celita's maternal bliss achieves consubstantial cloning in the *split-by-death-father-and-son* dyad. This myth of male homosexual origins collapses into chimerical hyphenation the father's death and its identifying clone effect upon the son's redundant making.

Juliano's adolescent flesh and Celita's predatory receptiveness (in their joint narcoleptic experience, lethal sleep, and conceptive merger) are theological and psychic markers of consubstantiality and infinite incest consanguinity. In killing narcoleptic Juliano (serving as the midwife who ushers him into death and takes his seed), Celita becomes his widow as he becomes the posthumous paternal surrogate of her future son. The son (Foción) achieves bipolar surrogacy with his dead adolescent father

(Juliano) by marrying his widow (his own Isis mother) in both her lethal and healing roles. In various traditions examined by Carl Jung, Isis marries her son Horus (later known as Gabritius) after putting together the corpse of her dismembered brother-husband, Osiris, and coupling with its restored phallus as he lies on a bier (she adopts the bird form of a kite). The widow's healing role in nursing her son's conception by a dead father is further transformed by alchemists into their marriage and the murder of the husband-son, killed by Isis with "the stroke of a viper" or *viperino conatu* (Jung, *Mysterium Coniunctionis* 19). Foción's *Anubis-Isis-Osiris* bond with his mother Celita puts him on both sides of her dual widow status with respect to the dead father and the son obtained through Juliano's conceptive death. She is transformed into the widow of the father in whom the son perishes before being born. Foción is thus (re)born under the crooked sign of disputed and shared substance or consubstantiality (Greek *homoousian*). He is an incest chimera infinitely consanguineous with his parents and with the homosexual brood he will madly pursue. The built-in polemic about the nature and consequences of his accursed sodomy comes back to the issue of the child's original substance: does it belong exclusively to the mother? Which of the two brothers gave it paternal seed? How is the father present in the son's reception in the womb—in the son's still unborn share of spirit and flesh? Hyphenated duality haunts Foción: whether male or female, maternal or paternal, fertile or barren, sacred or demonic.

Foción's circus theological and alchemical show of natures in clash will ultimately take him to New York to play dragon. The visit runs in synchronicity with Hart Crane's suicide off the coast of Cuba and a sermon delivered by Ricardo Fronesis at the steps of the University of Havana. During Christmas in Manhattan Foción performs in a sex trio with the incest adolescent hyphen-couple of brother-George and sister-Daisy (he hyphenates George's rear as the blond brother hyphens his toasted-honey sister's front). Brother George's preppie fixation on Hart Crane combines with his own search for the "possessive homosexual," making him a Crane clone in Foción's mythmaking and sex-hunting eyes.

As José Cemí listens to the New York Christmas story reported by Fronesis, he interprets for us Foción's tale according to Jung's notion of *synchronicity* (*unus mundus,* or one world), the highest principle of transcendental learning issued by psychotherapy in the twentieth century, succinctly rendered as that which "suggests that there is an inter-connection or unity of causally unrelated events, and thus postulates a unitary aspect of being which can very well be described as the *unus mundus.*"[1]

In his first public lecture ever, Lezama quotes Jung: "'One must follow the way of the waters'—Yung [*sic*] tells us—'in which one is always lead downwards, if one wants to exalt and renew the precious heritage of the father. . . . Man must descend into the waters in order to produce the miracle of the waters' revivification'" (*OC* 2:43). Baptism and the alchemical bath are as deeply and mutually embedded in Jung's writings as they are in *Paradiso*. According to Jung, alchemical bath and Christian baptism dialectically oppose and resemble suicide by water, the voyage into the *aqua permanens:* permanent oceanic water, as when Hart Crane plunges to his death off a cargo ship two hundred miles north of Havana into "the great marine mother"—in Foción's cynical epitaph (*P* 345/341). For his part, Foción survives his own plunge into the nightmare depths of Havana Bay, whose waters he pollutes with semen, as if he were mating with his beloved Fronesis, before coming face to face with a huge shark. His right arm is nearly lost as he fights the shark while dreaming of love with Fronesis before being rescued by a black swimmer.

Cemí thinks that, at the same moment of Fronesis's apocalyptic sermon to a chorus of bystanders at Havana University, the New York incest trio is performing their own sermon in bed and in the mirror. The implications of Cemí's thoughts in response to Foción's cynical tale of sexual exploits are grotesque. In Cemí's synchronicity script, Foción the dragon would be screwing St. George in the person of the adolescent brother George (at one point in Fronesis's sermon St. George is said to become the dragon's own replica). But since St. George is also made analogous to Antigone (Oedipus's sister and daughter), one is compelled to ask who, where, and in which position is she (the incest woman-actor) beside him—beside and beneath Dragon-Saintly-Oedipus-George.

Fronesis's sermon sets up Antigone's tragic will to give unlawful burial to her brother Polyneices in contrast with the docile unwillingness of the "choral masses" (such as the student bystanders) to rebel against any such laws. He claims that the applauding acquiescent chorus around him has replaced the dragons of old, who always went on to meet their fate as if on cue, sunk in their own stench and gloomy lake awaiting doomsday at the hands of heroes like Cadmus, St. George, Siegfried, and Tristan. Those ancient dragons never recoiled from their own fiery embrace and the hero's sword, just as Antigone never turned her back on her brother's brother-slain unburied body after Polyneices failed in his war to retake Thebes, their native city, and was killed in combat by his own brother, Eteocles. If Antigone and St. George are indeed alike in heroic duty, as proclaimed by Fronesis, her sisterly and unbreakable will to bury Polyneices—a will punished by having her buried alive and entombed—would be dragon-marked by a genealogy of incest in a family at war with itself and its polluted hyphens: a *father-brother* Oedipus whose children are *children-brothers-nephews* and *sisters-nieces* of the same *avuncular-brotherly-parent.*

The resemblance between Antigone and St. George affirmed by Fronesis is enhanced (but also threatened) by the knight's intercourse with the dragon's infernal awfulness and his eschatological bondage to the obliging beast he defeats but comes to resemble. The Christian apocalyptic Last Days theme is heard when José Cemí suddenly puts in the mouth of Jesus words nowhere found as such in the Gospels. Between Judgment Day and a "final banquet" to be held in Jerusalem, Cemí affirms, "Jesus's gloomy phrase *Woe to women giving milk and the pregnant, for they shall be put to the knife* is said" (*P* 334/330).[2] The aberrant notion that Jesus Christ should outclass Herod as a slayer of the innocent by ordering mothers to slaughter their unborn or newborn children distorts Matthew 24.17–20: "Let those who are in Judea flee to the mountains" (17), and "alas for those who are with child and for those who give suck in those days! Pray for your flight may not be in winter or on a Sabbath" (19). These words on the *birth pangs* (Matt. 24.8) of the approaching Final Days are repeated in Mark 13.17, and most tellingly in 2 Esdras 6.21: "Infants a year old shall speak with their voices, and women with child shall give birth to premature children at three or four months and these shall live and dance;" and also—and best suited for measuring Cemí's distortion—in Luke 20.34–37: "But those [sons] who are accounted worthy to attain to that age and to the resurrection from the dead neither marry nor are given in marriage, for they cannot die any more, because they are equal to angels and are sons of God, being sons of the resurrection." (Scripture is quoted here not in order to correct Cemí's version but to properly measure how it twists what the Gospels say about mothers and children in the face of Christian death and resurrection.) In Cemí's words (and presumably the author's own):

> It's undeniable that those nursing and pregnant women will harbor the secret thought of continuing the adventure of living in their children [in the face of Jesus' command to put them to the knife]. For the children they nurse or bear in their wombs, they will be forced to accept the destruction of their lives for the promise of resurrection. . . . [This] promise will even come to the pregnant mothers, to them all the more terrifying for their never having seen the face of their enwombed secret, that on that day they shall see the child whom they

> were not able to caress at the moment he was shown the earthly light, with a body which on the day of plenitude they will have to examine with eyes born to them for that moment of mortal recognition. They will have to content themselves with seeing a body that could not separate itself from their innards and whose life will be narrated to them by the lightning flash of eternal life, and not by their maternal cares. . . . And although they have lived in nature, on that day when their maddened reason must convince them of the terrible death of their children for the sake of life everlasting, they must be convinced that death is counter-nature, and that what was unknown to them, resurrection, is nature presented to them for the first time so that they will kill their children. (*P* 334–35/330–31)[3]

Such surrender of children's lives to their mothers under divine orders to destroy them (or their dying in the womb) is precisely what the Gospels neither proclaim nor foresee. Instead, it is announced that births will be facilitated and hastened, allowing children of the last generation to reach personal life status by themselves and separate from their mothers.

Inseparability from and between womb, breast, and maternal knife (as claimed by Cemí in aberrant fashion) is said by Fronesis—who agrees with it—to be "just as monstrous . . . as seeing St. George, the destroyer of the dragon, the monster, changed into a monster too, so as to enter the kingdom of heaven" (335/331). Kinship between Antigone and St. George (embedded in the saintly knight's own eschatological likeness to the dragon) brings us to Revelation 12 and its underlying mythic scheme linking the Septuagint Greek *drakon* (Hebrew *tannin*) with Satan, including the only reference in the Gospels to a war in heaven in which the Archangel Michel defeats the red dragon. This is the scriptural point where Fronesis's sermon comes to rest, in which St. George triumphs over the dragon who represents Satan in the role of Antichrist, personified by the heavenly beast who threatens to devour the woman's (Israel's) child Christ at birth.[4]

Other wondrous and ghastly things are watched on the Dragon Channel. Elsewhere in *Paradiso,* Cemí favors Fronesis's adoptive mother, María Theresa Sunster, as his friend's true mother over her sister (the vanished ballerina who gave birth to him and went off chasing after Diaghilev). The absent woman's maternity represents the missing head in Fronesis's descent from a "two-headed dragon" ("although the bedeviled ballerina is the one who looks with most tenderness at the Archangel who comes to destroy her" [*P* 286/285]). In Cemí's eyes, Fronesis is *two-mothered*—by the vanished sister who abandoned motherhood and by the faithful sister who adopted the maternal role. But he regards the vanished mother as wanting to be destroyed by the avenger St. Michael, who in scripture saves mother and child from the dragon who was awaiting birth in order to eat her son. Cemí, who earlier had Jesus calling for mothers to destroy their unborn or nursing children, now has a mother wanting tenderly to be destroyed by the Archangel Michael—as if she herself were the dragon he vanquishes into Hell in order to have her child saved. As a result, the New York burlesque threesome (where sister-incestuous St. George is speared in the rear by the dragon in Foción) now turns into St. Michel as the avenging son who kills his dragon mother.

In his guardian role watching over Foción and Fronesis, Cemí's versions of scriptural drama play a perverse game with Christian doctrine, covertly adapting it to the issue of a mother who gives birth to homosexual sons. In such queerly twisted fashion, the heterodox scriptural homilies found in *Paradiso* as delivered by Cemí and Fronesis articulate what has become known as homophobia. The specter of sodomy with Satan in the background is mirrored in misogyny. Fear of homosexuality in men and the women who mothered these men combines with ancestor worship: it is the family honor cast in the memory of the dead father that lies at stake in these patchwork doctrines.

## Stolen Temples

The Christian vanishing point reopens on Hellenistic/Pagan grounds. A famous spring (the Fountain of Salmacis tied to *hermaphroditea*) appears in Vitruvius's description of Halicarnassus and its architectural marvels. The entire passage has great and hidden significance as a fragment in the obsessive program of personal family vindication undertaken in *Oppiano Licario*—in whose pages a good chunk of the following text from *De Architectura* is lodged and blindly quoted in unacknowledged and adapted form:

> For just as on the right side there are the temple of Venus and the spring above described [Salmacis's fountain], so on the left wing is the royal palace which the King Mausolus had built to his own plan. From it there is seen on the right side the forum and harbour and the whole circuit of the walls; under the left there is a secret harbour lying hid under high ground, in such a way that no one can see or know what is going on in it, so that the king from his own palace could see what was necessary for his sailors and soldiers, without anyone else knowing. *14.* Therefore when, after the death of Mausolus, his wife Artemisia began to reign, the Rhodians were indignant that a woman

> should rule over the cities throughout Caria, and equipping a fleet they set out to seize the kingdom. It was reported to Artemisia. She hid the fleet in the harbour, concealing the rowers and the marines she had got together, and ordered the rest of the citizens to man the walls and to promise to surrender the town. These left their ships unmanned and penetrated within the wall. Artemisia, using an artificial outlet into the sea, suddenly led out her fleet from the lesser harbour and thus sailed into the greater. She then landed her soldiers and took the empty Rhodian fleet to sea. So the Rhodians, having no place to retreat, were surrounded and killed in the forum itself. *15.* So Artemisia, placing her own troops and rowers in the ships of the Rhodians sailed for Rhodes. But when the Rhodians saw their own ships come wreathed with laurel, they thought their fellow-citizens returned victorious and let the enemy in. Then Artemisia took Rhodes, killed the leading citizens, and set up a trophy of her victory in the city of Rhodes, having two bronze statues made, one of the city of Rhodes, the other of her own likeness. She had the latter figured as setting a brand upon the city of Rhodes. But afterwards the Rhodians, being restrained by a religious scruple because it is forbidden for trophies once dedicated to be removed, erected a building round the spot and protected it with a Greek outpost to prevent anyone seeing, and ordered this to be called "unapproachable" (*abaton*). (Vitruvius, *On Architecture* II.c.viii.13–15)[5]

The story of Artemisia's revenge in this, its only existing version, is regarded by Simon Hornblower as a "historical fiction" borrowed by Vitruvius and adapted from a lost "Rhodian patriotic source—such as Posidonious" (*Mausolus* 129). Ynaca tells the story in her own way (not using the names of Mausolus and Artemisia) after she takes Fronesis into Etruscan tombs at Tarquinia and inside the Cumean Gates. There they enter an underworld spanning the ancient Mediterranean and the Near East, from a spot attached to the Middle Ages and King St. Louis—"who would appear praying even as he swam with singing dolphins in the current by the river's mouth" (*OL* 355). Within such widening synchronicity between different historical times and geographies lies hidden the transfer of one of the seven wonders of the ancient world to Oppiano Licario's family tomb memorial, the Mausoleum, built by Queen Artemisia of Caria (who according to tradition died of grief) to honor her dead husband and brother. The most celebrated artwork in the Mausoleum is the so-called *Amazonomachy,* which depicts Artemisia as an Amazon queen at war. The Carian sister queen became a model of sustained grief in ancient tradition and European Christian piety. In a seventeenth-century devotional sonnet by Jean de La Ceppède, "Mausole" is named "Christ" and "Artemise," "L'Eglise"—or *Church* and *Temple* to her brother, whose bones she was believed to have swallowed in subtle powder mixed with wine in a golden cup, thus becoming his human sepulcher a little drink at a time.[6]

In *Oppiano Licario* the widow's role remains preeminent though thoroughly muted and encrypted. Ynaca is her brother's widow and his Li*Carian* queen. She is also widow and sister and mating mother to the sons and brothers and lovers with whom Oppiano mated posthumously through her. *Oppiano Licario*'s unnamed Carian queen stands above Ynaca in a secret mausoleum to widowhood. Lezama's Vitruvius fragment proclaims Athena in the warlike role of *Promakos*. It is also triumphant in proclaiming the "inaccessible" status of the *abaton* or sacred precinct in which the two stolen statues are taken to be worshipped, a stone enclosure whose human paragon is Ynaca's homosexual and celibate husband, the Oppiano clone architect known as craftsman Abaton Awalobit, custodian of the author's triumphant but injured dynastic imagination.

As claimed in the previous chapter, the complex status of homosexual male bachelorhood in Lezama's fiction is grounded upon the insistence to wed bachelor celibacy to heterosexual marriage under the aegis of the mother's widowed love. The bachelor son replaces the mother's dead husband—but not without supporting her widowhood by harboring deep matricidal anxieties of his own. Thus, widowed mother-worship is animated by the son's matrifocal conjugal and suppressed wish to commit matricide. This might explain (as wishful reversal) José Cemí's aberrant misconception of the Gospels' view of the Last Days as envisioning mothers slaughtering their unborn children.

In this complex son's worship of his dead father and mother's husband, a compulsory nexus between homosexual gay love and the institution and sacrament of marriage takes root in the fiction of Lezama Lima. To repeat what was said before: being gay in Lezama's fiction is refused autonomous existence from marriage—but someone else's marriage.

## Paternal *Vampironomy:* Injuring Injured Daedalus

A father who through his arts and magical craft dares to challenge solar power on wax wings worn by his son and who beyond his own mourning for that son lives on inside the labyrinth from within which that same and only born son mourns him. Such would be the twist of fate when Icarus reinvents Daedalus after fatherhood is lost to both of them once the father's overreaching magic kills the son—as it does happen in cryptic fashion in *Paradiso:* the son dies but survives as if the father had replaced him in the dying in a manner no less than sacrificial and more than a bit vampirelike.

Let us consider in legal terms that a case of paternal manslaughter of a son formally occurs when Daedalus gets Icarus to fly on wax wings and the flight ends in death. And let us further consider the liability and penalties incurred by Daedalus in circumstances where the person killed using his flying contraption—at his builder's behest and with all due warnings on his part—is not his son Icarus but a strange boy. Beginning with the latter case: on one hand, the liabilities and penalties that may result from the charge of manslaughter involving a youth who is not his son, possibly settled in court; on the other, the absence of any such legal recourse in compensation for lethal injury, possibly replaced by the feeling of mourning felt by Daedalus at the death of his son.

In the case of someone else's son dying while flying his machine, Daedalus can settle the issue and legally heal the injury through proper compensation without lessening in the least his sense of mourning. But in the case of his son's death, a more difficult and labored and nonlegal reparation for the injury may ensue—even if the father and crafter did properly warn his flying son not to go near the sun. In the event Daedalus could not get over the death of Icarus and kept it alive in his grief for a long time, he would be suffering from melancholia in Freud's conception of that illness. But there is no evidence in myth that Daedalus was for long grounded by feelings of loss and injury concerning the death of Icarus and his own role in it. And such is also the case in *Paradiso,* where in fact there is not a single reference to Daedalus in contrast with a few important references to Icarus—so important in fact that Icarus becomes perhaps the most significant mythical signature in Lezama's fiction. The signature of authorship in sustainable melancholia by which the son who in myth dies and is survived by his father becomes himself the survivor of that—his own—death now embodied in the father's incorporated life within the son's textual creations.

The intimacy of craft, execution, and performance between the artificer and his creations and their daring use is what this overwrought and sublime form of mourning between father and son exemplifies and endlessly expiates in the son's works. However, the incorporated bond between parent and sibling must exceed sublime articulations of the literary or textual sort; hence the endless melancholy impasse in the son's textual authorship. For the immaterial character of the injury in the incorporated textual personification—and personation—of the departed yet living father seeks materiality and thus claims for itself monuments, statues, secret gardens: all manner of erections and buildings as material evidence of triumph beyond fabricated text. Daedalus and Icarus embody the magical practices and interactive corporeal craftsmanship between actors who are in hands-on contact with matter as it takes shape in the sculpting of human figures and the construction of building, wings, and sails. Their master-pupil artisanal and thaumaturgic association joins together father and son, but with binding ligatures otherwise involved in crafts mediated by erotic energies mutually invested. The son's death, caused in close collaboration with his father's crafty designs and mastery, represents the embodied and twisted material simulation and enactment of a sexual clasp between them.

Sarah P. Morris has traced the incorporation of "Daidalos" into Greek culture and the mythic origins of his art. My purpose here is simply to underline the will to mastery and responsibility in the magical and technological designs of Daedalus in the wake of harms that he has—or might have—caused and injuries which his stature as inventor and craftsman could not help but to risk causing. According to legend and various mythical strands, Daedalus was involved in the arts of escape as much as in the dangerous craft of keeping unbound persons and agencies bound up and supernatural forces harnessed in constructed figures, as when Socrates says at one point: "If you have one of his [Daedalus's] works untethered, it is not worth much; it gives you the slip like a runaway slave. But a tethered specimen is very valuable, for they are magnificent creations" (Plato, *Collected Dialogues, Meno* 7d–98a). Jealous of his sister's son Talus (who some sources identify as his own son and who became his gifted pupil and rival inventor), Daedalus hurled him to death from the walls of the Acropolis. But Talus was transformed by Athena into a partridge in midfall. The youth flew off bearing his mother's name, Perdix. The story foreshadows the fall of Icarus, which is not blamed on his father Daedalus, but on his own folly in not following the advice not to fly either too close to the water or too near the sun. However, in earlier visual and epigraphic representations reaching back before the Athenian classical period, the figures of master and pupil are not so neatly distinct, the central motif in vases being a single depicted figure believed to be involved in rituals of initiation (perhaps metallurgical mysteries) in which the apprentice magician dives into water or leaps into the air to show fitness in joining a brotherhood. In the earliest vase depictions first showing the flying figure in ancient Greek art, it remains impossible to determine whether the winged man is Daedalus or Icarus. Also, much later, in the long-standing European tradition, emblems may show their joint flight, stressing the fatal disjunction between the father's proper path and the son's already befallen condition. In either case, the disjunctive but mutual fate between master father and disciple son shows a dual fall from which only one wretched being survives.[7]

Foción's dive into Havana Bay in *Oppiano Licario* could be seen as the submarine version of such an air plunge, if one takes into account that his encounter with the shark at a depth traditionally associated with the Morro Castle brings back Cemí's nightmare in "the aquarium of sleep" about encountering a similar shark threat under the guiding and protective finger of his father the Colonel. The father-centered dream is situated at the Morro Castle and its bulwark environs on the mouth of the bay. The Colonel enters his son's dream at the time when he is inspecting the castle, which "as an engineer he had rebuilt" (*P* 128/129). This happened at a time when the father and his six-year-old son seemed closer than ever, occasionally at the child's own risk, as when the Colonel submerged him in an ice-filled tub, in a scene that "had something of an ancient sacrifice," as he tried to shock the child out of his sickly bondage to asthma, without quite "knowing to which deity he was making the offering" (131/130). The Morro Castle and its environs evoke both the spot from which Talos takes his fatal flight in the trial imposed by Daedalus and also the imprisonment from which the craftsman and his son Icarus must escape as they attempt to flee the island of Crete by means of wings and sails invented by the father.[8]

The question becomes how the combined crafts of architecture and sculpture hold in place and bind together and then release from each other Daedalus the father and Icarus the son as mythical figures in the combined lives of José Cemí and Colonel José Eugenio. The comprehensive and enigmatic answer comes in chapter 12 of *Paradiso,* where four layered narrative strands combine into a dream unit in which, according to Cintio Vitier, Lezama places "José Cemí's dreams after his father's death" in a "new dimension beyond time and space" and "the terror and infinite nostalgia of the father's absence" (*EC* 672). The chapter's bedrock vampire narrative follows the career of a military tribune named Atrius Flaminius at the head of Etruscan legionaries fighting in Thessaly and Cappadocia under assault by witches, warlocks, and fiendish dwarfs and "ectoplasms" bent on destroying them by multiple mutilation. Besides such polluted death and the hands of animated rubbish, the Romans had already confronted and fallen under the viral charms of debauchery. The legionaries "had been corrupted with games of chance and languid Oriental influences," and tribunes like Flaminius himself had been bought into marriage by hefty dowries or else had chosen "to quench their appetites with the most select horsemen among their bodyguard" (*P* 373/368).

This picture of decadence and corrupt marriage corresponds to another of the narrative strands, in which a widowed retro Pre-Raphaelite music critic in his seventies marries a woman in her fifties. His first wife had shared with him a taste for fin-de-siècle art objects and "Nijinsky's best nights," while the second wife (possibly a younger feminist revenant of the first one) lost many pounds in secret while hiding the fact that, "like a crafty woman dedicated to espionage, she was a teacher of physical education" (377/372). The marriage (most likely kept celibate) reveals its own version of honeymoon in a droll snapshot of wife dietary regime upon her husband and his own loathing of her flesh: "The fish not much blessed by oil, lettuce, and the earthen yellow of papaya [Cuban slang for the vulva] were repeated so often in the meals that the music critic began to feel sick the moment he sat down at the table, he seemed to smell the cat savoring the skeletal comb of a porgy" (377/372). Soon the "infernal Circe" changes her papaya-with-fish menu for milkier stuff endowed with "somniferous virtues" until the husband sinks, first into "permanent somnambulism" and finally into cataleptic sleep inside a crystal urn. Thus, a Snow-White old widower (who loathes his new wife's flesh, but gets the stuff fed to him in a diet of her own concoction) is embalmed by her in a coma: "The wife learned that hibernation destroys the terrible drop-after-drop of time's flow; the safety of having her husband sleeping by her side frightened death away" (378/373). Although it is the mad wife who puts her husband in a coma in order to halt the passage of time, Eloísa Lezama Lima in her comments on *Paradiso* interprets the scene as her brother José's writing in crisis and in need to "to stop time" after their mother's death in December 1964. Indeed, the repeated use of "dormición" (dormition) to name the husband's urn coma suggests that Lezama had in mind the "sleep of the righteous" as traditionally applied to the Virgin Mary's ascending to heaven without actually dying. The crisis caused by the author's mother's death and symbols of the Virgin's reaching immortality without experiencing death may well represent his way of transcending sorrow, but they say nothing about the focal point of what actually unfolds in the narrative strand under discussion: the marriage of a man of advanced age, adverse to his wife's corporeal proximity, and her forced feeding him a condensed diet redolent of female genital substances.

In the end, *Paradiso*'s most complex instance of symbolic mourning, presumably written soon after the death of the author's mother, narrates in one of its layers a dismal allegory of marital dysfunction in which the aged husband resists connubial contact with the wife and in response she feeds him a double diet: first the sexual substances that he seems most repelled by and then a narcoleptic draught that puts him to sleep.[9]

Taking into account the seldom-explored influence of the spiritualist Allan Kardec on Cuban writers, one should observe Lezama's esoteric Christian spiritualism and the practice of table-rapping or "thrilling" in attempts to contact the souls of the dead. For instance, in one of chapter 12's narrative strands, a rocking chair becomes animated in the middle of a "compulsive patio," thrilled by disembodied laughter from unknown yet familiar spirits. Without any known or public adherence to *espiritismo,* Lezama is nevertheless frequently concerned with the mutually invasive contact between living persons and spirits in whose behavior after death distinct individual identities are believed to persist.

Spiritualism and madness dovetail in his fiction. María Poumier has observed that "the abundance of mad people in *Paradiso* is quite remarkable, as are the matter-of-fact dealings between the sane and the insane," and she adds that such contacts render most matters in the novel equivocal: "madness and sanity become reversible"; daily lives are "invaded by hallucinatory reveries in contact with one another, over and above those characters in whom they were first found as the reading progressed" ("Foción Erasmo Lima" 66). But what Poumier quite sensibly describes as madness may also express a feature of spiritualist personation removed from its manifest séance environment.

In the historical past represented in *Paradiso* and *Oppiano Licario,* spiritualism celebrates the reunion of souls in a single thrilled body: a spiritualized body, enraptured and redundant in its mourning by another person and in such joint action denying its own fall into oblivion. From this perspective, we will take a final glance at the bedrock narrative of injured Daedalus animated and reborn in his son's statue as the image of his own—the son's—inflamed solar death by his father's magical craft. (Latent syntactic ambiguity in this case is meant to signify the embedded duality of father and son in one single shape.) The tale of their injured and wistfully repaired union is lodged in the already discussed story of Atrius Flaminius and his Etruscan legionaries, besieged and mutilated in body and soul by ravenous troops sprung from Hell.

## Stoicism Queered: *Homo Necans: Homo Se Necans*

As Aeneas visits the underworld in *Aeneid* VI he comes upon Priam's son Deiphobus's embodied shade, "mutilated in every part of his body" ("brutally torn were his face and both his hands"), his head "had been ravaged at each side where his ears had been shorn off, and the nostrils had been cut close with a hideous wound": "et truncas inhonesto vulnere naris" (*Aeneid* VI.493–97). Aeneas can scarcely recognize his warrior friend, whom he knew had fallen as Troy itself fell and burned down as it was stormed by the Greeks, and to whom he had built a cenotaph on a strange shore, since he could nowhere find his body to take to its rest on home soil: "nequivi conspicere et patria decedens ponere terra" (*Aeneid* VI.507–8). The episode may serve as reference point for the most dismal encounter between father and son in Lezama's fiction—so often described by the author and his expert critics as the son's orphaned love's quest for the paternal figure lost in childhood.

In the story told in chapter 12, news of armies slaughtered in Capadoccia reaches Rome, causing suicide among young men trying to avoid military service in the far-off and bewitched province. As potential conscripts, the Stoic youths are said to be the "pointers of choral suicide"—or "indicadores del suicidio coral" (*P* 398/392). That such expedient recourse to choral—but nevertheless soloist—death might draw the line between Christian and non-Christian ethics appears to be the real issue, when suicide is next shown in its ghastliest shape as a father's preventive killing of his son.

A patrician Roman elder kills his son who has just enrolled in the army; he slits his throat "rather than have him snatched away by warlocks who would tear his nose off," and then he hangs himself from a tree where his nose is ravaged by frostbite and carrion birds before he descends into the underworld. But the mutilation scene is not exempt from ambiguity as to *whose* nose beside the father's gets eaten. It requires close reading as seen from the father's afterlife perspective:

> That nose on another face might pass right by him and he would barely recognize his noseless son, down in gloomy Orcus [reconociendo a medias a su hijo, que estaría en el fúnebre Orco, como desnarigado total]. . . . The son . . . retained the arrogant nose of a Roman patrician while the throat-slitting father lost his [as he entered Hell] with his hand held over the middle of his face, and now it is the son, down in the throat of hell's shadows, who passing by his father does not recognize him, and the father groans to see the afflicted

> neck, *while his son's nose stops him from transfiguring vision into embrace.* [Esa nariz podía pasar en otro rostro a su lado, reconociendo a medias a su hijo, que estaría en el fúnebre Orco, como desnarigado total. . . . Su hijo . . . retuvo su satisfactoria nariz de romano clásico. Pero el padre degollador perdió su nariz. . . . Tuvo que entrar en el valle de Proserpina con la mano abierta en mitad de la cara. Es ahora que el hijo, en la garganta de las sombras, cuando pasa al lado de su padre, no lo reconoce, y el padre gime al ver el cuello dolorido, *aunque la nariz del hijo le impide que la visión lo transfigure en el abrazo.*]. (*P* 398/392, my emphasis)

One may replace Rabassa's elegant translation ("his son's nose stops him from transfiguring vision into embrace") with the awkward but more accurate: "Even though the son's nose prevents [that his, the father's] vision would transfigure him [the father] by [and in] the embrace." For it seems clear that the son's intact nose (replica of the father's mutilated one) prevents the father from being himself transfigured by the posthumous embrace with his son. It being the case (in spite of Rabassa's all too neatly rendered version) that neither "visión" nor "abrazo" could be the direct object of "transfigure" (indeed the indirect and then direct object is the father himself—though not impossibly the son, whose *shade* or shape should represent the "vision" seen).

What obtains in the scene is the identity slippage between the murdering father and the son who somehow survives his murder and reappears in Hell bringing back to the father the signature resemblance that his father wanted to preserve by murdering him—but a signature ravaged and lost in obvious punishment. The entire scene in Hell is framed by the father's obsessed fears that his son has after all lost his nose, even though he killed him in order to prevent the warlocks from snatching the nose in battle. The father's guilt in killing the son in order to prevent the mutilation of the family's signature nose transforms itself into an impossible to resolve face-off between mutually ruined resemblances. Lastly, although rendered from the father's perspective, the wider angle and tight focus from which the mutilation scene is caught belongs to the son and not the father. It is the son's melancholic mourning that is being negotiated and vulnerably reinforced—rather than finally exhausted and discharged.

The scene stands as the precise instance of injury and at the point of demand for bodily restitution and compensation. The all too easy Freudian reading in terms of castration must be amended by means of underscoring the *material* form wherein the injury lies—compounded and beyond repair—in the actuality and symbols of posthumous flesh; but lies, also, quite within reach of repair: repaired if the symbolic bond between the human figure and the statue it requires for its own memorial support is to be recognized and executed in the marbled flesh. The missing resemblance and signature of fatherhood—in terms of aristocratic Roman social rank and in the particular case of a family's likeness and high breeding—demands *sculpted shape* beyond textual form. The notion of such a palpable and concrete realization of the injury's deletion back into wholeness (in the shape of the paternal signature of resemblance in the nose) manifests the way in which the son memorializes the father in one whole sculpted body. Such focus on sculpting and the restoration of mutilated shape renders complex the love-hate bond between the murdering father and the murdered son and the further issue of suicide. Self-recognition in the other's signature resemblance cannot escape the ghost writing of killing oneself for the other's sake, after having killed the other for his and one's own sake.

Such a tightly convoluted bond between resembling men seems to bind the issue of paternity in chapter 12 of *Paradiso*. But there's another side to the issue concerning, not resemblance in or through killing, but the homoerotic and virile pride of the living father. Upon hearing the bad news about suicide and murder back in Rome, the dying Flaminius thinks that whatever is done to replace death in battle with death by other means always leads to shame and, worse, "prevents kinsmen from recognizing each other in hell" (398/392). But it is not lack of recognition, but too much recognition, that haunts the meeting in hell between the father and the son whom he killed for the sake of avoiding his death by suicide or by mutilation in battle, and who then followed upon that murder with the disgrace of his own suicide. What obtains in this case of murder-suicide is the curse of punishment upon the killer father's fear of not being recognized by the son after he kills him in order to prevent the disfigurement of their *paternal* likeness. On the one hand, the son's murder does not succeed in preserving paternal resemblance beyond death; but on the other, one could ask whether such likeness itself might not be *enhanced* (as if sculpted on the family nose) by the father's murder of his treasured son. In any event, the story heard by Flaminius at the point of dying belies a tale of mismatched embodiment between two men and the wish for their sculptural resemblance erected in a single tomb memorial like the one Aeneas built in memory of Deiphobus's intact shape.

Besides this focal point of misidentification as too much identification, the story of Atrius Flaminius is very much a story of male gladiatorial nudity paired against the heavily weighted body of the armored foot soldier. While in the city of Miletus, the legionaries at his command are matched against enemy troops made up of gymnasts suggested to be naked, or nearly so, showing off like gladiators before the battle-hard phalanges, who are trained to fight together as a group and not as virtuosi athletes. The gymnasts seem to exceed strict military discipline, they are body actors who even in defeat are asked to entertain the winners with a circus performance. The gymnasts win even when they lose. Their implied Olympian nudeness shows up when Atrius Flaminius himself bathes naked in the Eurotas River, just as he and his troops must fight heavily weighted by the flint-stone ballast sewed on their battle gear in protection against being hoisted away into Hell by the mutilating warlocks. The flint-stone ruse was surmised by Flaminius from the Pythia's death gurgling words at Delphos after his soldiers had mangled her while trying to snatch from the woman's oracular rapture a clue to how to escape death far from home. But Flaminius dies not only away from home but away from battle itself.

Each narrative strand in chapter 12 ends up in death and inside the urn where the music critic lies at stake in Havana Auditorium, as if he were a high dignitary, a celebrity, a head of state. Near the end, in prelude to his final release from bridegroom coma into the arms of the Queen of Hell, he is replaced in the urn by two other corpses in succession: the body of the dead child who magically brought back images of boyhood to José Cemí's conscience as the gift of time regained, and the body of Flaminius (forever barred by his witchcraft death from dying in battle as so often mimicked in child-play). Being all at once a holograph picture and a vanishing point at the threshold of life's passage into death, the crystal urn cannot hold all these terminal confluences together in one grail scene. Except in the eyes of the critic's wife, for whom Flaminius replaces the husband in their joint death. Besides the wife, there is only one other witness to these deaths in—and by—synchronicity. It is the nightwalker fugueur and Oppiano alter ego whose sleepless eyes behold a child raised in repose: "the two little hands crossed on the chest held a flower as white as his gown. The pink of dawn on his cheeks had turned solemn in the rosy shades of a sunset sky. Death must have howled in joy as it threw herself upon the pinkness of a hare's mouth caught in a trap. It now seemed as if the gown had gained in length, as if its hem had found a resting place high in the clouds" (*P* 401/395).

Down through these clustered and choral deaths runs the meridian of injured consciousness in *Paradiso*'s Inferno. The architect of this vast palace of extravagant simulations is the injured crafter and magician whose solar contraption killed his only son as if by default. His awesome palace mausoleum Inferno houses the image of the father animated in the son's rebirth and erected in consubstantial memory to their injurious dissemblance—sublimely repossessed as resemblance and etched against the shadows of death.

## God Wants

On leaving the Five-Star Inferno in *Paradiso* let us imagine that someone in Old Havana had replaced the name *Trocadero* with *Daidaleion* on the block near the 162 door number—which to a large extent is what the man who wrote behind the door of the house so numbered did with the bulk of his literary work. (A similar trick could not be performed with Joyce, who was frequently moved from house to house by his father's penury and then by his own needs, beyond Dublin, during his life as a young and not-so-young artist.) A double caveat should be added to our street-name twist. First, *Daidaleion* would mean that a temple or sanctuary linked to a craftsman cult or guild stood nearby, whereas the man who lived at 162 had no craft peers in the neighborhood or beyond—if by peers is meant anyone trying to emulate what he set out to do to the novel and had already done to poetry as modes of extrasensory awareness. Second, the neighborhood presence of someone who had once lived there in the style of Daedalus would involve the scandal of his having murdered his nephew and pupil, son of his sister, out of jealousy (or perhaps his adoptive son, or the son of his sister with whom she was involved in incestuous union). The gifted young man, named Talus, survived the push from a rooftop nearby and flew away on the wings of the partridge he had become, and might have even changed sex in midflight. In this manner, Athenian Daedalus is twice involved in the death of a pupil of his own blood: first his sister's son and then his own. Legend has Daedalus murdering his nephew, who is saved, but myth has him doing something irredeemably lethal to his own son, Icarus, who plunges to death when his prosthetic wax wings are scorched by the sun. Daedalus seems blameless of his son's debacle—unless the harm caused by an artifact whose use itself inspires mad pursuits is blamed on its creator instead of its user—but, then, the boy son had little choice but to acquiesce to his father's wishes, due either to paternal compulsion or to his own youthful desire.

One way or the other, injurious guilt by association is older than most legal fictions—including fatherhood. And such is Daedalus's fiction in *Paradiso:* a fiction's fiction, wherein his name is never mentioned, but instead remains lodged like a fading mythical whisper inside three allusions made to Icarus and his fall. These three allusions belong wholly to Icarus, to his implied narrative alignment with José Cemí's role in conjunction with Oppiano Licario. The first allusion relates to Cemí's asthma; it ties together the mythological and fictional characters into one body frame linked by the wings and lungs: "When the asthma came, nothing did him more good than giving in to sleep, even if it was brought by the clouds of fumigatory powders that would dilate the branches of his lungs until equal harmony between interior and external space was achieved, like an architecture with a great deal of glass, which gives the impression that space has not been interrupted, or like some flying, invisible fortress where Icarus, now favored by the refraction, can keep his rib cage from melting" (232/232). Here architecture secures the joining together of inner and outer spaces by means of a trick in embodiment whereby the success in reversing the son's meltdown in the expansion of his lungs (as a sort of internal wings) is accomplished without jeopardy from the sun's scorching glare. It is in such architectural and sculptural device—of magical if not miraculous nature—where the handicraft of Daedalus's art manifests his otherwise unmentioned presence in *Paradiso*.

The second allusion concerns the symbolic rubric of Oppiano's last name, a patronymic drawn, not from the father's Icarus signature but from his son's fatal image, whose stamp carries the emblematic seal of disaster glued to the signature of lethal paternity: "Oppiano, from Oppianus Claudius, Stoic senator; Licario, Icarus, in the [Faustian enjoyment] cognitive splendor of his pride, not yet starting to deliquesce and come to ruin" (439/433). (Placed in brackets is the "Faustian" allusion in the original and discarded version.)

The third allusion unplugs Faustian overreach by framing the approaching death of Licario in Brueghel's painting *Landscape with the Fall of Icarus* as a marginal event: a trivial, unsung and lonesome catastrophe, so near and yet so far from the work routine of peasants, shepherds, and fishermen; a mere spot in the landscape: "When [Icarus] is already swimming in the bay against the waxen waves, his first surprise is the three peasants' apathy toward his feat. One continues to dream in his ageless task of plowing. Another, surrounded by sheep, unleashes his laughter, his back to the new swimming labors of Icarus: The fisherman, also impassive, he knows that one doesn't fish for. . . earth monsters" (456/449). In commenting on the scene, the *Edición Crítica* (532n39) aptly quotes W. H. Auden's poem "Musée des Beaux Arts" with its evocation of Icarus's fall against the unbroken pace of surrounding interests and labors:

In Brueghel's *Icarus*, for instance: how everything turns away
Quite leisurely from the disaster; the ploughman may
Have heard the splash, the forsaken cry,
But for him it was not an important failure; the sun shone
As it had to on the white legs disappearing into the green
Water; and the expensive delicate ship that must have seen
Something amazing, a boy falling out of the sky,
had somewhere to get to and sailed calmly on.
(*Collected Poetry* 45)

However, the comic irony in Licario's sense of waste (as he imagines the boy rising from the plunge and swimming in the liquefied remains of the stuff that once glued his former wings) would not extend any further in Auden's text. Certainly not in carrying the issue of worldly indifference toward Icarus's disaster into what strikes Auden as being radically disjunctive in the passions of the aged and the young:

How, when the aged are reverently, passionately waiting
For the miraculous birth, there always must be
Children who did not specially want it to happen, skating
On a pond at the edge of the wood:
They never forgot
That even the dreadful martyrdom must run its course.
(*Collected Poetry* 45)

Seen in retrospect from the poem's concluding section on Brueghel, youthful boyish death in Icarus has no claim to martyrdom. The poem alludes to Christological expectations among the aged and a corresponding lack of them in children, who are closer in age to Jesus's miraculous birth, but too busy with themselves and their sports to care.

By contrast, Licario's last thoughts, right after his evocation of Icarus's death, hinge on his passionate remembrance of a phrase ("recalled with mysterious violence since childhood") about not being Oedipus: "*Davum, Davum, esse, non Oedipum* [*sic: Davos, Davos sum, non Oedipus*]" (*P* 457/449).[10] One may question on psychological grounds the possibility of carrying over such a learned recollection from childhood to creeping senescence, except as a reworked screen memory of the Oedipus complex it passionately endeavors to reject while knocking on Heaven's Door. But Licario's Icarian Icarus fate exceeds psychologies of the ordinary or non-magical sort. One must accept the miraculous truth and moral lesson that his association with Cemí's dead father and his uncle Alberto is aimed at instilling in the reader and in Licario's own mirrored conscience of plural character and subjectivity: that at the point of his dying, aged Icarus remains a *puer,* an unfading child swaddled in dreams of parental and sibling fusion and in denial of dissemination and truancy—such as when Oedipus runs the full course from exposure to death to the unknowing murder of his father and marriage to the woman who was not given the chance to mother him.

Next to or beneath the Catholic anti-Oedipus and Icarus subject position in open disavowal of father-murder and mother-incest lies Uncle Alberto's Orphic saga. We have seen how Alberto's maternal uncle figure functions as alternate fraternal soul mate of the Colonel, José Cemí's father. In addition, Alberto's alternate role brings him down into a sexual underworld inhabited by sodomites who are implicated in his death. Sodomite guilt in this case is as much circumstantial and associative as Alberto's dwelling among bad sexual company is marginal, circumstantial, and a source of his own guilt by association. For it only takes the mere bad company of "raffish" homosexual men to darken with ambiguity and to injure Alberto's otherwise untainted virility. The paragon for such a conception of uninjured manhood is the Colonel himself, the man Alberto shadows and darkens with his charismatic and risk-taking play among hustlers and prostitutes. Yet Alberto does not do this to the Colonel, who remains without stain. It is rather the Colonel's immense aura of transcendent manhood that creates in his foster brother the anamorphic homosexual figure of his own uninjured though prematurely expired life. Alberto's brilliant recklessness and death-wish habits are the reverse picture of the Colonel's bad luck and the twist-of-fate odds of his sudden illness and death. One expects men like Alberto to die in the prime of their lives and even to be gay and even queer in more ways than one, but one does not expect a paragon of virtue like the Colonel to bite the dust, away from battle, unless by the pagan rules that made Apollo (and Daedalus) kill someone out of sexual envy.

Part Three

# Planet Cuba Up in the Clouds

In a time long ago I lived in the style of Adam.
What changed matters?
The eternal misery in the act of remembering.
If you only knew how to put together again
All those combinations,
Giving me back the country without the water,
I would drink it all
And spit it back at heaven.

Virgilio Piñera, *La isla en peso*

# 9 Gargling the Tribe

The tribe paradigm in Lezama's writing involves fluctuations and clashes between terms of identity stasis and breakup, between ingrained *homeliness* and *unhomeliness,* between a pillared or foundational sense of singular national identity and its fall into alienation and dispersal. This latter radical shift in identity fate will involve the prime contrarian vision of tribal Cuba uttered in Virgilio Piñera's poem *La isla en peso* (The island's burden). The poem is a savage mural where the vagabond and wandering sense encased in the etymology of planet (from Greek "I wander about"—as opposed to the belief in the fixed nature of the stars) collides and colludes with the value of *tribe* as symbolic investment in the ever-threatened homogeneousness of group identity under curse of collapse and scattering.

In Piñera's poem the island of Cuba in female hybrid shape falls rotten from celestial Paradise dreams and sinks into the nightmares of her castaway people as they drown in the Purgatorial bathhouse waters of the festering Caribbean. The macrocosmic Fallen Island image culminates in the microcosmic suicide of Adam's automaton act: "The rotten mangoes at the river's bottom blind my reason,/and I climb up the highest tree and jump down like a fruit." In the end, the suicide-rotten island human fruit afloat in her own tidal stew will find further Babel projection—at the limit of this text—in the warped words and gargling noises of Joyce's tribal *Wake.*[1]

## Babel Babble

I ride no further than half an hour by bike in good traffic from the tomb visited by Mallarmé's imaging sight where he found a tribal agenda that would have awakened Poe's bones in convulsive laughter and mad dancing had they heard of it—and just in case you are not familiar with the phrase from "Le Tombeau d'Edgar Poe," it goes like this: "Donner un sens plus pur aux mots de la tribu" (To lend purest sense to the words of the tribe). Lezama Lima recognized in Mallarmé's claim "the identity of the tribal chief," as he defines the grasping of pure words in their pristine iridescence as the act of reaching for "perverse magic" in the attempt to repossess the world through "naive animism"—this is how Mallarmé would have confessed to his listeners and readers that the "sense and reason behind common words" had been lost and had to be "found anew in their tribal sense" (*OC* 2:262). In the same 1948 talk at the Pen Club in Havana, reference is made to the opening line of "Don du poème": "Je t'apporte l'enfant d'une nuit d'Idumée!" (I bring you the child [fruit] of an Edomite night), words for the first among the oldest tribes (besides the Edomites, Scythians, and Chichimecs) in the *eras imaginarias* imagined in writing by Lezama. In Edom, he wrote: "Man slumbers, time is erased, from his flank a tree begins to grow, a new creature sprouts from its branches" (*OC* 2:835). But nothing of Mallarmé's dark conception of a bloodied poem-child torn from the androgynous male poet's own flesh is mentioned by Lezama, yet the Edomite primal ground cannot lie too far from where "poetry must splice together and darn the space left open by the Fall" (*OC* 2:762). It is no easy task to mend the primal wound, since—and here Lezama's phrases become typically gnomic and intractable: "At first, poetic utterance rested against a door hinge [bisagra], or upon a sign post or marker that allowed it access to what lied masked [embozado] behind the door hinge. But once this point of rest and access is lost, the poem is condemned to its own confluences and exceptions; to its own isolation, pleadings, which out of its willful dominance it succeeds in establishing within time's realm."[2]

This is one among a good number of imagist—and inherently narrative—accounts of poetry and the force of *poesis* in Lezama's work. It becomes evident that for him explaining the notion of image turns into rehearsing his own answer image-upon-image in redundant and circling fashion in order to show image-making as the origin and destination of expressive knowledge. (As if visual reasoning could not be aptly explained except in prolific visual and narrative terms.)

The tribal component always latent in such imagist origins may be grasped in Virgilio Piñera's contrarian effort to wipe clean the slates with his own brand of purifying the words of the tribe by going against the grain of both ordinary speech and hermetic wording:

I stop at certain traditional words:
Rain, siesta, cane fields, tobacco,

With a simple gesture, a bit onomatopoeically,
I run like a titan over their music,
And say: water, noontime, sugar, smoke.
(*Isla* 36)

But if this purifies, makes palpable, processes, consumes, and absorbs, what do the next imagist combinations do?

I combine:
Rain hitting horses' loins,
Siesta being dragged by a horse's tail,
Cane fields swallowing horses,
Horses stealthily vanishing in gloomy tobacco emanations,
The last gesture of Siboney Indians while smoke flows
   Through forked pipes
Like death's path,
The last Siboney hint,
As I dig this earth in search of Idols to make myself
   A history.
(*Isla* 37)

A history of tribal doom is told as if eye-filtered just a hairline short of hallucination and well beyond any attempt to reason with raw visual impact. These lines from *La isla en peso* mark a crossing point between Mallarmé's birth poem—removed from the flesh of his own androgynous insomnia—and Lezama's own behind-closed-doors search for the image's birthing room. In such iconic instances the tribal sense proves inalienable from the rival fear of losing home rule to *unhomeliness*—to the uncanny or *unheimliche*. Whatever was behind that door hinge is now lost, but the *now* where or behind which it lodged resonates even now and dwells somewhere as well as everywhere else. The word-map charting access to such places cannot be traveled on horseback, bike, or boat, but perhaps only by walking backward upon every footstep ever taken inside one's head.

George Steiner visits a former and now condemned familiar dwelling for the lost place in question, where "Shakespeare's stance in language" remains "a calm tenancy, an *at-homeness* in a sphere of expressive, executive means whose roots, traditional strengths, tonalities, as yet unexploited riches [the poet would] recognize as a man's hand will recognize the struts and cornices, the worn places and the new in his father's house" (*After Babel* 176). This is a place lost within a place still to be found to which in fact we will return soon in Lezama's imagined home dwellings. But the old "*housedness*" (as Steiner puts it) in language that opened up *in-housedness* beyond textual matter was unframed by modernism. After Mallarmé, he writes, "Nearly all poetry which matters, and much of the prose that determines modernism, will move against the current of normal speech" (*After Babel* 177). Despite the exaggeration (there is a good deal of poetry that matters and means plainly and simply) Steiner is correct when he writes that "the poet no longer has or aspires to native tenure in the house of words. The languages waiting for him as an individual born into history, into society, into the expressive conventions of his particular culture and milieu, are no longer a natural skin. Established language is the enemy. The poet finds it sordid with lies. The ancient metaphors are inert and the numinous energies bone-dry. It is the writer's compelling task, as Mallarmé said of Poe, 'to purify the language of the tribe.' He will seek to resuscitate the magic of the word by dislocating traditional bonds of grammar and of ordered space" (178). What segregates Lezama from the condition just described—in spite of his large and largely unfathomed share in it—is the claim he makes to recover, repair, and render answerable primal meanings, even in his often hermetic management of words; meanings earned through the agency of divine Catholic grace. The mystery to which his own often mysterious enunciations and dense phrases respond has escaped God's hands and remains at large, fumbling and bouncing in space. This cosmic trajectory he tries to intercept by moving into the path of the image in what he calls *vivencia oblicua*—a phrase plainly rendered as *life lived awry.* (*Vivencia* is not a common word; it has a philosophically freighted origin in *Erlebnis:* the preconceptual or ineffable living in—as well as through—life experiences in all their specific phenomenal tenancy.)

In the visual thickness of his prose, Lezama narrates in short scenes the dialectics between what he labels *ethos* (character) and *poesis* (world-making through visual words). By *poesis* he means almost the opposite of what Socrates explains about it in Plato's *Republic;* in words that may have actually echoed in Mallarmé's choice of *tribe:* "Shall we, then, lay it down that all the poetic tribe, beginning with Homer, are imitators of images of excellence and of the other things that they 'create' and do not lay hold on truth, but, as we were just now saying, the painter will fashion himself knowing nothing of the cobbler's art, what appears to be a cobbler to him and likewise to those who know nothing but judge only by forms and color?" (Plato, *Collected Dialogues, Republic* 600e5). In Plato, transparency rules imitation in *mimesis* to the point that, as Alexander

Nehamas writes, "it almost seems as if he believes that the painter lifts the surface of the subject and transplants it onto the painting" (*Virtues of Authenticity* 262). This leads to the limiting instance of mimetic transparency proposed by Socrates to Cratylus. The passage resonates in Lezama's fondness for doubling and matching characters and situations in face-off as his own method of grasping the image in theatrical action. As Socrates puts it: "Let us suppose the existence of two objects: one of them shall be Cratylus, and the other the image of Cratylus, and we will suppose, further, that some god makes not only a representation such as a painter would make of your outward form and color, but also creates an inward organization like yours, having the same warmth and softness, and into this infuses motion, and soul, and mind, such as you have, and in a word copies all your qualities, and places them by you in another form. Would you say that this was Cratylus and the image of Cratylus, or that there were two Cratyluses?" (Plato, *Collected Dialogues, Cratylus* 432b–c). Hence, the extreme claim for transparency in *mimesis* is posed as a Socratic question of choice: "If one could make both things, both what is imitated and the image, do you think that anyone would abandon himself to the making of images and consider that as his most precious possession in life?" (*Cratylus* 599a6–b1). Thus, the products of Platonic *mimesis* are images of real things, as the practice of *mimesis* rests on the image of a real practice (see Nehamas, *Virtues* 264).

Lezama might not object to this seemingly minimal claim, but his image practice keeps its extravagant relationship with *mimesis* at great and warped distance from imitation in transparency. Let us look into one such warped image spot and work backward through the path that led to it. I have claimed that *divine grace of the Catholic sort informs the image* in Lezama's writings, and here we have it in a microfiction at the point where *ethos* and *poesis* intersect. Just as Judith walks on her way to killing Holofernes: "Grace directs her steps, the other's dream [Holofernes's] seems to await her in order to be disturbed, she has killed as if blown [soplada] into it, she has walked without touching the grass. Grace has decapitated nature and laid her to sleep. She [Judith] continues in grace when she shows the errant head, held in her hands while she drifts away benevolently in her dream" (*OC* 2:761). Grace dwells here in both the iconographic object of what is visualized (Judith's blessed state and cruel actions) and in one's ability or talent to grasp her in her image of grace. If we could only read in both directions at once (as re-reading aspires to accomplish), we would read (forward) how a crystal Brazilian lizard decapitates a dragon with its tail and (backward) how

Judith grace-infused killing of Holofernes issues from (and transfigures) Benvenuto Cellini's "hot" resolution to kill his enemies. Further narrative oscillations across the textual spot—where Judith kills in grace—would lead (back) to images of flatworms at the ocean shore adapting to tidal ebb-and-flow currents and (forth) to King Adrastus of Thebes learning the course of a river in conquered territory at the same time that his babe son (Opheltes-Archimorus) is killed by a poisonous river snake (hence the oracular warning: "If you decipher me at the river, I'll bite you in the snake"). There remains for us to fathom the workings of a curse: as in "the species of secret enmity between the course of a river and the theory of a serpent" (*OC* 2:763). But this provides the key to nowhere except into further inward image cogitation and storytelling, disguised as labyrinthine reasoning, perhaps leading back to those shore flatworms whose species name (*Convoluta roscoffensis*), though unmentioned by Lezama, seems to accurately label the twisting path of the image in his poetic quest for visualized truth through multiple associations.

Let us next consider the issue of evasion in Lezama's writings on the image. By evasion is meant one's inability as a reader to grasp and then chase after how exactly his writing has missed the mark on a subject he deems transcendent. Once the apparent error in judgment or omission is established, the issue turns into what to make of it and how to explain Lezama's knowledge and practice beyond such mistakes and lapses as not just mere instances of wrongful thinking. The ultimate issue at stake is whether at such moments his writing falls into fantastical brooding in a hall of mirrors.

For instance, a saying in the so-called parable of talents (Matt. 25.26) is quoted in chapter 3 of *Paradiso: "I reap where I sowed not, and I gather where I have not strewed"* (*P* 41/41). It happens to be the same saying quoted in the essay "La dignidad de la poesía" in order to illustrate the workings of *vivencia oblicua,* or life lived awry—a concept whose definition proves next to impossible to isolate in one or two sentences (unless *vivencia oblicua* should be explained not conceptually but only in narrative performance: as a string of analogies and imagist propositions in flight). But since in the gospel quotation the meaning of *vivencia oblicua* comes pointedly attached to "*I reap where I sowed not, and I gather where I have not strewed,*" it helps to know that the saying is directly attributed by Lezama to Matthew himself as a "tax collector" who is keen on "measuring conducts" and whose "approaches to behavior" could not be deemed the result of "candor"—even as he "engenders perplexing and indecipherable versicles" (*OC* 2:766). Yet foxy and perplexing Matthew is not the author of the phrase in the Gospel, as neither is Jesus Christ, who puts it in the mouth of the master who in the parable entrusts his three servants with different amounts of silver coins, according to their ability, before he leaves on a journey. Then, upon his return, each servant is asked to render accounts of what has been done with the talents given, which were invested by the first two diligent servants and accrued monetary value through usury. But not by the third, who buried his master's money and now tells him as an excuse that he knew him to be a hard man, "reaping where you did not sow, and gathering where you did not winnow" (Matt. 25.24). And then his master answers him by saying: "'You wicked and slothful servant! You knew that I reap where I have not sowed, and gather where I have not winnowed? Then you ought to have invested my money with the bankers, and at my coming I should have received what was my own with interest. So take the talent from him, and give it to him who has the ten talents. For to every one who has will more be given, and he will have abundance; but from him who has not, even what he has will be taken away. And cast the worthless servant into the outer darkness; there men will weep and gnash their teeth'" (Matthew 25.26–30). There is no room for doubt in either the words of the master or the parable's teaching on the rewards of faithfulness or the punishment for laziness or the testing of disciples as they await the return of the Lord. But if there is any doubt, one would expect to find it explained by Lezama when he claims that Matthew "engenders perplexing and indecipherable versicles." Yet what becomes truly perplexing is the verbal run given to Matthew's presumed perplexity in Lezama's words on how the saying (which he lifts from its gospel parable context) illustrates *vivencia oblicua*. For *to reap where one has not sowed or gather where one has not winnowed* is said to "express the breakup of any causality in conduct," from which—obscurely—the imperative, the command which builds its own gravity in the causality of exceptions, escapes and gains strength: "Un rompimiento de toda causalidad en la conducta, del que se escapa para adquirir relieve un imperativo, una ordenanza que fabrica su gravedad en la causalidad de las excepciones" (*OC* 2:766). Opaque verbiage obscures the meaning of *to split cause from effect and thus rely on exceptions* as the apparent moral or aesthetic principle obliquely sought.

Skipping further verbiage, we get to Napoleon's mastery of obliqueness as he fights huge battles on land (at Wagram) with naval tactics that had failed at Trafalgar. Such oblique tactics against common cause-and-effect causality by Napoleon may correspond to King Adrastus's learning about the river's course on conquered enemy soil at the same time that he is bitten by his accursed fate when his son is killed by the poison of a river snake. The central issue in *vivencia oblicua* concerns release from determinism and the iron rule of cause and effect. But Lezama's writing awry of strict determinism—and his drifting from imagined scenario to scenario—implies his inability or lack of will or desire to address the issue head on. Is, then, Lezama's illustration of *vivencia oblicua* itself a sign of moral evasion camouflaged in mimicry?

Later in the essay "La dignidad de la poesía" the passage from Matthew is revisited and a moral and theological conclusion drawn from "to every one who has will more be given, and he will have abundance; but from him who has not, even what he has will be taken away" (Matt. 25.29). The lesson drawn is that those who have and those who have not should not feel content with excess or scarcity or even the total leveling of their status ("nadie conténtese con el exceso ni con la poquedad, ni aun el total arrasamiento"). This happens because both those who have and those who have not can be guilty and could turn ("rotar") into their drowning ("total anegamiento") (*OC* 2:771). For "it is as tragic to want to be richer as to want to be poorer. There are the new rich and the new poor, a detestable swarm [enjambre de detestos]" (*OC* 2:771). A lesson is thus drawn at odds with the strict and punishable distinction made in Matthew between those who have and may have more and those who act as if they have nothing and are thus punished with having even less than zero. To affirm that both the rich who become richer and the poor who become poorer are equally blameful before God according to Christ's parable in Matthew 25.14–30 goes against what the master (as the parable's stand-in for the Lord) rules. If the servant who buries the silver money and does not put it to gain or to "give birth" (*tuvko*) through usury stands for the "poor" (or Lezama's "nuevo pobre"), the parable blames him all the same for his fearfulness and lack of proper faith in God. The issue lies in Lezama's not recognizing that his judgment of the parable is at odds with the parable's professed teaching.

Lezama's odd (and—besides sexual or erotic meanings—queer) understanding of the parable rests on what he calls "lo inexistente sustantivo" (*OC* 2:771), in which what is substantive and nonexisting is declared to be a Catholic belief: "For Catholics, what does not exist [lo inexistente] not only is endowed with gravitation [no sólo tiene una gravitación] but becomes a substance, an overcoming of the Greek and senses-bound world [mundo griego y sensorial]; the nonexisting substantive is the development, without metamorphosis, by means of faith [el desarrollo, sin metamorfosis, por la fe]" (*OC* 2:771). This affirmation of unique Catholic spirituality precedes the one about the new rich and the new poor as equally blameful before God. It runs against the parable of talents' unbending and unkind judgment of the servant who is unable to invest his master's (and the Lord's) gift in silver money and fails to earn a better place in the Kingdom of Heaven to come.

Lezama's understanding of the parable of talents raises the question about the role of money, which he has so oddly misunderstood. He has misunderstood it insofar as the judgment of the master rules out any equivalence between the two diligent servants who profitably did invest his wealth and the idle and timorous one who ruinously did not. In the parable, new rich and new poor are sharply segregated as people when it comes to their share in the Kingdom of Heaven. The difference in kind between servants lies in what they did with the hard currency gift, which the parable has no problem making symbolically equivalent to the Lord's sign for his coming Kingdom. John Ruskin, for instance, in *Unto This Last,* would have criticized the master's gift of money in line with his view of the medium of exchange as the mark—and tying bond—of indebtedness:

> The disputes which exist respecting the real nature of money arise more from the disputants examining its functions on different sides, than from any real dissent in their opinions. All money, properly so called, is an acknowledgment of debt; but as such, it may either be considered to represent the labour and property of the creditor, or the idleness and penury of the debtor. The intricacy of the question has been much increased by the (hitherto necessary) use of marketable commodities, such as gold, silver, salt, shells, etc., to give intrinsic value or security to currency; but the final and best definition of money is that it is a documentary promise ratified and guaranteed by the nation to give or find a certain quantity of labour on demand. A man's labour for a day is a better standard of value than a measure of any produce, because no produce ever maintains a consistent rate of productibility. (*Unto This Last* 185)

Ruskin has his moral sight fixed on true wealth versus false wealth and the moral principle that human beings are the true wealth of a nation. The poor represent people who owe money to the rich, while the wealthy are carriers of the guilt of growing richer at the expense of others. In this view, the master's provisory gift of money to his servants carries with it the poison of indebtedness, since, even if the two trustworthy and enterprising servants become newly rich, their wealth is bound to generate the "illth" of new poor people attached to them by onerous salaries.

Another implicit critical view of the parable is found in Marx's general view of exchange as alienating. As he does in "Excerpts from James Mill's *Elements of Political Economy*," Marx would implicitly regard the master in the parable as the *alien mediator* which his divine counterpart in God already represents. He would then run through a series of linked equivalencies that read like a quick prolegomenon to the parable of talents:

> Christ originally represents (1) man before God, (2) God for man and (3) man for man.
>
> In the same way *money* originally represents (1) private property for private property; (2) society for private property; (3) private property for society.
>
> But Christ is God *alienated* and *man* alienated. God continues to have value only in so far as he represents Christ; man continues to have value only in so far as he represents Christ. Likewise with money. (*Early Writings* 261)

In this famously influential view, the Master-God dyad has set off a mediating chain of infinite length shackling the servants to the abstract and inhuman order of exchange and the nexus between monetary instruments and private ownership.

From the different and respective angles of paternalist socialism and nascent materialist communism, Ruskin and Marx allow us to better grasp Lezama's notion of "lo inexistente" and its "gravitation," which he attributes to Catholic belief. For what Lezama regards as "nonexisting" *does* certainly exist in Ruskin's and Marx's concurrent—though hardly similar—views on money. The nonexisting does exist, yet not as the immaterial gravity or weight of divine grace and its gifts, but as the spiritual wealth that money further abstracts into alienating dependence on exchange (Marx) and then corrupts in binding those who are owed (the poor) to those who exploit them (the rich)—as if the rich were the ones who were owed what they in fact have taken (Ruskin). In his not un-Christian view of the parable, Ruskin would regard the master's gift-money as tainted with the blood of suffering and the shreds of torn honor in stolen wealth that should belong to his servants—salaried or unsalaried. In fact, the nonexisting weighty substance of Catholic investment in God's gift of grace as understood by Lezama operates as a form of currency. No wonder it allows for the new rich and the new poor to be on the same boat bound for Hell.

At this point the moral and theological argument in "La dignidad de la poesía" reaches a critical view of those versicles of gospel teachings it calls "privativos o negativos" as it judges them in terms of character and poetry or *ethos* and *poesis* (*OC* 2:771). The chosen example is lifted from these words by Jesus:

> "Ask, and it will be given you; seek and you will find; knock, and it will be opened to you. For every one who asks receives, and he who seeks finds, and to him who knocks it will be opened. Or if he asks for a fish, will give him a serpent? If you then, who are evil, know how to give good gifts to your children, how much more will your Father who is in heaven give good things to those who ask him! So whatever you wish that men would do to you, do so to them; for this is the law and the prophets." (Matt. 7.7–12)

Lezama claims that the more "negative" such gospel affirmations become the more "inverse gravitation" hangs upon them. Namely, those gospel sayings that negate a certain outcome (that a person should not expect serpents when asking or praying for fish) "arrive by way of negation at that which is possible, and by way of the possible to the gravitation of that which is nonexisting" (*OC* 2:772). This means that asking, praying for, or expecting fish is never guaranteed not to get serpent instead. Getting serpent instead of fish lies in the realm where *poesis* establishes the "gravitation of the possible through the play of analogies and images of resemblance between fish, arrow in liquid; arrow, serpent of the air" and where, in "harmonious fluidity," the asking for fish initiates the granting ("*otorgamiento*") of serpents. This is why, "in the great moments of Hegelian idealism, negativity was the support of the absolute" (*OC* 2:772). However, neither analogical nor imagist fluidity are involved in the gospel conception of prayer and proper reward between God and those who pray—nor between parents and the children who ask them for nurture and sustenance. The question then is why poetry in all its dignity should disturb the firm grounds of religious and moral expectation among the needful believers who ask for something and expect to get what they ask in return—instead of getting its resembling though negative equivalent. Unless gone mad, needful believers really want bread, not stones; fish, not serpents. And if poetry does not disturb the affirmative rules and expectations (fish) against negative counterparts (serpents) that mediate between God, parents, and their faithful dependents, what exactly does poetry as *poesis* do—or want? What is poetry doing in such company—in the dialogue between spiritual and material modes of subsistence? Is the poetic analogical hazard of evoking and actually getting serpents when saying fish a gratuitous or frivolous imagining when set side by side with the stark moral and religious bonds proclaimed in Matthew 7.7–12? Is serpent-for-fish a real threat fulfilled by an evil God or by devious parents, or is it the conjuring of magical effects by poetic fancy? Is the latent imagist trick or correspondence between fish and serpent a poetic cousin of surrealist (disruptive) or Freudian (therapeutic) awareness, or a demonic artifact, a cosmic joke, an oblique speculation gone awry?

These questions will find no answer in the slippery surfaces, fractious syntax, and allusive currents of the essay written to illuminate the dignity of poetry. Such evasiveness would not matter if the prose at the service of the endeavor did not make almost constant reference to questions of great moral and religious consequence and pretended to answer them with profuse sententiousness. But, as I have tried to demonstrate by looking at passages in which gospel sayings are addressed and judged by Lezama, illuminating the dignity of poetry involves him in dialogue with virtual imagistic or poetical writings bearing on human conduct that are at odds with plain Christian belief and intuitive reasoning. A poem version of the Gospel of Matthew and even an opera are quite imaginable, but the transport of the gospel teachings and doctrines into such expressive media would have to answer questions of accuracy or inaccuracy with a high potential for moral and theological controversy.

The hermeneutic embarrassment and *queering* caused by the Lezama essay comes from the unawareness it displays concerning what it does to the discursive contents it transports from image to image into virtual infinity (that *walking backward upon every footstep ever taken inside one's head* mentioned earlier). Infinity rather than eternity is the end sought and reached by default for lack of means to arrest the flow of words: words coming from "only a madman, only a poet" (uttered by a Venetian prince disguised as Nietzsche—as it is written at the end of the essay). And also words: "in the dialogue between a delusional patient [enajenado] and his therapist." As in: "Is it true that you will leave in a children's carriage? Yes, of course. And the carriage will be made of gold? I do not deny it. And the carriage will be drawn by forty million deer made of diamonds? Who would ever doubt it? 'Certainly, I do not deny it, whoever doubts it,' that the possible infinity of poetry begins to distill its gravity, its lead plumb, of the nonexisting" (*OC* 2:792). This is convoluted and turgid; yet not the part about the children's fairytale, but rather this: "que comienzan a destilar su gravedad, su plomada de inexistentes, el infinito posible de la poesía." The plural "comienzan" ("they begin") lacks proper subject: Who begins? Who begins to distill, like compressed substance, the leaden stuff or lead plumb made up of nonexisting entities? The dignity that the alienist might accord his mad patient may include trying to understand such phrases. However, the allusion to poetic madness at the end of the essay on the dignity of poetry does not refer to the actual mind of a madman; it emanates from loose and meandering thinking at odds with the norms of prose, if prose is to render clear what is difficult, rather than running its own zigzag course interwoven with hermetic phrases. The essay on the dignity of poetry does not render purer the idioms of the tribe. It reads as if a private language had assured itself of oracular authority over its readers; as if one language contained other languages capable of expressing ineffable truths above and beyond its own ordinary means.

# 10 Babel Hustle and Flow

IN HIS ESSAY "Our Homeland, the Text" George Steiner identifies the "Adamic circumstance" with "a state of linguistic tautology" deployed over "a lasting present." So, on such strangely pleasured by *nomos* or law-grounded homeland, "things were as Adam named and said them to be. Word and world were one"—and upon such grounds for stasis a peace of "perfect contentment" locks in: "there is no summons to remembrance" as time flattens out with no wrinkles and "the present tense of the verb is also that of the perfect tomorrow." But then comes "the Fall of Man" and human speech gains "its ambiguities, its necessary secrecies, its power (the counter-factuals, the 'if' constructions) to dissent speculatively from the opaque coercions of reality" (*No Passion Spent* 308). In this view, the *fallen* behavior of language in the long shadow of Babel will bring back the force, warp, and queerness of myth narratives in which the proliferation of different tongues accrues viral tones and energies.

So there was only one language before the mad hustle to build a getaway into heaven. The attempt to reach God's abode brought about His punishment in the scattering of peoples and tongues. Adam and Eve's language had only a *few words* and one *common speech*. As George Steiner reminds us, Adam's "vernacular not only enabled all men [and women] to understand one another, to communicate with perfect ease. It bodied forth, to a lesser or greater degree, the original Logos. . . . The vulgate of Eden contained, though perhaps in a muted key, a divine syntax—powers of statement and designation analogous to God's own diction, in which the mere naming of a thing was the necessary and sufficient cause of its leap into reality" (*After Babel* 58). The common speech replayed and echoed the naming exactness of creation. A sign of prolific bounty in post-Babel speech confusion evinces not only scattering linguistic diversity but the lost touch with pure beginnings. From aping the language of creation without knowing it, speakers of new languages would have added words and word effects to each of their tongues. An internal differentiation of linguistic and rhetorical means went along with the external multiplication of different languages. The egregious hustle that drove men to climb up to heaven as if wanting to storm it and spy on its inner lives and schemes re-created language as the incurably hustling medium it needed to be in running ahead of God's wrath.

In his dedication to write at the tomb of fellow tribesmen in the craft of poetry, Stephan Mallarmé writes upon the unquiet resting place of Charles Baudelaire in a sonnet of canonical density and allusiveness as showcase of his poetic art—quoted next untouched as the reverse picture of the Adamic lingual stasis imagined by George Steiner in his homeland retrospective of primal Utopia:

> Le temple enseveli divulgue par la bouche
> Sépulcrale d'égout bavant boue et rubis
> Abominablement quelque idole Anubis
> Tout le museau flambé comme un aboi farouche
> Ou que le gaz récent torde la mèche louche
> Essuyeuse on le sait des opprobres subis
> Il allume hagard un immortel pubis
> Dont le vol selon le réverbère découche
> Quel feuillage séché dans les cités sans soir
> Votif pourra bénir comme elle se rasseoir
> Contre le marbre vainement de Baudelaire
> Au voile qui la ceint absente avec frissons
> Celle son Ombre même un poison tutélaire
> Toujours à respirer si nous en périssons.
> (Mallarmé, *Collected Poems* 70)

One could pry open the poem translating it line by line into its French base homeland and other ordinary tongues: layering the verses, arresting and stuffing their flow with lines in foreign tongues and script, gargling and shuffling without scansion or punctuation Mallarmé's fourteen flowing verses. The resulting artifact (tower, tort, ziggurat) would illustrate the imagist poetics that we have examined in Lezama's "La dignidad de la poesía" and stand as a microcosmic image of Babel and its polemical afterglow.

This solid though ephemeral multilingual shape—a sort of wedding cake—would soon crumble as matter into dust while its pure sonorous echoes in broken tongues made up with particles of the whole ensemble would somehow linger forever in the air in the wake of the Babel catastrophe it commemorates. (In this monstrous, scrambled, scrabbled, gargling shape, the monument sonnet would stand at the tomb of Eugenio Foción and his tutelary sodomite alter ego and anal god Anubis in Lezama's Hotel Paradiso.)

Let us now briefly entertain a film fantasy about Babel itself. The movie in question would be a Planet Hollywood–type production starring three scientists, two men and a woman, from different places on earth speaking English in place of their native languages. They have undertaken a voyage through time to the construction site of the Tower of Babel, but avoiding contact with the builders and workmen at the ziggurat. For some unexplained reason, they have chosen to arrive late, after the pyramid beehive structure has been abandoned. Perhaps their technological capabilities made it impossible for them to reach the actual site. So the threesome has chosen instead to access Babel by entering the space of Peter Brueghel's "Little" *Tower of Babel,* a 1563 painting hanging at the Museum Boijmans-van-Beuningen in Rotterdam (figure 3). This they have achieved after translating the painting into holographic layers of alternate worlds and epochs using *Matrix*-like gizmos. Upon reaching the tower, once inside the painting, the plan is to capture and record the echoes left behind by the builders before they fled. The idea is to contact, audit, and record what was being spoken at the site just before bedlam ensued once everyone ceased to understand everyone else, except, perhaps, those who belonged to the same craft or construction guild.[1]

The scientists know full well how difficult—perhaps impossible—it would be for them to break down and separate the scrambled sound layers before reaching bedrock in the layer or wave band spoken and understood by everyone who was laboring at Babel. After considerable suspense, digging through the echoing rubble of panicked utterances from the multilingual mob as it scattered in all directions, the woman in the group freezes in awe. Being the only one of the three with a literary education—as it happens, in French symbolist poetry—she thinks she hears as if through a gale of babbling noises the fourteen lines of "Le tombeau de Charles Baudelaire." This she is certain to have heard before all hell broke loose with a roar so mighty it made them all lose consciousness. (We may drop the fantasy at this point, avoiding perhaps an action film in which a rogue gang of deserters from some of the scattering groups—including some women they have managed to kidnap on their way—storms back into the tower.)

Figure 3. Peter Brueghel, *The Tower of Babel.* Museum Boijmans-van-Beuningen, Rotterdam.

The voices of women at the Tower of Babel building site is a nonissue within the short narrative compass of Genesis 11. Nor is gender at stake in the confusion of tongues engendered by man's pride in trying to reach heaven. However, women lie at the heart of the speculations that Claude Lévi-Strauss dedicates to Babel at the end of *Les structures élémentaires de la parenté,* speculations that would become highly polemical when *The Elementary Structures of Kinship* was published in the USA in 1969 at the height of the anthropologist's transoceanic fame. At issue here are not the points of controversy concerning the exchange or "traffic" in women—whether in Gayle Rubin's classic "The Traffic in Women: Notes on the Political Economy of Sex" (1975) or Hélène Cixous and Catherine Clément's *Le jeune née* (1975).[2]

Of utmost interest is how Lévi-Strauss construed language before Babel. With no God punishment in sight, at first, "the very nature of the linguistic symbol prevented it from remaining for long in the stage which was ended by Babel, when words were still the essential property of each particular group: values as much as signs were jealously preserved [précieusement conservés], reflectively uttered [prononcés à bon escient], and exchanged for other words [echangés contre d'autre mots] the meaning of which, once revealed, would bind the stranger, as one put oneself in his power by initiating him [le sens dévoilé lierait l'étranger, comme on se liait soi-même en l'initiant]" (*Elementary Structures* 496). What would follow Babel in language behavior was exchange as such, without the loaded reciprocity that had existed before, when everyone spoke the same tongue, but could not, nevertheless, belong to one and the same group or tribe. A common language did not prevent mutual strangers from crossing each other's path in need to transact, to trade words with the caution with which one might or ought to exchange gifts on such occasions. It is obvious that Lévi-Strauss does not wish to segregate talk among strangers before Babel from their mutual need to exchange as communicants by offering and accepting values other than words. (Though words, it is clear, were traded with all the care and caution with which one would trade values such as those involved in matrimonial exchanges.)

It seems that the uniform language before Babel did not eliminate the need to communicate and to transact between mutual strangeness among different social groups. On the contrary, it seems to have made speech as valued and loaded with promise or threat as when talk with a distant neighbor from across the valley would not seem just idle—or would not put on hold as if forever its own value to instill, buoy up, and compound further social value. The language intercourse before Babel, so speculated, is not alien to the hermetic—and hermeneutic—textures and deep imagist pools encountered across the fourteen seamless and *reflexively uttered* and yet *exchanged* (but forever singularly embroiled in their own verbal and image plot) in Mallarmé's Baudelaire sonnet. But, is this how the words of the tribe are purified? (Purified: as words had no need of being rubbed and burnished shining-clean before Babel.) The pregnancy of speech acts before Babel flowing from Lévi-Strauss's moral imagination proves as burdened with latent meaning as Mallarmé's retelling of Baudelaire's hard-core poetic ethos.

So our woman scientist from the film might have heard what she took to be, as it sounded in her ears, precisely Mallarmé's fourteen-line planetary word trip into infinity. Or she might have misheard it in the pre-Babel idioms that she searched for and was perhaps better trained to hear than her fellow time travelers, who were unfamiliar with poetry at its thickest imagist best.

In choosing the woman as the sole audience of either the sonnet or its pre-Babel correspondent speech sequence, I have reflected the role of women in exchange placed by Lévi-Strauss at the heart of his view on how symbolic trade in words and marriage alliances remained tied together before linguistic diffusion and after. I have also in mind the same issue in chapter 3 of *Paradiso:* the odd exogamous moment in the novel in combination with a crisis in marriage alliance and relationships among neighboring strangers outside Cuba.

## The Tribe Abroad

With unaccustomed southern unkindness, Roy Blount Jr. compares Havana to "an abandoned wedding cake that ants have moved into" (*Long Time Leaving* 265). Since distrust laced with disdain for Americans from northern Florida dominates the attitude of some Cuban immigrants, or criollos, living abroad in chapter 3 of Lezama's *Paradiso,* the tourist put-down witticism by an American southern humorist proves handy in framing the issue of cultural *schismogenesis* in reference to that chapter.

The big word (*schismogenesis*) means *coming about through splitting;* it was coined by Gregory Bateson and defined as "a process of differentiation in the norms of individual behaviour resulting from cumulative interaction between individuals" (*Naven* 175). There are two kinds of differentiation in schismogenesis. First, in the *complementary* case, an assertive person habitually interacts with a submissive one, whose adaptive submission to dominant assertion develops over time into a settled condition of interaction between the two individuals or their complementary groups. Second, in the *symmetrical* case, a standoff occurs leading to escalation, as when if "we find boasting as the cultural pattern of behaviour in one group, and the other group replies to this with boasting, a competitive situation may develop in which boasting leads to more boasting, and so on" (*Naven,* 177). Although boasting is not the only kind of symmetrical schismogenesis, it suits the situation we are about to examine, in which Cuban immigrants in Florida (mainly represented by the Andrés Olaya family) engage in play-and-counterplay interaction with the family of Dr. Frederick Squabs, a church organist native of North Carolina.

The sustained squabble between the Olaya and Squabs families avoids confrontation and remains latent and hidden, but it nevertheless ends in death. Besides differences in manners and social protocol, criollo Cubans and Floridians are divided by a deeper split in religious worldviews between Catholics and Protestants. These two antagonistic religious worldviews and cultural norms are described in Cintio Vitier's comments in the *Edición Crítica* of *Paradiso* (comments written in tacit agreement with the Cuban-Catholic side). At stake are "the Catholic and Calvinist Protestant conceptions of the will." So, on one side stands the Catholic, exemplified by "the act that gives itself up to the unforeseeable and trusts it as it trusts mercifulness," while on the other stands the Calvinist Protestant, based on "isolated stubbornness" and bound to "egotistical and pragmatic" faith (*EC* 651). National origins and religious faiths leave no room for negotiation. According to Vitier, definitive lines of contrast are drawn between "Anglo-Saxon Puritanism and a special kind of criollo refinement of Hispanic Catholic roots, proposed by Lezama as his own family wisdom and core element of his personal or life ethics."[3]

The contrast and confrontation between the Cuban criollo Catholic family headed by José Cemí's Olaya maternal grandfather and the American southern family headed by Dr. Squabs will end in two dismal events: the either accidental or preordained death by fall of the adolescent Olaya son and the subsequent elopement and disappearance of the Squabses' twelve-year-old daughter. The text of *Paradiso* makes it seem as if the two outcomes were tied together and as if Dr. Squabs's actions had caused the death of the Olaya senior son—as well as the loss of his daughter and his own sanity.

## Jesus and Money

The double catastrophe affects the Olaya family while living in Jacksonville, Florida, in the 1890s, where they await Cuba's liberation by war from Spanish colonial rule. At the opening of chapter 3, the girl Rialta (José Cemí's future mother) is seen perched on a branch reaching out for the "music" of "the bayberry stirring invisibly within the pod" (*P* 38/39). Although the girl of ten is reaching after the fruit to eat it, the ornate way in which her act of perilous overreach is rendered suggests that it is beauty itself that Rialta wants without knowing how or why, acting in "near somnambulism in the inscrutable vegetative gaze of her ten years" (*P* 38/39). Rialta is caught in the act by Florita, Mrs. Squabs, who admonishes: "*Rialta, don't steal the nuts*" (one of two phrases—together with "*Do you want to play the organ, Mr. Albert?*"—that the Olayas mimic in order to make fun of the Squabses' rigid officiousness).

Another phrase comes into play at a higher and more serious level of contact between the families: "*I reaped where I sowed not, and I gather where I have not strewed*" (*P* 41/41). The gospel phrase comes about quoted by Rialta's mother (Doña Augusta) in order to score a point against Florita's Protestant fatalism, by which the Squabs mother justifies herself for wanting only to prevent the theft of the nuts instead of the death by fall of the girl. For Florita believes that it is useless to exert her will against a deadly outcome (falling from a tree) already predestined to occur. Doña Augusta's words coincide with her imagining the silhouette of "Mr. Squabs's elongated hand [falling] across an organ pipe, or the same hand, reduced in size, caressing the black covers of a Bible" (*P* 40/41). But the mood of tongue-in-cheek melodrama surrounding Squabs's shadow silhouette does not distract from the issue at hand, laboriously worded in Florita's "improvised theology," echoing Calvin's "bony arbitrariness," as he tried to persuade King Francis I of France to convert himself and his whole kingdom over to the new Protestant faith: "And she [Florita] went on like that, in her foggy improvised theology, opposing destiny and will with the same bony arbitrariness with which Calvin wanted to unite rebellion and the dedication of his main work to his prince and sovereign lord" (*P* 41/41).

But Doña Augusta would have none of it. Shortened, her sly rebuttal to Florita comes to this: Calvinists put too much faith in their will ("*Your will*"); they put too much weight on choosing between god and evil, but choose, nevertheless, in order to reveal themselves as chosen only when proof of election comes in the form of material wealth. Therefore, if the reward for proving oneself chosen is such as being worldly successful, one would only sing praises for salvation to the sound of money: "We would only have that allegro cantabile of a counting house" (*P* 41/41). Doña Augusta supports her charge of Calvinist economic self-interest (linked to the Protestant belief in predestination as opposed to free will) upon the saying about money in the parable of talents from Matthew 25.26. Taking the gospel point as self-evident, she concludes by pitying the gloomy fate of Protestants, who are always waiting for something to happen in conjunction with their own will, and thus become "errant in relation to actions and good works," and as a result become "bleak," as opposed to a Catholic, "who knows that his action must flow along a certain path and that its twists and turns will be a wonderment and a mystery to him" (*P* 41/42). Bottom line: Protestants are out of touch with mystery. Having taken away the freedom of the will from human worldly affairs, Protestants are blind to the marvels of chance and sheer contingency—and thus out of tune with angelic sympathy. It should then be true that it pleases the angels and increases their watchful singing when, as Doña Augusta puts it, "a child reaches out across a branch to hear the amusing roll of those little spheres through the mystery of their pods" (41/42). Doña Augusta's words (and the author's) fulfill the grace and beauty suspended upon her daughter's leaning and reaching for the fruit in microcosmic concordance with the higher spheres of the stars reflected in the magical shells and the fruit within. Nothing can improve upon such visionary portrait of Adam's fall overcome and overturned in the gesture of a child. Rialta's gesture of overreach after the fruit upon the branch evokes the doctrine of *felix culpa:* blessed fault or fortunate fall, the notion that original sin and human suffering are linked to Christ's redemption and a greater good.

But what all this may have to do with the stern teaching of Jesus' parable of talents (and with the master's punishment of the idle servant who has uttered the words quoted by Doña Augusta in order to excuse himself) is quite another matter. That is to say: Jesus rejects from the kingdom of God the servant who did not invest the talents given to him by his master and who was thus punished for his lack of monetary speculation. The phrase so admired by Doña Augusta (and celebrated as "magical" and "Catholic" by Cintio Vitier in apparent agreement with Lezama's authorial intent) represents a piece of servant or subaltern lying, a twisting of the teachings of Jesus.

We should further ponder, not Augusta's inspired attempt at queering the saying in Matthew, by infusing magical intent into it, but what her author, José Lezama Lima, in whose dominant voice she distinctly speaks, may have in mind about wealth, money, and poverty in Christian scripture. After all, a strong Catholic reading of the parable of talents might rest upon blaming (not praising, as does Doña Augusta) the idle and faithless servant for surrendering his will to his master's prior script and predestined will to have his way with profit and increased wealth. In this other possible Catholic view, something good results from the master and lord whose money worth increases in the hands of his other two enterprising servants, whose fortunes improve as the result of their willingness to invest the talents that he lent them—all of it against a sense of preordained determinism, similar to the Calvinist theological bend rejected by Catholic Doña Augusta.

But such a pointed Catholic emphasis on actions and deeds, against Protestant bleak resignation to predestined fate, could also turn into a Calvinist argument. For Doña Augusta and the author who speaks through her regard as bleak and apparently defeatist a keystone feature of Calvinism, which in A. D. Nuttall's instructive words represents "one of the great puzzles of history," the question of "why a theology which taught that no one ever got to heaven by the exertion of his own virtue should have produced not a population of passive libertines but rather the most morally strenuous society the world has ever seen, that of seventeenth-century Puritanism" (*Alternate Trinity* 33). Rather than any passive inclination to libertine abandon, what Doña Augusta deplores in Mr. Calvinist Squabs and his wife is their joyless moral strenuousness.

Gloomy and eventually maddened, Dr. Squabs represents the automaton image of Puritan officiousness driven to church micromanagement and status hyperconsciousness and to the proper celebration of his daughter's birthday, the preparation for which causes the death of the Olaya family's youngest son. Could it be that behind Squabs's wretched defeat and the baneful consequences of his egotistic preparations for the birthday party looms the opposite Calvinist consequence, the triumph of capitalism (in Max Weber's theory) in alliance with the Protestant worldview born of the Reformation and best represented by Calvin's doctrine of election? It is not a facile exaggeration to claim in regards the parable of talents that the least Calvinist thing to do is to do nothing at all—and to excuse oneself, as the do-nothing servant does, by crafting a catchy and wily excuse (mysterious too) that goes: *I reaped where I sowed not, and I gather where I have not strewed,* as if it were the master's own brand signature. It is neither facile nor exaggerated, since the death by fall of the Olayas' youngest son is presaged by Doña Augusta herself when she fears that a gospel curse could bring down her husband.

In debating whether he should allow his son Andresito to play the violin at the fair organized by the Cubans, Andrés Olaya Sr. tells his wife that he has been reading the medieval German mystics in order to counteract Squabs's gloomy theology, and he then mimics the "symbolic expression of the organist" by saying something in Squabs's intonation and manner, but something that the organist himself would never have said in actual content: "'an image [says Andrés senior] on horseback slashing through the forest of the foe, carrying every "I" off his battlemented castle and penetrating it like the spark that prepares and illuminates the instant needed for the circles to touch. Let him go,' asking Doña Augusta for her consent" (*P* 57/58). A mimic voice parody and a satire of what Squabs would never have imagined saying leads to Andrés Olaya Sr.'s asking his wife for permission for his son to perform at the party. Doña Augusta will then tell a friend that when her husband gave his consent (she does not mention her own), he acted influenced by his own after-dinner conversations with Squabs, and that, "'even though he makes fun of the organist, all people who are made fun of, out of some kind of evangelical vengeance, have a decisive and terrible influence on the people who make fun of them'" (*P* 58/58). Superstitious or not, specifically Catholic or just an emanation of criollo Cuban wisdom, her apprehension will come to pass. That is to say, the chapter is scripted to show—as would a morality play—that the officious and dull Calvinist Dr. Squabs occasions the death of the Olaya son as well as his own calamity. In addition, whatever a gospel curse might actually be (according to Doña Augusta's pregnant foreboding), the doomed Squabs plot to fastidiously arrange for his own and everyone else's affairs exudes an aura of pathetic diabolism. One may ask: is then the defeatist Devil in Dr. Squabs a cloned Protestant of the Calvinist sort?

## The Devil's Party

Whether it should be God or the Devil that lies in the detail depends on who is talking to whom. Let's then carry through with the devilish or godly issue of justified or unjustified suffering and compensatory justice in the third chapter of *Paradiso*. Due to his insistence on calling Carlitos the carpenter away from his work in the construction of the elevator at the fair organized by the Cubans, Squabs becomes implicated in the faulty building of the railing that Andresito leans on and breaks as he falls to his death. Squabs's insistence on taking the carpenter away provides *cause* and *occasion* for the accident to unfold. The carpenter is the same young man who three years later, at age twenty-one, will run away and disappear with Squabs's daughter, still a minor. The question of ruined exogamy is raised as the Olayas lose a son and potential future husband and father, while the Squabses will lose the girl whose birthday caused her father to take away from the Cuban party the carpenter who will in the near future steal his pubescent daughter and destitute her as a decent Christian bride.

The question raised by the chapter's focus on free will versus predestination (and on the graceless and fatalistic view of human frailness espoused by Calvinists, as opposed to the Catholic openness to the illusions of magical agency) is whether the Squabs family's suffering is justified or unjustified. In their case, having brought about their own disgrace, their suffering is portrayed as justified—or well deserved. In Mr. Squabs's punctilious management of detail and his wife's display of submission to the predestined will of *their* God, the Calvinist family has been instrumental in its own fall into disgrace after having caused the death of the Olayas' youngest son. For their part, the Olaya Catholics remain blameless in their unjustified suffering—but not entirely. And here is where the notion of *schismogenesis* or *coming about through splitting* may prove useful. But proof of its usefulness requires a glance at the victim's father's youth, at Andrés Olaya Sr.'s origins in Cuban subaltern status anxiety.

The scenario in chapter 3 that precedes the family's tragedy abroad depicts the youth and apprenticeship of Andrés Olaya Sr. and his adoption by the Michelena family after his father dies. Elpidio Michelena (for whom Andrés works as business secretary) is a millionaire whose wealth in colonial days is said to have come from land and railroad investments. While dining at the Michelenas' farm, Andrés finds himself fooled by the Chinese servant who would not let him help himself with food before taking away each tray. Andrés asserts his rights of hospitality and rank by confronting the kitchen staff in a scene of grotesque comedy. He learns that the kitchen staff wants him to eat with them instead of their masters. Since the episode and the subsequent orgiastic night revelry at the farm occur in the 1860s in Matanzas province—which at the time was densely peopled with slaves tied to plantations—the servants' mock uprising against the young employee dinner guest raises the question of where the slaves or other blacks might be. Yet, even if not visibly or physically present at the farm, blacks show up at the site in the cult of Oschun, the orisha of fertility and seduction associated with the Vírgen de la Caridad del Cobre, who would soon be worshipped by the *mambises,* as the men who fought in Cuba's first war of independence that started in 1868 were called. Right after Andrés proves courageous in beating back and taming the kitchen servants, and as he explains the incident to his hosts, the childless Michelena couple asks him to pray with them, begging the Vírgen for children. Two kinds of increase result from the prayers: Andrés is adopted by the couple and is helped by the wealthy entrepreneur to profit in financial deals, and Michelena's wife gives birth to twins. (Although Oschun is not mentioned, the bountiful answer to the prayers gives proof of orisha power besides the Virgin's.) Thus, in the same chapter in which the loss of his son Andresito holds center stage, the young Andrés senior takes part in a successful twofold fertility act that results in two births for his boss and greater financial profits for himself.

Moreover, if we assumed that words invested in chaotic verbal and image display would yield money, or were themselves tokens of fiduciary thrust and potential value, the section in the third chapter about the orgiastic séance at the Michelena farm would amount to a magical cornucopia gained through a combined sexual and verbal orgy. In the scenes in Jacksonville, words find pointed investment in theological polemical exchanges and in mock phrases used among the Olaya brood for their own private jokes. By contrast, in the scene at Michelena's farm, words run amok and seem caught in a magical business in which what is staged or performed proves impossible to reduce to fixed mimetic meaning. An entire section more than five pages long (during the night of the dinner and later on) reads as if a mock epic battle involving servants and kitchen hands and cooks had joined an orgy in which a fat woman (probably Michelena's mistress) sings arias as she herself (and the Isolde who emanates from her singing and turns into a manatee) are attacked by a host of night birds called "las Nictímines," who act as a choreography of praying avian lesbians. It seems as if the millionaire's wealth is being shown off and scattered and wasted, and yet the expense in words and images—in its profligate expenditure of imagist energies and slippery meanings—signifies and issues its own counterfeit value. Words and images circulate as valuable only unto themselves and for themselves, as a private currency, and hence as a medium in which exchange as well as magical values are disowned through sheer excess and waste. The work of magic needs to be recognized in the affair because the prayers to La Caridad del Cobre—and to Oschun by default—have proven efficacious—either through comic irony or earnest intent. Therefore, the invisible presence of black popular and subaltern religion proves as contingent and efficacious to the fertile genetic outcome of twin-birth as magic itself proves affective within Catholic belief adapted to a Virgin cult whose powers are inalienable from the efficacy of miraculous agency.

Thus, a bottom line question: which one proves of greater efficacy, popular subaltern investment in higher Catholic sacramental magic or Catholic ecumenical faith in Yoruba magical means to gain wealth? Answer: Catholic and Yoruba are jointly and deeply invested in cultural capital under the averted blessing eyes of Rome and in subaltern tropical displacement to Cuba—as remembered in Cuban exile from Florida.

## Hegelian Numismatics: Heads, Thersites; Tails, Tiresias

Perhaps one way to enter the word-and-image maelstrom of the magical séance is to observe the pose struck by Thersites, the bad-mouthing Greek warrior in *The Iliad,* who appears visually quoted in arrest as the cook recoils under threat by the furious Andrés: "Manuel, arching his right arm like Thersites' shield, tried to protect himself with shameful postures" (*P* 47/47). This mimicked appearance by Thersites takes us back to his fuller presence in Lezama's 1961 essay on Ramón Meza's 1887 *Mi tío el empleado* (My Uncle the Employee), a novel of hustle and picaresque survival among immigrants from Spain in Havana, which Lezama surveys in terms of "tersitismo y claro enigma" (*OC* 2:1109–17).

But, what is *Thersitism?* The term was coined and rendered problematic by Hegel in the introduction to *The Philosophy of History* as he discussed the role of "World-Historical-Individuals" such as Julius Caesar. According to Hegel, these great men are observed by the "psychologists" who want to take them apart by scrutinizing their mundane needs. And he adds that even men of Caesar's stature must eat and drink and fall prey to sudden impulses and mood swings. Hegel quotes a proverb to the effect that "No man is a hero to his *valet-de-chambre,*" but he adds that it is "not because the former is no hero, but because the latter is a valet" (*Philosophy* 32). The valet servant stands for the psychologist who figures out the great man he grooms and cares for while failing to take on his greatness. Thersites fits in Hegel's mind the type of servile psychic reader of great characters. But in defining the nonheroic bad-mouthing Homeric warrior, Hegel turns the screw of the dialectic one notch: "His envy [Thersites'], his egoism, is the thorn which he has to carry in his flesh; and the undying worm that gnaws him is the tormenting consideration that his excellent views and vituperations remain absolutely without result in the world. But our satisfaction at the fate of Thersitism also, may have its sinister side" (32). One thing worries Hegel: that there might be wisdom in Thersites' willingness to take a pounding from the likes of Odysseus and to keep spitting foul words at the nonheroic face of the Trojan War effort. Hegel worries that in having fun at the expense of the old bastard's twisted ugliness, we might be laughing at our own ignorance of what it was he really bad-mouthed.

Enter Lezama, who obviously knew Hegel's text and coinage of "Thersitism"—most probably through direct reading. In typical fashion, having read Meza's published doctoral dissertation on Homer's poems, Lezama expands the single commonplace reference to Thersites in the thesis into a full-blown portrait. But—alas, *felix culpa!*—in the process he mistakes Thersites for Tiresias, the blind seer in Homer's *Odyssey* and Sophocles' Theban trilogy. But, beyond mere confusion, the mythical value of each figure increases. Lezama compounds the bad-mouthing warrior figure into the figure of what he calls "a man-woman-man," further compounded and mirrored in one of the characters from *Mi tío el empleado,* a count who behaves like an effeminate queer: "Coveo the count, bald, fatty, loud, a Thersites, a man-woman-man" (*OC* 2:1111). Here is schismogenesis with a vengeance. Thersites (a character who lives and dies by scurrilous boasting in fierce and escalating exchanges) splits up and becomes a character, Tiresias, whose clairvoyant blindness lies beyond reproach or error, but who also, in his interview with Oedipus, engages in the counterpoint revelation of the fatal truth to a hero whose servant or subaltern he is not, but whose slave he might have been: thus, Oedipus-stuck-on-Tiresias, a two-faced nonhero whose tragic fate and split life would again serve as emblem of schismogenesis—of birth through partition.

The Homeric Thersites in Meza's doctoral thesis is taken by Lezama into Shakespeare's *Troilus and Cressida,* which he sees as "the other face of Romeo and Juliette. On the reverse face one finds infidelity, sensuality, treason by the lovers, and the intervention of Thersites the wizard [hechicero]" (*OC* 2:1109). The slip-and-slide from one character to the other starts here, in seeing Thersites as a wizard or charmer, as he is never found in either Homer or Shakespeare. All the characters in Meza's novel are seen by Lezama "running in circles" around Thersites, whose deeds are listed but transformed into those of the blind soothsayer Tiresias: "Thersites, the one who unites and separates the serpents, who offers a cynical declaration to Juno in her polemics with Jupiter, who goes blind punished by Juno, who acquires the gift of prophecy from Jupiter, in order to be saved from Juno's punishment" (*OC* 2:1110). But it is of course Tiresias who twice sees two snakes mating—the first time he is turned into a woman and the second time back into a man—and who as a result is able to tell Zeus and Hera that women enjoy sex much more than men do, and in consequence, the angered Hera blinds him and Zeus compensates him with soothsaying gifts. (Perhaps Tiresias's answer about women's greater pleasure in sex is called "cynical" by Lezama because he regards the old seer himself as queer.)

The Thersites slip and resulting split into the compound figure of a foulmouthed warrior and the blind seer for whom T. S. Eliot in *The Waste Land* would coin a verb compounding suffering with foreseeing ("And I Tiresias have foresuffered all") defines two species of anxious social relationships in *Paradiso*'s third chapter. Thersites is found in the kitchen by the young Andrés Olaya in abject posturing as the result of the servants' and cook's plot to bring the guest employee down to their own lowly social rank. The comic episode of status warfare serves as overture to Olaya's promotion from secretary to adoptive son. The origins of the word *family* in *famulus* is thus etched in Olaya's character as he rises in rank above not only the servant crew but his own salaried status and gains access to economic prosperity among proprietors and investors with the help of his boss and adoptive father. (This happens to someone who was already the adopted orphan of his own extended family.)

The first aspect of social anxiety related to Thersites is solved in a manner favorable to Olaya. But the full view of the affair is not obtained unless the Hegelian comedy of Thersitism is appraised in the essay on *Mi tío el empleado*. In the novel, the hustling world of clerks and immigrant upstarts and the urban picaresque in 1890s Havana is given iconographic stamp in a compound figure whose focal attributes cut across sexes. Thersites becomes Tiresias as a travesty figure of grotesque and extravagant effeminacy in whom wealth, influence, frivolity, need, social climbing, and hustle converge and crystallize in motley garb and outright drag. Lezama's version of Thersitism originates in Hegel's *valet-de-chambre* scene between the servant's nonheroic consciousness and the master's heroic and apparent immunity to the corrosive worm of bedroom surveillance by subaltern characters only capable of lowbrow political wit. Differences between Lezama's Thersites-Tiresias double character and Hegel's Caesar and his garrulous servant are emboldened by twists in sexual condition and cross-dressing. By becoming Tiresias in addition to Thersites, the man who dresses Caesar in Hegel ends up cross-dressing Thersitism itself in Lezama. Specific anxieties concerning social rank in the kitchen actions of Thersites the cook are compounded by Thersitism's wanton release of the same kind of anxieties in gestures and actions through which sexual social decorum is now subjected to satire in his new double identity as Tiresias.

The present social world in Jacksonville shows the attenuated energies of Thersitism, but certainly in nothing like the burlesque mimics in Michelena's Bakhtin-worthy kitchen or the pandering hustle in the urban underworld of Meza's *Mi tío el empleado*. Yet the affirmation of Catholic status prestige that Doña Augusta directs at Mrs. Squabs proves satirically quite fierce. As when she shows off the slippers inherited from her uncle the canon and asks the Squabs daughter what she thinks the wearer's mouth looked like, and the girl answers, "Small and very red," and the answer is praised as a miracle of perceptiveness, possible only within a sphere of contingent and open responsiveness to chance—as distinctly allowed by Catholicism in its dispensation of grace through free will. But condescending praise is soon followed by put-down. It comes in the resentful afterglow of Doña Augusta's words, as the Squabs mother and daughter leave the house and the mother's imagination is seen as "a cross between a Pekingese and a chow," ready "to chew the canon's slippers thoroughly" (*P* 42/42). The satirical implication seems clear: Protestant uncomprehending dumbness toward the dressed-up marvels of Catholic ritual enacts a lapdog foot-biting social protest against a World religious view (the Roman) whose grandeur it cannot otherwise grasp.

## Grace, Disgrace, and Cultural Capital

We asked earlier whether the Catholic Olaya family was entirely blameless in its unjustified suffering for their son's death as opposed to the Squabs family's justified and blameful suffering for the loss of their daughter and the madness of her father. That is to say: blameful due to the Olaya father-driven guilt in having caused the son's otherwise accidental death as a mongrel version of the fall of Icarus. Let us recall that chapter 3 tells the story of the son's fall not as an accident but as caused by Dr. Squabs's actions in taking the carpenter away before he could finish his job with the wooden railing. But the nonaccidental cause of death is anticipated (and contradicted) by Doña Augusta's fear that her husband's mockery of Dr. Squabs's voice and mannerisms could bring upon him evangelical retribution. But in order for a revenge curse (such as the one she dreads) to work, it must be provoked or caused, as Doña Augusta's own sense of danger recognizes: provoked or caused without knowing it, as she superstitiously rather than theologically fears, her husband might have innocently brought the fall upon himself. If some members of the Olaya family were to believe that their son's death was caused by a curse of whatever kind—never mind an *evangelical* one—the acceptance of some measure of incurred blame on their part would seem inevitable. On the Squabs side, their own tragedy (and the Olayas' as well) would be seen as predestined, aside from any sense of guilt, if they acted according to the Calvinist norms of belief in predestination that the chapter scripts for them.

In the end, one must turn to Andrés Olaya Sr. for one last look at his grief. For if his mild mockery at Squabs's expense is indeed burdened by guilt in his own eyes, questions of self-doubt and self-blame would follow. Whatever these are, we could surmise the following: that, as he mocked Squabs with the voice and gestures of parody, Andrés senior acted as if his words assumed the role and space left empty by traditional words of brotherliness. After all, blood brothers and symbolic siblings do engage in remarkable banter on many occasions and risk breaking up their bonds by such actions. The lack of brotherliness in Squabs tests Andrés senior's own native talents beyond endurance. Native because his Cuban criollo ethos may itself be injured by its own deep-rooted dependence on brotherly exchanges and currents of mediated envy within and between families. Besides, in his own case, the Olaya senior head of family had to enter his own family twice, by birth and through adoption, and may have thus been, as it were, circumcised in his spiritual flesh by such tribal awakenings and reentries. Although he is no Daedalus in the act of removing the carpenter from his job and causing the death of his son Andrés junior as a parody of the fall of Icarus, Andrés Olaya Sr. shares with Mr. Squabs a measure of paternal guilt that the Calvinist is likely to dismiss in favor of predestined fate, but that he, wiser perhaps, might understand, but by a different name, as the blood guilt gargling of his tribe's Catholic-Cuban honor.

In gargled tribal ways, internal split-birth schismogenesis lies at the root of Cuban criollo, grown-above-subaltern, anticapitalist, Catholic, anti-Protestant, and newly aristocratic self-imaging. This form of proud deep-throat proclamation of elect breeding by Catholic innocents abroad rises in camouflaged colors of magical rhetoric while living in exile among late-day Protestants resigned to providential scripting. Over such grand and gnarled oceanic illusions flies on waxen wings the whole burden of familial tribal truth and honor in chapter 3 of *Paradiso*.

# 11 Discordance

> If juness she saved! Ah Ho! And if yulone he pouved! The ol-old stoliolum! From quiqui quinet to michemiche chelet and a jambabatiste to a brulobrulo! It is told in sounds in utter that, in signs so adds to, in universal, in polygluttural, in each auxiliary neutral idiom, sordomutics, florilingua, sheltafocal, flayflutter, a con's cubane, a pro's tutute, strassarab, ereperse and anythongue athall.
>
> *Finnegans Wake* (117.12–16)

PROOF OF discordance or something far worse is business as usual in Joyce's monster dream-book. In this passage (moving past historians and burned heretics and the universal language of sex and artificial instruments of lingual contact) we come to Cuba, or traces thereof, inserted in a French word for the occasionally intimate or privative human female part paired down to three letters from its English four, and from its masthead verb for *to have knowledge of*—so timely employed in the Bible whenever shameful parts mate for purposes at times risky if not downright fatal. As usual, Ronald McHugh's annotations to the *Wake* come handy: "*F* con concubine *Sp SL* cuba: cunt the pros & cons" (*Annotations* 117). A mistress and a whore are caught in some kind of slang tongue and dress-tooting that, in the first case, in Spanish, goes by *tuteo* or *tú-tú* familiar address among equals, when not used in willful disrespect to offend against proper formality. (Two other Cuba-related items beyond the pale of even the Irish are available for a bit of queering in "jambabatiste to a brulobrulo"—where Vico's Christian name gives us *Batista* dictatorship stammered and leading to *Bruno at the stake* burning, but not out of reach of a quite cryptic *mad Castro flambé*.)

## Profanology Queered

Profane language and lingual misshaping and abuse are the essence of the *Wake* as it spins off the planet's orbit into oblivion or the lifelong work of understanding its textures and ingrained layers of verbiage and cosmic privacies exposed and obscured upon the hardest pages ever committed to the art of storytelling. Language differs from lingual, plain and simple, as it does from word or parole, but with greater emphasis upon the fleshy organ involved in enunciation, besides the brain and the mind, unless the mind were to be conceived not as housed in the head but playing at large somewhere including the tip of one's tongue. It is at the point of that tip that profanity does its dancing. In the *Wake*, dreamscape and dream screen are in the dreamer's head only as far as dream shapes in the bedroom and beyond are parts of that mind expanded and *are* that mind itself—as much as its innermost image dream events are. The dreaming mind is the dreamer at large and confined and in passage between the annulled space gap lying between internal and external image embodiments and disembodiments.

If the world (as it happens in so many belief systems and religions) was profaned by accident or by the will of humans and their actions and made to fall from a primordial state of grace (as it was at the beginning, either under sacred will or natural causes), the art of *story-numbing* and *story-un-telling* and *queerology* in the *Wake* would be as lingual as the lower bodily functions are genital. In fact, the upper-cum-nether joining or bottoming-out-cum-upper-climbing congress between the lingual and the genital defines what I call *profanology* in the *Wake* as part of my programmed wish to apply some of its key features to *Cuba-as-lingual-linga-yoni-text*—or better: to Cuba as queer-sacred text or *Quba* (*Adam-cum-Eve-cubed-sacred* as desperate means to cleanse if not redeem Guantánamo).

That which was profaned was held sacred and inviolate before its desecration. It was taken out of or beyond the house of prayer, which Romans called *fanum*, or temple. But, within the *Wake*'s echo chambers, that name *fanum* tips over upon the tongue's tip and fans out into fanny-multiples of *ass* and God knows what else. Because the temple was already profane, profanology in the *Wake* profanes through repeated befouling, as if once were not enough, as if tiny residuals of sacredness remained in need of endless and profaning *queeronomy.*

As Richard Beckman has recently demonstrated, Joyce's "rare view" amounts to the nature of things in *rear view* or *reared* into view by the rear. God's rear becomes His voiced ocular stare at us after the fall, in the wake of things left and fallen behind. Thus, "the vaudevillian emphasis on the rear view and the view of the rear signifies the mode of the *Wake,* a mode in which the world is seen backwards and is observed with special attention to 'backwords' . . . and backsides. . . . *Finnegans Wake* is a book of life that goes nowhere"; it plows back and forth or "furrowards" and "bagwards" ("backwards to the prenatal amniotic sac or bag of waters") (*Joyce's Rare View* 12). The dreamer's head becomes planet as planet becomes boundless space bound in nutshell-like stem cells where the equivalent of originating episodes, bits of gossip, and clustered actions settle before being swallowed up into dream. The dreaming head is decapitated, but such a view of extreme severance from embodiment is meant to suggest the ubiquity of the detached head's bounded and infinite many-severed-heads spheres as well as the head's total and absolute encompassing of everything that transits through it without ever exiting its single-headedness (*pluriuniheadedness*).

We will next walk through the scaffold that connects *Paradiso* with the business of profane wording and rewording in the *Wake,* beginning with the quotation in the next section taken from a lecture by Joyce originally written in Italian. (We are in the business of building not a bridge to nowhere but *from* nowhere.)

## Profane Letters Reared in Bondage

While hired for the humane business of teaching his native tongue as foreign language abroad in Italy, James Joyce wrote and delivered in Italian a lecture now known in English as "Ireland, Island of Saints and Sages." The speaker's ambiguous—if not disputed—lingual ancestry becomes central to the talk and lends it peculiar urgency in today's rearview-mirrored world of quite real if often fantasized identities:

> The Irish language, although of the Indo-European family, differs from English almost as much as the language spoken in Rome differs from that spoken in Teheran. It has an alphabet of special characters and a history almost three thousand years old. Ten years ago, it was spoken only by the peasants in the western provinces on the coast of the Atlantic and a few in the south, and on the little islands that stand like pickets of the vanguard of Europe, on the front of the eastern hemisphere. Now the Gaelic League has revived its use. Every Irish newspaper, with the exception of the Unionist organs, has at least one special headline printed in Irish. The correspondence of the principal cities is written in Irish, the Irish language is taught in most of the primary and secondary schools, and, in the universities, it has been set on a level with the other modern languages, such as French, German, Italian, and Spanish. In Dublin, the names of the streets are printed in both languages. The League organizes concerts, debates, and socials at which the speaker of *beurla* (that is, English) feels like a fish out of water, confused in the midst of a crowd that chatters in a harsh and guttural tongue. In the streets, you often see groups of young people pass by speaking Irish, perhaps a little more emphatically

> than is necessary. The members of the League write to each other in Irish, and often the poor postman, unable to read the address, must turn to his superior to untie the knot. This language is oriental in origin, and has been identified by many philologists with the ancient language of the Phoenicians, the originators of trade and navigation, according to historians. This adventurous people, who had a monopoly of the sea, established in Ireland a civilization that had decayed and almost disappeared before the first Greek historian took his pen in hand. (*Critical Writings* 153–54)

In search of a response of sorts to this partial language map (or fractured landscape of linguistic and lingual partialities) let us imagine a mural in the act of being painted before us as we walk on the scaffold in front of it.

This pictorial view of a wall in the making represents in mimetic perspective the very opposite of the *Wake*'s Irish/Planet occupancy of space. It shows in panoramic ensemble pictures and scenes and word scrabbles from the *Wake*'s discernible plot as a worded or scripted dream event. The prime object of imitation being the dream, all the stuff represented in the mural is subject to scripted or lingual versions, running against the dream's palpable but delusional visual grain. Freud's distinction between primary and secondary processes obtains. In *topical* terms, the unconscious concerns primary as distinct from the preconscious secondary processes. In *dynamic* or *economic* terms, the psychic energy involved in primary processes flows freely and registers and binds itself into images facilitated by condensation and displacement reaching back into intrapsychic events and hallucinations labeled primitive or primal. (Dreams as well as early-infancy perceptual events represent iconic instances of primary processes in which need and desire impact themselves into images.) In secondary processes, psychic energy is bound or attached to more stable and represented forms, which, when related to the influx of unbound primary-process images, would never sustain a translation relationship with such primal contents. Put simply: going from primary to secondary processes is where and how the first great loss in translation occurs. In this specific representational scheme, the original fall (heightened to Fall) that is involved and retraced in the *Wake* becomes the echoing loss of that primacy shown in endless prime time as dreams are wordlessly replayed in the dreamer's own thoughts. But even in such inward and wordless thought-forms the loss is already registered. The loss grows further in size and consequence as words for the dream are scripted and given lingual shape as it happens in the *Wake*. Because of the increasing loss—as the dream is registered and shown in its own wake—the need to see and watch the dream stuff in naked visual shapes grows too. Though perhaps redundant, seeing *War and Peace* in mural form would be congruent with its panoramic and immense visual means, whereas seeing the *Wake* in pastiche or collage mural projection means to accommodate its dream cells into viewable but arrested resolutions of what was pure image flux.

The mural gimmick allows us to situate the *Wake* in linkage with *Paradiso* within the space of an island nation's linguistic and lingual past and present politics as addressed by Joyce in his 1907 lecture. (He spoke in Italian in his new home city of Trieste addressing his own language students at the Università Popolare.) The reinstating of Irish as national language brings up the question of creole speech, ethos, and lifestyle in *Paradiso*—and the presence of some form of monstrous planetary Creole in the bizarre lingual agglomerations of the *Wake*. In the context addressed in the lecture—and placed at the heart of *A Portrait of the Artist as a Young Man*—Irish acquires a potent measure of adversarial creole lingual impact upon English. Of course, Irish is no creole, but its native role against English makes it the *birth* and *rare-rearing* idiom of the homeland against colonial aliens. In this sense, Irish fulfils two core meanings of *creole* in Spanish *criollo*. The word connects with Portuguese *crioulo* for a "white" person born in the colonies, having meant originally a "black" born in the colonies as distinct from one brought by traffic from Africa. It relates to *criar* and to bring up a *cría* or *criado* at home. Born and reared at home, first as slave and then as master, in the colonies, away from the metropolitan and the traffic enclaves, *creole* becomes the epitome of transplant and translation beyond passage and traffic and thus marked by such displacements. Creole's lingual and cultural values are embroiled in these powerful tenancies of renewed homeliness and former uprooting.

The *Wake*'s incorporation of many languages into one whole amalgamation poses the issue of its performance as the Earth planet's unsung Creole. The ultimate bastard tongue punctuates and shuffles itself into being, and with each word it coins and impregnates, it performs at least two things. First, it underscores and reproduces the sudden lingual blast into mutual incomprehension among the builders of Babel as the afterimage echoes of their lost common speech still resonates in the new glossolalia entering their ears. The confusion of tongues at Babel registered the first episode of glossolalia in which the language-of-languages heard at the *Wake* takes creole roots. Second, the planet's bastard lingual matter tips on its pointed tongue and licks into the fertile ground verbal birth implants, newborn words of chimerical shape. The planet is planted local, even as it flies up into the clouds because the home grounds of its lingual home are enclosed and barred. The *Wake* is both in and out and banging at the door from both sides. The banging is profane both inside and outside the temple's door as it carries with it a wondrous load of filth and sinfulness always homegrown. But the heavy and rampant scatological contents in the *Wake* bear a different fruit besides their own fertile dirt. The bastard planet tongue so rooted at home as to resemble a lost primordial creole spoken between humans and their as yet not offended God is also the ultimate shape adopted by the alien tongue and the mark of strangeness in every language. Always at home with itself, each tongue occupies the lost planet of the one in which it is not spoken.

In *Paradiso* the issue of creole plays as follows. First, as criollo ethos, manners, lifestyle, idioms, humor, grief, and a certain stoicism in confronting calamity. Pursuing the sacred and profane analogy one step further, we may regard the *Edición Crítica* of *Paradiso* as the shrine where the host of creole sacred memories and currencies of expression are housed under Cintio Vitier's masterful stewardship. This makes the edition definitive as the gathering site or campground at which to go on reading the Book in whichever style one may choose (including a countercreole/creole amalgam such as the one you have been reading or enduring). The creole ethos habitat is thus framed and housed even as the Cuban culture it reflects is all but defunct.

A second creole aspect comes with the language and lingual values in *Paradiso* and the essays and poetry that may attend its reading as *Wake*. The issue turns paradoxical because there is no creole as such in Lezama's writing, unless it is what is called his *baroque* style and unique cultivation of allusions and image display. In which case, creole would represent the learned excrescence of a writer's hybrid readings in seventeenth-century Spanish literature and the idioms of its own national culture. By the same token, the existence of creole outside his work is also empty, for by comparison, Cuba has not developed or preserved any such autochthonous or homegrown language, in the strict sense in which creole exists elsewhere in the Caribbean. In reference to Joyce's remarks on the Irish language, creole Cuban would yield a historical fantasy. The Arawak, Taíno, and Siboney cultures would have survived the onslaught of colonialism and disease enough to leave a retrievable native tongue similar to the Irish language during the Gaelic revival. Indigenous extermination (and not any lack of will among nationalists with native or retro Taíno consciousness, as in the Dominican Republic) would mark the buried wound spot of the lost language whose entombed host names, nouns, and music mark the territory. But rather than native as such, the lost and suppressed Cuban counterpart (the equivalent of the "Sheltafocal" *cryptolect* or secret Irish language mentioned in the *Wake* near the reference to "con's cubane") would be an African speech brought and raggedly preserved in the black inflow into Cuba.

Remnants and traces of various African languages do survive in mostly urban settings in Cuba in association with popular religious practices. If from a Cuban perspective the national revival of Irish should evoke the restoration of a lost creole on its aboriginal Arawak soil, the historical fantasy would soon encounter a lost colonial connection with African peoples from various tribal nations brought to Cuba and distinct from the creole blacks already born there from a previous cargo. What is being suggested here is that the murky waters of planet and local creole in the native and alien dream spaces of the *Wake* would hit a sort of wall built with African blood, sweat, and tears. A transplanted-by-force and shackled hybrid African Arawak creole Titan would constitute the Cuban counterpart of the proto Irish Giant who lies beneath the pedestal of what is mourned and celebrated in Joyce's book.[1]

A consideration of creole in *Paradiso* leads to a phantasmal observance of loss and desired reparation. The whole purpose in inviting the Irish *Wake* to the Cuban party lies in recognizing the dubious and yet utterly compelling project of turning *Paradiso* into a national novel regardless of its often arcane phrases and themes. Here is where the planet comes into play. It plays in global absence at the macro level while playing also in dream but factual presence inside the microworld brewing in each detail and word cluster.

With regard to the nation or any of her parts as planet, Jean-Michel Rabaté's claim to associate Gabriel García Márquez's *One Hundred Years of Solitude,* Salman Rushdie's *Midnight's Children,* and Joyce's *Wake* as national novels proves useful in suggesting the inclusion of *Paradiso*—to which V. S. Naipaul's *A House for Mr. Biswas* could be added with perverse intent, given its staunch resistance to any attempt to nationalize its representations of Trinidad-Tobago cultures. According to Rabaté, in such a novel "an archetypal family bridges the gap between private and public realms, and sends us back to the same and different Heraclitean stream," where the hope of "delousing oneself" by bathing in the same river that won't repeat itself proves useless because the current carries what Rabaté sagely calls "its own life-affirming vermin." For what the residual mire of life in the flow carries is "a mixture of folklore, national history, mythical paradigms, all structured by the theatricalization of a wild and loose oral tale" (*James Joyce and the Politics* 106). Remove the magical realist component from the mix, and the act of oral discharge is what binds the resemblance between the *Wake* and *Paradiso* as national séances buzzing in novel shape. For all its overwritten and scriptural densities, *Paradiso* remains a lingual prodigy bound to a language warped by its scriptural mouthing and incubation and fall upon a DNA-humid Cuban page smelling of tobacco. The quotation that follows at the beginning of the next section on warp work addresses "surprises" warped as "subrises" and the woof work of *Cuba* upon this, the text under your nose.

## Incubus

In *Joyce's Book of the Dark* John Bishop situates us in the incubation zone for Cuba (text in brackets is Bishop's):

> Where this ascending progression of "subrises" leads will grow clear if we return to the opening pages of *Finnegans Wake,* and to the precise place at which our "reading [of the] Evening World" began—on the phrase "in bed" (3.17), in whose vicinity we learn that "*Hic cubat edilis. Apud libertinam parvulam*" (7.22–23 [L., "Here sleeps the public man. Near the small freedwoman"]). The Latin verb "*cubat*" in this construction ("sleeps") puts a new inflection on the phrase "in bed" (L. *cubile*) and in turn throws a new perspective everywhere across Joyce's "bog of the depths." For one of many possible Latin synonyms for the English "in bed" would be the phrase "*in cubato*" (which, from the verb *cubo, cubare,* would literally mean "in having gone to bed"). Because our hero's night-long drift through the dark in his own closed body of water takes place *in cubato,* his sleep necessarily becomes, everywhere in the *Wake,* an extended form of "incubation" (112.21, 397.34 [where the orthodox Eng. "incubation," historically deriving from the L. *incubare,* "to lie down upon," generates the meaning "to hatch" simply because birds "lie down upon" their eggs]). (374–75)

Cuba's *Cuba* lands in bed with Latin, as in a wine or olive oil or water tub to boot, as if fallen from its *mountain-rough* Arawak lingual gestures to Columbus and company, as in: "*Cuba!*" (Meaning something like "Move on, there is further *Cuba* over there!") The word also crops up in native names like *cubas* and *cubana* along the sierra regions across the eastern areas of the island first trodden by the two-legged and four-legged combined beast of conquest and plunder. The expletive *Cuba!*

in lingual gesture pointed intruders away toward other parts, perhaps even across the narrow straights between the island and Haiti, where the same *mountain-rough* voices named elevations and wild places. All this points ominously at Santiago de Cuba and the surrounding sierras and valleys west and north and farther east toward Guantánamo as places of wakeful unrest dream-work for the Arawak Titan counterpart of Finn Mac Cool, buried under Irish soil across the Dublin landscape, and the character known as HCE ("here comes everybody"), whose head lies at the Head of Howth promontory. Santiago's topography is saturated with places and erections of all sorts, from San Juan Hill and the Morro Castle boulder fortress at the mouth of the bay to the Cobre copper mine to the north, where the first successful slave uprising in the New World is claimed to have happened. The aforementioned aboriginal but hybrid Titan buried beneath the local topography, but also at rest and laid over its terrain, begins to fluctuate in appearance and substance: Arawak pure blood, creole black, and now a *cimarrón* runaway, who fled the copper mine into the wild mountains. (Nowadays his figure is sculpted atop Goat Hill, or Loma de los Chivos, as the heroic shape of man and horse fused into one in the colossal monument by Alberto Lascay Merencio.)

A momentous east-west rift befalls the hosting of the *Wake* on Cuban grounds, moving away from the eventual capital in Havana and back to the original focal point of conquest and settlement in the future Oriente province, so named after it was known simply as *Cuba* in early colonial times.

Disorientation sets in. Returning to the Orient's *Wake* primacy means moving backward into the earliest colonial and precolonial past, and forward into the future, in order to restore what was replaced when Cuba's first-landing planet signature naming in native blood-ink was reoriented and appointed as the only region on the island marked by one of the four cardinal points. Dangling Oriente, the Cuban crocodile's head, paws, and jaws; ridged-ribbed by peaks; twisted, queered, forced to look westward toward Havana. Such is the broadest and tallest and original planet-world Cuba for the *Wake* to stage its turmoil in troubled rest.

To the macrocosmic, epic view of Oriental landfall and rebellious Planet-Giant Cuba corresponds the bedroom incubation niche of the one person at rest—but far from stillness. Just as in the *Wake* the ground zero dreamer site resides in the couple's bedroom above the pub kept by the dreaming father, whose upper quarters he occupies with his wife, daughter, and twin sons, the corresponding site in *Paradiso* would primordially be the environment of the author's 1968 essay "Confluencias," spinning into dream space from its opening sentences: "I used to see the night as if something had fallen upon the earth, a descent. Its slowness kept me from comparing it with something descending a stair, for example" (99/1208).[2] But while the *Wake*'s chaotic domestic navel and dream nexus thunders with the living echoes of all havoc that creation wrecked, the room in "Confluences" offers shelter to the author's management of memories in the scripture of his last will.

In the incubation (but also postnatal and posthumous) night habitat of "Confluencias" the dream's emanation point does not belong anywhere except in the author's head: the author who now resides in the self-portrait scriptured a couple of years after the publication of the novel. The "Confluences" essay becomes a habitat cubicle and dream particle of *Cuba*. The site of the writing at the author's house at Trocadero 162 doubles itself up as the site of dreaming awake on Prado Street, at the grandmother widow's house where the key moment of recognition and epiphany occurs in the self-portrait. In reference to the *Wake*'s pub-incubation dream vortex, the Lezama authorship incubated in the essay recollects the confluences, the flow "riverrun, past Eve and Adam's" that opens and closes the Wake Book into cyclical reopening. The Lezama authorship is *river-run-flowed-flooded* by his life in penumbra, as he rests upon all the rest, the photo albums and smells and anticipated remains of his family history. A main river artery in "Confluences" flows from José Cemí and his maternal grandfather Andrés through the death of his teenage son Andresito—the pinpoint of the fall from earthly grace in the combined textual and lingual lives of José Lezama Lima and José Cemí. Their combined humors render in melancholic parody the Daedalus and Icarus tragedy retold awry in the third chapter of *Paradiso*. As already examined, the fall of both father and son takes up a good deal of that chapter. The sense of the Fall as blessed fault or *felix culpa* returns near the end of "Confluences" as the author remembers the opening of the "titanic" wardrobe by his grandmother, the widowed Doña Augusta, at the Prado Street house. The tuxedo suit worn by the young son violinist on the night of his death cascades out of the wardrobe and drowns the self-conscious Icarus child José Cemí in a rush of memories.

The effluvia and flow of memories make this scene the pillar and navel site of dream work in the allegorical nexus between mourning and melancholic bliss that holds together the fiction of Lezama Lima—and that at closure point moves it away from Joyce's chaos and toward Proust, in search of curing the jealousies that so often pollute memories by means of poetry's crafting of amnesia within rituals of remembrance.

The theological symbols of *Parousia* (second coming of Christ) and *Homoousian* (sameness in being or consubstantial) conjoin as the anagogical male pair at the Christian Trinity core of that poetic fiction. *Parousia* signifies and punctuates those moments where the death of the author's and José Cemí's father is felt in the son with the dual intensity of personal tragedy and the promise of Christian redemptive overcoming at the end of times. The second coming signals the highest anagogical figure of temporality in Lezama's work and its figural ultimate point of triumph in closure. *Homoousian* seals the relationship between father and son in one same substance. It happens in tragedy and disgrace as well as in moments of remembrance in the wounded memories of the son. It is present between Andrés and his dead son and between José Lezama Lima and José Cemí and their dead father. The Daedalus/Icarus son's loss to father as the father's loss to son is bound in one substance and in the promise of reunion when their split selves shall gather together once again at the end of times. Such is the redemptive Catholic overarching temporal and figural displacement as the retrospective nexus between the author's self-portrait in "Confluences" and the Jacksonville sections in the first and third chapters of *Paradiso*.

Just as *Parousia* and *Homoousian* represent anagogical instances of male pairing, *Trinity* centers on the mother and related figures of embedded womanhood in the son and his female siblings. The military camp house that is inhabited again in remembrance at the start of "Confluences" is where the story of *Paradiso* starts. In the bedroom, in a scene of corporeal crisis, the Trinity figure takes shape between the suffering child José Cemí and the trio of Baldovina and Trini and her husband, who are parental surrogates embodied in the son's Christ iconography of suffering. Obviously, four and not three people are involved, but the Trinity aura is unmistakable in the scene's pictorial halo. In chapter 6, the child José Cemí experiences nightmares while in bed with Baldovina the nanny and his sister Violante, and later on he is lured by Grace into a hole at the beach where female seduction requires the intervention of the same nanny and arouses the enmity of Thomas, Grace's brother. Dreams, nightmares, and sexual gaming engulf José Cemí in trinity bonding with females. The child and two bonding females are joined by a fourth male figure in whom attenuated aspects of the always-absent-present father are registered. The unfinished sequel of *Paradiso* in *Oppiano Licario* will transform José Cemí's trinity link with females into the joint dyad between the male self in Oppiano and the alternate self in his sister and wife

Ynaca Eco Licario. The double female role of sister and wife reinstates the Trinity in the couple.

## Warp Work

Warp occurs in the unfolding of sleep and makes it impossible to separate the sheer event character of dream stuff from its contents. The section in chapter 3 of *Paradiso* where the orgiastic séance at Michelena's farm takes place is sufficiently opaque in its descriptions to qualify as scripted or reworked dream work. As in the passage: "El cocotero tiene la mirada espejo que reproduce al hundirse el dedo en sus ondulaciones dictadas por el azar. Dos Reverencias se asombra del grito de un insecto, otro responde al díctico de frente blanca, y después tiene que cuidar las larvas asesinadas por la mano sumergida en el río [The coconut palm has a mirror glance that reproduces as one sinks a finger into its fortuitous waves. Two Obeisances is startled by an insect's scream, another responds to the deictic of a white forehead, and then must take care of the larvae murdered by the hand submerged in the river]" (*P* 50/50). The highly scripted scenario unfolding beyond comprehension makes the passage a dubious analogue for dream content. Enigmatic images stream forth, more as a dream further reworked into obscurity than as a dream recollected and retold. Ironically, nothing as elusive as this is ever told in the *Wake,* where all that happens as incident or scene is plain and ordinary, and then is taken up into levels of hallucination and darkly comic myth. It might be difficult to figure out what is happening at any given point in the *Wake,* yet what happens is always trivial and ordinary. But what happens at the Michelena farm could not happen as such anywhere or anytime. The images render actions and events as if they had already occurred in high metaphoric occlusion. Sure, someone dips a hand in the river and alters it where and when the act results in consequences, but the semantic aspect of larvae being murdered opens up a tunnel filled with undying speculative echoes. Dreams do not lure interpretation, interpretation lures dreams. Dreams therefore appear already interpreted and the interpretation that makes them so appear—as rendered into words—often lures further interpreting. Behind that hand-dipping in the river stands the magical lure of someone who wants us caught in the enigma of figuring out what he has dreamed upon the page.

By the same token, the obscurity in the *Paradiso* passage just quoted would certainly match the warp work characteristic of the *Wake* if the words were remade in homologous and echoing phonic shapes. A mild example of it follows, in which Cuba echoes in dress gear: "The wrinklings of her hydeaspects: potatorings boucled the loose laubes of her laudsnarers: her nude cuba stockings were salmospotspeckled: she sported a galligo shimmy of hazevaipar tinto that never was fast till it ran in the washing." (*Wake* 208.11–14). The dreaming factor in such passages is minimal. It concerns the need to unpack the made-up words in order to pinpoint what exactly is worn by the woman in question. But one can imagine what impact such phonic warping word-making and reworking would have on the already obscure *Paradiso* passage if its words were similarly altered soundwise on top of their already inscrutable and semantically unreal contents. This is why, besides such lexical and phonemic alterations, the phonic warp impact of the *Wake* upon *Paradiso* should affect only plot contents where dream-work story fragments join mythmaking as extrapolations of individual psychic stuff. This brings us to a brief inventory of the individual mind contents in a book from whose bottomless pages the individual subject and its character have been exiled.

## God-Awful Noise Incest

Beyond its dream enclosure, the *Wake* expands upon the struggle between parents and children dating from a time when there were no parents and children. What is commonly called "baggage" in anyone's psychic life lacks individual personal origins in the *Wake*. There is no one either to benefit from or to blame for his of her own psychic gifts or burdens. Instead, everyone is screwed up in everyone else. Social life and creation mesh in one bundle of guilt, dubious reparation, and atonement. The tragic consequences of such a mess remain intact even as the whole story comes to us in a buzz of comic grotesqueness and mute or ventriloquist laughter. Scandalous rumors and cross-questioning, such as: public urination and exhibitionism by an old peeping-Tom married man haunting nubile girls of questionable innocence; all sorts of incest stories circulating but never actually getting home anywhere except inside their own phrase coordinates. This only begins to map the sick scenes of *Wake* myth going back to Noah and the world from whose drowning he escaped into our accursed companionship.

Conjoined into one tainted stem cell, the sin-and-guilty Earwicker family casts a foul and corrosive gossip gloom upon the rest of a planet bursting with stories of origins fathered by earth-peopling incest redundancies and filial agendas to get even. Under "Theology" (and citing as sources "*Vico, Bruno, and Budge's notes to the [Egyptian] Book of the*

*Dead*"), James Atherton lists the following main axioms of the *Wake:* "*a)* Original sin was committed by God. It is simply the act of creation. *b)* 'Each civilization has its own Jove.' (Vico) *c)* Each Jove commits again, in a new way, to commence his cycle, the original sin on which creation depends" (*Books at the Wake* 53). Concerning Vico—in his account of "Poetic Metaphysics" under the general rubric of "Poetic Wisdom"—a tale of sublime origins in humans is told that can be made roughly the same for both Joyce, who patently took it into his *Wake,* and for Lezama, who does not use it in *Paradiso* or among his "imaginary eras," but who was quite fond of reading Vico.

The redundant enforcement of Vico's wisdom marks the matchmaking suture of *Paradiso* and the *Wake,* if we keep in mind that incorporation of esoteric matter reflects Lezama's whole-planet intellectual practice. What follows is a gloss of entries 376–79 and 388 in Vico's "Poetic Metaphysics" (*New Science* 145–52): So, as it came to pass, in their brawny dumbness, early humans could only create by means of their grossly physical imagination. This made them powerful and sublime in what they created and brought them the gift of *ecstasy* as first poets. Their task was to *invent sublime myths,* to *excite to ecstasy,* and *to teach the masses to act virtuously.* Changes in the upper air after the flood made the skies pregnant and moist, and soon huge thunderclaps and bolts of fire sent giants scattering up the mountains and into lairs, thunderstruck and ignorant of causes behind the sudden mayhem. More than ever sunk into their senses and ruled by animal passions, the mountain people buried deeper into their own bodies. Yet curiosity instilled in them the crude but accurate apprehension that it was all caused by Jove, who ruled over everything as he did the noisy and flashy skies. *Poco a poco,* in little steps, people learned to guide their impulses in the right direction, stopped wandering and using each other wantonly like beasts, and adopted the habit of marriage and of marrying not their own siblings. Echoes of the incest taboo first flooded into male ears in "the hundering blundering dunderfunder of plundersundered manhood" (*Wake* 596.2), before it settled for good inside the drumming caverns of the head, though only as a source of inner turmoil and perhaps the occasional recurrence of beastly promiscuity. (Whether, in the primal poetic soul, cosmic-rule ecstasy is ever sundered from potent feelings in promiscuous mating goes unanswered. Here lies perhaps the sutured but hurting fracture line between big primal passion and small modern lusts in Joyce's *Wake* under the curse of father-daughter incest.)

## Maiden Queer: Satan's Eve and Danae's Narcissus

Margot Norris has observed how in the *Wake* Vico's "myth of social and linguistic origin is essentially reversed": in Vico "thunder creates language and kinship laws while in the *Wake* the stutter serves as a symptom of linguistic breakdown and incestuous wishes" (*Decentered Universe* 57–58). In such purview, the issue of female sinfulness in Lezama's fiction as an aspect of Eve's umbilical mark on transgressions blamed upon her gender brings up the issue of father-daughter incest in *Paradiso* and *Oppiano* under the queer sign of lesbianism.

As already discussed in chapter 7, the orgy at Michelena's farm includes a set of six "Nictímines," or "lesbians," so named by Lezama, claiming that such was the plural bird-noun given to them in ancient Greece. In fact, the curse of father-seduction by lesbian daughters in *Paradiso* explains the choreography of lesbians as night birds. The curse rests on Ovid's story in *Metamorphoses* refracted in Sor Juana Inés de La Cruz's *First Dream* (a poem of the dark night just as the *Wake* is Joyce's dark lesson of the night).

At the onset of Sor Juana's *Dream,* birds of darkness are heard as the owl appears:

> With sluggish flight and song,
> jarring on ear and even more on spirit,
> shamefaced Nyctimene keeps watch
> by chinks in sacred portals
> or at those gaping openings
> of lofty, rounded windows
> best suited to her purpose:
> to desecrate the brightly shining
> holy lamps perpetually lit,
> extinguishing, even defiling them,
> while drinking in clear liquid form
> rich substance that Minerva's tree,
> constrained by press, has sweated forth
> out of her fruit, a tribute forced.
> (*Sor Juana Anthology* 172)[3]

In her split dream vision, the poet watches two daughters: Nyctimene, the one who in Ovid is turned into an owl after seducing her own father, and Minerva, the owl goddess Athena, daughter of Zeus-Jove (without mother) by way of wisdom and justified war. The desecrating lesbian daughter brings polluted incest into hallowed precincts on the wings of the transformed Nyctimene, a daughter by herself befouled, a sort of bird-nester thief who would steal from another daughter and bird-sister, Minerva, the substance of the latter's virgin bonding with her father Zeus.

However, one may ask: how can Athena's virginity and alliance with her Mighty Father ever be sundered from his own frequent actions as rapist? The godly enforcer of unwanted sex in Zeus-Jove acts as the founder of polluting mating with daughters of all kinds—of whom he is never the actual father. A frequent seducer or rapist of daughters, Zeus furthers the reach of father rape. Are such actions not the paragon of subsequent rapes by human fathers themselves? Zeus's sex with maidens is polluting even as it engenders powerful races and dynasties. By contrast, in the story of Eden, the primal parents are meant to sin on their own, in disobedience of God's command, but not by having sex with Him (except in certain so-called gnostic accounts of Eve's sexual misdeeds).[4] Whether in Greek myth god-seduction stories, or as demiurge, or embodied in Satan's Serpent form, the actions of a higher being reach down where it hurts: in the mother-daughter flesh of human beginnings. Such is precisely the father's gestating incest wound in the mother-daughter flesh that the *Wake* explosively mourns with the noisy instruments of chaotic laughter. In the grotesque and bawdy echoes of such laughter the earthly father's cuckolded anger at a mightier celestial Father is heard.

But are such primal scripts—or is any such foul stuff—present in *Paradiso* and *Oppiano Licario*? The answer is yes; for rape by a God-Father figure of the non-Christian sort is the primal sin in the biography of Ynaca Eco Licario (prominent female surrogate of José Cemí's author role in Lezama's fiction). Ynaca adopts the saga of the maiden-heifer Io as her own by means of the homophone personal pronoun for "I" or *yo* with gender-mixing results. The results are also quite disturbing upon the page—as in life what is felt or declared in what follows should have sent its sufferer to the care of psychiatrists. For it is written (late in the unfinished *Oppiano Licario*) that there is "rebelliousness"

> like a Promethean spark in Ynaca, in her refusing the god's [Jupiter] advances. Her movements are assimilated by one hundred eyes [the eyes of Argos]. It can be seen how, in signifying the goddess [la diosa] of the many hands and eyes, it would change once more the shape of the transformed animal [transformaba de nuevo el animal metamorfoseado], making it into a winged cow. It is the Io [Es el Io], measureless, rebellious who comes in Promethean aid [en ayuda prometeica] surrounded by eyes wanting to devour him and by flies who want

> to make him crazy. His face and anus are being chased and watched without a truce, reminding us that in the medieval Sabbath the Devil would show up wearing two masks, on his face and buttocks. She could be sublime without being ridiculous [sin dejar de ser ridícula]. Her punishment is at bottom as great as Prometheus's, it is born out of the same rebellion, she has not wanted to give herself to Jupiter, and thus withstands the greatness of the eyes that watch her and the flies that make her rump swollen. But Io is in me Licario's echo, from the family of the one who refused to mate with Jupiter: an image, my I is a double, my infused double who attempts the same as Licario but through the *dirita vía* [straight path]. (*OL* 394)

There is first the double nature of Ynaca and her brother as linked siblings and reciprocal widow figures to each other, given the fact that Oppiano Licario is not wholly dead and remains alive as his sister's widowed self and as her marriage spouse in the afterlife spiritualist realm. Io comes next, who adds yet another layer of gender-shifting maidenhood: to "I" and "me" and their joint eying in the eye of the self. The self is thus eyed by its own internal and external alternate gazes. The gendered ontology of the self is transfixed by surveying gazes from within and without, and the gazing eye is both ocular and anal. Ynaca (in whom the "I" of Io becomes the "Y" of pronoun "I/yo") is both man and woman fluctuating on the cutting edge of maddened incest sodomy.

Io's drama becomes a grotesque, pregnant, maiden-wandering avatar of the Narcissus life-and-death cycle in mirrored pastoral stillness. The Narcissus stillness is famously transported to the Nile Delta at the opening of Lezama's most important poem, *Muerte de Narciso* (1937): "Dánae teje el tiempo dorado por el Nilo" (Danae weaves time made golden by the Nile). Danae is seven fathers removed from the rape of Io by Zeus. She descends from the Zeus-raped, maiden-heifer, nymph-daughter of the river god Inachus. Afraid of an oracle, her father puts Danae out to sea in a chest accompanied by her maid. She is either already pregnant by Zeus or about to be, when he covers the chest with a golden shower. But Danae is never on the Nile Delta; she is taken to the island of Seriphos with her newborn child Perseus.

Rather than quibbling with Lezama's placing of Danae on the Nile, it should be noted that the pregnant maiden is only four fathers away from her male ancestors Aigyptos and Danaos and the terrible matter of the wedding-murder of the Danaides, first cousins of Aigyptos's sons. Perhaps the resonance *Danaos-Danaides* with *Egypt* in this context sparked Lezama's imagination and brought Danae to the Nile, where the impregnating gold shower became time-woven with Nile water turned into golden threads.[5]

A Christian-pastoral version of Danae's presence in the death of Narcissus scenario invites comparison with Eve's association with Narcissus in Milton's *Paradise Lost.* Although in *Muerte de Narciso* the lethal fixation upon his own beauty marks Narcissus as the embodiment of aesthetic as opposed to human generation, the antithesis itself puts him in contact with Eve's fecundity. In his comments on the poem, volume editor Emilio de Armas sees Narcissus as the poet personified, who crosses into mirrored death space in self-fecundation. As he puts it, in dialectical contrast with Danae: "Narcissus, son of a river, possess himself through the waters and achieves self-fecundation, which, as it excludes the masculine factor (Zeus) and the feminine (Danae), interrupts natural causality in order to establish the reign [reino] of the unconditioned poetic [lo incondicionado poético]" (Lezama Lima, *Poesía* 80n6). In the case of Milton's Eve, her inaugural moment of self-(mis-)recognition in *Paradise Lost* clones Narcissus's:

> As I bent down to look, just opposite,
> A shape within the watery gleam appeared
> Bending to look on me, I started back,
> It started back, but pleased I soon returned,
> Pleased it returned as soon with answering looks
> Of sympathy and love; there I had fixt
> Mine eyes till now, and pined with vain desire,
> Had not a voice thus warned me.
>
> (IV.460–67)

From a Christian (albeit queered) perspective, Zeus-pregnant Danae weaves a funereal golden gift to Narcissus, a gift tapestry whose threads are seminal and already enwombed in herself as her child Perseus—himself a hero on the side of poetic flight and against the lethal fixation coming from Medusa's coiled head and stoning glance. The Eve who in Milton emerges from her opening enthrallment under the spell of her own beauty, and who escapes from such Narcissus arrest to become the mother of humankind, is akin to Danae in her ability to escape the mirrored allurement of Narcissus. Milton's imagined glance into *Muerte de Narciso* would fix upon the death of one's mirrored desire for oneself (and one's own creations) Satan's infinite supply of insatiable and ultimately sterile desire. However, this does not mean that the poetic path to regaining Paradise is ever free in Milton from the desiring powers first possessed by Satan. For if God created first, Satan was first in recreating His work and first in occupying poetic agency on an epic scale.

## Queer Satan and the Gift of Another Skin

The lapidary voice in "Confluences" is best heard in "The night gave me the gift of another skin; it must have been the night's own skin" (99/1209). These words may well serve as one of several rubric epitaphs for the Lezama authorship: a one-line echo of Joyce's *Wake* and Sor Juana's *First Dream* registered inside the tomb of the author of *Paradiso* in Miltonic sublimity. The nightline speaks to the darkness in both Sor Juana and Joyce, as it goes on: "and I would turn about in that vast skin that stretched back, as I turned, to the mossy beginnings of time" (100/1210). In cosmogonies, primordial elements and realms are jammed into one another and require being sundered from their original embedment, often pictured as incest, until the work of division is done and a new cosmic fabric sewn. The skin of darkness worn by the author of "Confluences" as a gift from the night herself incorporates him into both the time before and the time after the break up of original incest in cosmogony. Wearing the night, like Milton's Comus, Lezama's authorial personhood impersonates cosmic elements and powers streaming back through his mind in the person of all the literary characters he created by feeding on his own soul. But in the kitchen, behind this one-man-banquet feast on his own character and flesh, raw family matters broil. Further back, into the tail end of the house, incest lingers in foul fragrance, bearing a dirt particle dropped from God's bad ass and lodged deep inside ancestral matter.

The Eden scenario transposes homebound incest from inside the cosmogony's encysted home body out into the barnyard, and further, among the trees, and by the river at night. As in Virgilio Piñera's *La isla en peso:*

> Night arrives smelling and everyone wants to mate.
> Smell knows how to tear off the mask of civilization,
> it knows that man and woman will find each other for sure
> in the banana grove.
> Oh, muse from paradise, protect the lovers!
>
> Heaven need not be won before enjoying it,
> two bodies in the banana grove are worth as much as the first couple,
> the hateful couple that served to mark the split.
> Muse from paradise, protect the lovers!
>
> (*Isla* 44)

Next, as the poem ends, "celestial powers" are rejected in favor of "earthly presences," and "earth" and "desire" are named human protectors of a group that does not carry "heaven in the blood's mass" and feels its physical reality only when being pelted by the rain. In mural amalgamation, the Island's recumbent body upon the sea is painted as if her figures and dramas had not separated themselves from one single substance and were still hitched together, sutured, bleeding colors by primal wounds where bodies were carved off from each other, but held on to the Island and her maternal burden. In the *Wake* the recumbent dreaming body is that of a legendary male giant, whereas in *La isla en peso* the femaleness of the earthly body that weighs down upon the waters retains its aboriginal androgynous wholeness in Eve's business with Satan.

> Under the rain, under the smell, under all that is real,
> a people gets done and undone in its own testimonies:
> a wake, a hoedown, a hand, a murder,
> mixed, embroiled, bound in perpetual riptide,
> saying high, showing teeth, banging kidneys,
> a whole people descends broken into pieces of manure,
> feeling the water all around,
> below, deeper, the sea nibbling its shoulders;
> a whole people keeps close to its own beast at the goodbye hour,
> howling in the sea, swallowing fruit, slaughtering animals,
> always deeper below, until knowing the Island's burden,
> an Island's burden in the love of its people.
>
> (*Isla* 44)

All in one corrupt body and from its own substance resurgent into self-healing and further injury, the cycle of being in the queerly Christian mongrel Caribbean goes on, on a cord line stretching forward into either absolute extinction or promised salvation. The combined world planet picture in the poem (as well as in *Paradiso, Finnegans Wake,* and *First Dream*) feeds from elements of sacred providential history, which are digested differently in each case, but without breaking ties with the religious scripts they have copied and queered. In *La isla en peso,* the severance from sacred Christian design and providential purpose puts the entire Nation's weight upon its people to suffer and to govern themselves by its burden. It is a dark vision of sovereignty in which the body of those sacred beliefs it has broken away from cannot vanish without the poem's losing the weight of a poetic wisdom it may have borrowed from Milton's Satan.

In *Paradiso* and *First Dream*, the passage from the skin-gift of Satan's darkness into dawn is the same, but the light that summons Sor Juana's dreamer back to consciousness awakes the woman poet into unbowed chasteness. To confess otherwise would topple the dream pyramid and the stone burden on whose pedestal the poet woman's Christian gaze rests upon the fallen world, a world she cannot see if not screened through her vows of chastity. The poetic soul dressed in woman's skin is the same in the dark night of *First Dream* as it is in the black forest where Milton's Comus assaults his Lady girl with all the force of his enchantments—and losses. The contested Manichaean grounds of *Paradiso* lie in between the unspotted woman's triumph over darkness in Milton's *Comus* and Sor Juana's awakened dreamer as woman-gendered self; in the poem's last phrase: "y yo despierta" (and I [feminine] awake). But behind this female consonance of wakeful victory over Satan stands Eve's Miltonic kinship with the Devil's huge simulations of Love's poetic gifts.

### At River's Mouth

The essay "Confluences" ends in benediction and in "ceaseless contemplation of the river," the river of Paradise, which in an ancient legend of India flows from unknown tributaries. It flows in circles and it boils and carries a lode of "tremendous confusion," sweeping all things into its waters: "Blessed are we the ephemeral who can contemplate movement as an image of eternity and follow intently the parabola of the arrow until it is buried beneath the line of the horizon" (121/1228). The imaginary congregation to which this fluvial benediction is addressed negates the unbounded poetic image of generation born from Narcissus in self-barren absorption before his mirrored image. The fluvial vision chooses death by other means besides and beyond Narcissus, who lies abstracted and detached from other selves while forever imprisoned within mirrored loneliness.

Fluvial hope flows inside other beings even as it wants to be fractioned by desires emanating beyond its own will to shape them and beyond its own reflection to shatter them. Fluvial flow wants itself to become roiled up in Being, being mixed, reduced to beings with all impure things and dissolved "riverrun, past Eve and Adam's" and rolling and falling upwards in letter clusters by the hundred: "bababadalgharaghtakammin arronnkonnbronntonnerronntuonnthunntrovarrhounawskawntoo hoohoordenenthurnuk!" (*Wake* 3.15–17)—as in the *Wake*'s echo of the lingual beginnings of World as Cosmos and Being, which Joyce could not resist parodying and lampooning as God's awful authorship rear-wind joke-blast upon humanity.

Literature makes a lot of noise at the expense of sounds it has stolen in echoes from (in the case of most authors dealt with in this book) religions in their tingling and chiming and queering unrest beyond doctrinal safe havens. Joyce rehearsed exile from such noises and rustlings by creating such a sonorous book it would quiet all others through its own self-oblivion. Thus, a circular terminal point was reached in the office of literature: to awe and scare the World Planet beyond the beaten paths of spooking itself on religious grounds and the soundtrack of worn-out scriptures. Literature defaulted through exhaustion on its own means to recycle religious myths and their political derivatives. Ill-fated letters streamed through the *Wake* beyond the Planet and made it burst like a bubble puffed up into one huge Nation gargling and choking like a tribe's lingual birth. Placing *Paradiso* in such terminal company may seem unwise or crazy, but it is the end of Things (in scatology and eschatology) that Lezama's novel addresses by extreme means.

The illusion persists about how nations in their programmed consensus as imagined communities can actually keep pace and follow certain extreme books as far as these lettered sound boxes may take them. It is that heavily political and cynical illusion that the book now under your nose, or fallen from your hands, wishes to shatter in order to clear the way for readers to become as naive and impolite as to brake up national covenants and factional deals in the politics of reading. Seeing the *Wake* and *Paradiso* above the Planet and up in the clouds as a loud but soundless and rumbling expletive against such politics comes in the next sentence that this one ends by silencing.

# Notes

## Introduction

1. Breslin writes about "I'm nobody, or I'm a nation" that "by refusing to choose between these alternatives, Shabine implicitly sees himself as both extremes at once: precisely by his inchoate lack of identity, he is representative of a people and carries its latent nationhood by synecdoche within himself" (*Nobody's Nation* 1).

2. "El Cometa Halley" (Arenas, *Adios a mamá* 81–107). See Olivares, "Twice-Told Tail," for a searching account of this tale.

3. *Before Night Falls* (DVD scene "Beauty Is the Enemy").

4. *Apocalypse Now* (DVD scene "He's really out there").

5. Besides James Frazer's *The Golden Bough,* seen next to his bed rest as a sort of bible, Kurtz would have been absorbed reading a book published too late for him to study: Neil Forsyth's 1987 *The Old Enemy: Satan and the Combat Myth.*

6. After naming such traits at different points in the poem, Spengemann reminds us that "Satan's voyage from the Hell in which God has imprisoned him to those most temperate regions . . . which he means to possess . . . is planned in Pandemonium, a council of colonial adventurers who have already been compared to mariners" (107).

7. Heidegger, "The Question Concerning Technology" (115). The word *Entgotterung* most accurately translates as *de-godization.*

8. Walcott, "Crusoe's Journal," *Collected Poems* (92); hereafter cited parenthetically by page number in text.

9. See Breslin's chapter "Adam's Amnesia: The Uses of Memory and Forgetting" (*Nobody's Nation* 102–26).

10. *Omeros* (244, 242, 245, 247).

## 1. A House in the Woods

1. Sophia's treatment at the Morell family *cafetal* was purchased with her sister's Mary's work as governess of Dr. Morrell's children. Mary's pained writings

on plantation slavery differed sharply from Sophia's enraptured effusions on nature (see Marshall, *Peabody Sisters* 274–77).

2. About the grandpa it is written: "He said he was an atheist, but he spent a lot of energy cursing [shitting upon] the Mother of God. Perhaps he did all this to irritate my grandmother, who would always devotedly fall down on her knees, even in the middle of the fields, to ask the heavens for something or other, which, in general, she did not get" (*BNF* 5/21).

3. "One morning the rooster was found dead; I think it was not as the result of the size of my cousin's penis, which was really quite small; I think the rooster died of shame from getting fucked when normally he was the one to fuck all the hens in the yard" (*BNF* 19/39).

4. "one of the pirate boats (whose legal name was 'immigrant frigates') that sailed away—full of Chinamen, Macaos, Negroes, Russians, Italians, Portuguese, all, like him, hungry fierce men, hungry fugitives, hungry dreamers, men who for the dream of fleeing their land grabbed up the only possessions they had, their bodies, and for the dream of escaping slavery sold themselves legally into slavery" (*PWS* 21/31).

5. Translator's introduction (Blumenberg, *Work on Myth* xx); first published in 1979 as *Arbeit am Mythos*.

6. "Bestial entre las flores" (*Termina el desfile* 144); the phrase is not rendered as such in Colchie's translation.

### 2. Pan's Labyrinth

1. *El verdadero Dios Pan* is an *auto sacramental*. The original reads: "La alegoría no es más/que un espejo que traslada/lo que es con lo que no es;/y está toda su elegancia/en que salga parecida/tanto la copia en la tabla,/que el que está mirando a una/piense que está viendo a entreambas./Corre ahora la paridad/entre lo vivo y la estampa." I translate "tabla" as "slate" where it could also be "board"; see comments on line 148 (*Autos sacramentales completos* 48 105).

2. See Borgeaud (*Cult of Pan* 42–44 passim) and Burkert (*Homo Necans* 86–87).

3. *The Devil's Backbone* (DVD scene 28). Scenes numbers are henceforth given in parentheses in the text.

4. McDonagh writes that in Victorian England "burial societies were a widespread phenomenon . . . offering the working class a means of ensuring for themselves and their families a decent burial through subscription to a common fund [they] were a form of mutualist financial organisation very much encouraged under the New Poor Law, as a way of facilitating self-help among the poor. They became, however, the focus of middle-class anxieties about working-class demoralisation and degeneracy" (*Child Murder* 113).

### 3. Lady in the Hot Seat

1. See Cynthia B. Herrup's *A House in Gross Disorder*, Stephen Orgel's "The Case for Comus" (31–32), and Roy Flannagan's "*Comus*" in Danielson's *The Cambridge Companion to John Milton* (23–24).

2. See "The Lady of Christ's" in John T. Shawcross's *John Milton: The Self and the World* (33–60). Besides young Milton's girly looks and his altogether queer immersion in Greek and Latin studies beyond all measure, Shawcross judiciously examines his friendship with Charles Diodati, given exalted poetic expression in "Epitaphium Damonis" (1638). Summarizing: "The view of Diodati . . . is [of] one who represented a dominant counterpart to Milton, one whose sexual life cannot be described but whose rough personality outlines—his excesses, his fickleness in friendship, his sensual nature, his drifting life—would not deny a rather promiscuous homosexuality. On the other hand, Milton would seem to be somewhere on the fringes of homosexuality through religious and ideological repressions of 'natural' attitudes toward sex, high-mindedness, and 'female' qualities of appearance, interests, and abilities" (55). See also Anna Beer's *Milton: Poet, Pamphleteer, and Patriot* for discussion of Milton's friendship. She writes: "In a society that demonised the act of sodomy, and in which, at the same time, it was perfectly possible to conduct and intimate relationship with another man without drawing any attention to one's activities, John Milton actively sought to elevate the emotional and erotic intensity of his writings connected with Charles Diodati" (51).

3. For the following sketches and quotations I rely on Tim Hilton's two-volume biography of John Ruskin cited in the text as *Early Years* and *Later Years* and on Paul Sawyer's *Ruskin's Poetic Argument.* See index entries in these books under Domecq, Adèle-Clotilde; Grey, Euphemia; and La Touche, Rose. (It proves far more accessible for the reader to find the Ruskin passages as quoted in these biographical and critical books than in the huge sum of his works—too often kept embalmed in special collections.)

### 4. A House of Sand

1. Nina Baym considers the dropped "w" change of spelling "a gesture of counterrepudiation" on the son's part against his paternal elders, "who had repudiated his mother for the sin of bearing children" (*Feminism and American Literary History* 43). When Elizabeth Manning married her neighbor Nathaniel Hathorne, she was two months pregnant with her first daughter, and the stain of illegitimacy upon mother and child proved indelible among her late husband's relatives.

2. For a full discussion of the Cuba Journals, see Megan Marshall, *The Peabody Sisters* (271–303), as well as Herbert, *Dearest Beloved* (7–58).

3. For factionalism behind witchcraft conflict in Salem, the groundwork study remains Paul Boyer and Stephen Nissenbaum's *Salem Possessed: The Social*

*Origins of Witchcraft* (1974). In his *Historia* ([1959] 1975) Fernando Ortiz provides a comparable study for Remedios, but without the detailed statistical mapping of factional conflict among locals in Salem analyzed by Boyer and Nissenbaum.

### 5. The A-Frame Agony

1. Keenly aware of the importance of spiritualism in Cuba, Fernando Ortiz wrote *La filosofía penal de los espiritistas: Estudio de filosofía jurídica* (1915).

2. Francisco Soto has convincingly shown how the Fortunato-Adolfina nexus as mutual doubles in *El palacio* returns altered in the marriage between Hector and his wife in *Otra vez el mar:* "Adolfina is presented as the feminine double of the adolescent Fortunato. This doubling pair reemerges not only in Hector / the nameless wife, but also in the figure of Tedevoro from canto 6 of *Otra vez el mar*" (*Reinaldo Arenas* 54).

3. Translations from the story are ours. See http://seds.org/Maps/Stars_en/Fig/auriga.html for Alpha Aurigae or Capella, and Timothy Gantz (*Early Greek Myth* 41) for the catasterism of Zeus's goat nurse Amalthea and her elevation among the stars. Given the errorless naming of all other stars and constellations in the story, the double mention of "Coppelia, la Cabra," strongly hints at the intention to misname the star. Francisco Soto offers a brief insightful analysis of "El reino de Alipio," calling it "an enigmatic tale" (*Reinaldo Arenas* 73). He points out that "uranology" may well stand as a coded name in reference to male homosexual emancipation in mid-Victorian England, in which regard Linda Dowling writes: "The cult of boy-love would find its literary expression in 'Uranian' poetry. This poetry, celebrating that Uranian or 'heavenly' love between males described in Plato's *Symposium* 180e, first appeared about this time [the late 1850s] in Oxford" (*Hellenism and Homosexuality* 114).

4. On *Aufheben* see Solomon's *In the Spirit of Hegel* (275).

5. Augustine writes: "It was Alypius indeed who kept me from marrying, with his unvarying argument that if I did we could not possibly live together with untroubled leisure in the pursuit of wisdom, as we had so long desired. For on that side of things he was quite extraordinarily chaste" (*Confessions* 6.12.21).

6. See *Farewell to the Sea* (27–33) and *Otra vez el mar* (34–39).

7. Olivares calls "telemaquía incestuosa" the Telemachus incest-seduction of his homecoming father, Odysseus, rather than, in reverse, the homebound incest roosting of the son with his mother, Penelope, during the years of absence by the father. Moreover, behind the fulfilled fantasy—or actuality—of the father's seduction by the son in *Viaje a la Habana* there is "another fantasy, that of Reinaldo Arenas himself: Ismaelito (veiled figure of Arenas' father) desires—and seduces—Ismael (figure of Arenas, the son)" ("Twice-Told Tail" 293). In going along with this splendid and mind-bending reading I have noted the difference in legal status between the unmarried Arenas mother and Ismaelito's once-married and divorced mother.

### 6. Son of Gorgo

1. Quotations in Spanish are given only when required by specific meanings and nuances. All *Paradiso* translations other than those by Rabassa are ours and taken from the *Edición Crítica* (*EC*). As explained preceding the list of abbreviations in the front matter, page numbers refer to the Gregory Rabassa English translation of *Paradiso* (Dalkey Archive, 2000) and the ALLCA/UNESCO *Edición Crítica.*

2. Rodríguez Feo sees in the letter just quoted Lezama's premonition "that his physical state would make impossible any attempt at evasion [escaping his sedentary life through travel] and that in years to come he would be prey to the immobility that so terrified him" (*Mi correspondencia* 32), but no explanation is ventured concerning the causes behind his friend's domestic entrapment.

3. See Cellini, *Autobiography* (338). The Cellini text in Rabassa's translation is slightly different from this translation (cited in full in the bibliography) of the *Vita*, from which I quote directly. The incident with Bandinello is briefly mentioned by Lezama in his diary of July 6, 1941 (*Diarios* 51).

4. See comments on *sincerismo* and Lezama's reading of André Gide in *Edición Crítica* (496n40).

5. Discussed in Diskin Clay, "The Origins of the Socratic Dialogue," Vander Waerdt, *The Socratic Movement* (41). On Socrates as Pythagorean in *Clouds,* see A. M. Bowie, *Myth, Ritual, and Comedy* (113).

6. For analysis of the polemic, see Rafael Rojas (*Tumbas sin sosiego* 126–27) and Duanel Díaz (*Los límites de origenismo* 106–20).

### 7. Mother Nero, Uncle Orpheus, and the Unborn

1. "Las imágenes posibles" is quoted from *Obras completas* (2:152–82). The essay is dated 1948. The made-up word "matria" suggests Lezama's knowledge of Bachofen's *Mutterrecht* or *Mother-Right.* The odd reference receives no comment in the *Edición Crítica.* Gustavo Pellón provides an insightful discussion of dragon nursing and Foción's admiration for the mythic beast and the breast (*Joyful Vision* 39–40).

2. *Introductory Dictionary* (109), quoting Lacan, *Seminar* (167).

3. See Dhalla, *History of Zoroastrianism* (89–90, 259–61, 391–96).

4. George Devereux analyzes Io's dream in Aeschylus's *Prometheus Unbound* as a symptom of incestuous wishes toward her father Inachus. His detailed reading rests on the assumption that, being a river god, Inachus would have to be *horned,* like Zeus and Argos Panoptes, who represent a more manifest joint threat to the royal maiden's chastity (*Dreams in Greek Tragedy* 26–53, 645–54).

5. See Maurizio Bettini, "The Bee, the Moth, and the Bat: Natural Symbols and Representations of the Soul" (*Anthropology and Roman Culture* 197–246).

6. Richard Buckle writes: "The dancer is reported to have stopped in mid number and placed his hands on his heart and said, 'the little horse is tired'"

(*Nijinsky* 407). *The Diary of Vaslav Nijinsky* (London: Gollancz, 1936) was translated and expunged by his wife Romola, who had published an earlier biography titled *Nijinsky* in 1933. Joan Acocella reports that Romola "deleted all references to defecation and much of the copious material on sex" ("Secrets of Nijinsky," *New York Review of Books*, January 14, 1999, 53–60).

7. In "Introducción a los vasos órficos" Lezama mentions "the plenitude of a *hieros logos* [as] a world of total religious reach shown as theogony where man emerges as a god"; he also refers to the *hieros logos* in terms of Demeter's presence in the underworld (*OC* 2:853, 858).

8. Cintio Vitier argues convincingly that Lezama's age at forty-three is the same as Oppiano's in 1953 (*EC* 525n7).

9. In a letter to Carlos M. Luis, Lezama praises Jacob Boehme's writing on Abraham's sacrifice and declares Kierkegaard's pages on the same subject "equally splendid" (*Cartas* 98).

### 8. *Paradiso* as a Five-Star Inferno

1. "Synchronicity: An Acausal Connecting Principle," *Essential Jung* (339).

2. The *Edición Crítica* (514n18) quotes: "la tenebrosa frase de Jesús *Ay de las mujeres lactantes y de las embarazadas porque serán pasadas a cuchillo,*" and refers to the same phrase (but not in italics in the manuscript) as "cross-out" ("tachada") or underlined. The note then suggests Matthew 24.19–20 as the probable source, but without bothering (or maybe avoiding) to check whether the words in italics actually exist in that or any other of the four gospels—but they do not.

3. In the original:

> Es innegable que esas mujeres lactantes o preñadas, tendrán la secreta idea de continuar en sus hijos la aventura del vivir. Tendrán ellas que aceptar, por los hijos que lactan o los que lleven entrañados, la destrucción de sus vidas por la promesa de la resurrección . . . cuya promesa llegará también hasta las madres preñadas, que ese día, en una promesa que es más aterradora, pues no han visto aún el rostro de su secreto entrañado, verán el hijo que no pudieron acariciar en el momento en que le enseñaban la luz terrenal, con un cuerpo que en el día de la plenitud tendrán que comprobar con unos ojos que les nacerán para ese momento de mortal reconocimiento. Tendrán que contentarse con ver un cuerpo que no logró desprenderse de sus entrañas y cuya vida les será relatada por el relámpago de la vida eterna y no por sus maternales cuidados. . . . Y mientras han vivido en la naturaleza, en ese día en que su razón enloquecida tendrá que convencerlas de la terrible muerte de sus hijos para que vivan eternamente, tendrán que estar convencidas de que la muerte es contranaturaleza, y que lo que era desconocido para ellas, la resurrección, es naturaleza que se les presenta por primera vez para matar a sus hijos. (*EC* 330–31)

4. See Neil Forsyth on Michael and the dragon, "Apocalypse and Christian Combat" in *The Old Enemy* (6 and 252–55).

5. The *Oppiano Licario* translated passage reads:

> Ynaca pointed toward the palace ruins and said to him: from the height of that tower, only the king could watch over a secret harbor and direct the movements of a fleet hiding there. The one who remained as the widow queen also knew of that secret. And then the rest of the subjects, those who did not wish to be ruled by a woman, declared themselves in rebellion. They sailed with a fleet to capture the widow. The queen ordered her troops to hide in that secret harbor, other soldiers wearing masks showed themselves falsely jubilant upon the high towers, as if ready to surrender the city. When the marines went ashore through the visible and walled-in harbor, the queen ordered that the channel be opened, and the sailors hiding in the secret harbor took over the fleet. Led by the queen, they reached the port at Rhodes, wreathed themselves with laurel. The queen exterminated the military high command and made slaves of the local citizens. The queen ordered two bronze statues erected, one showed her own figure as Minerva Promakos, as armed intelligence; the other showed the vanquished people turned into slaves, crying and begging for mercy. With the passage of time, these trophies were covered with metal plates and it became the duty to call them Abaton, the inaccessible one. (*OL* 376)

According to Strabo, Hecatomnos, the king of the Carians, "had three sons. . . . Mausolus, the eldest of the brothers, married Artemisia, the elder of the daughters. . . . Mausolus became king and at last, childless, he left the empire to his wife, by whom the above-mentioned tomb [the Mausoleum] was erected. But she pined away and died through grief for her husband" (*Geography* 14.2.17). Royal sibling marriage was rare in ancient Greece (Hornblower, *Mausolus* 358–63).

6. "Qui veut que ce soit la Roine Artemisia qui pulverisa le corps mort du Roi Mausolus son seigneur & mari, mélant céte chère cendre avec du vin dans une tasse d'or," Etienne Binet, *Des Attraits tout puissants de l'amour de Jesus-Christ, et du Paradis de ce monde* (Paris, 1631). References to Artemisia were frequent in sixteenth- and seventeenth-century French moral and devotional writings (I owe this information and text citations to Milad Duehi).

7. See the illustration of an emblem showing Daedalus in flight and Icarus falling in McEwen's *Socrates' Ancestor* (69). Sarah Morris discusses the uncertain identification of the flying or falling figures in archaic art (*Daidalos* 19, 354, and 257–68). She examines the Athenian context of the "Daidalos" legends and Attic traditions involving him, his sister, and Talos, either his nephew or adoptive son. See also Sergent: "According to Apollodorus, Talos the Athenian is the son of a sister of Daedalus named Perdix. But, in a different tradition . . . the name Perdix is given to the artisan-pupil himself—sometimes with the explanation that he was given this name because when Daedalus hurled him from the Acropolis, Athena out of pity changed him into a partridge" (*Homosexuality in Greek Myth*

201–4). Lezama's favorite sources for the story of Perdix and Daedalus are Ovid (*Metamorphoses* book VIII) and Garcilaso de la Vega's *Églogas*. My interpretation of the Daedalus-Icarus factor in *Paradiso* is "vampirized" from Alberto Moreiras, "Pharmaconomy: Stephen and the Daedalids," which in dealing with genealogies in James Joyce develops important clues in the story of Daedalus in his fiction.

8. See McEwen's *Socrates' Ancestor* (64–69) on the ancient Greek homology between sails and wings and their relation to architecture in the mythical legends about Daedalus in both Athens and the island of Crete.

9. Eloísa Lezama Lima writes about the passage: "José Lezama Lima wants to stop time; our mother has already died and he is in crisis" (*Paradiso* 1980 555n8). César López's chronology reads: "1964: on September twelfth his mother dies. On December fifth he marries María Luisa Bautista Treviño" (*OL* 106).

10. The phrase's faulty Latin is corrected by the editors of the *Edición Crítica* in a lengthy note (532–35n41) in which issue is taken with Enrico Mario Santí's essay "Parridiso" (1978), a bold and memorable reading of *écriture* taken at large, but also examined at work in pointed textual errors and odd quotations in Lezama's writing. The main issue lies in the editors' wish to trash Santí's claim of transcendent textual faults as symptoms of displacement from textual errors to errant thought; from textual twists as mere copyediting matter to their disruptive value as deviancy from prescriptive norms in culture and politics. See *Bienes del siglo: Sobre cultura cubana* (168–92) for a reprint of "Parridiso" and a rebuttal to the note in *Edición Crítica*.

### 9. Gargling the Tribe

1. For an interpretation of *La isla en peso* and the polemics attending its first reading by Piñera before a group of fellow poets, see Duanel Díaz's "*Orígenes*, Vitier, Lezama, *versus* Piñera, *La isla en peso, Ciclón*" (*Límites del origenismo* 121–86). Equally invaluable as a source of knowledge and interpretation of Piñera's work and the relevant biography is Thomas F. Anderson's *Everything in Its Place: The Life and Works of Virgilio Piñera*.

2. "En toda sustancia poética hay como un punto bisagra, como una señal adhesiva a un caudal que primero aclaró e hizo posible la existencia de lo embozado detrás de su bisagra. Al desaparecer ese análogo el poema queda condenado a su propia confluencia y a las excepciones, a los aislamientos, a las imploraciones, que por su voluntarioso predominio logra establecer en lo temporal" ("La dignidad de la poesía," *OC* 2:762).

### 10. Babel Hustle and Flow

1. See Boldrini's *Joyce, Dante, and the Poetics of Literary Relations* (84) for Dante's account of Babel in *De vulgari eloquentia*.

2. See Marcel Hénaff's *Claude Lévi-Strauss* (49) for a reconsideration of the polemic.

3. "Las concepción católica y protestante (calvinista) de la voluntad: como acto que se entrega o confía a lo imprevisible de la misericordia, o como empecinamiento aislado, egoísta y pragmático, respectivamente. Lo que aquí se contrasta es el puritanismo sajón y una especial fineza criolla, de raíz católica, que Lezama propone como sabiduría familiar y elemento básico de su concepción ética de la vida" (*EC* 651).

**11. Discordance**

1. I am familiar with two current manifestations of "kriollo" in Cuba. One is in Cuban hip-hop street culture and lyrics and the style of replacing "c" and "s" spellings with "k" and "z" for scriptural and iconic effect with the word "kriollo" in frequent display. The other involves the Kriollo Association in the provinces of Guantánamo, Santiago de Cuba, and Granma. When I met with members of the association in November 1999 in Havana, they claimed a membership of more than one hundred thousand Kriollo speakers. The creole language spoken by this people is said to blend Haitian Creole with the Spanish spoken in the provinces of eastern Cuba (formerly Oriente), such as Granma, Santiago de Cuba, and Guantánamo.

2. Page numbers in "Confluencias" refer to the translation in *José Lezama Lima: Selections* and to *Obras completas,* volume 2.

3. Ovid's *Metamorphoses* is the Nyctimene source for both Sor Juana and Lezama. In book 2, the crow tells the story of being displaced by the night owl as "Minerva's blameless attendant," and she says it was "Nyctimene, who became a bird as a result of a foul crime [who] violated her father's bed [and who is now a bird], but her guilty conscience makes her flee the sight of men and the light of day. She hides her shame in darkness, and is driven off by all the birds, from every quarter of the sky" (*Metamorphoses* 66). This happens in Lesbos, which in Lezama's mind links the daughter's seduction of her father as a lesbian sign among the ancient Greeks.

4. See Forsyth's *The Old Enemy* (236) for Seth's parentage by the demiurge in *The Apocalypse of Adam.*

5. See Gantz's *Early Greek Myth* for Inachus, Io, and their descendants (198–212) and for the story of Danae (298–306).

# Bibliography

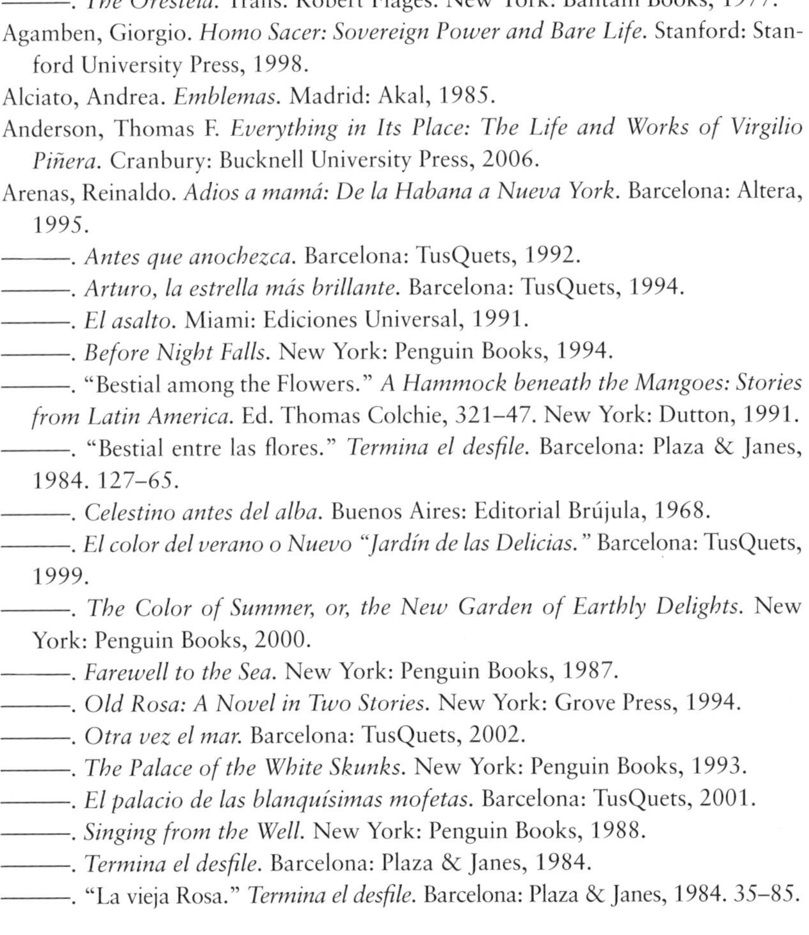


Aeschylus. *Choephoroi.* Ed. A. F. Garvey. Oxford: Oxford University Press, 1986.

———. *The Oresteia.* Trans. Robert Flages. New York: Bantam Books, 1977.

Agamben, Giorgio. *Homo Sacer: Sovereign Power and Bare Life.* Stanford: Stanford University Press, 1998.

Alciato, Andrea. *Emblemas.* Madrid: Akal, 1985.

Anderson, Thomas F. *Everything in Its Place: The Life and Works of Virgilio Piñera.* Cranbury: Bucknell University Press, 2006.

Arenas, Reinaldo. *Adios a mamá: De la Habana a Nueva York.* Barcelona: Altera, 1995.

———. *Antes que anochezca.* Barcelona: TusQuets, 1992.

———. *Arturo, la estrella más brillante.* Barcelona: TusQuets, 1994.

———. *El asalto.* Miami: Ediciones Universal, 1991.

———. *Before Night Falls.* New York: Penguin Books, 1994.

———. "Bestial among the Flowers." *A Hammock beneath the Mangoes: Stories from Latin America.* Ed. Thomas Colchie, 321–47. New York: Dutton, 1991.

———. "Bestial entre las flores." *Termina el desfile.* Barcelona: Plaza & Janes, 1984. 127–65.

———. *Celestino antes del alba.* Buenos Aires: Editorial Brújula, 1968.

———. *El color del verano o Nuevo "Jardín de las Delicias."* Barcelona: TusQuets, 1999.

———. *The Color of Summer, or, the New Garden of Earthly Delights.* New York: Penguin Books, 2000.

———. *Farewell to the Sea.* New York: Penguin Books, 1987.

———. *Old Rosa: A Novel in Two Stories.* New York: Grove Press, 1994.

———. *Otra vez el mar.* Barcelona: TusQuets, 2002.

———. *The Palace of the White Skunks.* New York: Penguin Books, 1993.

———. *El palacio de las blanquísimas mofetas.* Barcelona: TusQuets, 2001.

———. *Singing from the Well.* New York: Penguin Books, 1988.

———. *Termina el desfile.* Barcelona: Plaza & Janes, 1984.

———. "La vieja Rosa." *Termina el desfile.* Barcelona: Plaza & Janes, 1984. 35–85.

———. *Viaje a la Habana.* Miami: Ediciones Universal, 1990.

Augustine. *Confessions.* Trans. F. J. Sheed. Indianapolis: Hackett Publications, 1970.

———. *Las confesiones.* Vol. 2 of *Obras de San Agustín.* Madrid: Biblioteca de Autores Cristianos, 1951.

Auden, W. H. *The Collected Poetry of W. H. Auden.* New York: Random House, 1945.

Atherton, James S. *The Books at the Wake: A Study of Literary Allusions in James Joyce's* Finnegans Wake. London: Faber, 1959.

Banks, Russell. *Cloudsplitter.* New York: HarperPerennial, 1998.

Bartsch, Shadi. 1994. *Actors in the Audience: Theatricality and Doublespeak from Nero to Hadrian.* Cambridge: Harvard University Press, 1995.

Bateson, Gregory. *Naven: A Survey of the Problems Suggested by a Composite Picture of the Culture of a New Guinea Tribe Drawn from Three Points of View.* 1936. Stanford: Stanford University Press, 1965.

Baym, Nina. *Feminism and American Literary History.* New Brunswick: Rutgers University Press, 1992.

Beaupied, Aída. *Narciso hermético: Sor Juana Inés de la Cruz y José Lezama Lima.* Liverpool: Liverpool University Press, 1997.

Beckman, Richard. *Joyce's Rare View: The Nature of Things in* Finnegans Wake. Gainesville: University Press of Florida, 2007.

Beer, Anna. *Milton: Poet, Pamphleteer, and Patriot.* New York: Bloomsbury Press, 2008.

Bettini, Maurizio. *Anthropology and Roman Culture.* Baltimore: The Johns Hopkins University Press, 1991.

Binet, Etienne. *Des Attraits tout puissants de l'amour de Jesus-Christ, et du Paradis de ce monde.* Paris, 1631.

Bishop, John. *Joyce's Book of the Dark:* Finnegans Wake. Madison: University of Wisconsin Press, 1986.

Blount, Roy, Jr. *Long Time Leaving: Dispatches from Up South.* New York: Alfred A. Knopf, 2007.

Blumenberg, Hans. *Work on Myth.* Trans. Robert M. Wallace. Cambridge: The MIT Press, 1985.

Boldrini, Licia. *Joyce, Dante, and the Poetics of Literary Relations: Language and Meaning in* Finnegans Wake. Cambridge: Cambridge University Press, 2001.

Borgeaud, Philippe. *The Cult of Pan in Ancient Greece.* Chicago: The University of Chicago Press, 1988.

Boswell, John. *The Kindness of Strangers: The Abandonment of Children in Western Europe from Late Antiquity to the Renaissance.* New York: Pantheon, 1988.

Bowie, A. M. *Myth, Ritual, and Comedy.* Cambridge: Cambridge University Press, 1993.

Breslin, Paul. *Nobody's Nation: Reading Derek Walcott.* Chicago: The University of Chicago Press, 2001.

Brooks, Cleanth. *William Faulkner: The Yoknapatawpha Country.* New Haven: Yale University Press, 1963.

Brooks, Peter. *The Melodramatic Imagination: Balzac, Henry James, Melodrama, and the Mode of Excess.* New Haven: Yale University Press, 1976.

Brown, Peter. *The Body and Society: Men, Women, and Sexual Renunciation in Early Christianity.* New York: Columbia University Press, 1988.

Buckle, Richard. *Nijinsky.* New York: Simon and Schuster, 1971.

Burd, Van Akin. *John Ruskin and Rose La Touche: Her Unpublished Diaries of 1861 and 1867.* Oxford: Oxford University Press, 1979.

Burkert, Walter. *Homo Necans: The Anthropology of Ancient Greek Ritual and Myth.* Berkeley: University of California Press, 1983.

Butler, Samuel. *The Way of All Flesh.* 1903. New York: Penguin Books, 1966.

Calderón de la Barca, Pedro. *El verdadero Dios Pan. Autos sacramentales completos* 48. Pamplona: Universidad de Navarra, 2005.

Cellini, Benvenuto. *Autobiography.* Trans. George Bull. New York: Penguin Books, 1956.

Cook, Arthur Bernard. *Zeus: A Study in Ancient Religion.* Vol. 3. Cambridge: Cambridge University Press, 1940.

Coppola, Francis Ford. *Apocalypse Now.* 1979. DVD, Los Angeles: Paramount Home Videos, 1999.

Cornford, F. M. *Principium Sapientiae: A Study of the Origins of Greek Philosophical Thought.* New York: Harper Books, 1965.

Cottom, Daniel. *Abyss of Reason: Cultural Movements, Revelations, and Betrayals.* New York: Oxford University Press, 1991.

Crapanzano, Vincent. *Hermes' Dilemma and Hamlet's Desire: On the Epistemology of Interpretation.* Cambridge: Harvard University Press, 1992.

Crews, Frederick. *The Sins of the Fathers: Hawthorne's Psychological Themes.* New York: Oxford University Press, 1966.

Cruz, Sor Juana Inés de la. *Obras completas.* Mexico: Editorial Porrúa, 1985.

———. *A Sor Juana Anthology.* Trans. Alan S. Trueblood. Cambridge: Harvard University Press, 1988.

Cruz-Malavé, Arnaldo. *El primitivo implorante: El "sistema poético del mundo" de José Lezama Lima.* Amsterdam and Atlanta: Rodopi, 1994.

Dällenbach, Lucien. *The Mirror in the Text.* Oxford: Polity Press, 1989.

Danielson, Dennis, ed. *The Cambridge Companion to Milton.* Cambridge: Cambridge University Press, 1989.

Davidson, James. *Courtesans and Fishcakes: The Consuming Passions of Classical Athens.* London: HarperCollins, 1997.

Delcourt, Marie. *Héphaistos ou la Légende du Magicien.* Paris: Les Belles Lettres, 1957.

Deleuze, Gilles. *The Logic of Sense.* 1969. New York: Columbia University Press, 1990.

Derrida, Jacques. *Specters of Marx: The State of the Debt, the Work of Mourning, and the New International.* New York: Routledge, 1994.

Detienne, Marcel. "The Myth of 'Honeyed Orpheus.'" *Myth, Religion, and Society,* Ed. R. L. Gordon. Cambridge: Cambridge University Press, 1981. 95–111.

Devereux, George. *Dreams in Greek Tragedy.* Berkeley: University of California Press, 1976.

Dhalla, Maneckji Nusservanji. *History of Zoroastrianism.* Oxford: Oxford University Press, 1938.

Díaz, Duanel. *Los límites del origenismo.* Madrid: Colibrí, 2005.

Dickens, Charles. *Oliver Twist.* 1838. London: Penguin Books, 1996.

———. *Our Mutual Friend.* 1865. Oxford: Oxford University Press, 1998.

Diodorus Siculus. *Diodorus of Sicily.* Trans. C. H. Oldfather. Cambridge: Harvard University Press, 1935.

Dover, K. J. *Greek Homosexuality.* New York: Vintage Books, 1978.

Dowling, Linda. *Hellenism and Homosexuality in Victorian Oxford.* Ithaca: Cornell University Press, 1994.

Doyle, Laura. *Freedom's Empire: Race and the Rise of the Novel in Atlantic Modernity, 1640–1940.* Durham: Duke University Press, 2008.

Erlich, Gloria G. *Hawthorne's Fiction: The Tenacious Web.* New Brunswick: Rutgers University Press, 1986.

Euripides. *Iphigenia in Tauris. The Complete Greek Tragedies: Euripides II.* Trans. Witter Bynner. Chicago: The University of Chicago Press, 1957.

———. *The Complete Greek Tragedies: Euripides III.* Trans. William Arrowsmith. Chicago: The University of Chicago Press, 1957.

Evans, Dylan. *An Introductory Dictionary of Lacanian Psychoanalysis.* London: Routledge, 1997.

Faulkner, William. *The Hamlet.* 1940. New York: Vintage Books, 1961.

———. *The Mansion.* New York: Vintage Books. 1959.

———. *The Town.* 1957. New York: Vintage Books, 1961.

Fink, Bruce. *The Lacanian Subject: Between Language and Jouissance.* Princeton: Princeton University Press, 1995.

Forsyth, Neil. *The Old Enemy: Satan and the Combat Myth.* Princeton: Princeton University Press, 1987.

———. *The Satanic Epic.* Princeton: Princeton University Press, 2003.

Freud, Sigmund. *Totem and Taboo: Some Points of Agreement between the Mental Lives of Savages and Neurotics.* New York: Norton, 1950.

Gallagher, Catherine. *The Body Economic: Life, Death, and Sensation in Political Economy and the Victorian Novel.* Princeton: Princeton University Press, 2006.

Gantz, Timothy. *Early Greek Myth: A Guide to Literary and Artistic Sources.* Baltimore: The Johns Hopkins University Press, 1993.

Garff, Joakim. *Søren Kierkegaard: A Biography.* Princeton: Princeton University Press, 2005.

Glover, David. *Vampires, Mummies, and Liberals: Bram Stoker and the Politics of Popular Fiction*. Durham: Duke University Press, 1996.

González, Eduardo. *Cuba and the Tempest: Literature and Cinema in the Time of Diaspora*. Chapel Hill: The University of North Carolina Press, 2006.

———. "*Paradiso* y *Wilhelm Meister:* Goethe, Lezama y el dulce suplicio del abuso infantil." *Mal Estar* 3 (Nov. 2004): 68–74.

Hacking, Ian. *Mad Travellers: Reflections on the Reality of Transient Mental Illnesses*. Charlottesville: University of Virginia Press, 1998.

Hawthorne, Nathaniel. *The American Claimant Manuscripts: The Centenary Edition of the Works of Nathaniel Hawthorne*. Vol. 12. Ed. Edward H. Davidson, Claude M. Simpson, and L. Neal Smith. Columbus: The Ohio State University Press, 1977.

———. *The Blithedale Romance*. Ed. Annette Kolodny. 1852. New York: Penguin Books, 1983.

———. *The Scarlet Letter and Other Writings*. Ed. Leland S. Person. New York: Norton, 2005.

Hegel, Georg W. F. *The Philosophy of History*. Trans. J. Sibree. 1899. New York: Dover, 1991.

Heidegger, Martin. "The Question Concerning Technology." *Basic Writings*, 307–43. San Francisco: HarperCollins, 1993.

———. *Unterwegs zur Sprache. Gesamtausgabe*. Vol. 12. Frankfurt am Main: Klostermann, 1985.

Hénaff, Marcel. *Claude Lévi-Strauss and the Making of Structural Anthropology*. Minneapolis: University of Minnesota Press, 1998.

Herbert, T. Walter. *Dearest Beloved: The Hawthornes and the Making of the Middle-Class Family*. Berkeley: University of California Press, 1993.

Herodotus. *The Histories*. Trans. Aubrey Sélincourt. Baltimore: Penguin Books, 1969.

Herrup, Cynthia B. *A House in Gross Disorder: Sex, Law, and the 2nd Earl of Castlehaven*. Oxford: Oxford University Press, 1999.

Hilton, Tim. *John Ruskin: The Early Years (1819–1859)*. New Haven: Yale University Press, 1985.

———. *John Ruskin: The Later Years*. New Haven: Yale University Press, 2000.

Homer. *The Odyssey*. Trans. Richmond Lattimore. New York: Harper and Row, 1965.

Hornblower, Simon. *Mausolus*. Oxford: Oxford University Press, 1982.

Jager, Eric. *The Tempter's Voice: Language and the Fall in Medieval Literature*. Ithaca: Cornell University Press, 1993.

Joyce, James. *The Critical Writings of James Joyce*. Ed. Ellsworth Mason and Richard Ellmann. New York: Viking, 1964.

———. *Finnegans Wake*. 1939. New York: Penguin Books, 1999.

———. *Ulysses*. 1922. New York and Oxford: Oxford University Press, 1993.

Jung, C. G. *The Essential Jung*. Ed. Anthony Storr. Princeton: Princeton University Press, 1999.

———. *Mysterium Coniunctionis: An Inquiry into the Separation and Synthesis of Psychic Opposites in Alchemy*. Princeton: Princeton University Press, 1976.

Karlsen, Carol F. *The Devil in the Shape of a Woman: Witchcraft in Colonial New England*. New York: Norton, 1998.

Kerrigan, William. *The Sacred Complex: On the Psychogenesis of* Paradise Lost. Cambridge: Harvard University Press, 1983.

Kierkegaard, Søren. *Either/Or: A Fragment of Life*. New York: Penguin Books, 1992.

———. *Fear and Trembling*. New York: Penguin Books, 1985.

Klein, Norman M. *The Vatican to Vegas: A History of Special Effects*. New York: New Press, 2004.

Knoepflmacher, U. C. *Ventures in Childland: Victorians, Fairy Tales, and Femininity*. Chicago: The University of Chicago Press, 1998.

Lacan, Jacques. *The Seminar of Jacques Lacan*. Book 1, *Freud's Papers on Technique, 1953–1954*. Trans. John Forrester. Cambridge: Cambridge University Press, 1998.

Leibniz, G. W. *G. W. Leibniz's* Monadology. Ed. Nicholas Rescher. Pittsburgh: University of Pittsburgh Press, 1991.

Lévi-Strauss, Claude. *The Elementary Structures of Kinship*. Trans. James Harle Bell. Boston: Beacon, 1969.

Lewis, Matthew. *The Monk*. 1796. Oxford: Oxford University Press, 1983.

Lezama Lima, José. *Diarios*. Ed. Ciro Bianchi Ross. Mexico: Biblioteca Era, 1994.

———. *José Lezama Lima: Cartas (1939–1976)*. Ed. Eloíza Lezama Lima. Madrid: Editorial Orígenes, 1977.

———. *José Lezama Lima: Selections*. Ed. Ernesto Livon-Grossman. Berkeley: University of California Press, 2005.

———. *Obras completas*. Vol. 2. Ed. Cintio Vitier. Mexico: Aguilar, 1977.

———. *Oppiano Licario*. Ed. César López. Madrid: Cátedra, 1989.

———. *Órbita de Lezama Lima*. Ed. Armando Álvarez Bravo. Havana: UNEAC, 1966.

———. *Paradiso*. Havana: UNEAC, 1966.

———. *Paradiso*. Ed. Eloíza Lezama Lima. Madrid: Cátedra, 1980.

———. *Paradiso: Edición Crítica*. Ed. Cintio Vitier. Paris: ALLCA/UNESCO, 1988.

———. *Paradiso*. Trans. Gregory Rabassa. Normal, IL: Dalkey Archive Press, 2000.

———. *Poesía*. Ed. Emilio de Armas. Madrid: Cátedra, 1992.

Lieb, Michael. *Milton and the Culture of Violence*. Ithaca: Cornell University Press, 1994.

Linebaugh, Peter. *The Magna Carta Manifesto: Liberties and Commons for All.* Berkeley: University of California Press, 2008.

Lukacher, Ned. *Daemonic Figures: Shakespeare and the Question of Conscience.* Ithaca: Cornell University Press, 1994.

Lutyens, Mary. *Young Mrs. Ruskin: Unpublished Letters of Mrs. John Ruskin Written from Venice between 1849–1852.* New York: Vanguard Press, 1966.

Mallarmé, Stéphane. *Collected Poems and Other Verse.* Trans. E. H. and A. M. Blackmore. Oxford: Oxford University Press, 2006.

Mañach, Jorge. *Ensayos.* Havana: Editorial Letras Cubanas, 1998.

Marshall, Megan. *The Peabody Sisters: Three Women Who Ignited American Romanticism.* New York: Mariner Books, 2005.

Marx, Karl. *Early Writings.* Trans. Rodney Livingstone and Gregor Benton. Ed. Lucio Colletti. New York: Penguin Books, 1992.

McDonagh, Josephine. *Child Murder and British Culture, 1720–1900.* Cambridge: Cambridge University Press, 2003.

McEwen, Kagis Indra. *Socrates' Ancestor: An Essay on Architectural Beginnings.* Cambridge: The MIT Press, 1993.

Meza [y Suárez Inclán], Ramón. *Mi tío el empleado.* 1887. Málaga: Dador Ediciones, 1991.

Miller, J. Hillis. *Ariadne's Thread: Story Lines.* New Haven: Yale University Press, 1992.

Milton, John. *Comus. The Poems of John Milton.* Ed. John Carey and Alastair Fowler. London: Longmans, 1968.

———. "Nativity." *The Poems of John Milton.* Ed. John Carey and Alastair Fowler. London: Longmans, 1968.

———. *Paradise Lost.* Ed. Merritt Y. Hughes. Indianapolis: Odyssey Press, 1962.

———. *Samson Agonistes. The Poems of John Milton.* Ed. John Carey and Alastair Fowler. London: Longmans, 1968.

Moreiras, Alberto. "Pharmaconomy: Stephen and the Daedalids." *Joyce and the Return of the Repressed.* Ed. Susan Stanford Friedman. Ithaca: Cornell University Press, 1995. 58–89.

———. *Tercer Espacio: Literatura y duelo en America Latina.* Santiago: LOM Ediciones/Universidad Arcis, 1999.

Morris, Sarah P. *Daidalos and the Origins of Greek Art.* Princeton: Princeton University Press, 1992.

Mulhall, Stephen. *Philosophical Myths of the Fall.* Princeton: Princeton University Press, 2005.

Napier, David A. *Masks, Transformations, and Paradox.* Berkeley: University of California Press, 1986.

Nehamas, Alexander. *The Art of Living: Socratic Reflections from Plato to Foucault.* Princeton: Princeton University Press, 1998.

———. *Virtues of Authenticity: Essays on Plato and Socrates.* Princeton: Princeton University Press, 1999.

Norris, Margot. *The Decentered Universe of* Finnegans Wake: *A Structural Analysis*. Baltimore: The Johns Hopkins University Press, 1976.

Nuttall, A. D. *The Alternate Trinity: Gnostic Heresy in Marlowe, Milton, and Blake*. Oxford: Oxford University Press, 1998.

Ocasio, Rafael. *Cuba's Political and Sexual Outlaw: Reinaldo Arenas*. Gainesville: University Press of Florida, 2003.

O'Donnell, James J. *Augustine: A New Biography*. New York: HarperCollins, 2005.

Olivares, Jorge. "¿Por qué llora Reinaldo Arenas?" *MLN* 115.2 (2000): 268–98.

———. "A Twice-Told Tail: Reinaldo Arenas's 'El Cometa Halley.'" *PMLA* 117.5 (2002): 1188–1206.

Orgel, Stephen. "The Case for Comus." *Representations* 81 (Winter 2003): 31–45.

Ortiz, Fernando. *La filosofía penal de los espiritistas: Estudio de filosofía jurídica*. Havana: La Universal de Ruiz y Ca., 1915.

———. *Historia de una pelea cubana contra los demonios*. Havana: Editorial de Ciencias Sociales, 1975.

Ortiz, Ricardo L. *Cultural Erotics in Cuban America*. Minneapolis: University of Minnesota Press, 2007.

Ovid. *Metamorphoses*. Trans. Mary M. Innes. Baltimore: Penguin Books, 1968.

Park, Katharine. *Secrets of Women: Gender, Generation, and the Origins of Human Dissection*. New York: Zone Books, 2007.

Paz, Octavio. *Sor Juana, or, the Traps of Faith*. Cambridge: Harvard University Press, 1988.

Pellón, Gustavo. *José Lezama Lima's Joyful Vision*. Austin: University of Texas Press, 1989.

Person, Leland S. "The Dark Labyrinth of Mind: Hawthorne, Hester, and the Ironies of Racial Mothering." *The Scarlet Letter and Other Writings*. By Nathaniel Hawthorne. New York: Norton, 2005. 656–69.

Piñera, Virgilio. *La isla en peso*. Barcelona: TusQuets, 2000.

Plato. *The Collected Dialogues of Plato*. Ed. Edith Hamilton and Huntington Cairns. Princeton: Princeton University Press, 1961.

———. *Phaedrus and Letters VII and VIII*. Ed. Walter Hamilton. New York: Penguin Books, 1987.

———. *Plato: The Last Days of Socrates*. Trans. Hugh Tredennick. New York: Penguin Books, 1987.

———. *Plato: Early Socratic Dialogues*. Trans. Trevor J. Saunders. New York: Penguin Books, 1987.

———. *The Symposium*. Ed. R. E. Allen. New Haven: Yale University Press, 1991.

Pliny. *Natural History*. Trans. H. Rackham. Cambridge: Harvard University Press, 1959.

Poumier, María. "Foción Erasmo Lima: Elogio a la locura en *Paradiso*." *Unión Revista de Literatura y Arte* 8.25 (Oct.–Dec. 1996): 66–72.

Pucci, Pietro. *Odysseus Polutropos: Intertextual Readings in the* Odyssey *and the* Iliad. Ithaca: Cornell University Press, 1987.

Rabaté, Jean-Michel. *The Cambridge Companion to Lacan.* Cambridge: Cambridge University Press, 2003.

———. *James Joyce and the Politics of Egoism.* Cambridge: Cambridge University Press, 2001.

Rodríguez Feo, José. *Mi correspondencia con Lezama Lima.* Havana: UNEAC, 1989.

Rojas, Rafael. *Tumbas sin sosiego: Revolución, disidencia y exilio del intelectual cubano.* Barcelona: Anagrama, 2006.

Rosenberg, John D. *The Darkening Glass: A Portrait of Ruskin's Genius.* New York: Columbia University Press, 1961.

———. "The Devil and Mr. Ruskin." *New York Review of Books* June 29, 2000: 31–35.

Ruskin, John. *The Genius of John Ruskin: Selections from His Writings.* Ed. John D. Rosenberg. New York: G. Braziller, 1963.

———. *The Library Edition of the Works of John Ruskin.* Ed. E. T. Cook and Alexander Wedderburn. London: G. Allen, 1903–1912.

———. *Unto This Last and Other Writings.* New York: Penguin Books, 1997.

Salgado, César Augusto. *From Modernism to Neobaroque: Joyce and Lezama Lima.* Lewisburg: Bucknell University Press, 2001.

Santí, Enrico Mario. *Bienes del siglo: Sobre cultura cubana.* Mexico: Fondo de Cultura Económica, 2002.

Sawyer, Paul L. *Ruskin's Poetic Argument: The Design of the Major Works.* Ithaca: Cornell University Press, 1985.

Schmitt, Carl. *The* Nomos *of the Earth in the International Law of the* Jus Publicum Europaeum. Trans. G. L. Ulmen. New York: Telos Press, 2003.

Schwyzer, Philip. "Purity and Danger on the West Bank of the Severn: The Cultural Geography of a *Masque Presented at Ludlow Castle, 1634.*" *Representations* 60 (Fall 1997): 22–47.

Sergent, Bernard. *Homosexuality in Greek Myth.* Boston: Beacon, 1986.

Shakespeare, William. *Hamlet.* Ed. Neil Taylor and Ann Thompson. Arden Shakespeare, 3rd series. London: Arden Shakespeare, 2006.

Shawcross, John T. *John Milton: The Self and the World.* Lexington: University Press of Kentucky, 1993.

Shelley, Mary. *Frankenstein; or, the Modern Prometheus. Three Gothic Novels.* Ed. Mario Pratz. Baltimore: Penguin Books, 1968.

Sollors, Werner. *Neither Black nor White yet Both: Thematic Explorations of Interracial Literature.* New York: Oxford University Press, 1997.

Solomon, Robert C. *In the Spirit of Hegel.* New York: Oxford University Press, 1983.

Sophocles. *Antigone.* Vol. 2 of *Sophocles.* Ed. and trans. Hugh Lloyd-Jones. Cambridge: Harvard University Press, 1994.

———. *Electra. The Complete Greek Tragedies: Sophocles I.* Trans. David Greene. Chicago: The University of Chicago Press, 1957.

Soto, Francisco. *Reinaldo Arenas: The Pentagonía.* Gainesville: University Press of Florida, 1994.

———. *Reinaldo Arenas.* London: Prentice Hall International, 1998.

Spengemann, William C. "*Paradise Lost:* Milton's American Poem." *A New World of Words: Redefining Early American Literature.* New Haven: Yale University Press, 1994. 94–117.

Statius. *Thebaid.* Trans. A. D. Melville. Oxford: Oxford University Press, 1995.

Steiner, George. *After Babel: Aspects of Language and Translation.* Oxford: Oxford University Press, 1975.

———. *No Passion Spent: Essays 1978–1995.* New Haven: Yale University Press, 1998.

Stewart, Frank Henderson. *Honor.* Chicago: The University of Chicago Press, 1994.

Strabo. *Geography.* Trans. H. L. Jones. Cambridge: Harvard University Press, 1929.

Stravinsky, Igor. *Memories and Commentaries.* New York: Norton, 1960.

Suetonius. *The Twelve Caesars.* Trans. Robert Graves. Baltimore: Penguin Books, 1957.

Taylor, Marc C. *Altarity.* Chicago: The University of Chicago Press, 1987.

Toro, Guillermo del. *The Devil's Backbone.* 2001. DVD, Los Angeles: Sony Pictures Classics, 2004.

———. *Pan's Labyrinth.* 2006. DVD, Burbank: New Line Home Entertainment, 2007.

Vander Waerdt, Paul A. *The Socratic Movement.* Ithaca: Cornell University Press, 1994.

Vernant, Jean-Pierre. *Mortals and Immortals: Collected Essays.* Princeton: Princeton University Press, 1991.

Vico, Giambattista. *The New Science.* Trans. David Marsh. New York: Penguin Books, 2001.

Virgil. *The Aeneid.* Trans. W. F. Jackson Knight. Harmondsworth: Penguin Books, 1977.

———. *Virgil's Georgics.* Trans. Smith Palmer Bovie. Chicago: The University of Chicago Press, 1957.

Walcott, Derek. *Collected Poems.* New York: Farrar, Straus, Giroux, 1994.

———. *Omeros.* New York: Farrar, Straus, Giroux, 1990.

———. *What the Twilight Said.* New York: Farrar Strauss and Giroux, 1998.

Vitruvius. *On Architecture.* Trans. Frank Granger. Cambridge: Harvard University Press, 1970.

Walpole, Horace. *The Castle of Otranto. Three Gothic Novels.* Ed. Mario Pratz. Baltimore: Penguin Books, 1968.

Wineapple, Brenda. *Hawthorne: A Life.* New York: Random House, 2004.

# Index

NEW WORLD STUDIES

Vera M. Kutzinski, *Sugar's Secrets: Race and the Erotics of Cuban Nationalism*

Richard D. E. Burton and Fred Reno, editors, *French and West Indian: Martinique, Guadeloupe, and French Guiana Today*

A. James Arnold, editor, *Monsters, Tricksters, and Sacred Cows: Animal Tales and American Identities*

J. Michael Dash, *The Other America: Caribbean Literature in a New World Context*

Isabel Alvarez Borland, *Cuban-American Literature of Exile: From Person to Persona*

Belinda J. Edmondson, editor, *Caribbean Romances: The Politics of Regional Representation*

Steven V. Hunsaker, *Autobiography and National Identity in the Americas*

Celia M. Britton, *Edouard Glissant and Postcolonial Theory: Strategies of Language and Resistance*

Mary Peabody Mann, *Juanita: A Romance of Real Life in Cuba Fifty Years Ago* (Edited and with an introduction by Patricia M. Ard)

George B. Handley, *Postslavery Literatures in the Americas: Family Portraits in Black and White*

Faith Smith, *Creole Recitations: John Jacob Thomas and Colonial Formation in the Late Nineteenth-Century Caribbean*

Ian Gregory Strachan, *Paradise and Plantation: Tourism and Culture in the Anglophone Caribbean*

Nick Nesbitt, *Voicing Memory: History and Subjectivity in French Caribbean Literature*

Charles W. Pollard, *New World Modernisms: T. S. Eliot, Derek Walcott, and Kamau Brathwaite*

Carine M. Mardorossian, *Reclaiming Difference: Caribbean Women Rewrite Postcolonialism*

Luís Madureira, *Cannibal Modernities: Postcoloniality and the Avant-garde in Caribbean and Brazilian Literature*

Elizabeth M. DeLoughrey, Renée K. Gosson, and George B. Handley, editors, *Caribbean Literature and the Environment: Between Nature and Culture*

Flora González Mandri, *Guarding Cultural Memory: Afro-Cuban Women in Literature and the Arts*

Miguel Arnedo-Gómez, *Writing Rumba: The Afrocubanista Movement in Poetry*

Jessica Adams, Michael P. Bibler, and Cécile Accilien, editors, *Just Below South: Intercultural Performance in the Caribbean and the U.S. South*

Valérie Loichot, *Orphan Narratives: The Postplantation Literature of Faulkner, Glissant, Morrison, and Saint-John Perse*

Sarah Phillips Casteel, *Second Arrivals: Landscape and Belonging in Contemporary Writing of the Americas*

Guillermina De Ferrari, *Vulnerable States: Bodies of Memory in Contemporary Caribbean Fiction*

Claudia Sadowski-Smith, *Border Fictions: Globalization, Empire, and Writing at the Boundaries of the United States*

Doris L. Garraway, editor, *Tree of Liberty: Cultural Legacies of the Haitian Revolution in the Atlantic World*

Dawn Fulton, *Signs of Dissent: Maryse Conde and Postcolonial Criticism*

Nick Nesbitt, *Universal Emancipation: The Haitian Revolution and the Radical Enlightenment*

Michael G. Malouf, *Transatlantic Solidarities: Irish Nationalism and Caribbean Poetics*

Maria Cristina Fumagalli, *Caribbean Perspectives on Modernity: Returning the Gaze*

Vivian Nun Halloran, *Exhibiting Slavery: The Caribbean Postmodern Novel as Museum*

Paul B. Miller, *Elusive Origins: The Enlightenment in the Modern Caribbean Historical Imagination*

Eduardo González, *Cuba and the Fall: Christian Text and Queer Narrative in the Fiction of José Lezama Lima and Reinaldo Arenas*